T0294981

NEW ESSAYS ON CLINT EASTWOOD

New CLINT
Essays on EASTWOOD

Edited by LEONARD ENGEL
Foreword by DRUCILLA CORNELL

THE UNIVERSITY OF UTAH PRESS
Salt Lake City

Copyright © 2012 by The University of Utah Press. All rights reserved.

 The Defiance House Man colophon is a registered trademark of the
University of Utah Press. It is based on a four-foot-tall Ancient Puebloan
pictograph (late PIII) near Glen Canyon, Utah.

16 15 14 13 12   1 2 3 4 5

LIBRARY OF CONGRESS CATALOGING-IN-PUBLICATION DATA

New essays on Clint Eastwood/edited by Leonard Engel ; foreword by Drucilla
Cornell.
         p.   cm.
A companion to Engel's previous work, Clint Eastwood, actor and director: new
perspectives, this volume includes some of the films produced after the first volume
was published.
Includes filmography and index.
ISBN 978-1-60781-207-4 (pbk. : alk. paper)
1. Eastwood, Clint, 1930—Criticism and interpretation.
I. Engel, Leonard, 1936–
PN2287.E37N49 2012
791.4302'8092—dc23   2012017530

Printed and bound by Sheridan Books, Inc., Ann Arbor, Michigan.

Dedicated to the memory of my son
TOBIAS RAFAEL ENGEL (1993–2012)

CONTENTS

Foreword: Why Do We Turn to Eastwood Now? ■ ix
Drucilla Cornell

Acknowledgments ■ xi

Introduction: What Is Past, or Passing, or to Come ■ 1
John M. Gourlie and Leonard Engel

CHAPTER 1
"Landscape as Moral Destiny": Mythic Reinvention
from Rowdy Yates to The Stranger ■ 18
Robert Smart

CHAPTER 2
Thoroughly Modern Eastwood: Male/Female Power Relations
in *The Beguiled* and *Play Misty for Me* ■ 36
Brett Westbrook

CHAPTER 3
Clintus and Siegelini: "We've Got a System. Not Much, but We're Fond of It" ■ 53
Mike Smrtic and Matt Wanat

CHAPTER 4
Rawhide to *Pale Rider*: The Maturation of Clint Eastwood ■ 76
Edward Rielly

CHAPTER 5
Eastwood's Treatment of the Life of Creativity and Performance
in *Bronco Billy, Honkytonk Man, White Hunter Black Heart*, and *Bird* ■ 90
Dennis Rothermel

CHAPTER 6
"You Can't Hunt Alone": *White Hunter Black Heart* ■ 121
Richard Hutson

CHAPTER 7
The End of History and America First: How the 1990s Revitalized Clint Eastwood ■ 130
 Craig Rinne

CHAPTER 8
"A Man of Notoriously Vicious and Intemperate Disposition":
Western Noir and the Tenderfoot's Revenge in *Unforgiven* ■ 148
 Stanley Orr

CHAPTER 9
A Good Vintage or Damaged Goods? Clint Eastwood and
Aging in Hollywood Film ■ 168
 Philippa Gates

CHAPTER 10
Space, Pace, and Southern Gentility in *Midnight in the Garden of Good and Evil* ■ 190
 Brad Klypchak

CHAPTER 11
Mystic River as a Tragic Action ■ 204
 Robert Merrill and John L. Simons

CHAPTER 12
Lies of Our Fathers: Mythology and Artifice in Eastwood's Cinema ■ 224
 William Beard

CHAPTER 13
Eastwood's *Flags of Our Fathers* and *Letters from Iwo Jima*:
The Silence of Heroes and the Voice of History ■ 249
 John M. Gourlie

CHAPTER 14
Gran Torino: Showdown in Detroit, Shrimp Cowboys, and a New Mythology ■ 266
 John M. Gourlie and Leonard Engel

CHAPTER 15
Invictus: The Master Craftsman as Hagiographer ■ 277
 Raymond Foery

CHAPTER 16
Hereafter: Dreaming beyond Our Philosophies ■ 286
 John M. Gourlie

CHAPTER 17
Citizen Hoover: Clint Eastwood's *J. Edgar* ■ 290
 Kathleen Moran and Richard Hutson

Filmography ■ 295
Contributors ■ 299
Index ■ 303

FOREWORD: WHY DO WE TURN TO EASTWOOD NOW?

Drucilla Cornell

Few directors born and raised in the United States have focused as intensively and extensively on the burning issues of our times, such as revenge, war, justice, the possibility of love, virtue, and nationalism, as has Clint Eastwood. But it is not the breadth of his work that makes him so important. It is, rather, the unique way in which he has addressed these questions by connecting them to the question of what it means to be a good man in such difficult times as in the "America" of the twentieth and twenty-first centuries.[1] Eastwood takes us to some of the great images and symbols of the deepest fantasies of American life, through the classic genres of cowboy movies, police thrillers, and boxing heroics. What makes Eastwood so unique is that he reworks these Hollywood genres to a certain extent, by focusing on a fundamental question: What does it mean to live life as a good man in a complex and violent world? I am more than aware of the literature that has criticized the idea of the director as auteur, the originator and sole author of the narrative lines of his or her films. To engage in these classic Hollywood genres does impose real limits. But in Eastwood's case, his implicit return to the question of masculinity, and, particularly, to what it means to be a good man, breaks through those limits to some extent. This may seem like a strange conclusion, because has not so much of Hollywood presented us with the height of virtue, particularly masculine virtue? The answer is: Of course; but what Eastwood does is give us surprising perspectives on so-called heroic virtue. Indeed, in his classic film *Flags of Our Fathers*, the very ideal of the hero is called into question, and that questioning of heroism is underscored at the end of the film. Just when men think that they have it right, and are convinced that they are doing the right thing, they find the hubris of their self-righteousness turned against them.

Think, for example, of his underrated film *A Perfect World*. In that film, a classic American masculine fantasy, the hero of the Texas Rangers tries to rescue a young man from a situation of abuse, Butch Haynes, played by Kevin Costner, by placing him in a formidable prison for young people, which, rather than saving him, sets him off on a life of crime. I have written at length about this film elsewhere, so I will not describe the subtle unfolding of Eastwood's second attempt to rescue Butch but only emphasize that it fails completely, ending in Butch's death. The film ends with a surprising declaration from the so-called cocky characters that Hollywood has associated with the Texas Rangers. Eastwood turns away any attempts to comfort him, ending the movie with the following line: that he "don't know nuthin'. Not a damn thing." Not a very cocky way for a movie supposedly starring a Texas Ranger to end.

The undoing of masculine hubris that underscores character in these classic Hollywood genres is what makes Eastwood's work so powerful. But it would be a mistake to see Eastwood as an explicitly political director or as one who ties up complex narrative lines in easy ethical solutions. It is the struggle to engage with all the complexities of what it might mean to be a good man that makes Eastwood's own imagery so searing and emotionally compelling. We are oftentimes forced to engage with images of meaningless violence, including violence toward women, that portray the empty shell of the masculinity that traditional Hollywood genres have propped up as the basis of male heroism. Eastwood's ultimate strength as a director may be that he works through the stereotypes of masculinity so subtly that these stereotypes are ultimately called into question, even if, paradoxically, the male ideals that the characters seem to hold dear also drive the action.

In this rich collection, we find almost all of Eastwood's major movies reviewed, with excellent critical analysis and care for Eastwood's cinematic rejection of simplistic closure. The director does not attempt to give us an ultimate vision that leaves no place for the imagination of the audience: the very opposite is the case. The texts in this volume address the richness of Eastwood in his extraordinary work, not only as a director but also as an actor, and give rightful acknowledgment to his place of honor in the cinema of the United States.

■ Note

1. I put "America" in quotation marks because at the end of the day, America is a geographic designation that includes both North and South America. And if there was ever a director more deeply engaged with all the myths of what it means to be a North American man, it is Eastwood.

ACKNOWLEDGMENTS

This book has been a labor of love, and I am indebted to a lot of people for making it a reality. My friend and colleague John Gourlie has been the main inspiration. Truly, without his wise counsel and support this collection would not have come to pass, and his work in the introduction, on Clint's World War II films, on *Gran Torino*, and on *Hereafter* has been superb. My gratitude goes to all the contributors for their commitment and perseverance; they have written first-rate essays. In addition, I wish to express my thanks to Hans Bergmann, dean of Quinnipiac's College of Arts and Sciences, for his support. Many thanks go to Quinnipiac's fine library staff, particularly June DeGennaro, Linda Hawkes, and Janet Valeski, and to Mike Calia and Gary Pandolfi for their technical support. Thanks also go to editor Peter DeLafosse at the University of Utah Press for his patience, advice, and dedication to Clint and his work. Finally, a special thanks goes to my wife, Moira, for her understanding and constant support, and to Tessa and Toby, who have gotten into the act probably more than they ever wanted.

INTRODUCTION: WHAT IS PAST, OR PASSING, OR TO COME

John M. Gourlie and Leonard Engel

Contrary to F. Scott Fitzgerald's famous claim about there being no second acts in American lives, Clint Eastwood has had a terrific second act—or, more precisely, a series of amazing "second" acts, and they keep coming. He turned eighty-one in May 2011, continues to be as busy as ever, and shows few signs of slowing down. As one concession, though, after directing and starring in the highly successful *Gran Torino* (2008), he claimed that he will no longer act but will concentrate solely on directing, producing, and composing. However, apparently he has changed his mind and is planning to star in *Trouble with the Curve*, a forthcoming baseball movie, as a veteran scout.

Since we completed *Clint Eastwood, Actor and Director: New Perspectives* (Engel 2007), not only has Eastwood starred in and directed *Gran Torino* (2008), he has directed *Flags of Our Fathers* (2006), *Letters from Iwo Jima* (2006), *The Changeling* (2008), *Invictus* (2009), *Hereafter* (2010), and *J. Edgar* (2011). Eastwood's level of accomplishment is stunning for a filmmaker of any age, perhaps even more remarkable for one now in his eighties.

Our second collection of essays again looks at films that range over the course of Eastwood's career so that we might more fully appreciate and understand Eastwood as he continues to grow into an ever more accomplished storyteller, one who continues to sharpen his skills, deepen his power, and expand the range of his subject matter.[1] While our initial intention for this new book was to focus primarily on Eastwood's latest films, that impulse was broadened by the continuing enthusiasm of our contributors for Eastwood's work from its beginnings to its latest manifestations. This broad engagement with Eastwood's work underscores the degree to which his most recent work grows out of a lifetime of endeavor and accomplishment—all of which remains of interest. While each collection of essays can stand alone, together they form a broad perspective that illuminates the place where Eastwood's work began, the paths it followed as he grew, and the levels of artistic achievement the later work, in particular, attains. Accordingly, this collection seeks both to expand our understanding of individual films and to deepen our overall appreciation of Eastwood's artistry as, through the various stages of his career, he becomes an ever greater master of his craft.

From his beginnings in television to his iconic roles in Westerns and detective films, Eastwood has always generated star power as an actor. But his ambitions as a filmmaker grew over the years to encompass roles as director, producer, and eventually composer as well. Likewise, his continuous courage as a storyteller has led him from initially muted, small-scale, or offbeat productions to the treatment of major human themes on a broad canvas. Along the way, he has explored the dark corners of the psyche (*Play Misty for Me* and *The Beguiled*, both 1971); the unusual in subject matter (*Any Which Way You Can*, 1978; *Bronco Billy*, 1980); the artistically and personally meaningful (*Honkytonk Man*, 1982; *Bird*, 1988; *White Hunter Black Heart*, 1990); the extreme version of a character (all the Western avengers; *Tightrope*, 1984); tragic family issues (*Mystic River*, 2003; *Million Dollar Baby*, 2004; *The Changeling*, 2008; *Gran Torino*, 2008); the human sacrifice, national illusions, and nightmare horrors of war (*Flags of Our Fathers* and *Letters from Iwo Jima*, both 2006); the rare miracle of human brotherhood in history (*Invictus*, 2009); and, surprisingly, the afterlife (*Hereafter*, 2010). Eastwood's continuing star power as an actor-director and his financial acumen as a producer have brought him the freedom to extend this exploration throughout an exceptionally long and increasingly magnificent career.

In recent years, age and creative maturity have brought greater depth and power to Eastwood's work. In major films since *Million Dollar Baby*—films such as *Flags of Our Fathers*, *Letters from Iwo Jima*, *Gran Torino*, *Invictus*, and *Hereafter*—Eastwood expands his vision as a cinematic storyteller in remarkable ways. As different as certain of these films may be from one another, they share a common theme—the family of man. For example, *Flags of Our Fathers* and *Letters from Iwo Jima* depict the World War II battle for Iwo Jima, first from the perspective of the American marines and then from the perspective of the Japanese defenders. Significantly, the two films convey equal compassion for both sides in the combat. The cumulative effect is to liberate, say, American viewers from their own national outlook and to invite them to view "the enemy" as equally human and equally worthy—equal members of the same family.

Even sixty-five years after the Battle of Iwo Jima, this reformulation of American perceptions comes with a jolt, especially to those raised on the understandably nationalistic portrayal of World War II offered by Hollywood at the time and reinforced by most war films since. But both of Eastwood's Iwo Jima films offer a compassionate portrayal of family. In *Letters*, it is the straightforward device of Japanese soldiers writing letters from Iwo Jima to be sent to their families on mainland Japan. The film's story emerges as a flashback from the cache of such letters found undelivered on Iwo Jima years after the battle. In *Flags*, a complex nonlinear narrative unfolds, but it is still based on the search of a son for his father's hidden past as one participant in the famous photograph of Marines raising the American flag on Mount Suribachi during the battle for Iwo Jima. While the films explore differing conceptions of heroism and honor, they work in tandem to create a vision of shared humanity. In a combined perspective, the families of each film ultimately assume a role as representative of the "family of mankind." Given that the basic action of each film consists of American and Japanese soldiers killing each other, Eastwood's vision of their brotherhood—their belonging to the same family of mankind—is a remarkable achievement.

Eastwood sustains this vision of mankind's brotherhood in *Invictus*. Like *Flags* and *Letters*, *Invictus* also breaks the mold of the small-scale productions typical of Eastwood's earlier filmmaking. All three films are epic in scale. All three films address history. All three films portray actual people enacting actual events. In *Invictus*, Nelson Mandela, newly elected president of South Africa, asks Francois Pienaar, the captain of the national rugby team, the Springboks, to win the World Cup as a means of uniting black and white South Africans in a common cause. That the Springboks, a former emblem of white supremacy, gain the support of the black population, that in the moment of their victory they unleash an all-consuming joy powerful enough to unite warring races, and that Mandela's improbable strategy gives birth to the modern nation of South Africa constitute a miracle as soaring and as transfixing as the moment when the Boeing 747 roars over the stadium at 200 feet.

That Eastwood, who gained fame as the loner—the man with no name—has become a director capable of making *Invictus* is perhaps also a miracle of some order, one of exceptional artistic growth in a career spanning over forty years as a director and fifty-five years as an actor. With extraordinary dedication and unyielding ambition to expand and deepen his capabilities as a storyteller, Eastwood continues to make exceptional film after exceptional film.

While *Gran Torino* is not in the mold of epic history, it nonetheless exhibits a mythic dimension that expands it beyond the confines of its smaller-scale production. Making use of the character of the priest and of religious iconography, Eastwood renders the story of Walt Kowalski's growing engagement with his Hmong neighbors in Detroit into a myth for modern times. In bequeathing his Gran Torino to Thao at the end of the film, Walt fully acknowledges the Hmong teenager as his true son and heir, just as he has increasingly accepted the Hmong family next door as his adopted family. This story line of multicultural unity assumes mythic proportions in Walt's sacrificial death. As he is gunned down by a Hmong gang, he falls in a posture of crucifixion. In the funeral sermons at the beginning and end of the film, the priest places Walt's life in the context of the meaning of life and death. Such elements suggest that in *Gran Torino*, Eastwood is offering a story of mythic reach in its endeavor to express our fundamental values as a nation and as human beings.

Perhaps no single film like *Gran Torino*—or even a series of films like *Flags*, *Letters*, *Invictus*, and *Hereafter*—can by itself establish a mythic narrative capable of assuming the role that the whole genre of the Western has played as our national myth. Yet Eastwood is offering us a vision. In *Mystic River* and *Million Dollar Baby*, he offers us an emotional intensity that moves the very heart's core more deeply into compassion for human suffering and human failing. In *Flags*, *Letters*, and *Invictus*, he addresses world history with an underlying vision of human brotherhood that transcends warring nations and racial hatred. In *Gran Torino*, he formulates a mythic narrative of multicultural unity. In *Hereafter*, he examines the very mysteries of the afterlife itself—the shared destiny of all humankind. Most recently, in *J. Edgar*, he explores obsession and power in the person of J. Edgar Hoover, all but Director for Life of the FBI and a national figure emblematic of twentieth-century America. Taken together, these films trace the path whereby Eastwood has transformed his treatment of the family as an emotional and dramatic center into a lens capable of projecting an image of the family of mankind and its most profound values onto the canvas of history and into the realms of myth.

■ ■ ■

A great deal of attention has been paid to Eastwood and his films in recent years beyond their initial discussion in popular magazines and film reviews. Scholarly articles and books have appeared with perspectives ranging from the literary, philosophical, sociological, and historical to those of gender studies. In this wide-ranging vein, the writers in our collection seek to explore Eastwood's varied career. They do so in essays that examine Eastwood's body of work from the beginning of his acting career as Rowdy Yates in the television series *Rawhide* to his appearance in *Gran Torino* and from the beginning of his directing career with *Play Misty for Me* to *Hereafter*. Throughout, the essays seek to illuminate the variety and complexity of Eastwood's themes and his accomplishments throughout a lifetime of endeavor.

In chapter 1, "'Landscape as Moral Destiny': Mythic Reinvention from Rowdy Yates to The Stranger," Robert Smart examines the Western *A Fistful of Dollars* in the context of the seven-year stint Eastwood had on *Rawhide*. In the series, the emerging Eastwood hero blends attributes of Eric Fleming with elements of maturity in Rowdy Yates's own character. *Rawhide* avoided contending with the moral ambiguities of the Cold War period by remaining resolutely ahistorical. As the series plugged along, the main figures—Favor and Yates—find that they have to assert, sometimes invent, a moral order and code to deal with the problems they encounter. But in Leone's *A Fistful of Dollars* (1964; released in the United States in 1967), this moral ambivalence has been reframed in the persona of The Man with No Name, who embodies a strict and brutal moral code that often plays men's venalities against them until, at the end, they stand before a vengeful Stranger (Eastwood) who dispatches them once they are apprised of their moral culpability. This stark figure of vigilante justice is not a departure from the earlier series but a fuller development of the *Rawhide* years.

Often the critical attention afforded Eastwood's films has centered on various critiques of their penchant for vengeance and violence, especially that violence inflicted upon women. But the portrayal of gender, a major critical issue in Eastwood's films from the beginning, has, in recent studies, provided one of the most thoughtful and provocative avenues of investigation. Indeed, one particular book merits special mention—*Clint Eastwood and Issues of American Masculinity* by Drucilla Cornell. In this excellent study, Cornell carefully analyzes key films in Eastwood's canon and suggests that he has been dramatizing, both in the characters he portrays and in his directing, issues of masculinity drawn from early in his career. Eastwood, she claims, gives no easy answers to the issues. Rather, the power of his work "is that he presents his characters struggling honestly with ethical questions in all the complexity and urgency of real-life situations." His films

> cut us to the core of our being, not because they show us what it means to be a good man but because they illustrate so powerfully what a struggle it is to even make an attempt. His films have . . . a profound staying power in what they communicate about human relationships. They cut deeply beneath the surface of what we think we know about moral conflict and ethical commitment. The compelling depth of Eastwood's tragically scarred protagonists sears the flesh of the viewer, cuts more deeply than the salves of our psychic defenses can repair, and leaves an imprint on our very bones. (Cornell 2009, 189–90)

Sensitive to Cornell's insights, Brett Westbrook explores such issues in chapter 2, "Thoroughly Modern Eastwood: Male/Female Power Relations in *The Beguiled* and *Play Misty for Me*." Violence is prominent in both *The Beguiled* (1971) and, with Eastwood directing for the first time, *Play Misty for Me* (1971). *The Beguiled* is especially gruesome. Yet, despite having been made forty years ago, both movies are surprisingly modern in terms of the sexual boundaries men and women negotiate, the strategies they deploy, and the characters' ultimate goals. While most criticism of the films has been dismissive, even vehemently so, a closer look reveals an intricacy that touches on homosexuality, race, male privilege, and female empowerment still under discussion in the new millennium.

In chapter 3, "Clintus and Siegelini: 'We've Got a System. Not Much, but We're Fond of It,'" Mike Smrtic and Matt Wanat discuss Eastwood's early collaborations with director Don Siegel. The names in the title refer to the pet names Siegel and Eastwood had for one another. Smrtic and Wanat demonstrate the prevalence of a particular Siegel theme and the impact of Eastwood's iconography upon this theme. Specifically, the writers show that when Siegel first worked with Eastwood on *Coogan's Bluff* (1968), Siegel had already developed a complex and pervasive interest in the characters' negotiations of multiple and sometimes competing systems. Smrtic and Wanat illustrate the effects of Eastwood's presence upon this Siegel theme by comparing Siegel's procedural cop films in the period before Eastwood with films of the later period with Eastwood, an analysis culminating with Siegel and Eastwood's most famous collaboration, *Dirty Harry* (1971).

In chapter 4, "*Rawhide* to *Pale Rider*: The Maturation of Clint Eastwood," Edward Rielly examines Eastwood's early television series *Rawhide* (1959–65) in the light of his accomplishments in *Pale Rider* (1985), which Eastwood directed, produced, and starred in. Between the TV series and *Pale Rider*, Eastwood worked in films that included the Sergio Leone *Dollars* series; Don Siegel's *Coogan's Bluff*, *Two Mules for Sister Sara*, *Dirty Harry*, and *Escape from Alcatraz*; and his own directorial efforts, *High Plains Drifter*, *The Outlaw Josey Wales*, and *Bronco Billy*. The purpose of this chapter is not to chronicle Eastwood's learning curve from one project to another but, rather, to look at *Rawhide* and *Pale Rider* as bookends marking two crucial periods in Eastwood's career: first, the aspiring and always observant actor/director learning on the job and, second, the fulfillment of Eastwood's promise in *Pale Rider*, an extraordinary achievement that marks his clear arrival as a talented director and actor.

In chapter 5, "Eastwood's Treatment of the Life of Creativity and Performance in *Bronco Billy*, *Honkytonk Man*, *White Hunter Black Heart*, and *Bird*," Dennis Rothermel claims that—apart from the dominant themes of law, justice, vengeance, war, and violence in his films—Eastwood also focuses upon the issues of creativity and performance. Artistic issues lie close to the heart of a man who regularly combines his creative efforts as an actor, a director, and a composer in his films. Certain films offer ample evidence of Eastwood's admiration for country-western singers, jazz musicians, and other filmmakers. Rothermel maintains that Eastwood's treatment of the showman in *Bronco Billy* (1980), the singer in *Honkytonk Man* (1982), the filmmaker in *White Hunter Black Heart* (1990), and musician Charlie Parker in *Bird* (1988) reveals one of Eastwood's major concerns—the performer and the artist.

In chapter 6, "'You Can't Hunt Alone': *White Hunter Black Heart*," Richard Hutson, while focusing on *White Hunter*, examines a crucial period during Eastwood's filmmaking. Beginning with *Bird* in 1988 and continuing for a little over a decade to *True Crime* (1999), Eastwood seems to have been obsessed with characters deeply divided between the desire to do the right thing and impulses that thwart that intention. *Bird* provides a powerful example of the brilliant saxophonist, Charlie Parker, whose musical genius is always jeopardized by his drug addiction. *Unforgiven* presents a character who vows to follow the peaceful path advocated by his dead wife but then reverts to his unreformed self, an alcohol-fueled, brutal killer. In *White Hunter Black Heart*, Eastwood portrays the film director John Wilson, who is willing to jeopardize a film project and everyone within the company to go big-game hunting in Africa. After Wilson gets the actors and crew to Africa, he refuses to begin shooting the film until he shoots an elephant. Wilson is a profoundly contradictory character, asserting his independence by going to Africa yet, at the same time, defending Hollywood. He wants to play the role of the lone artist but ultimately, and tragically, learns that filmmaking, like hunting, is a collaborative act, the art of compromise among conflicting ideas, pressures, and personalities. Eastwood claims that he played the character, representative of John Huston and also of Eastwood himself, as a purely fictional character. Richard Hutson's view is that Eastwood used the film to engage in a serious meditation on himself as an actor-writer-director and the implications of being an artist in Hollywood.

Craig Rinne in chapter 7, "The End of History and America First: How the 1990s Revitalized Clint Eastwood," examines *Heartbreak Ridge* (1986), *Unforgiven* (1992), *In the Line of Fire* (1993), and *A Perfect World* (1993) in the context of American society and culture in the 1990s. In *Heartbreak Ridge*, Eastwood's character, Gunnery Sergeant Tom Highway, achieves redemption for a failed personal life and an unclear military career by participating in the 1983 invasion of Grenada. Certainly, the redemptive narrative is nothing new to Eastwood's characters, but the aged character played by Eastwood literally adds a new wrinkle to the story. The incorporation of the Grenada invasion adds an allegorical layer: The film is not only about Gunny Highway or Eastwood; it has something to do with the redemption of America.

The theme of the aging hero atoning for youthful sins, however, needed the 1990s to truly resonate. In 1989, the Berlin Wall fell, and as Communism crumbled, the United States seemed to have won the Cold War. Francis Fukuyama proposed that the end of history, ideologically speaking, had arrived; Patrick Buchanan argued that now was the time for a foreign policy that considered "America first." Not so coincidentally, Eastwood returned to prominence along with the Western and America's search for a new national identity and purpose after the Cold War. With the success of *Unforgiven* (including Academy Awards for Best Picture and Best Director), quickly followed by his starring in Wolfgang Petersen's *In the Line of Fire* and then directing and playing a supporting role in the critically acclaimed *A Perfect World*, Eastwood enjoyed a renaissance, reestablishing himself as a box-office star while establishing himself as a renowned director. This renaissance was based on his redemptive persona, for it meshed with America's tentative steps into the post–Cold War era. In all three films, Eastwood's characters grapple with the mistakes of their youth in narratives that refer to and rework American history. Such narratives allegorize a 1990s America that looks back at its Cold War past while exploring the new possibilities of its present.

While many scholars argue for the importance of Eastwood's *Unforgiven* (1992) to the canon of the American Western, few discern its complex relationship with film noir. In chapter 8, "'A Man of Notoriously Vicious and Intemperate Disposition': Western Noir and the Tenderfoot's Revenge in *Unforgiven*," Stanley Orr addresses Eastwood's evocation and subversion of the noir Western in *Unforgiven*. With recourse to several theorists, Orr provides an overview of the Western as a major "host-genre" for film noir. Orr begins by analyzing Western noir conventions in mid-twentieth-century films. He then examines how Eastwood's film reprises the noir Western, concluding with what some critics might term a "postmodernist parody" of the noir worldview. This argument turns upon the tensions between dime novelist W. W. Beauchamp (Saul Rubinek) and gunslingers English Bob (Richard Harris), Little Bill Daggett (Gene Hackman), and, especially, Will Munny (Eastwood). Defined by violence and vernacular dialogue, these hard-boiled figures—men of "notoriously vicious and intemperate disposition"—ultimately find themselves contending with Beauchamp's florid prose, which threatens to subsume the universe of the film. Orr concludes that *Unforgiven*, while in many ways an exemplary noir Western, ultimately transcends generic labels to deepen noir's darkly realistic vision of the self and the world.

In chapter 9, "A Good Vintage or Damaged Goods? Clint Eastwood and Aging in Hollywood Film," Philippa Gates discusses the actor as the epitome of tough American masculinity. Eastwood established himself playing vigilante heroes in Westerns in the 1950s and 1960s and then took the Western hero to the mean city streets in the 1970s and 1980s. Up to his late seventies, Eastwood continued to play leading roles in Hollywood films, surviving the kiss of death for a film star—old age. He has remained a contemporary icon of American masculinity despite the fact that conceptions of masculinity and heroism have undergone radical change since the 1960s—or, as this chapter argues, *because* they have. In over fifty years on-screen, Eastwood has transformed himself from being an ideal for young viewers to being one for an older generation. From the tough guy to the tough guy with the heart of gold, Eastwood offers fantasies of the golden years, embodying masculinity that is tested—and proved to be vital and valued. How did Eastwood beat the Hollywood clock? It was not by resisting the aging process, as Hollywood's leading ladies are expected to do, but by embracing it. In Eastwood's films since the early 1990s, such as *Unforgiven* (Eastwood, 1992), *In the Line of Fire* (Petersen, 1993), *Absolute Power* (Eastwood, 1997), *True Crime* (Eastwood, 1999), *Space Cowboys* (Eastwood, 2000), and *Blood Work* (Eastwood, 2002), much is made of Eastwood's age. According to Gates, Eastwood's aging face and body are presented as a spectacle for the audience to behold; thus his body's physical vulnerability is offered to audiences as an emotional sounding board. With this perceived vulnerability, Eastwood's tough-guy past is tempered, and his image is aligned with contemporary ideals of masculinity as physical and heroic but, simultaneously, sensitive and romantic. Eastwood thus becomes as much a hero for the early twenty-first century as he once was for the mid-twentieth. In his films of the last decade, he has transformed his image—from a man's man to a ladies' man, from tough guy to good father, from loner to lover—all through highlighting his aging body.

Brad Klypchak in chapter 10, "Space, Pace, and Southern Gentility in *Midnight in the Garden of Good and Evil*," examines Eastwood's manipulation of cinematic elements to depict Southern gentility. For the adaptation of John Berendt's novel *Midnight in the Garden of Good and Evil* (1994), Eastwood chose to shoot on location in Savannah, Georgia, thus drawing upon a prevailing sense of the historic South. Be it the Spanish architecture, the garden squares and their statuary, or the rich contrast between the green foliage and the drooping Spanish moss, the film creates an appropriate mood for its representation of Southern gentility. Eastwood uses the outdoor settings, long tracking shots, and limited cuts to move languidly through the travelogue-esque beauty that emanates from Savannah. Through these sequences, Eastwood eases the viewer into a pace of leisure and privileged serenity, characteristic of the Southern social elite.

Eastwood then juxtaposes scenes whose textures contrast with the idyllic image of Southern gentility. As the action moves indoors, an underlying sense of threat becomes evident as characters such as Jim Williams revel in both the beauty and the sordidness of society life. Contrasts in composition highlight the divide between a surface of gentility and the evils hidden beneath its thin veneer. The museum-like Mercer House enshrines ritual displays where hospitality and status are performed by rote. But Eastwood's treatment of the seedier elements of Savannah, including Williams's penchant for voodoo and the city's local drag circuit, reveals facets of Savannah quite different from its Southern charm. By manipulating space and pace so that they invite the viewer to reconsider Southern gentility, Eastwood expands upon the Berendt novel and its complexities of character and action.

In chapter 11, "*Mystic River* as a Tragic Action," Robert Merrill and John L. Simons argue that *Mystic River* (2003) is one of two tragedies Eastwood has starred in or directed. (The other is *Letters from Iwo Jima* [2006].) They first discuss the strategies Eastwood employs, especially in his Westerns and crime films, to approach but ultimately avoid tragic conclusions, with special attention to *Unforgiven* (1992) and *Million Dollar Baby* (2004), films often characterized as tragic but better understood as serious, but nontragic, actions. The core of their essay explains how *Mystic River* honors novelist Dennis Lehane's stated intention to write a classical tragedy by adapting his novel as faithfully as possible. The authors feel that the result is very possibly Eastwood's most distinguished film.

In chapter 12, "Lies of Our Fathers: Mythology and Artifice in Eastwood's Cinema," William Beard argues that *Flags of Our Fathers* (2006) is the most extended and articulate iteration of a theme that has been a distinguishing feature of Eastwood's cinema for many years. According to Beard, Eastwood typically accompanies his representations of heroic and superheroic characters and actions with indications of their artifice. Beard traces the history of this theme throughout Eastwood's work, illustrating its operation in four films: *Bronco Billy* (1980), *Heartbreak Ridge* (1986), *Unforgiven* (1992), and, above all, *Flags of Our Fathers*. *Bronco Billy* invests redemptive, social power in the entirely self-constructed and overly naive mythology of its hero. *Heartbreak Ridge* dramatizes the absurdity of the popgun invasion of Grenada, which was meant to counter our defeat in Vietnam. *Unforgiven* excavates the mythic power of the Eastwood cowboy hero to discover demonic passions incompatible with any kind of true heroism. And *Flags of Our Fathers* deconstructs the process whereby heroic nation-saving mythology is fabricated out of lies. In all of these cases, the films insist on the healing power, the practical success, and even the necessity of these mythologies. At the same time, the films substantially undermine such myths. The entire process demonstrates how very unusual and counterintuitive Eastwood's cinema actually is when examined closely. His uniqueness clearly emerges, Beard argues, in the contrast between the myth-destroying ethos of *Flags* and the mythic pieties of a nominally more liberal strain of "Good War" filmmaking as exemplified by Spielberg's *Saving Private Ryan* (1998), Ken Burns's *The War* (2007), and the Dream-Works/HBO series *Band of Brothers* (2001) and *The Pacific* (2010).

John M. Gourlie in chapter 13, "Eastwood's *Flags of Our Fathers* and *Letters from Iwo Jima*: The Silence of Heroes and the Voice of History," discusses how Eastwood offers to our picture of history both a second and a very different third cinematic view on one of the most revered battles of World War II. *Flags* (2006) gives us a multifaceted portrayal of the human encounter with a searing experience of war—specifically from the perspective of the U.S. Marines who fought at Iwo Jima in 1945. Focusing on the lives of the Marines who were photographed raising the American flag above Mount Suribachi, the film explores why these soldiers did not consider themselves "heroes," even though the American public indelibly fixed this image upon them. In theme and cinematic technique, *Flags* contrasts the Marines' lived experience to popular conceptions of "heroism." Closely following James Bradley's book, Eastwood's film searches into the souls of those soldiers performing the actions that we, as a nation, honor as heroic. It is a search that incinerates most of our conceptions and myths regarding heroism without diminishing the men who actually fought the battle.

Eastwood's companion film *Letters* (2006) presents the island battle from the perspective of the Japanese soldiers who fought it. Told in a straightforward, flashback narrative, the film opens with Japanese researchers in white overalls unearthing a cache of letters, written by the soldiers defending Iwo Jima and buried in the floor of their cave when defeat seemed certain. *Letters* provides an extended consideration of the concept of "honor" through the eyes of the Japanese soldiers facing death on the island. According to Gourlie, these two films serve as stories that reshape how we see our history. If we learn their lessons, such stories can perhaps lead us to create a new history, one where the accolades of "hero" and "honor" no longer signify that the blood of the world's youth has been spilled.

In chapter 14, "*Gran Torino*: Showdown in Detroit, Shrimp Cowboys, and a New Mythology," we examine the increasing emphasis on family in Eastwood's mature films. With family comes a sense of the past, often a dysfunctional past in which the normal bonds among family members have failed. Such failures of the past haunt the present-day action of

Gran Torino (2008). Their ghostly grip gives the film's action emotional resonance and depth of meaning. In addition, the multicultural social context of the film can be viewed against the backdrop of Eastwood's Westerns as another ghost of the past that haunts the present action. In *Gran Torino* a complex battle for possession of the neighborhood is occurring. No longer between White Man and Indian, this battle is now among various races and ethnic groups and is set not on the open plains but in a decaying city—Detroit. Sometime after the nineteenth-century cowboy stopped riding a horse, he began riding a pickup truck or, in this film, a Gran Torino, the prized possession of Walt Kowalski (Eastwood). In passing the keys to Kowalski's Hmong "son" at the end of the film, Eastwood seems to present a new mythology to replace the decayed and broken one of the past. The price of this new mythology of American manhood is Eastwood's sacrifice of himself as the embodiment of all that symbolizes the old conception of American manhood—war hero, craftsman, middle-class homeowner—and by extension, Western gunman and hero. The film suggests as much in its image of Walt's death, where his body lies riddled with bullets in a crucifixion pose. As heir to the Gran Torino, the Hmong youth rides with Walt's dog into the sunset of America—this time along the waters of the Great Lakes.

Is Eastwood working toward a new mythology? The film seems to suggest that a man's true family may not simply be his bloodline kin. It might not even be among his own race or ethnicity but might include those of other ethnicities, such as the barber, the construction boss, and even those as "foreign" as the Hmong neighbors. In suggesting that the keys to American manhood can be passed to immigrant sons of another race, Eastwood seems to be laying out a narrative of such a mythology. In its larger implications the film embraces humanity. In its mythology, the principle "All Men Are Created Equal" truly includes all men and all women—of whatever ethnicity or race—in the American community.

In chapter 15, "*Invictus*: The Master Craftsman as Hagiographer," Raymond Foery states that *Invictus* (2009) is a powerful tribute to Nelson Mandela in which Eastwood explores the nature of political leadership within the dynamic of cinematic language. After briefly surveying Eastwood's portrayal of the antihero (as both actor and director) in his earlier films, Foery argues that with Mandela, Eastwood has a genuine hero, one might even say a saint. This is the premise of the film and the approach Eastwood takes toward constructing the narrative. Thus, *Invictus* is a kind of cinematic hagiography, or at least one chapter in the story of the life of this particular, saintly individual, a man so revered that he provokes responses like the one Matt Damon's character gives to the question of what the great man might be like: "He's not like anyone I've ever met before." Carefully constructing his dramatic narrative and choosing meaningful camera shots and angles, Eastwood's disciplined directorial style at times mirrors that of his larger-than-life subject and at other times contrasts with it. The ultimate effect is to capture the brilliance of Mandela's leadership as it entrains Captain Francois Pienaar and the Springbok rugby team in order to guide them in a strategy to unify the country through their athletic victory in the World Cup. Foery's analysis demonstrates how Eastwood's own brilliance as a director seamlessly creates the cinematic strategies that render both the humility and the grandeur of Mandela's character while endowing the film's action with dramatic intensity and deep meaning.

In chapter 16, "*Hereafter*: Dreaming beyond Our Philosophies," John Gourlie examines Eastwood's treatment of a most unusual subject matter—the near-death experience and a psychic medium who can communicate beyond the grave. While such material is highly unusual, Gourlie argues that Eastwood nevertheless pursues certain of his traditional themes—human isolation and silence—as the main characters, the French journalist Marie, the psychic George, and the bereaved youth Marcus, are driven by their experiences out of mainstream society to the lonely edges of existence. Indeed, the subject matter of *Hereafter* enables Eastwood to probe the meaning of life and death more openly and directly than in any of his other films. For Eastwood, this meaning is found ever more clearly in the bonds of the human family. Symbolizing these bonds, the journalist, the psychic, and the young boy essentially unite in the drama as the elements of such a family. The heroic truths of life are no longer embodied in "the stranger" or "the man with no name." Instead of a hero's guns ablaze in a quest for vengeance, it is the kiss that Marie and George share at the film's end that bespeaks life's values and truths. In their embrace, the film implies that love, communication, and human bonding constitute life's core values and truths. The film further implies that these values and we ourselves have currency not only in the "here" but in the hereafter as well. If it is nothing else, *Hereafter* is a testament to the artistic distance Eastwood has traveled as a filmmaker, and it especially reflects the courage and daring with which he has undertaken this creative journey.

In chapter 17, "Citizen Hoover: Clint Eastwood's *J. Edgar*," Kathleen Moran and Richard Hutson point out how Eastwood throughout his career (as actor and/or as director) has emphasized the outsider, the maverick, who refuses to play by the ordinary rules of being a cop or being an artist of one sort or another. This protagonist has deeply divided commitments, or oppositions, that often lead to destruction. In *J. Edgar* (2011), by contrast, Eastwood presents a pathologically focused character, one so obsessively single-minded in his view of the world that it is almost impossible for him to imagine simple matters of humanity. Eastwood's Hoover has difficulty thinking about anything other than his job as the chief law officer of the land. Thus, early in the film, J. Edgar appears to be the ultimate insider, a man in a highly important administrative post who wields unprecedented power over others, including U.S. presidents. However, by the end, Hoover works so intensely as an insider, operating so completely inside a "closet" of power, that he is finally an outsider. He is America's chief lawman who almost always works outside the laws of the land. To a surprising extent, he ends up a geriatric, pop psychology version of Dirty Harry: the lonely enforcer of the nation's morals, even as he is constantly breaking her most basic laws. The film is a critique not only of J. Edgar Hoover's distorted understanding of justice but perhaps also of the pathological potential inherent in the avenging heroes Eastwood himself embodied earlier in his career.

■ ■ ■

As unlikely as it might have seemed at the time, say, of *High Plains Drifter*, Eastwood's films have now reached a pitch where they portray an artist's vision of life, its tragedies, and finally—however obscured, denied, or beset—its ultimate value. And looking back, we can see throughout the many films of Eastwood's career a developing sensibility that has so grown in power and capacity that it unfolds an artistic vision worthy of his maturity.

As the writers in this collection explore Eastwood's films anew, a common thread is their respect for Eastwood's sustained commitment to cinematic storytelling. In its own way, each essay examines certain films of Eastwood's career, and collectively, they illuminate his achievements as a filmmaker. In examining his Westerns and detective films, these essays suggest how Eastwood put his individual stamp on those particular genres.

And in examining his more recent films, the essays suggest how he has used family, history, and myth to transcend generic conventions and to project a hard-won vision of humanity united beyond the chasms of its ethnic, racial, and national conflicts. In light of the artistic vision of Eastwood's maturity, the essays seek to extend and enrich our understanding of his achievements by illuminating the pathways he took. Cumulatively, they remind us of his lifelong devotion to perfecting his artistry and his powers as a storyteller. As Yeats wrote, it is as though Eastwood's soul increasingly found the way to sing more loudly, whatever the tatters of mortal dress, to us his audience—we lords and ladies of Byzantium—of what matters, "of what is past, or passing, or to come."

■ Note

1. We have updated our remarks on Eastwood's films for the current introduction. However, for a fuller overview and discussion of Eastwood's life and work, we refer the reader to our "Introduction" in our first collection (Gourlie and Engel 2007). In the current introduction, where we briefly describe each chapter, we have frequently drawn upon the language of the contributing writer. Likewise, we have drawn in several places upon our own perceptions and language from the 2007 "Introduction" in reaffirming our understanding of Eastwood's accomplishments.

■ Bibliography

Beard, William. 2000. *Persistence of Double Vision: Essays on Clint Eastwood*. Edmonton: University of Alberta Press.

Brauer, Ralph. 1975. *The Horse, the Gun, the Piece of Property*. Bowling Green: Bowling Green State University Press.

Cornell, Drucilla. 2009. *Clint Eastwood and Issues of American Masculinity*. New York: Fordham University Press.

Eliot, Marc. 2009. *American Rebel: The Life of Clint Eastwood*. New York: Harmony Books.

Engel, Leonard, ed. 2007. *Clint Eastwood, Actor and Director: New Perspectives*. Salt Lake City: University of Utah Press.

Foote, John H. 2009. *Clint Eastwood: Evolution of a Filmmaker*. Westport, Conn.: Praeger.

Frayling, Christopher. 2000. "The Making of Sergio Leone's *A Fistful of Dollars*." *Cineaste* 25, no. 3: 14–23.

Gallafent, Edward. 1994. *Clint Eastwood: Filmmaker and Star*. New York: Continuum.

Gourlie, John M., and Leonard Engel. 2007. "Introduction." In *Clint Eastwood, Actor and Director: New Perspectives*, ed. Leonard Engel, 1–23. Salt Lake City: University of Utah Press.

Hughes, Howard. 2010. *Aim for the Heart: The Films of Clint Eastwood*. London: I. B. Tauris.

Jardine, Gail. 1994. "Clint: Cultural Critic, Cowboy of Cathartic Change." *Art Journal* 53, no. 3 (Fall): 74–75.

Johnstone, Iain. 1981. *The Man with No Name*. New York: Morrow Quill.

Kael, Pauline. 1994. *For Keeps: 30 Years at the Movies*. New York: Dutton.

Kehr, David. 2004. "Eastwood Noir." Based on *American Masters Documentary*, aired September 27, 2000. PBS, http://www.pbs.org/wnet/americanmasters/episodes/clint-eastwood/eastwood-noir/582/.

Kitses, Jim. 2004. *Horizons West: Directing the Western from John Ford to Clint Eastwood*. London: British Film Institute.

Koehler, Robert. 2000. "Clint Eastwood: From Oaters to Auteur." *Variety* 380, no. 2: Arts Module, F-12.

Miller, Jim. 1987. "Clint Eastwood: A Different Kind of Hero." In *Shooting Stars: Heroes and Heroines of Western Film*, ed. Archie P. McDonald, 182–95. Bloomington: University of Indiana Press.

O'Brien, Geoffrey. 2003. "Fallen World: *Mystic River*." *New York Review of Books*, December 18, 67–70.

Schickel, Richard. 1996. *Clint Eastwood: A Biography*. New York: Vintage, a Division of Random House.

———. 2010. *Clint: A Retrospective*. Intro. by Clint Eastwood. New York: Sterling Publishing.

Sheehan, Henry. 1992. "Scraps of Hope: Clint Eastwood and the Western." *Film Comment*, September/October: 17–27.

Smith, Paul. 1993. *Clint Eastwood: A Cultural Production*. American Culture, vol. 8. Minneapolis: University of Minnesota Press.

Thompson, Richard, and Tim Hunter. 1978. "Clint Eastwood, Auteur." *Film Comment*, January/February: 24–31.

CHAPTER 1

"LANDSCAPE AS MORAL DESTINY": MYTHIC REINVENTION FROM ROWDY YATES TO THE STRANGER

Robert Smart

> The commercial value of the West—for fiction and for
> film—resides in the movement between proclaimed
> absence and textual presence, in the nostalgic portrayal
> of an image and era marked as passing if not passed.
>
> —BILL BROWN

In a recent review of an essay collection by Joyce Carol Oates in the *New York Times Book Review*, Louisa Thomas notes that "here violence is a fact, and survival isn't confused with redemption" (2010, 13). Much the same could be said of the first of Sergio Leone's "spaghetti Westerns," which rescued Clint Eastwood from a moribund acting career in the Western TV series *Rawhide*, whose basic episodic formula had changed little since its debut in January 1959. "Rowdy Yates, Idiot of the Plains" is how Eastwood would later characterize his role on *Rawhide* (Schickel 1996, 109). Nonetheless, a career as long as Eastwood's invites questions about origins, exegetic arguments that attempt to bring a historical sensibility to current work by sifting through the sometimes serendipitous choices and developments over the previous sixty years of work for clues about how the "iconic" Eastwood character was born. The development of Eastwood's character Rowdy Yates prior to his evolution into The Stranger or The Man with No Name is key to understanding what Eastwood found attractive in Leone's description of the *Dollars* film idea, and it is instructive for the later developments of Eastwood's long creative career.

In this brief filmic exegesis, I mean to examine Eastwood's transition from Rowdy Yates to The Stranger in Sergio Leone's 1964 *A Fistful of Dollars* (first screened in the United States in 1967 because of a copyright snafu with Akira Kurosawa, whose *Yojimbo* was the immediate inspiration for Leone's first low-budget blockbuster). Most specifically, I want to argue by triangulation for a transition to *A Fistful of Dollars* from *Rawhide* that is more nuanced than the usual (brief) commentaries on the *Rawhide* years, first by exploring the serial Western form and developing a critical lexicon that provides a means for us to understand the sort of apprenticeship Eastwood underwent between 1959 and 1966. The key focus of this first leg of the critical triangle will be the *Rawhide* years. From there, once the context for Eastwood's "gamble" on a role in a low-budget Western directed by an Italian who spoke little or no English is established, *A Fistful of Dollars* will be examined with an eye to understanding why this decision was really no gamble at all. Thence, and finally, we move to a discussion of Eastwood through his work on the *Dollars* trilogy, after which he was anyone but the "Idiot on the Plains." What should become clear is that Eastwood's apprenticeship in the television Western serial gave him a powerful and creative understanding of the mythic landscapes and stories that fed the classic Western form and encouraged him to reinvent both himself and that form in subsequent films. The success of that process is inarguable; the specific origins of his successful reinventions might not be so obvious.

■ The West, the Western Serial, and *Rawhide*

> In *Rawhide*, I got to play every day. It taught me how to pick up and run, how to make things up, wing things in there.
>
> —CLINT EASTWOOD, 1985

When Clint Eastwood accepted the role of ramrod in the Western serial *Rawhide*, his career "had actually been in decline" (Frayling 2005, 43);[1] the main role of trail boss in the series (which was originally titled *Cattle Drive*) was played by actor Eric Fleming, whose screen credits also did not mark him as a big name draw to the show. Intended as a series that would draw audiences from the most popular Western series on television at the time, *Wagon Train*, which starred actor Ward Bond, *Rawhide* was CBS's attempt to create a new setting for the serial Western without fussing with what was obviously a profitable and popular formula. In fact, television playlists for 1958–59 featured several Western serials, at least one of which still holds the record for longest-running network serial, *Gunsmoke*. Other popular series included *Cheyenne, Maverick, Bronco, Lawman, The Rifleman, Wyatt Earp, Sugarfoot,* and *Have Gun Will Travel*.[2] Unlike all of these other shows, *Rawhide* and *Wagon Train* rely on the pilgrimage formula, relatively unchanged from Chaucer's *Canterbury Tales*, in which the cast of characters, united by a single-minded purpose (moving cattle to the northern stockyards, or leaving civilization behind for a new home in unknown territory), encounters a number of incidents that threaten their progress toward completion of this purpose and, for the most part, who prevail through a combination of pluck, luck, and providence.

In the other Western serials, the formula focuses on a location, a relatively new town (Dodge City in *Gunsmoke*, for example) or a hardscrabble ranch or farm (the McCains's ranch in *The Rifleman*), or on the single traveler/adventurer/picaro type who wanders from city to city encountering various characters and villains who test his skills, usually his skills with a gun (*Maverick*, *Sugarfoot*, and *Have Gun Will Travel*, e.g.). In all of these settings (and repeated weekly), the survival of the settlement at the end of the episode satisfies the episodic formula, something that historian Richard Slotkin among others has correctly pegged to the politics of the time. The late 1950s were an uneasy time, and these serial Westerns embodied "the central paradox of America's self-image in an era of Cold War, 'subversion,' and the thermonuclear balance of terror: our sense of being at once supremely powerful and utterly vulnerable, politically dominant and yet helpless to shape the course of crucial events" (Slotkin 1998, 383). The formulaic resolutions of these Westerns seemed blessedly unambiguous compared with the geopolitics of the age. We will return to this connection later, but for now it is important to recognize that the power of these satisfactory endings lay as much with the expectations of a Cold War audience as with the rapidly tiring elements of the Western serial (Slotkin 1998, 381).

In his provocative and insightful collection of essays on film, Stanley Cavell describes this reliable formula for the serial Western in terms that aptly capture the difference between a show like *Rawhide* and a show like *Gunsmoke*; it is worth quoting at length:

> If classical narrative can be pictured as the progress from the establishing of one stable situation, through an event of difference, to the re-establishing of a stable situation related to the original one, serial procedure [i.e., the Western serial] can be thought of as the establishing of a stable condition punctuated by repeated crises or events that are not developments of the situation requiring a single resolution, but intrusions or emergencies—of humour, or adventure, or talent, or misery—each of which runs a natural

course and thereupon rejoins the realm of the uneventful; which is perhaps to say, serial procedure is un-dialectical. (1988, 258)

In most Western serials, the "stable situation" is the town or the homestead, a vulnerable location that is threatened by the untethered, hostile elements that usually arrive out of nowhere to threaten the lives of the settled. These are most often outlaws or strangers from other lands, and the most pressing need in each episode is to reestablish the sanctity and stability of the city or ranch or homestead. In serials like *Rawhide* and *Wagon Train*, however, the spatial dimension of the show is already in flux: the herd and the twenty–twenty-five men charged with bringing it to a northern stockyard for sale are moving, often through indistinct or unknown territory, hostile territory on occasion.[3] The parts that need stabilizing after threat from outside the group are the relationships in that group, most especially among and between the main characters of the story. In the case of *Rawhide*, the chief relationship is between Gil(bert) Favor, trail boss, and his ramrod, Rowdy Yates.

In both kinds of serials, the action is ahistorical, with few references to actual events outside the narrative; the focus is on the tensions between settled and unsettled in the case of the majority of the Western serials or between the necessarily tight relationships of the key characters in the pilgrimage formula of serials like *Rawhide* and the unplanned or unusual events that threaten those relationships from the outside. According to critic Edward Gallafent,

> History cannot give meaning to the different personalities of what these two characters [Favor and Yates] could do or be, because the "stable condition" of the series has no way of, or perhaps interest in, addressing this. Most obviously, no liaison with a woman can be permanent—and neither of them can die. . . . [N]o great moment of change can be evoked, no emphasis on the uniqueness of any specific event in history (which can be a crucial event in the drama of the Western), no movement between the different qualities of past and future. (1994, 13)

This timeless, mythic quality will become an important legacy for Eastwood when he moves from this aging serial to his Italian adventure with Sergio Leone, but at this stage of the conversation, the importance of this strict focus on the key relationships restricts the action in the episodes (or "incidents," as they are almost all called) by implicitly guaranteeing that there will be a reconciliation and return to "normalcy" at the end of the episode, especially with audiences as well informed about how these serials work as those in the 1950s were. As Gallafent further notes, this return to stasis "is the *donnée* of a particular series [because it] either locates the action in an unspecific historical present, or offers a simple cyclical pattern based around the seasons of TV scheduling" (1994, 12).

This general ahistoricity, however, is also freeing in a particularly significant way for a burgeoning director like Eastwood. While supposedly set in the 1860s, when plenty of historical elements could have tied the series to its setting and time, the series floats through the nineteenth century, barely noting changes in technology (transportation and communication, for example), business (the changed landscape of American capitalism after Jackson, for example), or history (the changed American South postwar or the renewed Indian wars that eventually "solved" the "Indian problem"). Instead of using the moment of the drama to reflect on current issues and fears, *Rawhide* cycles a limited number of plot threats to heighten the mythic dimension of the serial. Episodes such as "Incident at Superstition Prairie" (December 2, 1960) or "Incident of the Haunted Hills" (November 6, 1959) play on Native mysticism, at a time, incidentally, that the people who were associated with these mysteries and legends were disappearing. "Incident of the Golden Calf" (March 13, 1959) adapts Old Testament narratives to the "modern West," while episodes like "Incident of the Prodigal Son" (October 19, 1962) focus on well-worn plots that drive straight to the central relationships of the series, all with the implicit promise that these relationships will survive and thrive. The setting of the series supports this timelessness: vast prairies, stark mountain ranges, tumbleweeds, threatening cliffs, all highlighted on occasion by spectacular *Lear*-like storms that emphasize the vulnerability of the stable center in such inhospitable terrain. This last point also frustrated Eastwood, who was developing a director's eye for setting and the potential that change in setting has for becoming dialogue, moral dialogue that foreshadows action (Schickel 1996, 126). The studio relied on a limited number of stock shots of the Arizona landscape and of the cattle drive, in which director Bill Warren insisted "that cattle on the move always had to traverse the screen in the same direction" (Schickel 1996, 112). Predictability and conformity trumped realism, something Eastwood would never allow to dictate in his subsequent breakout work in the Western genre.

There is one historical element, however, that does find its way into the series, albeit almost unnoticed, and once established, it has ultimately little to no impact on the development of the series. It comes in the third (1960) season, in "The Incident at Poco Tiempo" (December 9), when we learn not only that Rowdy Yates joined the Confederate Army when he was sixteen years old but that his father, Dan Yates, was as bad a husband as he was a father. We also learn that Gil Favor served as a Confederate captain during the war.[4] However tempting these tidbits are for establishing a more historically bound story, they are all but forgotten the next week.[5] Nothing remains of these provocative personal histories from episode to episode because the essential formula for the Western serial is not progressive, or in Cavell's term, "dialectical." Each episode (with some few exceptions, for example, when the cattle drive finally does come to its elusive destination, Sedalia, Missouri, for the first time in the third season) illustrates the risks that threaten the central relationships of the series, the dependence of men on each other for their survival, and the return of stasis to those relationships completes the moral trajectory of each episode. All is well, and the audience waits for another week for another threat.

By the time the series ended in 1966, Eastwood was more than ready for something new. His era of serial Westerns had clearly run its course, and *Rawhide* in particular had suffered from being left in the hands of several unimaginative directors after Bill Warren left the show in 1960. In addition, the departure of the show's lead, Eric Fleming, after season 7, while it would seem to have opened the door for Eastwood to realize much of what he had wanted to try, produced little in the way of real change for the new lead or for the tired formula of the series. And by 1966 the country had added a "hot" war to the twenty-year-old Cold War: Vietnam.[6] But when Clint Eastwood left for Rome in April 1964, on his "gamble" with Italian director Sergio Leone, he had learned several key elements of the Western that would mark his later work. As he described this moment in 1971 to Stuart Kaminsky, "In TV, I saw so much that I *wouldn't* do" (Kapsis and Coblenz 1999, 10). First, he understood that the Western formula should not subsume the central character—that would be the surest way to becoming moribund and stale. The character becomes the formula, in a way, something that must have occurred however incompletely to Leone as he watched the one episode of *Rawhide* and saw in Eastwood something that none of the many directors and producers of the show had been willing to see.

Second, Eastwood's long-standing desire to shift dialogue away from the character to the landscape reflected what he had learned in watching the formulaic settings of *Rawhide* elide any possibility of depth and complexity in the stories. This is how Richard Schickel describes Eastwood's growing understanding of this signature shift:

> When the company was on location in Paso Robles earlier that [third] season shooting a cattle stampede, Clint was in the middle of it thinking, God, there are some great shots here, and I'm in a position to get them. So he went to [Bill] Warren and pointed out that if he was given a hand-held camera he could ride low in the saddle or even dismount, and move among the animals, getting close-ups that the stationary cameras, set up on the periphery of the action, could not possibly obtain. (1996, 126)

The answer was no, of course, but the incident reveals much about this young actor/director's learning process, especially about the potential for landscape to carry moral meaning, at least as well as substitute for spoken dialogue.

Eastwood also came to appreciate the renewability of the Western mythos, a point over which he and Sergio Leone especially agreed. This regeneration was not so much a matter of adding new elements to the timeworn genre as it was a need to reduce the stories to essential elements and then stylize the action to highlight the fluid power of the Western to define and reaffirm the moral architecture of this American myth. Richard Slotkin explains the point this way:

> The consonance between the formal character of the gunfighter Western and its ideological content is a genuinely poetic achievement. It gave the gunfighter films ideological and cinematic resonance and made the heroic style of the gunfighter an important symbol of right and heroic action for filmmakers, the public, and the nation's political leadership. (1998, 379–80)

This is a fundamental tension that the typical Cold War Western serial had avoided but which Eastwood came to understand was key to the survival and renewal of this quintessential American narrative genre. In Eastwood's and Leone's revision of the American Western, the camera would tell the story, mixing landscape and action together in the service of mythopoesis. *A Fistful of Dollars* would prove a powerful and popular amalgam of everything that Eastwood had learned from his years on *Rawhide* with everything Sergio Leone wanted to create from his lifelong affection for the American Western.

- A Palimpsest: Remaking the Western

> I kept thinking, . . . wouldn't it be great to play the hero sort of like the villain is normally portrayed, and give the villain some heroic qualities.
>
> —CLINT EASTWOOD, 1993

The only episode of *Rawhide* that Sergio Leone is known to have watched before he offered the role of The Stranger to Eastwood is number 91, which originally aired on November 10, 1961 (Frayling 2005, 83). We do not know exactly what he saw in this typical serial episode, but his later comments revolve around the figure of Eastwood's character and Leone's interest in the "catlike combination of indolence and menace . . . in Clint's movements" (Schickel 1996, 131). This now iconic character mix was something that Eastwood had long wanted to develop in Rowdy Yates but had been prevented from doing because of a rigid production regime and because the 1950s Western serial did not countenance that sort of complexity in the moral trajectory of the weekly stories. He was by all accounts, however, prepared to make the most of this European hiatus: "I'll go over there and learn some stuff. I'll see how other people make films in other countries" (in Schickel 1996, 132). And he arrived convinced that the stiff and awkward dialogue in the script that had been delivered to his home needed to be cut in favor of some of the ideas that he had been developing while on set for *Rawhide*.

The man that Eastwood was leaving the United States to meet had also arrived at this juncture through serendipity and kismet. Sergio Leone was the son of a cinephile artistic director, Vincenzo Leone; at age seventeen he entered the vibrant Italian film industry he loved and which had ostracized his father because of his socialist politics. After a long apprenticeship making "sword and sandals" epics as second-in-command with American actors who were past their prime in America, Leone put together the money (such as it was) and the talent to take an excursus into a film genre he had loved since childhood, the Western. The details of this meeting

between two artists at the end of the journeyman portions of their careers
have been detailed several times: the fact that Eastwood was not the studio's first choice—just the one contender willing to accept $15,000 for the
job uncontested; that Eastwood picked up most of his wardrobe in California on Rodeo Drive before leaving for Rome and that he brought his
Rawhide guns with him for the first film; and that Leone, despite his inability to speak English, was quickly willing to make his work with the lanky
American star a collaboration.[7] In 1984, Eastwood characterized his working relationship with the excitable Italian director this way:

> I spun off Sergio, and he spun off me. I think we worked well together. . . .
> He liked dealing with the kind of character I was putting together. The
> character [The Stranger/Joe] was written quite a bit different. I made it
> much more economical. Much less expository. . . . My theory to Sergio
> was, "I don't think you have to explain everything. Let the audience imag-
> ine with us." (Kapsis and Coblenz 1999, 91)

We can see a number of important developments here: the actor's voice is
directorial—Eastwood's collaboration with Leone brought his insights and
instincts about how to revision the moribund Western genre to bear on the
Fistful of Dollars screenplay.[8] More so, we can hear the careful delineation
of the new aesthetic that the film would come to embody in Eastwood's
description of the work he did with Leone: less spoken dialogue, more
depiction, greater reliance on landscape as dialogue, and clear focus on
character.

Martin Scorsese suggests that what Leone brought to the partnership—
in addition to a new directorial attitude toward working with actors—was
an Italian operatic sense. In a 2004 interview, he spoke admiringly about
Leone's work in the *Dollars* trilogy, noting that "Leone created new masks
for the Western, and he set new archetypes for a genre that needed fresh
influences. . . . [I]t was like the revision of a genre, in a way—or more like
an evolution of a genre, because the western genre was getting old at the
time" (in Frayling 2005, 201). Eastwood, himself, recognized that the stylization of the Western that he helped Leone realize came from a distinctly
Italianate source: "[The Italian Westerns] changed the style, the approach
to Westerns. They 'opera-cized' them. . . . They made the violence and the
shooting aspect a little more larger than life, and they had great music and
new types of scores" (in Frayling 2005, 101).

While the aesthetic had changed at the hands of Eastwood and Leone, the Western archetype remained very visible:

> The standard plot involved this loner riding into an isolated Southwestern shantytown—ruled by warring factions or clans (usually one Mexican, one gringo, divided by interests rather than values)—being seriously beaten up by one or both before defeating the strongest villain in a ritualized "settling of accounts." The gunman-trickster was distinctively dressed, he posed a lot, and he had distinctive weapons as well. (Frayling 2005, 177)

The emphasis in this formula is on spectacle, and the focus is on the main character, the loner. The setting is anarchic and indistinct: it could be virtually anywhere within the Western mythic landscape.[9] The camera is not stationary but always moving, making us and the main character, Joe or The Stranger, essentially spectators, voyeurs in this earthbound hell.[10] In this new "operatic" Western, sounds are loud, actions are slow and stylized, and the focus rarely shifts away from the main character who will be the precipitant figure in the story, the one who makes everything happen. The key question at this point is why he does what he does.

At least at first, there is little in the story that reveals anything about why The Stranger does anything, aside from his oft expressed desire to serve himself by making money from anyone who will pay for his services. The Stranger is framed by two characters, and they, for a time, are triangulated by a key sympathetic element in the film: Marisol, who is married to a Mexican peasant and has a young son. The sympathetic Sancho Panza character is the cantina keeper Silvanito, who develops a grudging admiration and respect for the tight-lipped stranger, while the archenemy is one of the Rojo brothers, Ramon, whom we learn early in the film is a brutal killer without morals or scruples. Ramon has kidnapped the lovely Marisol from her husband and in an act that reveals how little value communal laws and customs have for such thugs, dissolves her marriage to her peasant husband, sending both him and the son off into their penury. The constant wailing of the distraught son pierces the soundtrack early and often, preventing the movie from settling into a too familiar and formulaic track and ensuring that the plight of this peasant family is never too far from the mind of the audience.

We see all this in fairly rapid order, following the "'rhetorical' use of the camera, which tended to linger on, and extend, the visual clichés of the

Hollywood Western as if they were a part of the liturgy" (Frayling 2005, 178). The scoring of the movie is striking, even after fifty years: it is a "memorable, up tempo musical score with unusual orchestration, echo effects, choral interludes, a Fender Stratocaster guitar, a catchy melody, and amplified natural sounds" (Frayling 2005, 178). In fact, the regular association of particular sounds with specific actions in the story (gunfights with specific trumpet crescendos, e.g.) almost makes the film like Sergei Prokofiev's classic musical opera *Peter and the Wolf*, where the specific musical signature tells the viewer what is about to happen. The action shifts between the Baxter gang (gringos) at one end of town and the Rojos at the other, for a time with The Stranger standing between the two in Silvanito's cantina, plotting how to make money from the two rival gangs. In quick order he offers his services to the Rojos and later to the Baxters, each time for a good deal of money. His role as spectator in the film is most fully developed in this first third of the movie, as he spies on Ramon Rojo's murder of a troop of soldiers in an arms deal gone wrong, spies on Marisol, and eavesdrops on the conversations between Ramon and his older brother Don Miguel Rojo. These spectator interludes provide The Stranger and us with information necessary for understanding the final quarter of the film, and they cut down on explication time, reinforce the outsider role of The Stranger, and cause us to speculate that there may be more to his motivations than simple greed.

The rapidity of events in the final third of the movie, from The Stranger's surprising offer to Marisol and her family to the final showdown with Ramon and the Rojo gang, became a trademark of Leone's "spaghetti Western" trilogy, rising from his belief that the audience came to see Westerns for the showdowns and gunfights (Frayling 2005, 145). It is in these final, dramatic scenes that the pedigree of the Western genre becomes clear. Each re-creation of the Western, I argued earlier, is a palimpsest, carrying with it—no matter the aesthetic or technical innovation—the DNA of the earliest films of the genre. Nowhere is this more evident in *A Fistful of Dollars* than in this final third of the film. Most revealing, perhaps, is The Stranger's sudden change of heart regarding the hapless Marisol and her family, kept in the audience's mind by the repeated squalling of her young son. Just after the middle of the story, when he has the opportunity to take up Marisol's cause against her captor Ramon, The Stranger returns her to captivity, dashing any hope we might have had that he was operating from more noble scruples than self-enrichment. Then suddenly he returns her to her husband and son when the Rojo gang is out chasing after a ruse that he and Silvanito set up. Handing her what appears to be all the money that he has made to date from the rival gangs, he sends them on their way to safety. When Marisol questions him, twice, about why he is acting so counter to the persona he has cultivated thus far in the movie, his answer resonates from within the established genre: "Why? Because I knew someone like you once, and there was no one there to help. Now get going!"

Here is where Leone's homage to the Westerns he so loved is clearest. In Edward Gallafent's analysis,

> The Americanness presented by Eastwood in this [part of the] film is expressed in two very traditional impulses of the Western hero—to support the little (powerless, unarmed, or old) man against the threat of the gunman, and to defend the family. . . . The vagueness and the impatience here [in the scene with Marisol's family] may be more than simply the gruffness of a man committing an act of generosity. They point to the degree to which the impulse to defend the "traditional" values now floats entirely free of any place with which it can be firmly identified or any narrative that can be realized or remembered—it has indeed to operate in the face of a surrounding world of unrelieved brutality. (1994, 17–18)

Thus the traditional elements of the Western genre are re-visioned within a structural aesthetic that is part Italian opera, part parody, and part homage. The same is true of the final showdown between the brutal and nihilistic Ramon and his gang, where every part of the Rojos' arrogant and violent world is systematically destroyed by The Stranger. The comic elements of this opposition, like The Stranger's inversion of Ramon's oft repeated celebration of the rifle over the six-gun, are part of the Leone/Eastwood aesthetic, a way of paying homage to and transcending the formulaic Western at the same time. The end result in *A Fistful of Dollars* is the realization of the character that Eastwood sought to craft out of his Rowdy Yates character but was prevented from doing, framed within the Western fantasy that Sergio Leone had nurtured since his childhood. For both Italian and (years later) American audiences, *A Fistful of Dollars* returned the Western to its point of origin, to the essential elements of the Western mythos. In an interview with Christopher Frayling, Leone made his intentions in this film project plain: "The basic idea, of course, was to use some of the conventions, devices, and settings of the American western film and a series of references to individual Westerns—to use these things to tell *my* version of the story of the birth of a nation" (2005, 31). That the trilogy is still studied by film students and cinephiles everywhere would suggest that both he and Eastwood succeeded in their "gamble."

■ From Story to Character: Mythopoesis and the West

> It's the climate that does it, that and the infernal distances . . . induces people to shoot persons in high places. . . . [I]t's a savage country, really.
> —ENGLISH BOB, in *Unforgiven*

In the May 17, 2011, Arts section of the *New York Times*, Seth Schiesel reviews the newest blockbuster video game, *Red Dead Redemption*. I would not have read the review necessarily (not being a video game player myself) were it not for the obvious resonances in it with this examination of the Western and the Eastwood/Leone refashioning of that venerable genre. The caption beneath the large, dramatic image from *Red Dead Redemption* reads, "The good, the bandits and the coyotes" (Schiesel 2011, C1), an obvious paean to the third film in Leone's *Fistful* trilogy, *The Good, the Bad, and the Ugly*. The reviewer's description of this virtual West is worth quoting at length:

> Like our own, the world of *Red Dead Redemption*—its cantinas, dusty arroyos, railway stations and cragged peaks—is one in which good does not always prevail and yet altruism rarely goes unrewarded. This is a violent, cruel world of sexism and bigotry, yet one that abounds with individual acts of kindness and compassion. Like our own, this is a complex world of ethical range and subtlety where it's not always clear what the right thing is. (2011, C1)

It is not difficult to see in this reviewer's comments virtually every element of the genre that we have considered in this essay: the powerful landscape, the moral ambiguity that can only be clarified by individual violence, and the yearning for a simpler way of life unthreatened by outsiders and desperadoes. The fact that no Western video game has yet become widely popular, the review notes, is not because the action is too arcane or the characters are uninteresting: it is "because there has never been a western game that has been truly made well. And that may be because the Western, perhaps more than any other genre, exposes how much more work is required to make a realistic game than to make a 'realistic' film" (Schiesel 2011, C4).

Dan Houser, one of the creators of *Red Dead Redemption*, explains that "Westerns are about place. . . . They're not called outlaw films. They are not even called cowboys-and-Indians films. They're called Westerns. They're about geography" (in Schiesel 2011, C4).

It is in this connection that the creation of a virtual West coincides with the long-running fantasy Western serial that Eastwood worked in during the first part of his career and with the childhood fantasy West of John Ford that Sergio Leone paid homage to and transcended in *A Fistful of Dollars*. This is the idea that Eastwood understood about the potential for landscape to become language, and it is the reason that his first efforts at collaborating with Sergio Leone on the *Fistful* project were on reducing the talk, the dialogue, and expanding the view—letting the camera do what stilted dialogue and stock scene footage could not. It is not surprising that the next "frontier" should be a virtual one or that the venue for this $85 million video blockbuster—made in a time when the nation is again troubled by foreign wars and domestic unease—should be the Old West. The West was always an invented place, a panorama upon which could be projected the aspirations and anxieties of a uniquely American culture, one that translated itself clearly into a postwar Italy, in the mind of a young Italian cinephile.

In an interview from the 1980s, Leone described his fantasy film, the one he always wanted to make as a postscriptum to his work with Eastwood:

> [A] dance of death, [in which] I wanted to take all the most stereotypical characters from the American Western—on loan! The finest whore from New Orleans; the romantic bandit; the killer who is half businessman, half killer, and who wants to get on in the new world of business; the lone avenger. With these five most stereotypical characters from the American Western, I wanted to present a homage to the Western at the same time as showing the mutations which American society was undergoing at that time. (in Frayling 2005, 31)

The key to understanding the Eastwood/Leone collaboration post-*Rawhide* lies in Leone's final statement of intention: that he wished to look back in homage at the long history of the genre and that he also wanted to revive the genre and link it to its particular moment culturally and politically. What the serial Western ignored so diligently, the film addressed aesthetically, responding to the nation's worry and unease about the new geopolitical threats facing America. Edward Gallafent has summed up this new dimension of Western filmmaking:

> I argued that the defense of civilization in *A Fistful of Dollars* amounted to sending a family away to America, a potent image. There is also a subdued possibility of some release from the world of the film for The Stranger—there is a border across which he too could pass. (1994, 25)

For viewing audiences increasingly distressed by the conflict into which the nation had sent its sons and husbands and brothers, the film resonated powerfully, something the film critics at the time failed to see.

We know from this critical distance that as a cultural location, the West was modal, an amorphous marker that we could use to measure our distance from the overcivilized East and through which we could articulate national anxieties and aspirations. Its border was Turner's frontier, and once he pronounced it "dead" in 1893, the West became most clearly a cultural landscape rather than a literal place on the continental map, an interior landscape that embodied a strict moral code most often enforced through violence. The particulars of this code shifted from generation to generation, starting ten years after Turner's obituary for the American frontier with the 1903 release of *The Great Train Robbery*, but in all successive re-creations, the essential elements of the original formula remained the same. In this way, every Western movie has been a palimpsest in which traces of the earliest myths and stories are still discernible. The genius of the Eastwood/Leone collaboration is that they recognized this fact early on.

■ Notes

1. Essentially, a ramrod was the second-in-command, for which (at least according to George C. Duffield, a trail boss from 1866 who kept a diary that was partial inspiration for the *Rawhide* series) Yates would have been a bit young and inexperienced. Disciplinary orders would have been handed down from the trail boss to the ramrod for execution; ironically in the series, it is the aptly named Rowdy Yates who often needs disciplining from his patient superior.

2. When CBS hesitated before renewing *Rawhide* after its initial ten episodes had run, Eastwood played a role in an episode of *Maverick*, a series that played the Western formula much more humorously than did the other serials.

3. It is remarkable how few specific locations are mentioned in many of the *Rawhide* episodes, especially in the first three years of the show, almost as though the action is taking place in a parallel universe, one without the usual compass points that we rely on to know where we are.

4. In my recent immersion into the film history of the Western, I have been struck by the easy assimilation of the Confederate veteran or renegade into the stock characters of the serial and movie Westerns. If this particular trope has not yet been explored by students and aficionados, it should be. Eastwood certainly retained this part of his *Rawhide* identity in the character he helped create for *A Fistful of Dollars*, who is another Confederate veteran, perhaps renegade, and then developed it more fully when he directed and starred in *The Outlaw Josey Wales*, where Wales's Confederate background frames the foreground of the story. The ending of the movie allows Wales and the other vagrants he has attracted to him to finally leave this thorny bit of history behind them.

5. After all, the men and the cattle are headed north to Missouri, one of the most contested spots in the West both ante- and postbellum.

6. "By the late 1960s and early 1970s, cultural forces, including those engendered by the Vietnam War, were effecting changes in American society that rendered the traditional western hero increasingly outmoded" (Gourlie and Engel 2007, 3).

7. Concerning costume, the trademark poncho was Leone's addition, something purchased locally in Spain, as were the trademark cigars, which Eastwood hated to smoke.

8. The original title was to be *The Magnificent Stranger*, but this was changed to *A Fistful of Dollars* not long into production. The final title of the film is frankly a bit puzzling, almost like an unfinished aphorism or common saying: "A fistful of dollars will buy you any justice you like" or "For a few dollars more [the title of the second film in the trilogy] you can corrupt anyone."

9. This is a point that is both ironic, since the real sets are anywhere but the American West, including Rome, Spain, and Almeria, and pointed, since this matters little within a mythic landscape, since any landscape—real or imagined—must conform to the moral and aesthetic dimensions of the imagining presence.

10. The character, as many have pointed out, does in fact have a name—Joe, despite the publicity that created the legend of the "Man with No Name." But exactly what sort of name is Joe, which in the movie is spoken most often by Piripero, the undertaker and almost certainly a figure from the Italian commedia dell'arte tradition?—especially when placed in the autobiographical context of Leone's memories of American G.I. Joe's invading Italy, "who chased our women and sold their cigarettes on the black market" (in Frayling 2005, 18). In my reading of the film, "Joe" is not a real name at all but a generic name for Americans.

The stationary cameras of the serials offered an uncritical reality, something unchanged and unchangeable, while the dynamic camera work in Leone's films suggests the opposite by locating the sensible center with the audience. We are forced to make sense of things, forced to pay attention to scene and setting, mostly by following a virtually silent "hero" through a number of adventures.

■ Bibliography

Altman, Rick. 1984. "A Semantic/Syntactic Approach to Film Genre." *Cinema Journal* 23, no. 3 (Spring): 6–18.

Borden, Diane M., and Eric P. Essman. 2000. "Manifest Landscape/Latent Ideology: Afterimages of Empire in the Western and 'Post-Western' Film." *California History* 79, no. 1 (Spring): 30–41.

Cartensen, Vernon. 1982. "Making Use of the Frontier and the American West." *Western Historical Quarterly* 13, no. 1 (January): 4–16.

Cavell, Stanley. 1988. "The Fact of Television." In *Themes Out of School: Effects and Causes*, 235–71. Chicago: University of Chicago Press.

Cremean, David. 2007. "A Fistful of Anarchy: Clint Eastwood's Characters in Sergio Leone's *Dollars* Trilogy and in His Four 'Own' Westerns." In *Clint Eastwood, Actor and Director: New Perspectives*, ed. Leonard Engel, 49–76. Salt Lake City: University of Utah Press.

Denby, David. 2010. "Out of the West: Clint Eastwood's Shifting Landscape." *New Yorker*, March 8.

Erisman, Fred. 2007. "Clint Eastwood's Western Films and the Evolving Mythic Hero." In *Clint Eastwood, Actor and Director: New Perspectives*, ed. Leonard Engel, 181–94. Salt Lake City: University of Utah Press.

Frayling, Christopher. 2005. *Once Upon a Time in Italy: The Westerns of Sergio Leone*. New York: Henry N. Abrams.

Gallafent, Edward. 1994. *Clint Eastwood: Filmmaker and Star*. New York: Continuum.

Gentry, Rick, and Clint Eastwood. 1989. "Clint Eastwood: An Interview." *Film Quarterly* 42, no. 3 (Spring): 12–23.

Girgus, Sam B. 1994. "Review: Representative Men: Unfreezing the Male Gaze." *College Literature* 21, no. 3 (October): 214–22.

Gourlie, John M., and Leonard Engel. 2007. "Introduction." In *Clint Eastwood, Actor and Director: New Perspectives*, ed. Leonard Engel, 1–23. Salt Lake City: University of Utah Press.

Jardine, Gail. 1994. "Clint: Cultural Critic, Cowboy of Cathartic Change." *Art Journal* 53, no. 3 (Autumn): 74–75.

Kapsis, Robert E., and Kathie Coblenz, eds. 1999. *Clint Eastwood: Interviews*. Jackson: University Press of Mississippi.

Landy, Marcia. 1996. "'Which Way Is America?' Americanism and the Italian Western." *boundary 2* 23, no. 1 (Spring): 35–59.

Lenihan, John H. 2002. "Teaching the Western." *OAH Magazine of History* 16, no. 4 (Summer): 27, 29–30.

McClain, William. 2010. "Western, Go Home! Sergio Leone and the 'Death of the Western' in American Film Criticism." *Journal of Film and Video* 62, no. 1 (Spring): 52–66.

McGregor, Gaile. 1993. "Cultural Studies and Social Change: The War Film as Men's Magic, and Other Fictions about Fictions." *Canadian Journal of Sociology* 18, no. 3 (Summer): 271–302.

McVeigh, Stephen. 2007. "Subverting *Shane*: Ambiguities in Eastwood's Politics in *Fistful of Dollars*, *High Plains Drifter*, and *Pale Rider*." In *Clint Eastwood, Actor and Director: New Perspectives*, ed. Leonard Engel, 129–56. Salt Lake City: University of Utah Press.

Minus, Ed. 2010. "Westerns." *Sewanee Review* 118, no. 1 (Winter): 82–90.

Nelson, Rob. 2010. "Clint Eastwood, Who He Wants to Be: Honoring The Man with No Name at Lincoln Center." *Village Voice*, July 6.

Rogin, Michael. 1990. "'Make My Day!': Spectacle as Amnesia in Imperial Politics." *Representations* 29 (Winter): 99–123.

Schickel, Richard. 1996. *Clint Eastwood: A Biography*. New York: Vintage Books.

Schiesel, Seth. 2011. "Way Down Deep in the Wild, Wild West." *New York Times*, May 17.

Scott, James. 2010. "The Right Stuff at the Wrong Time: The Space of Nostalgia in the Conservative Ascendency." *Film and History* 40, no. 1 (Spring): 45–57.

Siebers, Tobin. 1993. *Cold War Criticism and the Politics of Skepticism*. Oxford: Oxford University Press.

Slotkin, Richard. 1998. *Gunfighter Nation: The Myth of the Frontier in Twentieth-Century America*. Norman: University of Oklahoma Press.

Smith, Paul. 1993. *Clint Eastwood: A Cultural Production*. Minneapolis: University of Minnesota Press.

Thomas, Louisa. 2010. "Literary Compass, Review of *In Rough Country: Essays and Reviews*, by Joyce Carol Oates." *New York Times Book Review*, July 18, 13.

Westbrook, Brett. 2007. "Feminism and the Limits of Genre in *Fistful of Dollars* and *The Outlaw Josey Wales*." In *Clint Eastwood, Actor and Director: New Perspectives*, ed. Leonard Engel, 24–48. Salt Lake City: University of Utah Press.

Worden, Daniel. 2007. "Masculinity for the Million: Gender in Dime Novel Westerns." *Arizona Quarterly* 63, no. 3 (Autumn): 35–60.

Chapter 2

THOROUGHLY MODERN EASTWOOD: MALE/FEMALE POWER RELATIONS IN *THE BEGUILED* AND *PLAY MISTY FOR ME*

Brett Westbrook

"Don Siegel hates women—and fears them." So states critic Karyn Kay (1976, 32) in her article about *The Beguiled*, a 1971 Siegel-directed film starring Clint Eastwood. By association, at least for Kay, so does Clint Eastwood. Siegel and Eastwood collaborated on six movies— *Coogan's Bluff* (1968) and *Two Mules for Sister Sara* (1970), followed by three films all in 1971: *The Beguiled, Play Misty for Me* (directed by Eastwood), and *Dirty Harry*.[1] The last was *Escape from Alcatraz* (1979). With few exceptions, Kay's comments sum up (at the extreme end) the general critical attitude toward both filmmakers, particularly in terms of portrayals of women.[2] Eastwood's spaghetti Westerns along with the Dirty Harry movies and similarly violent *policiers* are particularly damned as films in which expendable and interchangeable women are raped and humiliated, tossed aside, left out, silenced, and ignored. Even a film like *Sudden Impact* (1983, dir. Eastwood), in which a woman exacts revenge for rape, abetted by the Eastwood character, could not dislodge either Eastwood's movies or his on-screen and off-screen personas from the presumption of woman-hating.

Statements from star and director have been regularly quoted by critics as evidence that the unrepentant misogyny comes from within. One of the favorites comes from Siegel about *The Beguiled*: "Women are capable of deceit, larceny, murder, anything. Behind that mask of innocence lurks just as much evil as you'll find in members of the Mafia. Any young girl who looks perfectly harmless is capable of murder" (quoted in Smith 1993, 79). Critics take up this theme of misogyny, seeing it in almost every Eastwood film and especially those associated with Siegel. An early article about *The Beguiled*, for example, even has *misogyny* in the title, making clear author Karyn Kay's point before the first line, "*The Beguiled*: Gothic Misogyny." Kay claims that *The Beguiled* is another example of Siegel's attitude toward women: in "film after film, he depicts females as manipulative and evil, plotting to destroy men" (1976, 32). In fact, "all Siegel females," according to Kay, are "vile, murderous shrews when aroused" (1976, 33). For Paul Smith, the "misogynist gesture" of *Two Mules for Sister Sara* becomes the "driving force in the next Eastwood–Siegel collaboration" (1993, 78), *The Beguiled*. The Dirty Harry movies only cemented the male chauvinist reputation, despite Harry Callahan's reluctant-yet-genuine affection for the doomed Kate Moore (Tyne Daly) in *The Enforcer* (1976).

The critical voice denouncing Eastwood's filmic misogyny has been softened somewhat thanks to more "sensitive" movies like *Unforgiven* (1992), *A Perfect World* (1993), *The Bridges of Madison County* (1995), *Million Dollar Baby* (2004), and *The Changeling* (2008). The general critical consensus is that these more recent incarnations of the Eastwood character represent a linear cinematic evolution for Eastwood, from woman-hater to woman-lover, and are, therefore, surprising and new. William Beard, for example, terms *Bridges* a "radical departure" (2000, 42) from the usual Eastwood model of relationships. Eastwood may be backsliding, however, falling back into the "usual" pattern of gender relations as star and director with the women in *Gran Torino* (2008) again brutalized and relegated to the backseat of the family car.

Two early Malpaso films, however, call into question that progressive understanding of Eastwood's development as a filmmaker, from misogynist to feminist (or some approximation thereof). While both *The Beguiled* and *Play Misty for Me* are generally included in discussions of Eastwood films, they are often approached as outliers, quirky little movies on the boundaries of the Eastwood oeuvre. William Beard, for example, refers to them as "two strange films of 1971" (2000, 5). They do deviate from formulas established in Eastwood's Westerns and Dirty Harry films. The former takes place during the Civil War, with Eastwood as Cpl. McBurney, a wounded Union soldier inserted into a girl's school in the South behind Confederate lines. *Misty*, set contemporaneously in Carmel, California, stars first-time director Eastwood as David Garver, smooth jazz radio DJ. In both movies, the male characters contend with their own sexuality in relationship to that of the female characters, more successfully in the latter than the former, in which McBurney dies.

A first screening might mark the films as early examples of the woman-hating/fearing cinema decried by Karyn Kay and others. In *The Beguiled*, for example, the Eastwood character cynically exploits the dreams and desires of the three oldest women in the school and is not above kissing a twelve-year-old to get what he wants. In *Misty*, the swinging Dave Garver is just out for a good time, while the main female character, Evelyn Draper, is clearly psychotic, determined to manufacture an exclusive relationship with Garver or if that does not work out, kill him and his pretty girlfriend, too. Both men are victimized by these shrill, possessive women. Understanding both *Beguiled* and *Misty* as woman-hating, woman-fearing films, however, requires a kind of procrustean criticism, one that lops off bits of movies to make them fit an imaginary Eastwoodian bed. A closer look reveals that both movies evince an entirely modern conception of gender relations. In *The Beguiled* the presentation of particularly female sexuality and sexual expression is so modern as to be anachronistic, while *Misty* limns the kind of gender relations reflected in current discussions of equitable power dynamics between the sexes.

Criticism of *The Beguiled* and *Misty* generally focuses on a particular marker for misogyny: hysteria. Even more specifically, the female characters become hysterical in response to their own sexual arousal, stirred up into murderous frenzies by the mere presence of a studly man. According to Kay, McBurney's fatal mistake is that he "doesn't know Siegel females" morph into "vile, murderous shrews when aroused" (1976, 33). Even Gina Herring, who does her best to recuperate *The Beguiled* from Kay's article, concedes that "the movie does perpetuate some stereotypes about female sexual repression, jealousy, and hysteria" (1998, 215). William Beard notes the "film's peculiar hysteria" (2000, 121), while Foster Hirsch claims that the Eastwood character is "held prisoner in a house of hysterical women" (1981, 136). And Paul Smith is simply blunt: "The females are hysterical" (1993, 79).

The argument that hysteria is evidence supporting a charge of misogyny rests on the assumption that hysteria is inherently a criticism specifically of women. According to Janice Haaken, "Hysteria is thought of as an excessively emotional reaction, one in which emotion overrides rational reasoning" (2003, 222). And although hysteria "is not inherently a female condition," women still "carry the lion's share of emotions that are culturally designated as excessive or abnormal" (Haaken 1998, 61). Hysteria in this view can offer no understanding or insight. According to Victor Jeleniewski Seidler, "It is already assumed that emotions are 'subjective' and 'personal' and so cannot be sources of knowledge" (2007, 11). Further, men are never hysterical themselves. Violence, possessiveness, and a heightened emotional state in men are not explained as overreactions. Dennis Bingham contrasts the women's "stealthy, veiled and indirect" actions with McBurney's "'masculine' confrontations" (1994, 202). As Janice Haaken puts it, the standard take is that woman is "positioned as prone to emotional excess" while the man functions as "her steadying influence" (2003, 222).

In her remarkable book on gender and memory, *Pillar of Salt: Gender, Memory, and the Perils of Looking Back*, Haaken questions not whether a particular response is or is not hysterical but whether these reactions indicate some kind of failing or problem. How much of a response, exactly, is an *over*reaction? What if emotional excess makes sense under the circumstances? The young schoolmistress Edwina especially seems to exemplify hysteria for the critics, no more so than when she finds McBurney having sex with the sexually precocious teenager Carol.[3] In a rage fueled by jealously and sexual repression, so goes the conventional wisdom, she *deliberately* sets in motion the events leading up to the amputation of McBurney's leg. McBurney is "thrown down a spiral staircase by Edwina" (Knapp 1996, 40), or more deliberately she "shoves McB down the stairs" (Kay 1976, 33). Or more mildly she "pushes him down a long circular staircase" (Herring 1998, 214) or just "down a flight of stairs" (Bingham 1994, 199). The critics want to have it both ways—that Edwina is somehow both hysterical (i.e., in a nonreasoning state) and calculating enough to deliberately cause McBurney's fall. Both states cannot obtain simultaneously.

According to Haaken, in fact, "hysteria enlists the body to communicate the ineffable" (2003, 222). When Edwina first makes the discovery, she cannot even look at the couple, much less engage in a rational, that is, non-hysterical, discussion about her assumption of exclusivity, for example. She backs out of the room, averting her eyes from the betrayal that is Carol's naked flesh. Still unable to look at him after he manages to get out of Carol's room, Edwina flails at McBurney, arms windmilling. Her long hair is loose and flies in her face as she finally finds her voice, screaming at the hapless McBurney desperately trying to placate her. The landing is so small that there is no room for a hobbling McBurney to avoid her fury, and he falls down the stairs.[4] Edwina's inarticulate screaming and flailing express the humiliation and horror of McBurney's betrayal in the only way open to her.

While Edwina is cited with great frequency as an example of hysteria, the rest of the inhabitants at the Farnsworth school seem equally "overly" emotional. As McBurney becomes increasingly violent toward them and as Southern troops leave the vicinity, the women resort to what Bingham refers to as the "furtive, euphemistic approach," deploying their "feminine wiles" (1994, 202). Everyone except Edwina conspires to lure McBurney to his death. Even though he has threatened all of them, spurned Miss Martha for Carol, and killed little Amy's turtle in a drunken rage, McBurney accepts the offer of a conciliatory dinner, using the occasion to announce that he and Edwina plan to marry and leave the school. But is it in fact "hysterical," that is, irrational and excessive, for the women at the Farnsworth Seminary to protect themselves against McBurney? He has demonstrated his, to them, lechery. He is in possession of the sole firearm, and he has behaved toward them with great violence. The alternatives are to bear up under the constant assault to their womanhood or take action. These women and girls have survived years of war, with all its deprivations. A nonhysterical reaction, one supposedly rational, with everyone using his or her words, would not make sense for any of the female characters. In effect, then, the hysterical reaction *is* the logical reaction. Critically, hysteria functions as evidence of Eastwood and Siegel's misogynistic take on women. But what if it is not? Haaken asserts that "there is something amiss in this contempt for hysteria—in the rejection of emotional excess and irrationality" (1998, 61). While critics like Karyn Kay and Paul Smith deride Siegel and Eastwood for their misogyny, they participate in this contempt without questioning the conventional wisdom that these apparently excessive responses offer no insight and are the response of women exclusively.

In addition to her interrogation of the problematics of female hysteria, Haaken argues that male "hysteria posed a dilemma for professionals, who were generally averse to social controversy or direct challenges to convention" (1998, 142)—here the convention that men are not emotional. McBurney, however, is just as highly sexualized as the women in the school. He starts seducing them even before entering the gates of the seminary. Even though he can hardly walk, McBurney manages to kiss the twelve-going-on-thirteen-year-old Amy within the first few minutes of the film, ostensibly to distract her from a passing Confederate patrol. It is an entirely creepy moment. He picks up on Carol's promiscuity, Edwina's fantasies, and Miss Martha's sexuality with the alacrity of a mind reader. Despite the fact that McBurney's virtually instantaneous response to a houseful of females, ages thirteen–forty, is almost 100 percent sexual, this approach is not labeled hysterical. Nor is his reaction to the amputation of his leg. He is, of course, horrified. He gets drunk, gets his hands on the only firearm available, and demands sexual access to all the women. It is a rampage of threats and smashed china. As Richard Schickel puts it on the *Beguiled* DVD, McBurney "goes through the house like a dose of the plague." Even after this rampage, McBurney manages somehow to convince Edwina to marry him. Instead of condemning him as an oversexed maniac, however, Gina Herring refers to McBurney as "a charming scoundrel" with only his "masculine charm" (1998, 214) to save him. Paul Smith sees the character as merely a "suffering hero whose only crime appears to have been his sexual philandering" (1993, 79), while Bingham argues that the "Eastwood protagonist is forced into a passive role in relation to women" (1994, 200). Similarly, McBurney's postamputation machinations do not fall into the category of "furtive" for Bingham, despite his using the promise of marriage as a means of escape.

The focus on the sexuality in the movie, sexual expression, motivation, and so on keeps the critical discussion on the surface. The tug-of-war is more complicated than McBurney versus Farnsworth, than deciding who is under- and who is oversexed. The exploration of sex and sexuality was big box office in 1971. Hit movies that year included *The Last Picture Show* (Bogdanovich), *Carnal Knowledge* (Nichols), and *Klute* (Pakula). Sexuality, particularly men's sexuality, was a significant portion of the Hollywood landscape in 1971—at least according to receipts, Oscars, and Golden Globes. Only *The Beguiled*, however, was set more than one hundred years in the past. While Hollywood is never a good place to go looking for history, the overlay of sexuality in *Beguiled* is so contemporary that it is anachronistic, pushing the film out of time and space, completely draining the movie of credibility.

In the 1860s, there was precisely one narrative of white, female middle-class sexuality—that women, at least nice women like those at the Farnsworth Seminary for Young Ladies, do not *have* a sexuality, *any* sexuality. Even if Edwina did harbor a fairy-tale notion of her future instead of one centered on duty and child rearing, premarital sex would be nonnegotiable. And anyway, Prince Charming does not expect Snow White to put out. Nor would the mistress of a Southern school have sex with some stray Yankee who landed on her doorstep. The cult of Southern womanhood in the late nineteenth century subjected particularly middle- and upper-class women to a strict regime under which sexual activity was relegated to the category of necessity. Likewise, McBurney's uncanny, Spock-like, mind-melding abilities are far-fetched at best. Women were not known to have fantasies. His detection of their longings indicates a modern (Hollywood) understanding of what makes women tick. Cinematic techniques, like flashbacks to Miss Martha's incestuous longings and her fantasy of three-way sex with McBurney and Edwina (culminating in a bizarre Pietà-like tableau), are equally clumsy, providing an all-too-convenient psychological explanation for why these women behave the way they do. In the 1860s, biology was destiny. Concepts of sexuality simply did not exist (Briggs 2000; Cott 1978; Welter 1966).

Psychoanalytical explanations, however, cannot save the narrative in *The Beguiled*, which is deeply flawed. The women at the Farnsworth Seminary could easily overpower one man, especially once he is down to only a leg and a half. He has to sleep, has to eat, and would be vulnerable at any number of points. The movie does try to make McBurney intimidating. He manages to get his hands on the single firearm in the whole school, but it is only a small one-shot pistol that has to be reloaded after every shot. He gets drunk, waves the pistol at everyone, and makes demands about having sexual access to any- and everyone, though he does narrow it down to any young lady who desires his company. They could, apparently, just say no. Martha tries to menace him with a hatchet, which he knocks out of her hands. Picking it up again does not seem to occur to her. By the end of the rampage, when he smashes Amy's pet turtle to bits, he successfully alienates everyone except Edwina. The entire display is utterly unconvincing, as is Edwina's siding with McBurney, a second courtship that occurs entirely off-screen. Within the narrative scope of the movie, this kind of behavior should alienate her, too, not prompt her to defend him, much less agree to marry him.

The script, an adaptation of the Thomas Cullinan novel of the same name, was put together by Albert Maltz, one of the Hollywood Ten, whose first script after being blacklisted was *Two Mules for Sister Sara*, a Siegel/Eastwood collaboration. Siegel hated it, claiming that Maltz and cowriter Martin Rackin saw the story "in terms of crude and stupid burlesque," leaving it up to him to "humanize it" (quoted in Higham 1971, D-11). Siegel apparently thought just as poorly of Maltz's script for *The Beguiled* (cowritten with Irene Kamp), this time claiming that Maltz imagined the narrative as a "romantic love story" in which McBurney runs off happily ever after with Edwina.[5] The feeling was mutual, as Maltz and Kamp used the pseudonyms John B. Sherry and Grimes Grice. The remnants of the script's first iteration seem evident as the movie devolves from what Ian Nathan calls "an astonishing sweep of Grand Guignol grizzliness" (2008, 123) into a romance of sorts. At the final dinner, staged by the conspiring women of the Farnsworth Seminary as a reconciliation, McBurney offers feeble excuses about having been drunk and reveals his plans to marry Edwina and leave the school. While this could perhaps be one last bit of maneuvering on McBurney's part, his being able to somehow re-woo Edwina is as implausible as his threatening everyone into submission with a one-shot pistol. Of course, he is a dead man hobbling by the time he announces his plans to run off with Edwina (so to speak). He staggers outside the dining room and dies of mushroom poisoning. The pupils, under the exacting tutelage of Miss Martha, sew him up in a shroud while Edwina watches. They all suppose he died of heart failure, and that is that—back to French lessons and practicing one's etiquette for after the war.

The original novel provides much more in the way of motivation for the women, why they do not simply overpower him and turn him over to any passing army. The sexually precocious Alicia (Carol in the film) fears being exposed as the daughter of a "fancy woman." Emily believes that she has given away important tactical information and McBurney will reveal her to be a traitor to the Southern Cause. Maria Deveraux (left out of the movie) believes that McBurney will convince her mother that she contributed to her father's death. The adaptation, however, focuses almost exclusively on an overplayed, hothouse version of sex in the Old South to the exclusion of narrative coherence. Dennis Bingham claims that "*The Beguiled* after all is a Hollywood film that throws up more contradictions than can be recuperated" (1994, 202). While he laments the apparent dissolution of the masculinity of the Westerns and the Dirty Harry series, the actual contradictions in the movie stem from the overlay of a 1960s-era pop *Playboy*-driven psychology, reinforced by art house cinema techniques that impose a "modern" understanding onto a nineteenth-century story. It is at the very least an ambitious film from both Siegel and Eastwood. Even though it is "soaked," as reviewer Philip Wuntch puts it, "in blood and dimestore Freud" (1971, 24), the character of McBurney—tuned into women's emotions, talkative, charming, highly sexualized—sets up a significant counterpoint to the stony, virtually wordless masculinity of the Man with No Name and Harry Callahan.

Just as much of the criticism of *Beguiled* focuses on the sex and apparent hysteria, critics writing about *Play Misty for Me* generally focus on the neurotic Evelyn Draper and the development of the "relationship," for lack of a better word, with swingin' DJ Dave Garver. Lost in this discussion is the relationship that Garver works to develop with Tobie Williams. That relationship stands in direct contrast to the psychotic need Draper has to possess Garver, as it is based on feminist ideals of equity and partnership that still shape relationship discussions today. Even further, Williams's fears about their being a couple reflect very modern thinking about the nature of the self within a relationship.[6]

William Beard posits a fundamental maleness in the Eastwood universe. This "talismanic invincibility" is "an absolutely crucial and constitutive aspect of the Eastwood ur-persona" (Beard 2000, 1). For Beard, "Eastwood's starting point is that of a heroic persona who, amid the ruins of classicism, adopts the role of a regressive and uncommitted centre of masculine power within the socially nihilistic period of the 1970s" (2000, 12). In this view, masculinity is under siege, as evidenced by Garver's inability to get rid of Draper and by his sensitivity in general. The siege comes from the political Left, which by 1971 had apparently left white, middle-class, straight masculinity reeling from an apparent loss of status. For Adam Knee, this "refiguration of white masculinity" means that the main character must "defer to blacks, gays, and, most centrally, women" (1993, 89). Bingham finds in the Siegel/Eastwood collaborations a

> reclamatory spirit, as if grabbing back the standards and traditions the white patriarchy perceived it had lost to feminism, the civil rights movement, anti-Vietnam protest, sixties youth culture, the so-called sexual revolution (in particular the short-lived tolerance of homosexuality in the 1970s), the civil-libertarian decisions of the Supreme Court led by Earl Warren, and the "permissive philosophy" in general. (1994, 189)

All of these cultural changes are terrible—for white, middle-class straight men. But what if there were alternatives to the kind of masculinity promoted by Beard and others as somehow primal and immutable?

Apparently, white, heterosexual masculinity is so completely entrenched in violence and divorced from emotion that no reasonable alternatives exist. In other words, when white, straight men have to stop being jerks, they lose, which leaves a power vacuum. Knee argues that "Evelyn appears as a threat precisely because she has taken on traditional masculine characteristics, of the very type David is being forced to give up" (1993,

91)—which turns him into a girl. As a "result of being forced to repress traditional masculine tendencies," apparently like promiscuity, Eastwood/ Garver (completely conflated by Knee and others) is "starting to become hysterical" (Knee 1993, 98). The whole situation leaves Garver a "disconcerted, humiliated, and ultimately frightened figure of weakness" (Beard 2000, 125).

What Garver and Draper have is a failure to communicate. Garver believes that he does the responsible thing by letting her know up front that he is "hung up" on a "nice girl." Draper understands that he does not want to "complicate his life." She seems to agree to the terms, and they have sex. When she comes over the next morning with groceries and without an invitation, he reiterates his understanding of their postcoital situation, "the deal about no strings." She again agrees but reminds him that she "never said anything about not coming back for seconds." And they have sex for the second time. At this point, Garver believes that they have an understanding, that he will call her if he wants to see her—and sleep with her—again. However, Draper understands such a statement as "playing a game," which is "really not necessary." When a neighbor objects to the early a.m. conversation being held outdoors, Draper's facade of normalcy slips; she swears at the neighbor and in the same moment beams at a confused Garver.

The "nice girl" Garver is hung up on, Tobie Williams, returns to Carmel from Sausalito, where she had gone to think things through. Upon her return, Garver begins to pull back from Draper, refusing to take her calls. She escalates her efforts to maintain a connection, playing games of her own—snatching his car keys to make him chase after her as if they were children, appearing at his house naked underneath her coat (very much the adult), and finally a weak suicide attempt. It is her presumption on his availability that goads Garver into what he hopes is the last conversation they will have. He goes to Draper's house, determined to have a talk. She interrupts, putting him off to admire her new lounging pajamas, so that she can offer him food, and finally so that she can give him a present—a pair of shoes. It is a cringe-worthy scene. Draper kneels on the floor to take off his shoes and put on the new ones: "It's Madame Butterfly time. First, friendly neighborhood geisha remove honorable shoes." Garver, utterly horrified at her subservience, lurches up out of the chair. Draper's first assumption is that she has "done something wrong." Garver only wants "to be straight" with her, insisting again that they have to talk, a proposition she rejects, begging him to "be nice to me instead." While Garver stays on the defensive—"I never lied to you"—Draper escalates the accusations: jealousy (the picture of Williams on his dresser); accusations of his having used her sexually—"all dressed up in my little whore suit"; belittling him—"You're not even good in bed!" Draper sets a land-speed record moving through a veritable catalog of relationship maneuvers.

The insanity picks up again that evening, when Draper drives over to Garver's house determined to ferret out the other lover in his bed. He is alone and still refusing to agree that they are in love with each other. Draper has a tantrum, flinging herself on his bed: "It's not true! It's not true!" His saying something like this must be another game, a coyness required at the beginning of a love affair but quickly dropped. Because Garver believes that he has "been straight" with her from the beginning, he cannot understand her protestations about love any more than Draper can take in what Garver is trying to communicate. This is not a question of Garver's giving up some kind of ur-masculinity; nor is it about Draper's occupying a traditionally masculine prerogative. It is about speaking different languages.

Draper occupies a liminal space between a post–World War II, rigid gender regime that condemns any girls who are "not nice" and women's lib—or the Hollywood version anyway. She winds up being a monstrous sort of Franken-femme, miniskirted and available for premarital sex, even initiating the pickup in the bar, yet still assuming that intercourse really does mean exclusivity, domesticity, submission: she cooks for him, buys "lounging pajamas" to make herself attractive to him, buys him presents. Her prerogative is that he is available to her without silly games, like calling first. When he does not play along, Draper becomes frantic, resorting to attempted suicide to keep Garver close at hand. Drucilla Cornell argues that Garver demonstrates "a man's blindness to a woman's view of what goes on in a sexual relationship" (2009, 3), while Laurence Knapp claims that Garver is unable to "comprehend or withstand the emotional and psychological demands of a woman" (1996, 48). Both statements seem to assume that Draper represents every-woman, that all women make these types of demands, and that expecting some kind of reciprocity in a relationship constitutes a demand in the first place.

Garver's relationship with Tobie Williams, however, reveals quite clearly that he does know what it all means. While the Donna Mills character does not get nearly as much screen time as Draper, her relationship with Garver is clearly the desirable one, the one toward which he strives, one that would describe an equitable relationship in 2011. Before the beginning of the film, Williams left Carmel because of Garver's well-known promiscuity. His fellow DJ, Sweet Al Monte, for example, is positive Garver will get "that Frisco gig" because a woman is making the decision. In a later scene, Monte wants to double-date with Garver: Monte, his girlfriend, Garver, "and one of them hens you can dig up." When Garver finds out that Williams is back in Carmel, he takes her for a walk to find out why she left. She brings up this redhead, that blonde, how she would wait up wondering where he went after his show was finished. Her response is not to blame Garver, or demand that he change to fit her needs, or nag, or just give up and take whatever behavior he dishes out. Her response has to do with herself, her identity within the parameters of that particular relationship. She could see what their being together was making of her, and she rejected that person: "You know, the thing I hate the most in the whole world is a jealous female. . . . [A]nd that's what I was getting to be. That's why I had to split. I was starting to be one of my most unfavorite people. I hated it. I know you did, too." Williams's question to Garver, then, is how to be in a relationship together and not lose who she is as a person.

In her 2004 discussion of the functioning of relationships, thirty years after the movie appeared, Jessica Benjamin describes the "idea of complementary relations." These are the "push-me/pull-you, doer–done-to dynamics that we find in most impasses, which generally appear to be one-way—that is, each person feels *done to*, and not like an agent helping to shape a co-created reality" (Benjamin 2004, 9). Draper feels *done to* by Garver's refusal to stop playing games and agree to the relationship of her imagination. Williams's response, on the other hand, sees Garver's behavior in terms of the choices he makes. The conversation is not accusatory or blaming; instead, it assumes that both people exist and that being in a relationship means that both people necessarily change. Benjamin refers to this interaction as the "principle of reciprocal influence" (2004, 11). Just as the ineffective communication between Garver and Draper leaves everyone vulnerable, understanding the reciprocity in a relationship "opens the space of third-ness, enabling us to negotiate differences and to connect" (Benjamin 2004, 11). This is the thoroughly modern aspect of the male/female dynamic in *Play Misty for Me*. The question of maintaining one's personhood still drives the relationship industrial complex even today: *Sex and the City, Cosmopolitan, Oprah,* Dr. Phil, how-to, self-help, and even ismymaninlove.com.

Despite her strong attraction to Garver, Williams is completely unwilling to disappear, to be that subservient neighborhood geisha or the seething jealous female. In her discussion of *Bridges of Madison County*, Cornell sees in the film "a crisis of femininity that precludes a woman's self-assertion outside of fulfilling the masculine fantasy" (2009, 92). While that is an insightful point about *Bridges*, this same sort of question was raised almost a quarter of a century earlier in *Misty*. Garver does not want any of the supposedly male fantasies offered by Draper—domestic diva, sex-pot, miniskirts, or friendly neighborhood geisha. Williams's strong position would seem an obvious counterbalance to Draper's deranged notion of an ideal relationship, yet Williams is consistently left out of the discussion. For example, Adam Knee argues that Draper functions "as an over manifestation of the threat posed by the flourishing of the women's liberation movement" (1993, 91). Bingham agrees, claiming that the movie "finds literally horrifying the prospect of women as autonomous sexual agents" (1994, 197). Paul Smith summarizes the movie's "proposition: that if women expect sexual liberation, they cannot also try to tie men down into committed relationships; women's punishment for wanting both is madness and then death" (1993, 83). All of which beg the question: Why doesn't any of this happen to Williams? She wants, though does not expect or demand, a commitment from Garver, and she does not wind up mad or dead. In fact, if either woman is a product of women's lib, it is Williams. She uses a still-current vocabulary to discuss her deep concerns about the relationship. She sets good boundaries, ones that Garver actually respects. She says that she needs time to "figure out where I'm at." Garver agrees to back off. The conversation, much less the outcome, simply could not happen between Garver and Draper.

Instead of seeing the thoughtful conversation that actually happens on-screen (and still apparently pining for Harry Callahan), Adam Knee is certain, since this is Clint after all, that there is a "violence seething beneath the surface" (1993, 92). For his part, Beard seems just plain disgusted that the Eastwood/Garver character "has forsaken the harsh world of male combat for the perfumed one of poetry, soft music, and women; who has displaced conflict and mastery from the rocklike, masculine world of violence into the soft, feminine one of sexual relationship" (2000, 130). Beard is notably relieved when "the character does indeed rediscover his violent masculinity" (2000, 130) during the fight with Draper that ends in her death. Critics such as Knee, Beard, and others seem utterly unable to disassociate masculinity from violence. In fact they cling to this association, lament its absence, and are determined to see it in Eastwood's movies even when it is not there. Dennis Bingham sees the sad passing of that cherished brand of masculinity, unfeeling and always violent, starting with *Unforgiven*: "It will be difficult after all to recuperate Eastwood. His career, with all of its missteps, has illustrated a twelve-step withdrawal program from masculinism. The fact that no one in the mid-1970s would have believed that Eastwood could be written about in this way may offer some hope" (1994, 243). Except both *The Beguiled* and *Play Misty for Me* do make an entirely different statement from that of *Dirty Harry*. Audiences could see that in 1971, no need to wait for the "sensitive" films like *Bridges of Madison County*. And in between came movies such as *Paint Your Wagon* (1969), *Breezy* (1973), *Thunderbolt and Lightfoot* (1974), *Tightrope* (1984), *White Hunter Black Heart* (1990), and *A Perfect World* (1993). Drucilla Cornell, one of the few critics to see past the cultural insistence on a single Eastwood version of masculinity, notes that "from the beginning of his directorial journey he has been more complicated than he has appeared, working with some of the most sophisticated literature that addresses the meaning of straight white maleness throughout the history of the United States" (2009, 1). Why isn't that obvious? What gets in the way of our seeing? Eastwood himself understands the question in terms of variety: "I could have gone the easy route and been portrayed as Clint Eastwood, the guy with a gun in his hand, making some smart remark somewhere. That's fun for a moment, but then there's other parts to life, too" ("*The Beguiled, Misty*, Don and Clint," 2001). The variety and complexity of masculinity in Eastwood's movies, those other parts to life, could have both started and sustained a conversation about options for being male in post–World War II America. Still, we seem to cling to an absolute association between violence and masculinity, seeing it where it does not exist.

So, why Clint Eastwood? Why does this perception of a stone-faced, silent masculinity persist in the face of direct evidence that his films have actually been suggesting ideas about all sorts of masculinities practically from the very beginning of his career? There are various explanations. James Neibaur in his exploration of the tough guy in movies argues that Harry Callahan offers something for everyone (men, that is): "a throwback to the stereotypical authoritarian male," allowing men to "latch onto the Eastwood character who remained in control without budging." Those who embraced the counterculture and disdained the man "secretly admired his having the gall to battle such forces so unflinchingly" (Neibaur 1989, 196). Pauline Kael is not quite so kind. She cites an interview with Sergio Leone describing what he saw in Eastwood:

> When Michelangelo was asked what he had seen in the one particular block of marble which he chose among hundreds of others, he replied that he saw Moses. I would offer the same answer to your question—only backwards. . . . What I saw [in Eastwood], simply, was a block of marble. (quoted in 1985, 14)

Culturally, we seem to chisel out of the block that is Eastwood an endless stream of violent, woman-hating/fearing characters. In a 2009 article on the then seventy-eight-year-old actor/director, *London Times* writer Andrew Billen speculates: "Perhaps we only assume that Eastwood is a sexist, perhaps all the time he was a new man" (2009, para. 22). Perhaps one of these days, the rest of us will finally catch up.

■ Notes

1. *Misty* was Eastwood's directorial debut, but he was taking no chances. To keep his mentor close at hand and available for consultation, Eastwood cast Don Siegel in a small role, telling the anxious first-time actor, "Don't worry about it. If I screw up as a director, I've got a good director on the set" (in Knight 1974, 171).

2. For an exception, see, most notably, Drucilla Cornell's thoughtful and open-minded *Clint Eastwood and Issues of Modern Masculinity* (2009).

3. The scene with McBurney and Carol is remarkable, not the least for its soft-core porn imagery in 1971, featuring the allowable views of a woman's nakedness (hips, breasts, rear end), but also for how acrobatic the crippled McBurney manages to be.

4. That Edwina somehow deliberately backs him up so that down is the only way to go cannot be supported by what happens on the screen. She is simply not that calculating.

5. Higham quotes Siegel about the original script: "I was horrified by the softness and sentimentality of his treatment and I showed him a print of 'Rosemary's Baby.' I said, 'If you'd written this script, Mia Farrow wouldn't have given birth to the devil. She'd have given birth to healthy blond twin sons'" (1971, D-11).

6. I agree with Drucilla Cornell's rejection of "a theory of the subject that pretends to tell us exactly how we are limited and constituted so that, underneath it all, we cannot find even a remnant of the subject who creates" (2009, ix). While she refers to Eastwood as actor/director, I refer to Tobie Williams. The idea applies to characters, both fictional and otherwise.

■ Bibliography

Beard, William. 2000. *Persistence of Double Vision: Essays on Clint Eastwood*. Edmonton: University of Alberta Press.

The Beguiled. 1971. DVD. Dir. Don Siegel. Universal, 2009.

"*The Beguiled*, Misty, Don and Clint." 2001. On *Clint Eastwood American Icon Collection*, disc 1. DVD. Perf. Clint Eastwood. Universal Home Video.

Benjamin, Jessica. 2004. "Beyond Doer and Done To: An Intersubjective View of Third-ness." *Psychoanalytic Quarterly* 73: 5–46.

Billen, Andrew. 2009. "How Dirty Harry Became a New Man; at 78, Clint Eastwood Is Still a Republican and Likes to Play the Tough Guy. But He Is Also a Doting Father and a Champion of Great Female Roles. Andrew Billen Met Him; Clint Eastwood." *Sunday Times*, February 28, http://entertainment.timesonline.co.uk/tol/arts_and _entertainment/film/article5814534.ece, accessed September 9, 2010.

Bingham, Dennis. 1994. *Acting Male: Masculinities in the Films of James Stewart, Jack Nicholson, and Clint Eastwood*. New Brunswick, N.J.: Rutgers University Press.

Briggs, Laura. 2000. "The Race of Hysteria: 'Overcivilization' and the 'Savage' Woman in Late Nineteenth-Century Obstetrics and Gynecology." *American Quarterly* 52, no. 2 (June): 246–73.

"Cinema: Killer! *Fatal Attraction* Strikes Gold as a Parable of Sexual Guilt." 1987. *Time Magazine*, November 16. Accessed September 7, 2010.

Cornell, Drucilla. 2009. *Clint Eastwood and Issues of American Masculinity*. New York: Fordham University Press.

Cott, Nancy F. 1978. "Passionlessness: An Interpretation of Victorian Sexual Ideology, 1790–1850." *Signs* 4, no. 2 (Winter): 219–36.

Cullinan, Thomas. 1969. *The Beguiled*. New York: Avon Book.

Fatal Attraction. 1987. DVD. Dir. Adrian Lynch. Paramount.

Foery, Raymond. 2007. "Narrative Pacing and the Eye of the Other in *The Bridges of Madison County*." In *Clint Eastwood, Actor and Director: New Perspectives*, ed. Leonard Engel, 195–203. Salt Lake City: University of Utah Press.

Haaken, Janice. 1998. *Pillar of Salt: Gender, Memory, and the Perils of Looking Back*. New Brunswick, N.J.: Rutgers University Press.

———. 2003. "Pleasures and Perils of Looking Back: Response to Fogel, Grand, Kahane, and Namir." *Studies in Gender and Sexuality* 4, no. 2: 208–25.

Herring, Gina. 1998. "*The Beguiled*: Misogynist Myth or Feminist Fable?" *Literature Film Quarterly* 26, no. 3: 214–20.

Higham, Charles. 1971. "Suddenly, Don Siegel's High Camp-us." *New York Times*, July 25, D-11.

Hirsch, Foster. 1971–72. "*The Beguiled*: Southern Gothic Revived." *Film Heritage* 7, no. 4: 15–20.

Kael, Pauline. 1985. "Pop Mystics." In *Hooked*, 14–17. New York: E. P. Dutton.

Kay, Karyn. 1976. "*The Beguiled*: Gothic Misogyny." *Velvet Light Trap* 16 (Fall): 32–33.

Knapp, Laurence F. 1996. *Directed by Clint Eastwood: Eighteen Films Analyzed*. Jefferson, N.C.: McFarland and Co.

Knee, Adam. 1993. "The Dialectic of Female and Male Hysteria in *Play Misty for Me*."
     In *Screening the Male: Exploring Masculinities in the Hollywood Cinema*, ed. Steve
     Cohan and Ina Rae Hark, 87–102. London: Routledge.

Knight, Arthur. 1974. "*Playboy* Interview: Clint Eastwood. A Candid Conversation with
     the World's Number-1 Box-Office Star." *Playboy*, February: 57–58, 60, 62, 64, 66, 68,
     70, 72, 170–72.

Nathan, Ian. 2008. "Clint Eastwood: The Man in Movies." *Empire*, July: 121–31.

Neibaur, James L. 1989. *Tough Guy: The American Movie Macho*. Jefferson, N.C.:
     McFarland.

Play Misty for Me. 1971. DVD. Dir. Clint Eastwood. Universal, 2009.

Seidler, Victor Jeleniewski. 2007. "Masculinities, Bodies, and Emotional Life." *Men and
     Masculinities* 10, no. 1: 9–21.

Smith, Paul. 1993. *Clint Eastwood: A Cultural Production*. Minneapolis: University of
     Minnesota Press.

Welter, Barbara. 1966. "The Cult of True Womanhood: 1820–1860." *American Quarterly* 18,
     no. 2 (Summer): 151–74.

Wimsatt, W. K., Jr., and M. C. Beardsley. 1946. "The Intentional Fallacy." *Sewanee Review*
     54, no. 3: 468–88.

Wuntch, Philip. 1971. "Screen: Gothic Horror of *The Beguiled*." Review of *The Beguiled*, dir.
     Don Siegel. *Dallas Morning News*, April 24, 24.

Chapter 3

CLINTUS AND SIEGELINI: "WE'VE GOT A SYSTEM. NOT MUCH, BUT WE'RE FOND OF IT"

Mike Smrtic and Matt Wanat

Clint Eastwood has often acknowledged his artistic debt to director Donald Siegel. Given the ongoing popular and critical interest in Eastwood's films, therefore, one might expect to find many detailed analyses of Siegel's influence on Eastwood's body of work. Unfortunately, this is not the case. Although some critics have noted the connections between Eastwood and Siegel's directing strategies and visual styles, there is in Eastwood criticism almost no mention of the influence of Siegel's dominant themes upon Eastwood's work. Similarly, critics generally have failed to consider the impact of Eastwood's presence, in the five Siegel-directed Eastwood films, upon Siegel's own long-standing thematic preoccupations.

More seriously, few contemporary critics assess Siegel's full body of work in any detail, leaving us to wonder whether critics and fans discussing *Dirty Harry* (1971) or *Escape from Alcatraz* (1979) are even aware that, prior to his work with Eastwood, Donald Siegel had already displayed a commitment to revising and expanding the police procedural and prison film genres in his earlier films. The following essay describes Siegel's dominant theme of individuals or groups struggling to negotiate complex systems and considers the effects of Eastwood and Siegel's collaboration in terms of this central Siegel theme.

Consider, as a starting example, two Siegel prison films, one made prior to his work with Eastwood and the other after four collaborations. Fourteen years before the release of his first film with Eastwood, Siegel directed *Riot in Cell Block 11* (1954). Ostensibly a prison reform film inspired by producer Walter Wagner's incarceration for "shooting at the genitals" of his wife's lover (Siegel 1993, 157), *Riot in Cell Block 11* is more interesting as a meditation on the complications of

individual and collective agendas within systems of authority and procedure. The film is a minor masterpiece of balance, economically crosscutting
between the demands of rioting inmates, led by unstable Dunn (Neville
Brand) and less stable Carnie (Leo Gordon), and the sympathies, thwarted
by public politics, of Warden Reynolds (Emile Meyer). Additionally, the
film includes well-rounded characters from within the various echelons of
the prison, each also negotiating systems wherein everything and everyone
is numbered and controlled.

The mise-en-scène of the film is replete with evidence of the limitations of any human agenda, suggesting that the authorities are as bound
as the inmates to systematized institutional realities. Lighted switchboards
for "Blocks" and "Towers" regulate all activity within the walls, and sig-
nage proliferates, warning guards "No Loafing at Desk" and inmates and
guards alike "Don't Slam Gate." Yet, while these signs represent systematic
rigidity, they also suggest the inevitability of human agency within the system, that rules and codes will be broken, negotiated, transformed. Therefore, in addition to the balance with which the film interrogates systems
of authorities and criminals, the film also complicates what might be an
otherwise facile celebration of individual rebellion. There are no clear win-
ners or even endings, just constant layers and processes of intra- and intersystemic negotiation, until two weeks after the warden and the governor
agree to the prisoners' demands, the state legislature repudiates the agreement, and the film ends with the Warden Reynolds telling the now more
deeply incarcerated Dunn that the publicity will help the continuing cause
of prison reform, opening the systemic microcosm within the walls to the
macrocosm of politicians and public to whom the prisoners have been trying to speak.

Cut forward twenty-five years to *Escape from Alcatraz*, the fifth and
final of the Eastwood films Siegel directed. Like *Riot in Cell Block 11*, *Escape
from Alcatraz* deals with the dehumanizing effects of a prison, the impen-
etrability of its walls, and the personalities of jailors and inmates. However,
unlike the earlier Siegel film, *Escape from Alcatraz* focuses on the Eastwood
character, Frank Morris, thus abandoning most of the balanced treatment
of adversaries and ensemble action in favor of a film in which supporting
characters and systemic relations are most relevant insofar as they bear
directly on Morris's point of view.

As this brief comparison suggests, Siegel's general thematic concern
with individual and collective negotiation within systems has bearing on

his work with Eastwood, but Eastwood's presence also transforms the typical Siegel theme. In either case, the mutual influence of Siegel's ideas upon
Eastwood and Eastwood's presence upon Siegel's ideas merits close consideration if we are to deepen our knowledge of these two film artists and
their relative and collaborative positions in cinema.

■ Eastwood and Siegel

Clint Eastwood's presence in American cinema now seems undeniable and
undeniably rounded. Described by Christopher Frayling as an "herbivore
who has become the most famous film actor in the world by pretending to
be a carnivore" (1992, 23), Eastwood the performer, director, and public figure has acquired an image increasingly varied. Essays in this and Leonard
Engel's previous collection (2007), along with numerous books, account
for the diversity of Eastwood's ideas as a director, and critical interest in
Eastwood's directorial work has grown steadily. Similarly, books by Smith
(1993), Bingham (1994), Beard (2000), and Cornell (2009), along with a
number of essays in Engel's previous collection, examine Eastwood's iconography as a cultural construction. In fact, part of Eastwood's success, as
evidenced by the attention now given his later work, has involved reinvention of self-image, though one consequence of Eastwood's continuing success at reinvention has been a dearth of critical attention to the intersection
of the actor's early iconography with the work of Don Siegel.

   Along with Sergio Leone, Siegel is surely the most important director to Eastwood's development as actor, director, and icon, and while the
effects of Siegel's directing style upon Eastwood's have been frequently
noted, there has been very little discussion of Siegel's dominant themes
and the effects of Eastwood's iconography upon these themes. In fact, with
the exception of *Invasion of the Body Snatchers* (1956) and *Dirty Harry*,
Siegel's body of work has fallen into critical neglect. Our essay begins to
rectify this neglect and to closely read the intersection of Siegel's themes
with Eastwood's star presence.

   In a postscript to Stuart M. Kaminsky's *Don Siegel: Director* (1974),
which along with *A Siegel Film* (Siegel 1993) remains the best book-length
work on the director, Sam Peckinpah characterizes Siegel as a master of
his craft "maniacal in his continuing battle against stupid studio authority"
(1974, 300). Biographically, Peckinpah's claim may be auteur-era hyperbole,
but textually, Siegel's work demonstrates a pervasive thematic interest in
individuals' negotiations of multiple and sometimes competing systems,

both in terms of systems of codes by which characters live and in terms of institutionalized systems that shape and limit the range of characters' actions. Rarely a simple celebration of the isolated rebel against some authority, the theme occurs across multiple characters and systems within any given Siegel film, with variation according to story and genre. However, when it is brought to bear on his first and fourth films with Eastwood, the procedural police films *Coogan's Bluff* and *Dirty Harry*, the Siegel theme becomes increasingly focused on and by the iconography of Eastwood, and what emerges is both a narrowing of the range of Siegel's questions and a singular and charismatic playing out of the theme in terms of Eastwood's characters.

Whereas our research approach was inductive, beginning with screenings and rescreenings of more than thirty Siegel films, we limit our discussion here to procedural police films *The Lineup* (1958), *Madigan* (1968), *Coogan's Bluff* (1968), and *Dirty Harry* (1971), which should suffice to demonstrate the Siegel theme of people in systems and Eastwood's effect on the theme.[1]

■ *The Lineup* (1958)

When Siegel and screenwriter Sterling Silliphant were hired to direct a theatrical version of the 1950s television program *The Lineup*, they departed from the standard police procedural framework of the series to construct the film, instead, around the characters of two professional criminals, cultivated mentor Julian (Robert Keith) and aspiring protégée Dancer (Eli Wallach), and the duo's efforts to collect packages transported unwittingly by innocent tourists as part of an international drug smuggling operation headed by The Man (Vaughn Taylor). The objections of producers Frank Cooper and Jaime Del Valle to this drastic reimagining of a successful franchise led to a number of structural compromises in the final film (Siegel 1993, 210–11), which retains its recognizable generic investigative framework for the first twenty minutes and sporadically thereafter but finally refocuses its full attention upon the career criminals and their ultimately unsuccessful reconnaissance assignment. This off-kilter sense of balance ironically inverts the structure of the typical police procedural, as the increasingly marginal efforts and methods of the police force become of secondary interest to the delineation of hierarchical criminal systems, their context-dependent protocols, and the dire consequences for criminal professionals who misread the codes of these systems.

"How far can you go with this special stuff?" asks Dancer of his partner Julian as the pair fly into San Francisco to execute "a tight one," during one of many conversations between the two men that identify them as professionals and depict them as partners participating in a system of criminal protocol and ethics. The topic is "English Grammar and Usage," a manual Dancer studies as they prepare to land, and Julian replies, "It sets you up, remember that. How many characters you know hang around street corners say, 'If I were you?'" Julian's role is here established as that of the seasoned expert guiding the newcomer toward achieving professional distinction within the criminal community ("If he continues to listen to me, he'll be the best"). Dancer is an impulsive pupil, whom his teacher deems a "pure psychopath," yet thinks of himself as a tradesman and often pauses from procedure to reflect on matters of professional preference: He likes his getaway cars to be inconspicuous and have freshly stolen plates; he is always on time, does not like people "coming on too big," and does not take notes on the job. As for money, "Dancer derives no particular feeling from it," Julian tells Sandy (Richard Jaeckel), the driver whom they both treat like an amateur and outsider because of his drinking problem. The depiction of Julian and Dancer as professionals who treat their life of crime as "work" (a theme Siegel revisited in 1964's *The Killers*) structurally systematizes their criminal behavior, and by exploring the nature of their personal partnership the middle section of Siegel's film effectively becomes a small-time crime "procedural," turning an otherwise generic set of drug recovery runs into a professional development exercise.

In addition to the criminal unit constituted by his partnership with Dancer, Julian also displays an awareness of the duo's respective position within a much larger criminal system, with its own set of protocols, codes, and hierarchies. When they meet The Man to turn over the recovered drugs, they also have to explain a collection shortfall caused by a little girl powdering the face of her doll with the heroin concealed inside. This procedural snafu ironically highlights the operational shortcomings of The Man's smuggling system, but Julian understands that he and Dancer are accountable to The Man nonetheless and warns Dancer to be careful of the abstract system of criminal codes and power that lies beyond the domain of their subcontract partnership: "Sure you can take him. It's what he represents that you can't take, not even you." Julian's own sense of professionalism is epitomized by the small book he carries, in which he records the last words of the team's victims, as well as the attention to mission protocol

he exhibits in keeping Dancer on course as they carry out their reconnaissance agenda, telling him to "take your time and keep it impersonal"
and promoting a respect for procedural adherence and tact that Dancer at
times finds amusingly old-fashioned.

Dancer's meeting with The Man serves as the key dramatic encounter
of the film, a showdown in which his efforts to negotiate and adopt a personal system of professional codes of conduct come into fatal opposition
with The Man's enforcement of a larger, more diffused and arbitrary system of criminal protocol. After making the drop at the arranged place and
time, Dancer decides to stay behind to explain things to The Man, a risk
that elicits the response, "Nobody ever sees me. That's going to make you
dead. Maybe you'll make it to the airport, maybe you won't, but your time
is borrowed." In Dancer's confusion at not being accepted or understood,
he makes a fumbling attempt to explain himself further, hoping that cir-
cumstantial context can accommodate his actions within The Man's system
and allow him to evade The Man's decree of violation and consequence. But
he loses his professional cool along with his recently elevated diction, slipping desperately back into the street gangster argot he has been learning
to avoid: "Julian and I will blow. . . . Julian and I don't want no beef with
you. . . . When it got goofed up like that, I couldn't drop a short shipment
without some explanation, could I?" When The Man answers his submissive plea with stony silence, Dancer, in blind rage at his actions and justi-
fications not being accepted by a higher authority, pushes the wheelchair-
bound Man to his death over the edge of a skating rink balcony.

Following this explicitly symbolic rejection of The Man's power, Dancer
discards all trappings of professional formality and restraint, reverting to
the persona of the antisocial lone gangster as he lashes out impulsively at
all systems and dismisses the benefit of any collaborative protocol or plan.
He tells Julian: "From here on in, I'm running the show. Me. You're in the
backseat, that's where you stay." This repudiation of their partnership coincides with a dramatic car chase by the now Fury-like San Francisco police
force, terminating in an elevated dead end on the partially constructed
Embarcadero Freeway. As they reach a final impasse, Dancer mocks Julian's
book of "famous last words" before killing him, parroting The Man's own
final speech as he shoots, in a final symbolic rejection of the two father figures of different criminal families. Dancer then releases his child hostage
and tries to escape over the edge of the freeway but is shot by police and
falls to his death, bouncing off several levels of freeway embankment on

his way down. Dancer's literal dead end follows his rejection of two over-lapping systems of criminal protocol, one based on personal camaraderie and the aspirational assimilation of professional codes, the other on professional submission to a set of impersonal codes justified with contextual power. Like *Riot in Cell Block 11*, *The Lineup* casts a dispassionate eye upon individuals negotiating for authority within complex and highly dynamic systems, but whereas the oppositional systems in *Riot* are discretely demar-cated, *The Lineup* focuses on individuals trapped at the unstable nexus of a system within a system, for whom negotiations of sublevel protocol lead to conflict with codes enforced from above.

■ *Madigan* and *Coogan's Bluff* (1968)

Siegel spent much of the 1960s working in television, directing a number of pilot episodes, producing the series *The Legend of Jesse James* for 20th Century Fox, and directing some of the first made-for-television features at Universal, including *The Killers* (1964), *The Hanged Man* (1964), and *Stranger on the Run* (1967). He returned to theatrical feature-directing at Universal with *Madigan* (1968), which resumes the analysis of "systems within a system" in the domain of the police procedural and is the first of three films we will examine in which police officers in professional crisis are required to execute complex intra- and intersystemic negotiations in bids for active authority.

Superficially, *Madigan* is concerned with two separate narrative arcs: the public efforts of Detectives Dan Madigan (Richard Widmark) and Rocco Bonaro (Harry Guardino) to capture a killer who steals their guns and later shoots two policemen, and the private struggles of Police Commissioner Anthony Russell (Henry Fonda), who uncovers departmental corruption and must decide upon and administer an appropriate institutional response. The film's structure alternates between these two plot strands, employing parallel crosscutting for thematic juxtaposition but also diffusing the narrative focus of the film across two sets of characters, conflicts, and resolution patterns. From a screenplay significantly entitled "Friday, Saturday, and Sunday" (Kaminsky 1974, 202), *Madigan* effects another of Siegel's refinements of the procedural genre by focusing on the resolution of internal crises within the police system and elaborating the ways in which professional status is dependent upon the contextual options open to individuals at different hierarchical levels of the system.

Siegel and cinematographer Russell Metty embed Madigan and part-ner Bonaro within a gritty mise-en-scène that reinforces the materiality

of their professional existence and locates their ongoing pursuit of killer
Barney Benesch (Steve Ihnat) within a landscape of train tracks, beat-up
patrol cars, city streets, dive bars, low-rent apartments, and movie theater
back rooms. In this streetwise investigative zone, Widmark's portrayal of
Madigan seems the very physical embodiment of "work," from the film's
opening chase, in which Madigan's unsuccessful rooftop pursuit of Benesch
leaves him exhausted and sweating, to the final shoot-out sequence in
which he bursts into Benesch's hideout, violently sacrificing himself to
reclaim the professional standing lost in the film's opening sequence. The
depiction of Madigan and his milieu is most strikingly contrasted throughout the film with the lush aristocratic surroundings of Commissioner
Russell, whose office and apartment appear spartan and orderly and whose
reserved demeanor discloses almost none of the personal turmoil swirling
beneath its surface.

This visual contrast is employed most strikingly in the first section of
Madigan, which delineates, largely through parallel crosscutting, the hierarchies of the police system, the relative statuses of those within it, and the
degrees of authority available to those at each level. Madigan and Bonaro
return to the local precinct office following Benesch's escape to wait upon
Lt. James Price (Frank Marth), who announces sarcastically: "I woke up
the District Commander, and he woke up the Borough Commander. Now
the Borough Commander woke up the Chief of Detectives, and the Chief
Inspector, I can assure you, has already presented the glad tidings to Police
Commissioner Anthony X. Russell." As hipbone is connected to thighbone,
so flows the authority of the police chain of command, and Madigan and
Bonaro will be prevented from recommencing their search for Benesch
until news from headquarters arrives to reinstate them to active professional status. Price also tells them that they will be fined five days' pay for
losing their guns, in accordance with departmental protocol. Madigan and
Bonaro may be the early-rising risk-takers on the force, but authority in
the police system is hierarchical, and they (and we) must wait for another
scene, in which Russell and his high-ranking associates debate the matter
further before deciding that the detectives will have seventy-two hours to
bring in Benesch.

Throughout the film, Madigan is acutely aware of the limited options
available within this bureaucratic police system for tracking down Benesch ("Now we're down to terrorizing old ladies") and thus makes use of
a number of external resources to locate his target, employing, in turn,

bookie Midget Castiglione, street punk Hughie, and an assortment of other unofficial informants, including daylight drunks and subway dispatchers. Though Madigan never explicitly breaks the law, Siegel explained elsewhere the rationale for Madigan's disregard of police protocol: "A man in the kind of a jam he's in isn't going to stand on formalities" (quoted in Bogdanovich 1997, 763). Madigan's own ancillary "system" leverages personal obligations, often described as "favors," out of a desperate need to capture Benesch quickly, but these actions are also inscribed within an implied critique of the detached moral rectitude of those higher up in the police system, most notably Russell, of whom Madigan says, "With him, everything's either right or wrong; there's no in-between." Unlike Russell's own crises in the film, which are depicted as philosophical and moral, Madigan's efforts to reassert his status through means external to the police system are depicted as utilitarian correctives to the unrealistically rigid worldview espoused by men like Russell, not as a moral response to the inadequacies of the system itself.

Although Madigan's professional use of personal relationships ultimately leads him to Benesch, his relationship with wife Julia (Inger Stevens) is depicted as part of a personal system in direct competition with his professional identity and requiring constant negotiation. Julia feels socially isolated because of the nature of her husband's work and suggests to Madigan that his job is incompatible with her emotional well-being: "Why didn't you think of me once in a while? Maybe there's some kind of life I want." In her husband's absence, Julia watches television so much "it's coming out of my eyeballs" and disdains the idea of going out alone. On two occasions, moments of potential physical intimacy between the couple are interrupted by the symbolic intrusion of Madigan's work into their domestic space, including a phone call from partner Rocco, who ironically is shown on the other end of the line enjoying a home-cooked meal at the kitchen table while Madigan and his wife bicker in their cluttered bedroom.

The Captain's Party, a police-sponsored public event that sanctions a temporary intermingling of the personal and professional systems, becomes the unlikely stage for Julia's reaffirmation of her relationship with Madigan and, in some ways, his final failure to accommodate her into his professional world. Madigan briefly interrupts his hunt for Benesch to don a tuxedo and pass his wife into the temporary company of colleague Ben Williams (Warren Stevens) so that he can get back on the job. Upon leaving the event, he encounters Commissioner Russell in the only physical meeting of these men in the film and delivers a confused monologue that conveys uncertainty about his current systemic status: "I just left the wife. Just left her. As a matter of fact, I'm on my way uptown right now. I didn't want her to miss the party; she's been looking forward to it. I was just going to call my partner." Although this stumbling rationalization indicates Madigan trying to demonstrate sensitivity to his wife's needs, the comedy here emerges from his exposure to Russell at this vulnerable moment, appearing to be disregarding his duty, when he is in fact, as we shall see, disregarding his wife.

The evening ends in narrowly averted marital crisis for Julia when chaperone Ben attempts to take advantage of her following the party. Julia, intoxicated with champagne and the high of an evening away from the TV and within the company of others, leads Ben on slightly but refuses his gradually more forceful advances and tearfully breaks down to demand he take her back to the hotel. Ironically, Madigan never learns of this possible threat to his marriage or the implicit marital reaffirmation that Julia's rejection of Ben symbolizes—she calls the precinct office the next morning to tell him that she loves him, but the message is received as an afterthought by Madigan, who is preoccupied with Benesch's capture.

After leaving the Captain's Party, Madigan is forced to confront a final symbolic violation of the professional system that ultimately requires his complete commitment to this system above all others. Benesch uses one of the stolen guns to shoot two policemen who identify him on the street, killing one of them. The significance of this systemic breach perhaps propels Madigan to act with a directness unseen in the film up to this point, as he arrives the next morning with extra determination at the police stakeout of Benesch's apartment, refuses to put on a protective vest, and demands to enter first as "the senior man." Madigan bursts in first but is mortally wounded before Bonaro kills Benesch, his self-sacrifice a final validating reclamation of his professional standing.

Ultimately, the success of *Madigan*'s analysis of hierarchical police systems and the difficulties of reconciling both professional and personal needs is a result of its balanced and diffused structure and multiple-character narrative. Although we do not have time here to explore in greater detail the other relevant narrative arcs in the film, most specifically those involving Commissioner Russell and Chief Inspector Charlie Kane, *Madigan* resonates significantly not as a story of the man-against-the-system but as an analysis of the men within the system, expanding upon Siegel's earlier explorations of these themes to measure the direct consequences of competing systems in personal terms.

Released the same year as *Madigan*, *Coogan's Bluff* marks Siegel's first collaboration with Clint Eastwood. When discussing the film, few critics have failed to note what Christopher Frayling calls Eastwood's "individualist of frontier mythology" at odds with the "pen-pushers" of the city (1992, 77), as Coogan, an Arizona lawman, is ordered to New York City to bring back convict Ringerman (Don Stroud), whom he attempts to extradite without going through proper channels and loses after being ambushed by Ringerman's friends Linny (Tisha Sterling) and Pushie (David Doyle). Along the way, Coogan locks horns with Lt. McElroy (Lee J. Cobb) of the New York Police Department (NYPD) and becomes involved with probation officer Julie (Susan Clark) as he tries to redeem his professional honor by hunting and apprehending the fugitive. East and West, urban and rural, the crime film and the Western—each juxtaposition figures into the film's version of the Siegel theme, but most important is the intersection of McElroy's procedural policy, Julie's sympathetic behavioral psychology, and Coogan's predatory behaviorism. Moreover, in the case of each system (procedure, therapy, the hunt) human factors intrude and complicate, which replicates Siegel's typical interest in the collision of systems and negotiations of individuals therein, but in a way that ultimately privileges Coogan's point of view.

Indeed, the film begins and ends with Coogan's predatory method insofar as, with the eventual capture of Ringerman in Manhattan's Fort Tryon Park, the film comes full circle back to Coogan's original apprehension, in Arizona, of Navajo fugitive Running Bear (Rudy Diaz). In the opening scene, Coogan ignores orders and tracks his prey, finding an abandoned boot labeled "Navajo Reservation," apparently left by Running Bear to lure him in. Like bugling cavalry, Coogan drives his jeep into Running Bear's crosshairs, but this is the first of Coogan's many bluffs, for he soon circles his jeep to create dust cover that allows him to sneak up on his disoriented prey. Coogan's later capture of Ringerman mirrors each of the elements from the Running Bear scene: the bluff, the prey's attempt to use high ground, the prey's loss of viewing privilege. Following Linny, whom Coogan has abused into revealing Ringerman's hideout, Coogan bluffs her, saying, "I'll be right behind you," before disappearing, leaving Linny and then Ringerman in states of confusion mirroring Running Bear's.

Several important elements emerge from the opening and closing scenes, the most significant being the drama of ambush and bluff in predatory relations, a predatory motif that also figures into romantic relationships as Coogan sexually hunts Julie and Linny but also bluffs each, using the women for information. Likewise, the hunter Coogan is preyed upon by urban cabbies, hotel employees, and hippies, though each underestimates him as a country rube. In fact, Coogan is constantly underestimated by the subsystems of the city, and by shysters and bureaucrats therein, and this underestimation becomes part of his method, for example, when he teases Linny's name out of Ringerman's mother (Betty Field), who, though dismissive of the official police, seems distracted by Coogan's being a "cowboy." Likewise, Coogan gets Linny's address by using her probation officer, Julie, whom he treats to a combination of predatory sexuality and western courtship.[2]

Coogan's bluffs represent the ruses of a hunter seeking his quarry, but they also point to the dishonesty with which others cling to their respective systems. The lesson that Coogan and, in large part, the film offer to Julie and McElroy is not so much that their systems are wrong as that their systems are complicated by unacknowledged human nature. In this respect, the film presents Coogan as a better behavioral psychologist than Julie is, not only because Coogan can sniff out his prey like one would an animal but also because Coogan seems to know that others become hypocrites within their systems. In McElroy's case, after Coogan is first told the procedure he must follow to get Ringerman from the ward, Coogan dismisses all of it by saying, "You could get him," and one wonders why McElroy does not simply do so. Later, after Coogan is accused of ruining the stakeout for an undercover officer (James Edwards), McElroy defends his procedure: "We've got a system. Not much, but we're fond of it. We don't like it when some two-for-a-nickel cowboy thinks he can bend it out of shape." But he goes on to inadvertently reveal more human motives: "You blew a stakeout. It involved a lot of time and trouble and discomfort for Sgt. Wallace." The scene plays comically as one begins to realize that the issue for McElroy is less the superiority of his system than the comfort of his officers. Opposite this revelation of the human motives behind NYPD procedure is Coogan's more germane predatory behavioral method: "You learn a lot about a person when you hunt him."

While Julie's behavioral psychology—comically described as psychophysiological autogenesis—might seem closer to Coogan's method, her system is also undermined by the personal. After Coogan is nearly beaten to death at Pushie's bar, Julie berates him for ruining Linny's parole but cannot help adding that she knows Coogan slept with Linny, whom she calls a "painfully graphic little girl," making it clear that Julie is not angry out of pity for her client but, rather, out of jealousy that Coogan—who earlier asked the reluctant Julie, "Still running?" when she dodged his advances—has decided to pursue another.

In short, Coogan's influence reveals the human motives beneath systems: McElroy's procedural and Julie's sympathetic-psychological. Therefore, each character must be reconciled to Coogan before he flies away with Ringerman. McElroy accepts the human factor within his procedural system and is reconciled when he gives Coogan an incriminating western hat, left at Pushie's bar where, without jurisdiction, Coogan has killed a man. And Julie is reconciled when, coming to see Coogan off, she wears red, which an earlier discussion has established as "the color of pity."[3]

Coogan, however, must also be reconciled to procedure, and after apprehending Ringerman in the park, he agrees to follow the original protocol McElroy mapped out for Ringerman's release, and in the process, he earns the respect of McElroy, who on the flight deck addresses him as "Sheriff" where he has earlier disparagingly called him "Wyatt." This reconciliation follows Coogan's apparent need for the NYPD: whereas at Pushie's bar sirens both scatter Coogan's assailants, thus saving him, and send Coogan running like a fugitive, in Fort Tryon Park, the police sirens turn Ringerman back toward Coogan, hence running the prey back into the arms of the hunter. It remains unclear whether or not any recognition of this inspires Coogan's reconciliation of his methods with the NYPD, but there is some acknowledgment on Coogan's part that he has failed by not following the original procedure. Less clear still is Coogan's recognition of his flaws in handling Julie. Indeed, right after Coogan has forced Julie to see veiled envy in her pity for Linny, he slams the door furiously, which is match-cut to his kicking in Linny's door. While Coogan seems to understand the animalistic behavior of humans, he never really controls his own.

At the end, apprehending Ringerman on the ridge of the park known as "Coogan's Bluff," Coogan seizes the cityscape for his own. Earlier, overlooking the Cloisters with Julie, Coogan turns his gaze upon the city itself: "Trying to picture it the way it was, just the trees and the river, before people came along and fouled it all up"; and the events at the end, particularly the point-of-view shots where Linny and Ringerman struggle to find Coogan in the forest, confirm his erasure of the foul human from the natural place while mirroring his mastery of Running Bear's perch at the opening of the film. However, the result, like the message, is hardly pristine. Indeed, the extent of Coogan's animalistic behaviorism is misanthropic, and his use and pursuit of Julie are underwritten with the real enigma of his personality, which Julie (and later Linny) seeks to understand but which is ultimately not clarified: Does Coogan want Julie, or does he simply use her? Why is she part of the hunt? Does her pity finally atone, in his or the script's apparently sexist reasoning, for his being stabbed once for trusting a woman? Julie's seeing Coogan off at the end answers none of these questions. Nor does his giving Ringerman a smoke on the helicopter, a gesture he refused Running Bear earlier, atone in any satisfactory way for the misanthropy underlying his methods.

Eastwood's Coogan brings an imbalance to the questions this particular Siegel film raises about individuals in systems. While the film struggles to reconcile McElroy, Julie, and Coogan to the effects of the human upon each of their respective systems, we do not find Coogan's reconciliation convincing, nor does the systemic characterization seem convincingly balanced.[4] This imbalance occurs not only because *Coogan's Bluff* is a star vehicle but also because of the charismatic effect of Eastwood's performance. For one thing, the entire first part of the film is comic, regarding both male–female relations and colliding systems, and much of the comedy hinges on Eastwood's knack for curiously judgmental facial expressions, as if everything either amuses or annoys him and ought to do the same to us. More important, Eastwood introduces an element previously unfamiliar in Siegel's body of work, where even Elvis in *Flaming Star* (1960) monopolizes less thematic interest in the individual. The result of Eastwood's participation is a new system in the Siegel theme, a particularly charismatic return of the star system wherein the other individuals in the story become less parallel instruments of theme than support or adversity for the protagonist. Nowhere is this clearer than in *Dirty Harry*, which in the context of Siegel's work and the procedural cop film depicts the intersection of person and system in a uniquely existential and individually focused way.

■ *Dirty Harry* (1971)

Critics tend to read *Dirty Harry* as a political film, and a number of readings have described, condemned, or defended the film on these grounds.[5] Whatever their differences, most of these readings share the assumption that *Dirty Harry* is best read as the product of 1971, teetering between New Left and New Right. Because consensus tends to characterize *Dirty Harry* as sociopolitical allegory and to speculate about the film's effects on audience in terms of appeal within a specific political milieu, little or nothing has been written on the film's roots in Siegel's procedural plots and thematic preoccupation with systems, a curious omission given that *Dirty Harry* functions as a rather extreme example of Siegel's interests.[6] *Dirty Harry* is a transitional film, but not solely of the sociopolitical sort that has obsessed critics. Rather, *Dirty Harry* marks the transition from the more balanced explorations of competing legal and criminal systems we see in *Riot in Cell Block 11*, *The Lineup*, and *Madigan* to cinematic landscapes dominated by the presence of Eastwood himself.

The opening scenes of *Dirty Harry* establish the film's relationship to the genre of the police procedural by focusing on the investigative and strategic response of the San Francisco police department to the actions and demands of the anonymous killer known as Scorpio (Andy Robinson). Inspector Harry Callahan's professional status is conveyed to the viewer beneath the opening credits, as he arrives on the murder scene, silently seeks out Scorpio's abandoned rooftop vantage point, and retrieves a spent shell casing with a ballpoint pen before placing it inside an evidence collection envelope. Callahan's subsequent meeting with the Mayor (John Vernon), Police Chief (John Larch), and Lt. Bressler (Harry Guardino) positions him within a hierarchical law enforcement system of professional accountability and protocol, as he and his superiors meet to discuss the police department's investigative progress and plans for dealing with Scorpio's ransom demands and capture. "The city of San Francisco does not pay criminals not to commit crimes; instead we pay a police department," intones the Mayor before Callahan is called in, setting the stage for what in other films with a similar procedural opening (such as *The Lineup*) would become a reassuring briefing on matters of police technique and technology.

Callahan's entrance, however, serves not to distill into one character portrait all of the police system's implicit moral, organizational, and procedural virtues but, rather, to introduce a critical voice to challenge the system's grounding logic and methodology. Callahan answers the Mayor's generically appropriate question, "What have you been doing?" with the eyebrow-raising response, "Well, for the past three quarters of an hour, I've been sitting on my ass in your outer office, waiting on you," and from this point onward, Siegel's film will leverage Eastwood's iconographic persona to open up a space within the procedural for a representative of the system to criticize it from within. Callahan's attempts to explain to the Mayor several technical points of the investigation (including the use of identification files and ballistics methods) are interrupted by his superior officer Bressler contextualizing the department's progress in more concrete terms, and Callahan's frustration with this procedural jockeying sets the stage for an outright disagreement with the Mayor: "Wait a minute, do I get this right? You're going to play this creep's game?" Callahan's alternative suggestion for dealing with Scorpio ("Why don't you let me meet with the son of a bitch?") is followed by an exchange in which the Mayor and Callahan debate the meaning of *intent* and in which the Mayor's "policy" of avoiding trouble is contrasted with Callahan's own personal standard: "I shoot the bastard, that's my policy." Siegel's experienced handling of Eastwood's outsider persona renders the professional wrangling in this scene comic, yet notably Callahan's challenges to the system at this early stage are posed not by a lone wolf but by a professional within the system who uses the system's own language, protocol, and standards to challenge its underlying assumptions and critique its procedural inadequacy.

During the first half of the film, Callahan is depicted as occupying a contradictory position within a law enforcement system that seeks to restrict his scope of action yet simultaneously requires his transgressive persona to accomplish tasks beyond the grasp of its standard operating procedures. Immediately following this contentious mayoral briefing, Callahan interrupts his lunch, Magnum drawn, to stop a bank robbery single-handedly because the police whom he has summoned to deal with the situation have not yet arrived. Yet after congratulating him for this "pretty good pinch" and passing along the kudos of the Police Chief, Callahan's boss, Lt. Bressler, assigns him to work with rookie officer Chico Gonzalez (Reni Santoni), effectively implementing a check on Callahan's tendency toward unsanctioned professional conduct: "You're working with Gonzalez, or you're not working. Now that's straight from the Fifth Floor, you got it?" In later scenes involving a potential suicide jumper and a ransom exchange, Callahan accepts assignments seemingly beyond the call of duty for other officers of indeterminate rank depicted in the film, yet he is also repeatedly reined in by the system's voices of authority, told to "play it straight, do what you're told." Perhaps it is this operational cognitive dissonance that accounts for Callahan's ironic attitude toward his job and figures of authority in the film or even his begrudging acceptance of the nickname "Dirty Harry," which references his assignment to "every dirty job that comes along" but additionally designates him as an uneasy fit within the clean lines of the police system.

It is Callahan's enlistment in the ransom exchange for Scorpio's fourteen-year-old kidnapping victim, however, that symbolically places him at the mercy of two incompatible systems and precipitates the professional crisis that initiates the film's shift from the procedural to the personal. When Bressler offers Callahan the courier job, he also prohibits Gonzalez's participation, presumably because of the junior officer's inexperience, although the scene also implies that Gonzalez has learned enough from Callahan to perceive the police system critically, as Gonzalez asserts in Callahan's own outsider tongue that Harry is getting "the shit end of the stick." Callahan, procedurally isolated by the police system, now makes use of resources unsanctioned by Bressler, enlisting Gonzalez's unofficial aid, along with a borrowed radio transmitter and a concealed switchblade knife (of which Bressler disapprovingly comments: "It's disgusting that a police officer should know how to use a weapon like that"). The exchange operation itself constitutes acceptance on the part of the police system of Scorpio's own system of codes, referred to several times by Scorpio himself as a "game" and which requires Callahan, being followed at some distance by Gonzalez, to move from place to place, the city of San Francisco becoming a physical map of Scorpio's illogical requirements.

By the time Callahan reaches the final meeting place, the cross in Mount Davidson Park, the landscape of the city (previously a showcase for police presence, as the pursuit of Scorpio engages helicopters and rooftop surveillance) has disappeared into a pool of black night and obstructed point-of-view shots, leaving the police system's representative without a system to protect him. In this indistinct, unmappable visual space, we see Harry's face, an oval on a black screen, now at the complete mercy of Scorpio, who commands Callahan from offscreen to "freeze, just like a statue." Scorpio emerges from the darkness only to beat the powerless Callahan viciously before informing him that the rules of the game have changed and that in fact he is going to kill both Callahan and the kidnapped girl. Scorpio has violated the terms of his own deal, and as he readies his gun to kill Callahan, the mortal threat reveals the human consequences of the unraveled logic of the police system, which by taking Scorpio's system seriously has put Callahan's life in jeopardy. Only through Chico's armed intervention and Callahan's own switchblade skill does he survive this scene, wounded, powerless, and alone, at the base of the cross. In the abstracted empty space around Callahan's supine figure, the police system's ineffectiveness has been made explicit, and in the next sequence, wherein

Scorpio is cornered in Kezar Stadium, Callahan steps decisively outside the professional system, achieving the transformation from a conflicted and constrained professional into an iconic hunter.

Unleashed in Kezar Stadium, Callahan first dismisses the need for a search warrant and then dismisses his fill-in partner, DiGiorgio (John Mitchum)—"Go on out and get some air, Fatso"—after DiGiorgio has thrown up the lights and Callahan has again wounded Scorpio on the football field. The scene is extraordinary, encapsulating and abandoning Siegel's theme of individual cop within procedural system, as Callahan jettisons all semblance of police officer in favor of predator. However, although the throwing up of the lights releases Callahan and us from the darkness that has pervaded much of the previous twenty minutes of the film, Callahan's apprehension of Scorpio in the stadium neither restores police presence to the cityscape nor presents Callahan the hunter as any realistic alternative. In fact, the execution of the drama—from Lalo Schifrin's score to the football lights to the waving of the grass beneath the helicopter shot that closes the scene with Scorpio writhing beneath Harry's foot—is not only beyond the professional imperatives constraining police procedure but also fundamentally unheroic and unreal, undermining any clear sense of diegetic insularity or realism without ever really offering the comfort that might come from seeing this scene as formally self-reflexive or the product of Harry's mind.

What emerges from the Kezar Stadium scene is a far less realistic or human approach to the question of Harry's relation to the systems of the police or Scorpio than that which starts the movie. Whereas at the beginning Callahan participates, though cynically and rebelliously, within the force, a number of scenes after Kezar Stadium show Callahan off the clock, no longer answerable to procedure or kidnapper's timetables, now simply stalking Scorpio after a more abstract system, the "law" of Miranda rights and search warrants, secures Scorpio's release by technicality. However, just as Inspector Callahan and the procedural constraints of police work give way to wraithlike hunter and abstract legality, Scorpio's command of the cityscape through "demands" gives way to the prey's increasing tendency to cling to his rights and the press in response to his being stalked.

While the inadmissibility of Scorpio's rifle, obtained by illegal search, suggests Scorpio's continued manipulation of the law, it also shows his increasing dependence upon it, a dependence that begins with his begging for a lawyer when Callahan is torturing him in the stadium. Stalked by

Callahan in the well-lit schoolyards of day and the cavernous strip clubs of night, Scorpio turns the press to his advantage by paying to have himself beaten and then publically blaming Harry; but his manipulation of the system becomes more erratically executed, and more masochistic for that matter, and it is clear that once Harry's actions are divorced from systematic constraints, Scorpio's system is doomed.

When Scorpio kidnaps a bus full of children and warns authorities not to intervene on the Sir Francis Drake Boulevard route to the airport, his doing so recalls his directions to Callahan during the previous money drop but with the weight of vulnerability now shifted from Callahan to the killer, as Callahan refuses to be the Mayor's "delivery boy" and, instead, awaits the bus on a railroad bridge that overstretches the route and the limits of plausibility. Callahan mounts the bus, which Scorpio crashes into the Hutchinson Rock Company, where Callahan chases him on foot through the quarry and shoots him after Scorpio takes his last hostage, a boy fishing in a quarry sump. Here Callahan repeats the film's famous "Do you feel lucky?" speech from the bank robbery sequence at the beginning, but where the speech was playful earlier, complete with Albert Popwell's bemused bank robber, it now becomes menacing, punctuated in the script by the direction "His face contorts in anger" (quoted in Siegel 1993, 364), a pretext to Harry's killing Scorpio with his last bullet. As Scorpio floats in the sump, distant sirens approach, and Callahan throws his badge into the water before the camera pulls back to reveal not the approach of the police cars but, rather, Callahan alone, isolated in the quarry.

Siegel (1993, 366) and others have written about Eastwood's reluctance to throw the badge, which Eastwood associated with Harry's quitting. Certainly, the throwing of the badge symbolizes Harry's abandonment of some element of the job, if not the job itself, but given the abstraction of the last half of *Dirty Harry*, the symbolism transcends Harry's decision. The film resolves by pitting Harry's predatory system, finally unleashed from the bureaucracy of procedure and law, against Scorpio's manipulation of systems, and this puts Scorpio on the defensive. With this in mind, it is easy enough to see why many call *Dirty Harry* a reactionary celebration of assertive individualism within a flawed legal system. However, it must also be noted that the film's style becomes increasingly unrealistic in the second half, with more prolonged dissolves that move the pacing away from the tighter action exposition of the procedural half into a kind of cinematic dream state of Scorpio's manic behavior and Eastwood's iconic stance awaiting the final showdown. Likewise, the cityscape that dominates the procedural half of the film gives way to natural and industrial margins where even a site as iconic as the Golden Gate Bridge seems only another leg of the bus's existential journey to the quarry, further centering Eastwood. Coupled with an increasingly ambivalent characterization of time and space is the elimination of other police from the action, with Callahan refusing to do his superiors' bidding and Chico deciding, in a dreamy rooftop convalescence center, to become a schoolteacher. Through these shifts in style and action, the movie reorganizes itself around Eastwood's and Robinson's performances as hunter and prey and, particularly, around the visual iconography of Eastwood, beginning with Kezar Stadium and culminating with the famous "Do you feel lucky?" speech as refrain.

Dirty Harry's shift from thematic exploration of men in systems to iconic dreamscape of retributive violence marks a partial revision of Siegel's previous interests, which are now organized around Eastwood's emerging iconography. In retrospect one can see this change coming in *Coogan's Bluff*, where the jokes about Coogan's dealing with urban methods give way to a dark and concentrated study of Eastwood as hunter. With *Dirty Harry*, however, this thematic transition comes of age, and the Siegel plot, with its previous balance of characters, is made almost irrelevant by an emerging icon whose presence, even in the first *Dirty Harry* movie, always borders on the extradiegetic realm one generally expects only from parody and self-reflexive experimentation.

The degree of abstraction inherent in Eastwood's iconography, here simultaneously intradiegetic and extradiegetic, is no doubt part of the seduction and also accounts for the ways in which *Dirty Harry* can be seen as both existentially open and single-mindedly propagandistic. However, we think it most important to note that the thematic preoccupations underlying *Dirty Harry* come as much from the history of genre and Siegel's body of work as they do from any 1971 political discourse. *Dirty Harry* does not invent or reflect a discourse so much as it transforms Siegel's themes.

■ Conclusion

Siegel followed up *Dirty Harry* with his first film since 1968 not to feature Eastwood, the heist film *Charley Varrick* (1973), a thematic summation and apparent career valedictory on the theme of professionals negotiating complex and competing systems. Charley Varrick (Walter Matthau) is a small-time bank robber unexpectedly propelled into the big leagues when a routine rural bank job nets a dangerous windfall of Mafia money. Outsider Varrick must manipulate a vast network of interlocking systems, including police, Mafia, and bank forces, in addition to a renegade coconspirator, in order to create enough diversionary noise within the global environment to ensure his safe escape and evade further pursuit. The film's original title, *Last of the Independents*, which is also the motto of Varrick's decoy crop-dusting enterprise, hints at the pride the film takes in his meticulously strategic success, while simultaneously intimating that his adept maneuvers showcase a vanishing brand of professional skill.

Opposite *Charley Varrick*'s elegiac tribute to the Siegel theme, one might consider Siegel and Eastwood's final collaboration, *Escape from Alcatraz*, a prison film, like Siegel's *Riot and Cell Block 11*, but with notable differences. In this final Eastwood/Siegel film, an ensemble of escapees are pitted against the authoritarianism and cruelty of the Warden (Patrick McGoohan), but the film emphasizes Eastwood's character Morris, and Morris's encounters with authority serve mostly to establish that the Warden is full of hubris and that Morris will eventually defeat him. Though impressive in its use of location, score, photography, and Eastwood, *Escape from Alcatraz* demonstrates the effect of Eastwood's star presence on a common Siegel theme of individuals' negotiations of systems. In 1954's *Riot in Cell Block 11*, this theme drove plot, characterization, photography, editing, and setting in an integrated and complex way. In *Escape from Alcatraz*, these narrative elements are driven mostly by Morris's mission and mood in response to a cruel authoritarian and an "inescapable" rock.

The power and limitations of Eastwood and Siegel's collaborations deepen, or ought to deepen, our understanding of each artist. Through close analysis of Siegel's body of work and Eastwood's position therein, we not only recover a neglected Hollywood director but also extend our understanding of an important Hollywood artist and icon, Clint Eastwood. Although Eastwood's insertion into established Siegel themes seems to have narrowed the diegetic breadth of their application, Eastwood's iconography also extends these themes into an extradiegetic realm of mass cultural myth. One wonders, for example, if *Unforgiven*'s reexamination of generic imperatives and personal roles and obligations would even be possible without Eastwood's iconography, but one ought also wonder to what degree Eastwood's iconography has unexamined roots in Siegel themes that predate Eastwood's career. At the very least, there is far more to Eastwood's dedication of *Unforgiven* "To Sergio and Don" than first meets the eye.

■ Notes

1. Though we emphasize the procedural crime film, the Siegel theme is evident
across genres, from the sci-fi *Invasion of the Body Snatchers* (1956), wherein relational and
professional identities collapse amid a macrosystemic shift from the human to the alien, to
the delinquency film *Crime in the Streets* (1956), wherein relationships within and among
gangs, police, neighbors, social workers, businesses, and families are mapped according
to spatial-systemic territories within the mise-en-scène. Even the Western *Flaming Star*
(1960) demonstrates the theme, applied in this case to a generic preoccupation with white/
Indian relations common in fifties miscegenation plots and "pro-Indian" Westerns.

2. After the incident with Ringerman's mother, Coogan is arrested for "imper-
sonating an officer," but if he has impersonated anything here, he has impersonated a
"polite" cowboy in a "fancy hat." Elsewhere Coogan uses legal authority to his advantage,
both revealing the inconsistencies of the system and recognizing that he is part of it, for
example, when he tells Julie that the real complaint of Piute Sheriff McCrea (Tom Tully) is
that Coogan will someday have his job.

3. Red is the color Julie wears when Coogan first encounters her letting herself be
sexually harassed by a client in order to "get through" to him; red is the color that Pushie
wears when he coldcocks Coogan and again when Coogan beats him; and red is the color
Coogan brings up during a conversation with Julie, overlooking the Hudson, wherein
Coogan tells her about a cop, him perhaps, who was stabbed because he let a wife embrace
with her husband. "The color of pity is red," Coogan grimly jokes: "It was all over the
floor, pity."

4. Certainly, later Eastwood films would address the sexism inherent in some of
the unresolved predatory sexual relations—Siegel's *The Beguiled* (1971) would punish the
Eastwood protagonist alongside female hypocrites, *The Enforcer* (1976) would attempt to
articulate the Dirty Harry persona through a female partner (Tyne Daly), and numerous later films would address female points of view—but during the late sixties period
in which the Eastwood brand was being established, one of Eastwood's effects upon the
Siegel themes seems to be the elimination of balance, gendered or otherwise systematic.

5. Pauline Kael (1973, 388) famously associated the movie with fascism, and William
Beard has described it as a "primitive form of conflict resolution and order restora-
tion" (2000, 19). Meanwhile, Christopher Frayling (1992, 89–90) cites Robert Reiner on
the film's interplay of reactionary response to rights with its appeal to disenfranchised
groups, which introduces one of the political ambiguities of *Dirty Harry*, i.e., its tendency
to celebrate rebellion and defend the disenfranchised, on one hand, while seeming to
advocate aggressive assertion of the law, on the other. Whereas Daniel O'Brien (1996, 112),
like Siegel (1993, 373) and Eastwood, has dismissed political readings, others have delved
deeper into the film's political complexities—most notably Smith (1993) and Bingham
(1994), who chart the disavowal of politics as part of the film's politics, and Wanat (2007),
who reads the film as subtly self-conscious. Beard has also called the franchise "self-
consciously mythic and reflexive" (2000, 19), though he, like Smith (1993, 101–2), tends to
attribute greater degrees of self-consciousness to later Eastwood films.

6. Frayling, after noting that Siegel's *The Lineup* combines "the 'police procedural' with the film noir, in a Bay Area setting," adds of *Dirty Harry* that "those very procedures which had been the subject of the 1950s cycle of cop movies, had now become the enemy" (1992, 88–89), but this observation only begins to describe the effect of the emerging Eastwood iconography on the Siegel plot.

■ Bibliography

Beard, William. 2000. *Persistence of Double Vision: Essays on Clint Eastwood*. Edmonton: University of Alberta Press.

Bingham, Dennis. 1994. *Acting Male: Masculinities in the Films of James Stewart, Jack Nicholson, and Clint Eastwood*. New Brunswick, N.J.: Rutgers University Press.

Bogdanovich, Peter. 1997. *Who the Devil Made It: Conversations with Legendary Film Directors*. New York: Alfred A. Knopf.

Cornell, Drucilla. 2009. *Clint Eastwood and Issues of American Masculinity*. New York: Fordham University Press.

Engel, Leonard, ed. 2007. *Clint Eastwood, Actor and Director*. Salt Lake City: University of Utah Press.

Frayling, Christopher. 1992. *Clint Eastwood*. London: Virgin.

Kael, Pauline. 1973. "Saint Cop." In *Deeper into the Movies*, 385–89. Boston: Little, Brown and Co.

Kaminsky, Stuart M. 1974. *Don Siegel: Director*. New York: Curtis.

O'Brien, Daniel. 1996. *Clint Eastwood: Filmmaker*. London: Batsford.

Peckinpah, Sam. 1974. "Don Siegel and Me." In Stuart M. Kaminsky, *Don Siegel: Director*, 299–301. New York: Curtis.

Siegel, Don. 1993. *A Siegel Film*. London: Faber and Faber.

Smith, Paul. 1993. *Clint Eastwood: A Cultural Production*. Minneapolis: University of Minnesota Press.

Wanat, Matt. 2007. "Irony as Absolution." In *Clint Eastwood, Actor and Director*, ed. Leonard Engel, 77–98. Salt Lake City: University of Utah Press.

Chapter 4

RAWHIDE TO *PALE RIDER*:
THE MATURATION OF CLINT EASTWOOD

Edward Rielly

Clint Eastwood did much work between his early television series, *Rawhide* (1959–65), and the film *Pale Rider* (1985), which he directed, produced, and starred in, that helped him grow into one of film's most acclaimed actors and directors. That work included the Sergio Leone–directed films *A Fistful of Dollars* (1964), *For a Few Dollars More* (1965), and *The Good, the Bad, and the Ugly* (1966); such Don Siegel films as *Coogan's Bluff* (1968), *Two Mules for Sister Sara* (1970), *Dirty Harry* (1971), *The Beguiled* (1971), and *Escape from Alcatraz* (1979); and his own directorial efforts, including *High Plains Drifter* (1973), *The Outlaw Josey Wales* (1976), and *Bronco Billy* (1980).

The purpose of this chapter, however, is not to chronicle Eastwood's learning curve from one project to another but, rather, to look at *Rawhide* and *Pale Rider* as bookends marking two crucial periods in his career: (1) the always observant actor and aspiring director learning on the job and (2) the fulfillment of Eastwood's promise in *Pale Rider*, an extraordinary achievement that marks Eastwood's clear arrival as a superb director and actor. Of course, Eastwood, having arrived as a genuine film artist, continued to grow, doing some of his best work in later years, including *Unforgiven* (1992), *Million Dollar Baby* (2004), and *Gran Torino* (2008), although these later works are beyond the scope of this chapter.

Clint Eastwood has acknowledged that his years as Rowdy Yates on *Rawhide* provided a "great training ground" (Cahill 1999, 124). The series went on the air on January 9, 1959, halfway through the season, the year in which the Western was at its all-time peak, with twenty-three weekly Western series taking up about one-fourth of prime-time hours (Schickel 1996, 105). Charles Marquis Warren, who had brought *Gunsmoke* to television, was the initial producer of *Rawhide* for CBS and directed some of the early episodes. The series starred Eric Fleming, like Eastwood getting his first big break in television, as trail boss Gil Favor. Eastwood was second-in-command, the ramrod named Rowdy Yates. Other regulars included Paul Brinegar as Wishbone, the cook; Sheb Wooley as the scout, Pete Nolan, who regularly took over the drive when Favor and Yates were absent; James Murdock as Mushy, a naive and not overly bright assistant to Wishbone; Robert Cabal as Jesus (pronounced Hey Soos), the wrangler in charge of the remuda; and Steve Raines as Jim Quince, one of the drovers.

The series, which featured ongoing cattle drives, a variety of well-known actors in guest spots, and a lot of interaction between Favor and Yates in something of a father–son relationship, achieved considerable success during the early part of its run, ranking sixth in the Nielsen ratings for the 1960–61 season. It remained reasonably high the following year, thirteenth, but then slid to twenty-second in 1962–63 and forty-fourth the next year (Schickel 1996, 126). Not insignificant in the audience's initial reaction was the catchy opening song by Dimitri Tiomkin and Ned Washington, who had won an Oscar for their theme song for the film *High Noon* (1952). The *Rawhide* song, with its memorable lyrics ("Roll 'em, roll 'em, roll 'em, keep those dogies rollin' . . . Rawhide . . .") was sung by Frankie Laine. During the 1964–65 season, *Rawhide*'s popularity remained low, and after the season Fleming left the show. The Eastwood character was promoted to trail boss, and new characters were introduced, including the veteran actor John Ireland and Raymond St. Jacques, the latter becoming the first African American regular in a Western series. The changes, however, did not boost the show's popularity, and the final original episode, "Crossing at White Feather," aired on December 7, 1965. It was episode number 217.

The series was enormously beneficial to Eastwood in a variety of ways. In addition to the financial rewards of a regular paycheck (his first as an actor), he proved popular with the audience, especially the younger audience, and most notably with girls, who did not regularly watch Westerns. The series made Eastwood a star, much in demand for personal appearances (usually with Brinegar and sometimes Wooley as well) at rodeos, fairs, and other events. Eastwood also tried his hand at singing, recording three singles, starting with "Unknown Girl" backed by "For All We Know" in 1961, and an album, *Rawhide's Clint Eastwood Sings Cowboy Favorites* for Cameo Records. In February and March 1962, Eastwood with Fleming and Brinegar visited Japan, where the series was extremely popular (McGilligan 1999b, 115). In the same year, Eastwood made a guest appearance on the television show *Mr. Ed*, which starred a talking horse. The appearance demonstrated his growing personal star status apart from his Rowdy Yates role.

Very much an acting neophyte when he started on the series, Eastwood proved an observant student, learning from the many producers and directors who worked on *Rawhide* during its run. Although initially not a particularly nuanced actor, Eastwood nonetheless portrayed an appealing character: handsome, soft-spoken but given to occasional hotheadedness, and very much an individualist able to stand up to Favor when he thought the trail boss wrong but usually fiercely loyal to him. Before long, however, as Eastwood later noted, he was seeking an acting style that suited both him and his acting ideal, a certain ambiguity that he termed a "mysterioso quality," which kept viewers wondering what the character was thinking (Cahill 1999, 125). That quality he would continue to refine throughout his acting career.

As the *Rawhide* series progressed, Eastwood tried to give the Rowdy Yates character greater depth. Some of Eastwood's comments have been critical of the role, at least in the early stages of the series, referring to him, for example, as the "idiot of the plains," a phrase that Richard Schickel uses as the title for the chapter on this period of Eastwood's life in *Clint Eastwood: A Biography*. Patrick McGilligan observes,

> It was on *Rawhide* that the actor first introduced and began to perfect the slouched stance, the slow burn, the half-feral smile and—in moments of crisis—the vein that bulged like a continental divide in the middle of his forehead. As Rowdy's participation in plots grew and varied, Clint began to demonstrate surprising authority, precision, mocking humour and emotional nuance. (1999b, 113)

McGilligan quotes Ted Post, who directed Eastwood in about two dozen *Rawhide* episodes, describing the fledgling actor as "a young man truly struggling to master the craft of acting, trying hard to understand it" (1999b, 112).

At the same time that Eastwood was developing a more nuanced acting style, he was thinking much about being on the other side of the camera. His directorial mind-set showed up in a variety of ways, including his observations about camera shots. At one point while riding among the cattle during filming of a stampede scene, he decided that the stampede could be filmed more vividly from a camera carried within the herd rather than shooting from outside. He said to the director and producer, "I'd like to take an arriflex, run it on my horse and go right in the middle of this damn thing, even dismount, whatever—but get in there and really get some great shots, because there are some beautiful shots in there that we are missing" (McGilligan 1999a, 24). The answer was no, supposedly because allowing an actor also to film action would violate union rules. Eastwood disagreed sharply with that explanation, believing instead that they simply did not want to change the way they were functioning. That resistance to change in favor of the status quo was especially galling to an actor who already was seeing ways to be more innovative and wanted to put them into practice.

Lighting was another concern that the aspiring director thought much about, especially the tendency of directors to overlight their scenes. "I had heated discussions with the producers," Eastwood later said: "They wanted to put around 900 lights on you, and they were also convinced that you needed that much light" (in Pavlovic 1999, 144). When Eastwood later was able to exercise directorial control himself, he would favor more natural lighting. Striking examples include the lighting of indoor nighttime scenes in *Unforgiven*, where the viewer's vision is impeded by realistically limited lighting. So inside the saloon when William Munny is ostensibly beaten because he has violated the town's no-gun rule but even more so because he is assumed to be in town to carry out killings contracted for by the resident prostitutes, much remains in shadow, including Munny's face as Little Bill confronts him.

One of the characteristics of *Rawhide* that Eastwood especially appreciated was its commitment to realism. He noted about the show, "We did honest stories, pretty much the way they happened. Now and then we may have rearranged things to heighten the drama, but in general, we respected historical truth" (in Yoggy 1995, 278). Realism, of course, is especially relative in a television series. It was difficult to capture the epic sweep of genuine cattle drives featuring several thousand cattle on a small screen, and much of the time the cast made do with a small herd on a studio ranch where a lot of the cattle scenes were filmed. In addition, certain details of everyday life on a cattle drive were consciously removed, as Eastwood himself admitted, apparently in deference to the sensibilities of the show's family audience. Horse droppings, for example, were immediately cleaned up, and scenes of a bull mounting a cow were assiduously avoided (Schickel 1996, 112).

Still, the show was far more realistic than most, and that was clearly the intent of Charles Marquis Warren, who based the series partly on a diary kept by an actual drover, George C. Duffield, on a drive from Texas to Iowa in 1866. Viewers generally agreed that the show seemed realistic, although many might not entirely agree with Jeff Rovin, who states in *The Great Television Series* that *Rawhide* "was the closest that television had ever come to creating an authentic sweat-and-blood Western" (1977, 61). For Warren, the key to being historically accurate was keeping the camera's eye steadily on the cattle, as real drovers could never forget their primary obligation to the herd. Contrasting his show with another series, *Wagon Train*, with which it is often compared, Warren claimed, "With us, the herd is primary. We're always up against the elements, and we never leave them entirely behind. For instance, the *Wagon Train* people come across their exploits, and, suddenly, the wagon train disappears while they tell their story" (Rovin 1977, 61).

Trying to convey a sense of true grit would become one of Eastwood's continuing efforts in his Westerns. That commitment was another of the lessons he learned from his early series.

Eastwood's observations of what the various *Rawhide* directors and producers did and did not do fed his desire to try directing. Eastwood cleared his plan first with series lead Eric Fleming, who gave his blessing to Eastwood's ambition, and the producer apparently signed on as well, assigning Eastwood some tuning-up work directing trailers for the series. But when it came to actually directing an episode, the producer reneged on his promise, offering as a reason that actors on other series had gone over budget directing and, therefore, CBS had established a policy against actors directing (Henry 1999, 99; McGilligan 1999a, 24–25). That response left Eastwood's directing ambitions delayed but still very much alive.

By the time that Eastwood began *Pale Rider* (1985), he had learned a great deal about directing (including how to direct his own acting), and he put his knowledge to work in a film that would become a genuine Western classic. Eastwood had already accumulated experience directing Westerns: *High Plains Drifter* (1973), *The Outlaw Josey Wales* (1976), and the modern Western, *Bronco Billy* (1980). Of the three, *Josey Wales* is the most nuanced, its title character combining the trauma of losing his murdered wife and son, his burning desire for revenge, and a rebirth of family spirit as he tries to aid a variety of people in the latter part of the film. That list includes a young Rebel, Jamie, who along with all of the guerrilla fighters except for Wales surrenders to Union forces. The surrender turns into a massacre, with Jamie escaping but mortally wounded. Wales cares for Jamie until he dies and later befriends an elderly Cherokee named Lone Watie, a young Navajo woman, and two women from Kansas who are trying to reach a Texas ranch after the men in their party are killed by Comancheros. Arriving at the ranch, they face an attack by Comanches until Wales talks the chief out of attacking with a live-and-let-live plea for peace and understanding.

Even this brief, partial summary illustrates that *The Outlaw Josey Wales* demonstrates a growing ability on Eastwood's part to achieve both breadth and depth in his films, although the epic sweep of the film yields a somewhat disjointed plot. The film was not well received by reviewers, although Michael Coyne praises it highly and in considerable detail in *The Crowded Prairie: American National Identity in the Hollywood Western*. Unfortunately, Coyne seriously undervalues *Pale Rider*, dismissing it as minimalism disguised "as superficial and/or pretentious mysticism" and, referencing the film's parallels to *Shane* (1953), as "not so much homage as plagiarism" (1997, 173–79, 186).

Coyne, however, stands largely alone in his complete denigration of *Pale Rider*. In fact, reviews of *Pale Rider* usually were positive. Patrick McGilligan writes that "a combination of nostalgia for the western genre, which had lapsed in fashion and commercial viability since the 1960s, and the rising tide of recognition for Clint-the-artist, gave the film Clint's most unanimous reviews since *Bronco Billy*." McGilligan also quotes the *Chicago Tribune* reviewer Gene Siskel, who claimed, "This year [1985] will go down in film history as the year Clint Eastwood finally earned respect as an artist" (1999b, 378).

When Eastwood began *Pale Rider*, he was prepared to synthesize a wide range of directorial (and acting) abilities in order to create a film that is profound, multilayered, aesthetically mature, and deeply engaging. Although the Western as a genre was widely seen as being in decline, Eastwood chose to make another Western because, as he once said, "it's a genre in which you can analyze new subject matter and moralities; you can take it in different directions, otherwise it gets into a rut" (in Aaker 1997, 182–83). In a similar vein, Eastwood noted in a 1985 *Rolling Stone* interview that "you can still talk about sweat and hard work, about the spirit, about love for the land and ecology. And I think you can say all these things in the Western, in the classic mythological form" (in Cahill 1999, 127). This new Western, therefore, could be, and, in fact, became, a mixture of realism and myth and, as Richard Schickel puts it, a middle road between "dull archetype" and "revisionism" (1996, 403).

Eastwood fits *Pale Rider* into the classical Western tradition by creating an extensive set of parallels between his film and *Shane*, almost universally accepted as one of the greatest of Westerns. Most of the parallels, however, come with a difference as well, reflecting the director's aesthetic principles and his desire to make the Western both classic and contemporary.

The main character is a mysterious loner who arrives suddenly and at an opportune time to help a band of miners (farmers in *Shane*) try to secure their lives, homes, and livelihood against a powerful miner (in *Shane*, ranchers) who controls the town. The new arrival professes to be (and dresses the part of) a preacher except when he must face the villains in the climax of the film. At that point, he gets his guns out of a Wells Fargo lockbox, transforming himself back into a gunfighter complete with black hat. Similarly, Shane had traded his gunfighter's buckskins for farmer's clothing when he took off his guns, only to re-dress himself as a gunfighter before facing the Ryker brothers, including Rufus, clearly the boss and an earlier version of LaHood, who in *Pale Rider* is accompanied by a son rather than a brother.

There is a love triangle in both films, but in *Shane* the hero and the wife, Marian Starret, remain platonically proper. In *Pale Rider*, the Preacher has a onetime sexual encounter with Sarah Wheeler, who along with her daughter, Megan, lives with Hull Barret. Hull thus parallels Joe Starret of *Shane*, both as the newcomer's host and quasi-employer and as the persuasive leader of the miners (farmers) in keeping them united against their powerful adversary. Both pairs of men also bond through a shared and physically challenging enterprise: removing a stump in the earlier film and breaking a boulder in order to explore the gravel underneath for gold in the latter. Megan takes the place of *Shane*'s Joey as a young admirer, even worshiper, of the hero, although, unlike *Shane*, *Pale Rider* is not portrayed primarily through the young admirer's point of view. Also in both films, one member of the community goes into town without the other miners (farmers) and is killed by the hired gunfighters (Marshal Stockburn and his six deputies in *Pale Rider* and Jack Wilson in *Shane*).

In *Shane*, the hero's arrival includes no explanation, although stylistically his approach is handled with skilled camera work, framing him within a deer's antlers; in *Pale Rider*, the Preacher seems to appear in direct response to Megan's prayer after LaHood's men raid the miners' camp and kill her dog. As she prays at her dog's grave, she inserts her own personal reflections and plea within the lines of the Twenty-Third Psalm. As she gets to the lines "For Thou are with me. Thy rod and Thy staff, they comfort me," she adds, "But we need a miracle." She continues with the prayer and her insertions: "If you don't help us, we're all going to die. Please? Just one miracle? Amen."

As Megan prays, a distant rider appears in a dark, shadowy vista. As Megan concludes the psalm and her personal pleading, the rider is presented, no longer in darkness but in a beautiful scene of blue sky and patches of snow as he descends through woods, having come, like Shane, from the mountains, themselves a traditional religious symbol representing the abode of God and, in Psalm 121, the source of help (with mountains replaced by hills in some versions of the Bible).

The parallels go on and on, but the point of them is not to create a sort of filmic roman à clef so that viewers can compile a list of which characters and incidents in the earlier film are referenced in the later. Instead, Eastwood is paying tribute to the Western tradition and positioning his film within that tradition, but he is also, in part through differences within those parallels, taking the film and the genre forward.

Some of the elements found in *Pale Rider* had appeared in Eastwood's films before. Mysticism is one of them, with the nameless protagonists of the Sergio Leone films and *High Plains Drifter*, but in *Pale Rider* mysticism is wedded to mythology in a much more profound and positive way. The Preacher appears presumably from a place beyond the normal mortal world, but there is no nihilism or cynicism about him. In *High Plains Drifter*, the townspeople are hardly worth the helping, but not so in *Pale Rider*, where the miners are at least as meritorious as the farmers in *Shane*.

Eastwood has referred to the Preacher as an archangel, noting that "he inspires them [the miners] with the courage to resist and defend their rights" (in Henry 1999, 100). For Eastwood, "*Pale Rider* is kind of allegorical . . . though he isn't a reincarnation or anything, but he does ride a pale horse like the four horsemen of the apocalypse, and he could maybe be one of those guys" (Frayling 1999, 135). One might wish for a more definitive statement by Eastwood than that, but clearly Eastwood intends to build on the tradition of Western mythology with a mysticism more positively developed in this film than in the earlier ones.

The allegory is not a simple good-versus-evil rendition. The Preacher is altruistic, but there is more to him than that. He is willing to sleep with the woman Hull wishes to marry, although Eastwood does not actually show that occurring.

Certainly, there is no turning the other cheek when the Preacher learns that LaHood has contracted with Marshal Stockburn and his deputies to get rid of the miners by getting rid of the Preacher. Despite Hull Barret's efforts at building and maintaining unity, ultimately his efforts will fail without the Preacher and his guns. LaHood understands the role that the newcomer is playing in giving the miners confidence, although he may not yet appreciate fully the Preacher's gunfighting ability when he notes that "a man without spirit is whipped" and explains that a preacher "could give 'em faith."

The Preacher's purpose seems to include a heavy helping of revenge as well. In an early scene, viewers get a look at the Preacher's bullet wounds in his back. Gradually, the past relationship between the Preacher (or whoever he was previously) and Stockburn comes out. When LaHood describes the Preacher, Stockburn recognizes the description as fitting the man he once knew but apparently dismisses the similarities as coincidence, as he believes that the man he knew is dead. Stockburn should know, as he and his deputies were the men who shot the Preacher. Yet the film never gives an ultimate answer to whether the Preacher had died and now has returned in a resurrected form or whether he somehow managed to survive the six bullet wounds. Eastwood's rejection of the "reincarnation" interpretation may lay open the possibility of survival, but then there is the "archangel" claim. Archangels do not die, but there are precedents for depicting an angel as formerly human, for example, in Mormon belief.

The Preacher ultimately makes clear that he is going off on a personal matter as well as to help the miners. He says to Sarah, "It's an old score. It's time to settle it." When she wants to know who is calling his name, he responds, "A voice from the past." The distant calling, however, hardly seems to be coming from Stockburn himself or his deputies, as if the voice itself is a mystical summons.

As the climactic moment approaches, two relationships undergo further development. First, Megan professes her love for the Preacher, which he tries to deflect as a generic, nonsexual love, although he certainly knows what she really means. Megan is not put off, though, and makes her meaning clear. The scene (along with the overall substitution of a fourteen-year-old girl for Joey) contributes to sexualizing the film much more than *Shane*, a quality of the film discussed by Stephen McVeigh in his essay "Subverting *Shane*: Ambiguities in Eastwood's Politics in *Fistful of Dollars*, *High Plains Drifter*, and *Pale Rider*" (2007, 150). The Preacher tells her that she should practice loving for a while before making love. She says that she will wait for him, but the Preacher says, "You wouldn't want to spend your future on a man like me." Megan then accuses him of loving her mother and angrily tells him, "I hope you die, and I hope you go to hell." The angry response parallels Joey's anger after the fight between Joey's father and Shane.

The latter half of her denunciation is especially interesting given the allegorical nature of the film. If he is akin to the rider of the pale horse of the Apocalypse, the Preacher's mount biblically is identified in Revelation 6:1–8 as death, with hell (sometimes translated as Hades) following behind. That biblical passage is what Megan is reading at the dinner table when the Preacher rides past her window on his first entry into the mining camp. The victims of the Preacher's guns, Stockburn and his men, soon will meet death and presumably hell. Where the Preacher goes on his final ride back up into the mountains is surely more akin to some sort of heavenly existence, although it is hard to imagine any traditional view of that afterlife quite meshing with the Preacher's persona.

In the final shoot-out, after killing four of LaHood's men and the six deputies, the Preacher faces Stockburn close-up so that the marshal can recognize him, a recognition punctuated with the marshal's, "You. You!" The Preacher shoots him six times, exacting precise revenge for his own wounds, and then, plucking a second gun from his belt, adds a seventh bullet to his forehead, mimicking Stockburn's final shot into the murdered miner, Spider Conway.

Prior to the climax of the film, Megan's admiration for the Preacher returns when LaHood's son attempts to rape her. The scene also suggests the possibility of a gang rape as a group of LaHood's miners surrounds the younger LaHood as he struggles with his intended victim. Fortunately, the Preacher arrives in time to rescue her and reclaim his position in her eyes of hero, now a desexualized hero rather than a potential lover.

Few people are completely saints or sinners, perhaps even archangels, and the Preacher also occupies that realistic middle ground. As noted earlier, altruism and revenge combine in his motivation as he confronts Stockburn. Sometimes, though, goodness is unalloyed, as in his efforts to dissuade Megan from pining for him, a relationship wrong for several reasons, from the difference in their ages to possibly a metaphysical difference (angels traditionally do not have intercourse with humans, although that apparently did not apply to the Preacher and Sarah any more than did the tradition, based on chapter 6 of Genesis, that angels in antiquity had intercourse with women who thus gave birth to giants).

There also is considerable goodness in the Preacher's decision, paralleling Shane's, to try to prevent the Hull/Joe Starret figure from almost certain death by trying to face down professional killers. Shane resorted to hitting Joe over the head with a gun, eliciting Joey's anger at what he saw as a dishonorable way of fighting. The Preacher seemingly acquiesces to Hull accompanying him, but after dynamiting LaHood's hydraulic mining facilities, he fakes a dropped stick of dynamite. When Hull dismounts to throw away the stick, the Preacher runs off his horse. Both heroes clearly believe that the end does justify the means so long as the end is to save the life of a good man. The stratagem could have been costly for the Preacher, for after disposing of Stockburn and his deputies, he is about to be shot from ambush by LaHood when Hull, having walked all the way to town, shoots LaHood. The film gives no hint that the Preacher cannot be killed despite his ability to disappear in the blink of an eye (or in a quick camera shift).

The destruction of the mining facilities concludes another theme of the film, the ecological evils of hydraulic mining. Eastwood's attempt to update the Western again comes into play here as he takes aim at a mining technique that involved the use of water cannons to shoot water under great pressure, thus eroding large portions of land in the search for gold. LaHood is raping the land, paralleling the attempted rape of Megan. The community of small miners, on the other hand, uses simpler, less intrusive techniques as they pan for gold. Many books have chronicled the controversies and legal issues involving hydraulic mining throughout the second half of the nineteenth century, including Robert Kelley's *Gold vs. Grain* (1959), although usually the conflict was between hydraulic miners and farmers, whose agricultural efforts were harmed by a mining process that ripped apart the land and often led to serious flooding.

As Paul Smith notes in his *Clint Eastwood: A Cultural Production*, Westerns had often presented issues involving the land and its use but usually dealt "with ecological questions in only gingerly and sporadic fashion, by and large displacing them onto the familiar power struggles between homesteaders and land barons, communities and railroads, settlers and 'Indians,' and the like" (1993, 51). *Shane* follows this traditional pattern, but

Pale Rider, as Joe Huemann and Robin Murray explain in "Hydraulic Mining Then and Now: The Case of *Pale Rider*" (2006), takes an ideological stand in favor of respecting the land itself. In Eastwood's film, again to quote Smith, "scenes of the moonscape effects of Lahood's [*sic*] methods are juxtaposed with the quiet industry of Hull Barret and his companions working by hand" (1993, 53).

Eastwood also demonstrates his talents as a director in other, more technical ways. His use of camera shots harkens back to his lament regarding a cattle stampede in *Rawhide* that the filming was too external to the action, too static. The early scene in *Pale Rider* when LaHood's men ride into the miners' camp and cause great destruction demonstrates creative camera work that gives a vivid sense of immediacy, pulling the viewer into the maelstrom of action occasioned by the attack. Quick changes in camera angles and camera shifts, even occasional blurring of the image, mimic the rapid, terrifying experience of miners suddenly caught in a situation that is both frightening and dangerous.

Camera shots elsewhere in the film also are used to considerable effect. There is the juxtaposition of shots of Megan praying at her dog's grave and the approaching rider already mentioned. The Preacher's mystical nature is further hinted at by his sudden appearances and disappearances, the result of both well-planned camera use and careful editing, as when he appears on horseback, then disappears, and then reappears again on foot during the scene when Hull is being beaten by LaHood's men in town early in the film. Later, the telegrapher notices the Preacher on horseback and then, once a train has passed, his disappearance. The suddenness of these movements proves startling to those who have seen him, as if they cannot completely believe their eyes. In each instance, there is just the bare possibility of a rational explanation. The man preparing to attack Hull momentarily takes his eyes off the rider, and it is perhaps conceivable that during the quick passing of the train the rider rode just far enough to be out of sight. Throughout the film, Eastwood hints at the mystical but refrains from definitively affirming a mystical reality. It remains up to the viewer ultimately to come to a decision about what constitutes reality within the film. The line between deliberate inconclusiveness and trickery is a fine one, but Eastwood as director has learned to walk that line without falling off.

Eastwood pulls all of this together in *Pale Rider*, along with his own acting performance. Still a loner, as are some of Eastwood's most memorable earlier roles, and an otherworldly one at that, the Preacher has a moral depth beneath his generally succinct actions and words. Capable of uniting and inspiring the ecologically and morally sound miners in danger of being driven away from their land if not killed, the Preacher has an ability to engage in interpersonal relationships far beyond that of some of Eastwood's earlier characterizations. The Preacher is committed to both the communal and personal good, the latter clearly evidenced in his behavior toward Megan, whose romantic interest in him he kindly but firmly deflects. As director and actor, Clint Eastwood has matured by *Pale Rider* into an accomplished artist in both categories.

Pale Rider is far from the end of his accomplishments and growth, but it marks a major arriving. In *Pale Rider*, Rowdy Yates is still around, but he has grown much and has put his learning to very good use.

■ Bibliography

Aaker, Everett. 1997. *Television Western Players of the Fifties: A Biographical Encyclopedia of All Regular Cast Members in Western Series, 1949–1959.* Jefferson, N.C.: McFarland and Co.

Cahill, Tim. 1999. "Clint Eastwood: The *Rolling Stone* Interview." In *Clint Eastwood: Interviews*, ed. Robert E. Kapsis and Kathie Coblentz, 117–29. Jackson: University Press of Mississippi.

Coyne, Michael. 1997. *The Crowded Prairie: American National Identity in the Hollywood Western.* New York: I. B. Tauris.

Duffield, George C. 1924. "Driving Cattle from Texas to Iowa, 1866." Ed. W. W. Baldwin. *Annals of Iowa* 14: 243–62.

Eliot, Marc. 2009. *American Rebel: The Life of Clint Eastwood.* New York: Harmony Books.

Frayling, Christopher. 1999. "Eastwood on Eastwood." In *Clint Eastwood: Interviews*, ed. Robert E. Kapsis and Kathie Coblentz, 130–36. Jackson: University Press of Mississippi.

Henry, Michael. 1999. "Interview with Clint Eastwood." In *Clint Eastwood: Interviews*, ed. Robert E. Kapsis and Kathie Coblentz, 96–116. Jackson: University Press of Mississippi.

Huemann, Joe, and Robin Murray. 2006. "Hydraulic Mining Then and Now: The Case of *Pale Rider*." In *The Landscape of Hollywood Westerns: Ecocriticism in an American Film Genre*, ed. Deborah A. Carmichael, 94–110. Salt Lake City: University of Utah Press.

Kelley, Robert L. 1959. *Gold vs. Grain. The Hydraulic Mining Controversy in California's Sacramento Valley; a Chapter in the Decline of the Concept of Laissez Faire.* Glendale, Calif.: A. H. Clark.

McGilligan, Patrick. 1999a. "Clint Eastwood." In *Clint Eastwood: Interviews*, ed. Robert E. Kapsis and Kathie Coblentz, 21–41. Jackson: University Press of Mississippi.

———. 1999b. *Clint: The Life and Legend.* New York: St. Martin's Press.

McVeigh, Stephen. 2007. "Subverting *Shane*: Ambiguities in Eastwood's Politics in *Fistful of Dollars*, *High Plains Drifter*, and *Pale Rider*." In *Clint Eastwood, Actor and Director: New Perspectives*, ed. Leonard Engel, 129–56. Salt Lake City: University of Utah Press.

Pavlovic, Milan. 1999. "Clint Eastwood Interviewed by Milan Pavlovic." In *Clint Eastwood: Interviews*, ed. Robert E. Kapsis and Kathie Coblentz, 137–52. Jackson: University Press of Mississippi.

Rovin, Jeff. 1977. *The Great Television Series*. New York: A. S. Barnes.

Schickel, Richard. 1996. *Clint Eastwood: A Biography*. New York: Alfred A. Knopf.

Smith, Paul. 1993. *Clint Eastwood: A Cultural Production*. Minneapolis: University of Minnesota Press.

Yoggy, Gary A. 1995. *Riding the Video Range: The Rise and Fall of the Western on Television*. Jefferson, N.C.: McFarland and Co.

Chapter 5

EASTWOOD'S TREATMENT OF THE LIFE OF CREATIVITY
AND PERFORMANCE IN *BRONCO BILLY, HONKYTONK MAN,*
WHITE HUNTER BLACK HEART, AND *BIRD*

Dennis Rothermel

Themes of law, justice, vengeance, war, bravery, and violence frequent
Clint Eastwood's films—those in which he stars but does not direct,
those in which he stars that he also directs, and also those that he directs
but does not star in. The dominant mold for his films follows the peren-
nial screen persona of the filmmaker as an actor. A focus on the life of
creativity and performance arises in four films that are among the filmmaker's low-budget efforts that he has produced and directed: *Bronco
Billy* (1980), *Honkytonk Man* (1982), *White Hunter Black Heart* (1990),
and *Bird* (1988). These films about creativity and performance wander
far away from the more dominant screen persona, the stalwart hero of
action films and Westerns. But these four films lie close to the heart of
the man who happens regularly to combine his creative efforts as an
actor, a director, and a composer in the films that he makes, even as he
does not act in one of them and all four come before he began composing scores for some of his films. Evidence of Eastwood's admiration for
country-western singers, jazz musicians, and filmmakers abounds in
the extensive collection of published interviews, and these comments
are particularly effusive when he talks about music, acting, and performing in reference to these films.

Clint Eastwood consistently has been generous in providing interviews, particularly during the period of promotion of his newest film.
Interviewers note that he is taller in life than he appears on film, that
he is soft-spoken, and that he is willing to talk openly and at length
about his work in film but not about his private life. That boundary was crossed once during a televised interview, resulting in the
squint-eyed, stern glower for which Eastwood's action film screen

persona is renowned.[1] Terri Gross, on her radio interview show *Fresh Air*, asked for him to speak in the calmly-seething-in-anger, clenched-teeth, no-nonsense delivery that is also a trademark of the action film persona. Eastwood obliged, but pointedly with a telltale touch of mirth in his voice— "I don't know what you're talking about."[2] Humor and humility prevail in the interviews.

Interviewers often conceive of the same questions, which receive patient responses that do not vary much. Those consistencies provide a look into how the filmmaker understands his work. Aspects of his way of going about filmmaking get mentioned consistently: that he works— proudly—with a tight budget and precise schedule, always coming in under budget and ahead of schedule;[3] that he is efficient in his work on the set, both in terms of getting the shot he wants quickly, typically on the first take, and with his personal company of collaborative Malpaso crew, who know his inclinations well enough that he can indicate with a gesture what he wants;[4] that he eschews excessive coverage of a scene and keeps the ratio of footage shot to footage surviving in the final cut very low;[5] that he does not rehearse his actors, with the exception of allowing for rehearsal on the set, which he films and often keeps as the take he prefers because that is how he will get fresh and unstudied performances;[6] that he commands cinematography, lighting, casting, and editing with his own particular intention and considerable technical expertise;[7] that he prefers contrasting, dark images, with backlit figures, even though it makes transfer to video difficult;[8] that his mise-en-scène is nonflamboyant, though varied appropriate to the theme of the film;[9] that he aspires to a theme-variant but understated style, understated acting, and minimal dialogue;[10] that the Malpaso crew and actors enjoy a congenial community on sets that are quiet, friendly, relaxed, and yet efficient;[11] that he is flexible and collaborative in the production but mostly committed to realizing the script he begins with, for which he has worked out in his head before shooting how to do the entirety, though never with a storyboard;[12] and finally, that there is an apparent alternation between large action-film productions that Eastwood typically stars in but does not direct and the smaller, seemingly personal films that he directs, though not always with a role for himself.[13]

This is an interesting collection of traits—and all emerging from the filmmaker's assertions in interviews. Another recurring aspect to Eastwood's interviews offers contrast to Eastwood's congenial participation: evasiveness. Typically the filmmaker responds to a question he does not feel inclined to answer by taking the conversation onto an entirely different topic.[14] Often enough, his initial response is, "No, I don't think so. . . ." For an interviewee who otherwise is attentive—and consistent—in how he acquits his role, this redirection can only be deliberate. It shows how the filmmaker thinks the question and the questioner misconstrue his work. Reading these passages of redirection carefully, the secret of this filmmaker becomes evident—Clint Eastwood is first and foremost *an actor.* He delights and exults in the task and artistry of the actor. Those redirections in the interviews are all toward wanting to talk about the importance of the complexities and nuances of story and character, which are not just the actor's concerns but what actors crave.[15] He is particularly amused by the perception at the time of his first directorial effort that film critics were hardly ready to acknowledge that he was an actor much less a director.[16] Orson Welles was among the first to spot Eastwood's accomplishments as a filmmaker, in 1982.[17] Welles's imprimatur notwithstanding, Eastwood's artistry as a filmmaker has only very slowly gained recognition. The actor who chose to become a filmmaker can relate this story of popular criticism resisting his claim to being a filmmaker—decades later—with the same gently obliging mirth with which he can clench-teeth "I don't know what you're talking about" for Terri Gross. The difference, though, is how much Eastwood wants to talk about what genuinely matters to him, which is not the screen persona with the trademark glower and clenched-teeth delivery.

These redirections, to answer in terms of what makes for an interesting story and character development, come in response to a variety of suggestions: that the film discussed reflects current events or developments in his own life or work;[18] that there is political symbolism in a character or in what is said or done;[19] that there is an auteur's worldview underlying any one or all of the filmmaker's oeuvre;[20] that a film symbolically reflects upon the nature of the artist or of cinema itself;[21] that there is an artist's dilemma in the alternation between ungratifying, large action-film productions and the personal films with smaller budgets and audiences;[22] and—easily the most grating confusion—that there is spiritual or political or philosophical identity between the role the filmmaker plays as an actor with the spiritual, political, or philosophical outlook of the film or filmmaker.[23] It is this last confusion that will most befuddle the man who takes himself to be an actor, first and foremost. An actor delights in playing a variety of challenging roles.

What attracts Eastwood to a script is this same promise of a milieu in which an actor can shine—a story and characterizations with depth and development. At a crucial juncture in his career, when it had been revived in Sergio Leone's trio of outré Westerns, Eastwood declined the fourth opportunity, *Once Upon a Time in the West* (1968), because, as much as he liked Leone's spectacle, Eastwood craved character and story, more than what could prevail in the Leone spectacle.[24] The partnership with Don Siegel likewise had its limits for Eastwood.[25] Everything that has been noted as included in the set of traits of Eastwood as filmmaker falls into place as conducive to the actor's concerns, to the actor's perfect milieu. An efficient, quiet, congenial set is the perfect atmosphere for an actor to feel primed and at ease. The consistently low number of takes per shot, especially the one and only take during a "rehearsal," endears actors and keeps them at once primed and spontaneous. Meeting a schedule sustains attention to the project, with promise of not impinging upon private lives and professional commitments. The cinematography, mise-en-scène, lighting, and editing adapted to the theme of the film constitute an extension of acting—as if the compositional elements of the image were extensions of costume, makeup, voice, and gesture. As with the predilection for understated acting, these elements are purposive yet never ostentatious in Eastwood films. Dark, shadowy images encourage an audience to perceive and comprehend depth, complexity, obscurity, just as much as flat, bright lighting, best amenable to video transfer, already primes an audience for cliché, automatic reactions, nothing left unrevealed, shallowness—and a laugh track.

Finally, completing projects efficiently, under budget, ahead of schedule, with short postproduction (because it was shot to meet the script and envisioned in Eastwood's head) ensures a low threshold of box-office success to make a profit. Especially for low-budget projects, that the film reliably will not cost more than projected grants Eastwood variance from studios that might otherwise insist upon interfering in ways that undermine the actor's perfect milieu and specifically to impose clichéd characterizations. Eastwood shares with Woody Allen this combination of reliable efficiency in completion of the project, a typically low budget, and a pretty much guaranteed audience at least to meet a low threshold of fiscal success.[26] He also shares with Allen the persistent confusion of screen persona with the filmmaker within the critical and scholarly literature. Allen is a *writer-director*, though often also an actor in films, like Eastwood. Eastwood *finds* scripts he wants to direct, which he alters rarely and then usually to condense rather than to expand or to substitute. Both Allen and Eastwood work with fine cinematographers, though Allen with a much greater predilection for long sequence takes. Both create the splendid milieu for actors to thrive in, with story and characterization imbued with complexity and substance, to include a nearly ever-present tone of black humor.[27]

Eastwood works within the terrain of Hollywood. He exercises constraint and thus has success in dealing with studio committees, without the cantankerousness of John Ford, who also identified "the committee" as the constant threat of mediocrity.[28] But Eastwood learned very early in his career to create his own production company, Malpaso, within Warner Brothers as a means of buffering control of his projects from studio influence.[29] So long as his Malpaso films make money, the arguably uniquely long-term relationship that Eastwood has had with Warner Brothers thrives both for the studio and for him.[30] Forming his own production company was something that Ford decided to do late in his career, with his Argosy Pictures, only after Darryl F. Zanuck mangled *My Darling Clementine* (1946).[31]

Until that point, Ford had trusted his skill in what he called "cutting in the camera" to prevent studio interference—that is, not shooting the shots or master cover shots that could be used in postproduction to inflect a scene differently from what Ford had intended.[32] This resulted in a much lower ratio of exposed footage to the final cut. Eastwood shows that same parsimony and specifically identifies the small amount of film stock that Ford used on *The Grapes of Wrath* (1940) as a sign that Ford knew precisely what he wanted before shooting began.[33] Ford's purpose, though, had been to constrain how postproduction could subvert his intentions, which was not something Eastwood needed to worry about once he had established his own production company early in his directorial career.

Like Ford, Eastwood often shoots on location, though not for the sake of authenticity but for the sake of how suitable a landscape is for the story. For Ford, Monument Valley became the suitable look for all of the American west. Eastwood's Dust Bowl–era Oklahoma in *Honkytonk Man* is shot in Nevada and California. Various locations in the United States and Canada suffice for unnamed small-town America in *Bronco Billy*.[34] Like Ford, Eastwood thinks in terms of how his audience can comprehend his construction of the film. Ford's films typically embed a deeper layer of meaning somewhat disguised by more popular effects on the surface. Eastwood became fond of a line that he gets to deliver, as John Huston–like John Wilson, in *White Hunter Black Heart*, "I won't make eight million popcorn eaters pull me this way or that."[35]

Nevertheless, he is attentive to an audience, though an audience he conjures up as appropriate to what he wants to accomplish in a film, rather than as predictably entertained by whatever empirical methods the studio committee thinks to trust.[36] The special advantages of small budgets and reliability in meeting budget and schedule help to keep the need for popularity low. He shows no regret in losing that part of his loyal audience who have expectations of macho heroism.[37]

Eastwood's sly traversal of the terrain of Hollywood cinema charts out possibilities for variance without penetrating the periphery. He is well studied in the catalog of accomplished Hollywood actors and specifically how an earlier generation distinguished themselves with identifiable styles and gained the frequent opportunity to play out of character, such as Eastwood relishes. Eastwood has a fix on them all individually: Marlon Brando, James Dean, Lawrence Olivier, Jackie Gleason, Jack Benny, Clark Gable, Claudette Colbert, Bette Davis, Barbara Stanwyck, Gary Cooper, John Wayne, Humphrey Bogart, James Cagney, Kirk Douglas, Burt Lancaster, Henry Fonda, Spencer Tracey, Buster Keaton.[38] This is a long list, very carefully chosen, including more predecessors than contemporaries. It shows Eastwood's study over time looking for this singular accomplishment of major Hollywood actors inclined to embrace the actor's challenge of a portrayal not obviously within their established range.

Eastwood particularly admires Hollywood stars who have the courage to attempt something contrary to their established screen persona.[39] Getting roles with more challenge accrues to the movie stars who have bankability, while it is more difficult for actors who have had less success in Hollywood to avoid being typecast.[40] Eastwood bemoans the lack of roles with substance for actresses in Hollywood, particularly when an actress survives beyond a certain age, in contrast to contemporary French cinema and compared with what Davis could do.[41] Very much in contrast to the norm for A-list action film actors, Eastwood has chosen parts for himself in his own films and those directed by others that align with his age rather than continuing to portray much younger men.[42] This, too, betrays the actor interested in new acting challenges and not the same bankable screen persona continually.

Eastwood acknowledges a reputation for luck—in how the weather complies with his needs on location and in how his audience follows him along his wanderings within the terrain of mainstream cinema.[43] But of course, God helps those who help themselves. Being ready to adapt to the weather is a function of having a tight and devoted company always ready to move quickly. Keeping that audience always in mind, from the initial reading of the script through to the completion of editing, creates the intentional pathway for an audience to latch on to and to comprehend.[44] In speaking of his luck, without sanguinity, Eastwood knows it could run out—especially on the audience issue.[45] His nonchalance easily has more to do with having made his first big pile of money on *Every Which Way but Loose* (1978) than with his vantage point at the far end of a long life and career.

Eastwood is equally well studied in the styles and methods of a generation of Hollywood filmmakers prior to his: John Ford, William Wyler, Howard Hawks, George Stevens, William Wellman, Alfred Hitchcock, John Huston, Frank Capra, Tay Garnett, Jacques Tourneur, Anthony Mann, Preston Sturges, Raoul Walsh, Laslo Benedek.[46] For all of these, story and character were primary, and for most, style was subdued, if not invisible. Again, it is an extensive list of filmmakers that Eastwood is able to cite who exemplify the primacy of nontrivial story and character. It betrays a conscientious and prolonged study of this one model of filmmaking that he admires, which will include invoking continued success to be able to take on a variety of projects, including atypical films that otherwise would not get produced.[47]

As much as Eastwood traverses the terrain of Hollywood cinema freely, without the usual hindrance of intervention executed in the name of multimillion-dollar fiscal responsibility, his storytelling remains within how Gilles Deleuze delineates the organic narrative, in contrast to the opening up of a crystalline narrative in European film and American independent film.[48] Organic narrative relies first on organic descriptions—objects in the image are presumed to have indexicality in the diegesis. Hints of ghostlike images notwithstanding, Eastwood's films sustain a diegesis with sparse injection of metaphor. Crystalline descriptions are purely visual and sonic, detached from placement in a reality, such as the flashing lights in Jean-Luc Godard's *Alphaville* (1965).

Second, in organic narrative, the relation between real and irreal may be ambiguous, but it always matters. The hints of ghostlike presences in *High Plains Drifter* (1973), *Pale Rider* (1985), and *Unforgiven* (1992) still matter—Is he a ghost or not? Is the Stranger a relative to the murdered Marshal Duncan, or is he Duncan?[49] Is the Preacher with the bullet wound scars on his back the avenger of the man that Stockburn is sure he saw gunned down, or is he that man's ghost? Are Will Munney's inexplicable reforms from a vicious killer into a farmer, back briefly into that methodical killer again, and then once again into the peaceful family man all the natural fluctuations of an erratic psychology or miraculous divine intervention? In the crystalline narrative, it does not matter—the separations between one set of contingencies and another allay one another rather than competing for status as reality, such as what has to be the heuristic capitulation in any reading of David Lynch's *Mulholland Drive* (2001).

Third, organic narration maintains an orientation within a plausible continuum of time and space, even through fragmentation of the time line in flashback and flash-forward. Science fiction and supernatural elements offer not a contrast to the supposition of a physical continuum but an expansion of what the physical realm contains. The crystalline narrative abandons the obligation to sustain this continuum and the rule of causality that applies to events within it, such as Peter Greenaway exploits in *The Tulse Luper Suitcases* films (2003–4). Though Eastwood adapts to fragmented time lines easily, these narrative shifts will parse out strictly coherently for the audience to decipher.

Fourth, the organic narrative establishes and sustains an expectation of truth, not so much as what promises to be *the* truth about anything but, rather, *a* truth that is the epistemological unity of the world and actions that the narrative depicts. Crystalline narrative undermines this expectation and abandons the promise of a world in which there is a truth to what happens, such as Orson Welles announces as a surprise revelation in *F for Fake* (1973). So it will seem clear that Eastwood's cinema remains strongly centered in what Deleuze calls the organic narrative.

But we can extract a different point from a different text by Deleuze, "Literature and Life," which resonates with an essential element in Eastwood's films. It happens to be exactly what baffles the filmmaker when his critical and scholarly readers insist upon taking characterizations in his films as generalities—which is the consistent mistake of the set of confusions that Eastwood attempts patiently and politely to divert, to talk about story and character instead. Literature indulges fabulation, rather than fantasy, Deleuze writes, when it

> discovers beneath apparent persons the power of the impersonal—which is not a generality but a singularity at the highest point: a man, a woman, a beast, a stomach, a child. . . . Health as literature, as writing, consists in

inventing a people who are missing. It is the task of the fabulating function to invent a people.[50]

This distinction between the projection of generalities in fantasy—which is how fantasy pervades Hollywood cinema—and the fabulation that we expect of nonjuvenile literature finds Eastwood on the side of fabulation, against the fantasy-machine manufacturing of Hollywood.

Just as in his interviews, we can see more carefully into Eastwood's comprehension of his own genuine role and endeavor in looking past the dominant themes and pause over his treatment of the showman in *Bronco Billy*, the singer in *Honkytonk Man*, the filmmaker in *White Hunter Black Heart*, and the jazzman in *Bird*. These four films reveal what more truly, and perhaps more privately, concerns Eastwood—the performer and the artist. But of course, with the proviso just posed above, we shall see that these are just stories, not confessions, not expositions of types, but tales of *a* showman, *a* singer, *a* filmmaker, and *a* jazzman. In each case this need not align with any real person at all. But in all four cases, these are persons who are missing from the culture's imaginary; they are fabulated persons.

One salient pitfall evident in both popular criticism and scholarly commentary on Eastwood films is the presumption that the role Eastwood plays in films defines the philosophical worldview of the film or the filmmaker. Careful attention to the variety of Eastwood's acting should dispel that mistake, and his repeated comments in interviews about what matters to the actor will underscore that. A second salient pitfall is that Eastwood the filmmaker—director and producer—makes films with a focus upon the historical-cultural settings, which then are taken as the filmmaker's central purpose and which differ with each film, as if warmed-over cultural anthropology travelogues fit into the variety of appeals within the popular movie market.

Facile receptions of this sort treat *Bronco Billy* as an enjoyable tale of high jinks about a traveling troop of jolly carnival actors playing out Western fantasies as they traverse small-town Americana. *Honkytonk Man* becomes the tale of a country music singer who escapes the Oklahoma Dust Bowl and finds redemption by struggling against the ravages of tuberculosis to record his soul-felt tributes to his roots in Nashville before succumbing. *White Hunter Black Heart* becomes the melancholy story of hard-living, premier 1950s Hollywood director John Huston, on location in the African jungle filming *African Queen* with Humphrey Bogart and

Katherine Hepburn. *Bird* becomes the biopic that relates the tragic story of the celebrated star of the frenetic American jazz scene in the 1940s.

A conservative tradition in film studies recapitulates the interchangeable discourse of Hollywood studio story consultations—in which hackneyed conceptual traits are mixed as if ingredients in a stew. Industry-attentive criticism thus typically bears no distinction in depth of insight from the one-sentence movie blurbs composed in the same clichés that one finds in *TV Guide*, however much this tradition of commentary may yield longer discussions to include close readings. However much this approach to film commentary may be adequate to exhaust what mainstream Hollywood films mean, the frailty lies not so much in the absence of critical distance as in the blindness of reinforcement of a shared set of standard conceptual frameworks that prevents detection of more interesting, subtler, more sophisticated if recondite threads of meaning that imbue some films in spite of the hegemony of Hollywood film meaning-construction. That Eastwood, in particular, has cultivated a personal way of making films that critical and theoretical responses have failed to acknowledge makes his case all the more interesting.[51]

In his classic essay "The *Auteur* Theory," Peter Wollen explains the emergence of a kind of critical approach to popular cinema emanating out of the *Cahiers du Cinéma* editorial ruminations of François Truffaut and others and the spread of that approach to American and British film commentary.[52] The substantial discoveries lie in the recognition of authorship where no one has suspected it, that is, among the journeymen Hollywood directors who were presumed to be subservient to Hollywood studio control of subject, character, casting, script, and mise-en-scène, leaving the director as an on-site glorified technician. In some cases, nevertheless, the irrepressible imprint of a vibrant and consistent personal worldview and/or cinematic style persists, albeit sometimes subdued beneath the garish fabric of studio production values. The point in the auteur theory, scholarly approach is to look carefully for the concealed personal elements of meaning and particularly not just to ignore the variation of film subjects, settings, casting, and genre but to look purposively across these industry striations in order to isolate and tease out that recondite core of meaning more purely on its own.

Howard Hawks becomes the demonstration case for Wollen's essay, and Hawks happens to be one of Eastwood's filmmaking heroes, particularly for the sake of what does register in Eastwood's interview remarks—the importance of substance in character and story—which also stands as the salient force of meaning-construction that Wollen identifies in Hawks. So, these four Eastwood films—*Bronco Billy*, *Honkytonk Man*, *White Hunter Black Heart*, and *Bird*—provide exactly the diversity of subject and setting in which to look for that core of recondite meaning that the filmmaker harbors close to his thinking and intentionally not overtly shouted out so that everyone in the films' audience tires of hearing it upon even the first enunciation. Moreover, in his interviews, Eastwood proffers up his own interconnection of these four films, which he speaks of consistently in terms of what attracted him to the material—character and story.[53]

■ *Bronco Billy*

In a scene that arises late in the film, long after the initial establishment and development of the central characterizations, Bronco Billy arranges to meet Sheriff Dix to negotiate the illegal release of Leonard James, the cowboy rope trickster for Bronco Billy's Wild West show. Leonard's arrest for brawling revealed his desertion from the armed forces, avoiding service in Vietnam. Bronco Billy had chastised Leonard for being a coward and declared that he hereby washed his hands of his plight, in earshot of the sheriff and deputies in jail. But he had other things in mind, namely, this rendezvous with the sheriff away from all other observers.

The sheriff is a vain, insecure man who relishes the power he exerts over prisoners and subordinates alike. He is in constant need of affirmation of his superiority, and he thinks himself to be a quick-draw artist and brave enough to test himself against Bronco Billy. Without flinching, and with only a hint of the Eastwood trademark scowl of contempt, Bronco Billy concedes the test of courage, manhood, and skill that the sheriff clearly treasures. It is, of course, a juvenile fixation on this skill test of courage and manliness, one that governs the sheriff's self-image and behavior. Bronco Billy exploits the sheriff's juvenile passion to maneuver him into relinquishing Leonard.

Eastwood films occasionally exhibit flat characterizations that evoke our immediate scorn, such as the feckless motorcycle gang in *Every Which Way but Loose* or Maggie Fitzgerald's relatives in *Million Dollar Baby* (2004). How different, though, is Dix's fascination with speed and courage from the pointed lesson that Little Bill Daggett delivers to W. W. Beauchamp in *Unforgiven* about the folly of relying upon speed in a gunfight. Staying calm and taking careful aim are what he trusts. As flat as is the characterization of Sheriff Dix, Little Bill's is considerably more substantial, more vigorously sadistic even without Dix's vanity. Formulation of a consistent stereotype for Eastwood's Western lawmen thus will not emerge easily.

The importance of Sheriff Dix's fixation upon speed and courage in the draw derives from the popular representation of Western heroes. Bronco Billy's Wild West show relies upon the same popularized notions of the Western hero that Dix fantasizes himself to fit, even though Bronco Billy has no experience either as a cowboy or as a lawman. But the difference is how Bronco Billy understands shooting skills as sideshow tricks and how Sheriff Dix is consumed by the fantasy. Bronco Billy's fascination is in the show, in performance for an audience, for which his shooting skills have purely instrumental and not intrinsic value, least of all as a proof of virility.

Sheriff Dix and Bronco Billy negotiate a payment for Leonard's release, consisting of the entirety of Bronco Billy's money stash, $1,100, more than the rest of the troop would realize he had accumulated. But it is a modest sum, and it is a testament to Bronco Billy's frugal management of meager resources that he would have kept this amount in reserve. His loyalty to Leonard is enough to tap out the reserve, even though losing Leonard from the troop would not in itself bring about the demise of the show. As much as Bronco Billy will play up his unity with the man and the role he plays in his show, this moment away from his audience and his collaborators shows the careful reflective difference between the role and the man's self-understanding. It is thus with the role as performed that he gains gratification, with being a performer but not indulging a fantasy.

Studio advisers urged appending a scene later in the film, where Bronco Billy would return to the sheriff's town, confront him alone again, and this time pummel, defeat, and humiliate him, reduce him to shock and tears, and so on, such as would restore the screen image of Eastwood's Western and action-hero screen persona.[54] This would better guarantee a market for the film. Eastwood demurred, and for good reason. Sheriff Dix is captive to a juvenile fantasy of masculinity and courage, a fantasy promulgated by a long history of the culture's representation—and primarily in Hollywood Westerns and action films, particularly in the extension of that tradition in the films Eastwood made with Sergio Leone and Don Siegel.

Bronco Billy lives a fabulation, a role that he has designed for himself and which he not just portrays but enacts wholeheartedly both in his show and always. It is not a role that came to him naturally but one that he appropriated as he pleased from fragments in the culture, one he feels at home with and which offers him absolutely no measure of conflict with how he sees himself as part of that culture. Indeed, his shoestring operation is fabulously removed from the economic and ideological structures of that culture. The sole purpose in his keeping the show alive can only be for the sake of Bronco Billy's living that fabulation. It is a fabulation, Billy's conscious fabulation, and he encourages the other members of the troop likewise to create and to follow their own freely invented fabulations. Bronco Billy knows when it is important to show his bravery and prowess, knows when it does not matter, and knows when he need not do so. He thus is the crafter of his persona, the one who has invented it and controls it, and very explicitly in contrast to the juvenile fixations of Sheriff Dix.

Dix is representative of a somewhat artificial type, contrived for the sake of this moment in the narrative, to expose what may be dominant in the culture but what, nevertheless, does not apply to Bronco Billy, even as one would perhaps expect it to be likely to his character. Having Bronco Billy return to give Dix his comeuppance would thus validate Dix's *fantasy* and undermine Billy's carefully chosen and ongoing *fabulation*. Eastwood realized that this abstention from an easy invocation of his popular macho screen persona would likely risk losing part of his loyal audience, but it would be a following he was willing to jettison.[55]

Bronco Billy's freely fabulated persona comes replete with costumes, argot, attitude, philosophical outlook, and purpose. He is always in costume, ready for that day's show, but he has no outfit to dress down in when he is out of character. As with his costume, the argot of the Western hero is how he always speaks. It is a corny idiom full of the catchphrases and clichés appropriated from the movies but not in the least realistic to the historical referents of the Westerns. It is an argot exactly appropriate to a touring Wild West show. The attitude is upbeat, reverting to anger only on the hint of disloyalty and then bent upon resolving it or cutting ties right then and there. The philosophical outlook rests upon moral and social authenticity, but without any taint of religious or political ideological slant. Bronco Billy's purpose is to have a healthy, constructive influence upon children, at an age when they are still impressionable. The target of his show and thinking is univocal: the "'lil' pardners."

Bronco Billy forgives Leonard in an instant for his past flight from military duty and, more seriously, for having kept his legal liability secret from him. The sole complaint he has, which does not mitigate the forgiveness, is that Leonard's past actions undermine how he can set a good example for "the 'lil' pardners." Billy finds moral orientation in that projection of the good example. Without that purpose there would be no coherent and sustaining drive to his show. Though he is clearly a practical-minded show-man, the life he has fabulated bears no potential for significant wealth. The show's marginality is established in the opening images of the film, an extreme long view of the troop arriving in their old vehicles at the location of the seasonal carnival, where they set about the long, hard work of unpacking and assembling their tent. That long view returns during their travels from one site to another, at the end of the film, and at that moment when the blazing tent is clearly out of their control. The entourage makes its way tenuously in a world much too large to retain their impact for long. It takes very little for the marginal operation to face eliminating jeopardy.

The earnestness of Bronco Billy's outlook arises in the sequence of his encountering some young boys admiring his cowboy-decorated automobile, toying with their quick awe of his heroic stature, and then inviting them to his show. He hands them free tickets, but with the deliberate encouragement that they bring along their folks—who, of course, would be paying full admission. It is for the "'lil' pardners" that he does this—and the impact of the show will be all the more cemented if mom and dad are there to share it. The opportune stoop to promotion allows Bronco Billy to keep the show alive, to provide for his troop, and to continue to have an impact upon lil' pardners wherever he goes. The low-angle, wide-angle point of view of the boys looking up to the silhouetted tall man in the Western outfit captures the American flag atop a pole up in the corner of the image. The patriotism, though, is an incidental ingredient of Bronco Billy's outlook. It comes along without implications for any partisan political agenda. When later he will enlist the workers in the mental hospital where he has always provided free shows to sew a new tent for him out of the American flags that they make for profit, that new splattering image of the nation's icon will likewise come along as nothing more than one accidental, innocuous, and deadpan humorous touch flagrantly devoid of irony.

In the next scene, Bronco Billy surprises a bank holdup, which gives the film the one instance of full-fledged, even self-parodic, Eastwood scowl when the miscreants knock down a young boy, his piggy bank smashing in his fall—the wanton bullying of a "'lil' pardner" just when the boy is at the bank to deposit his hard-earned savings. The boy's fall is as perfect an affront to his targeted moral purposes as can be imagined, which instigates Bronco Billy's scowl and reflex intervention. Billy unleashes his fast-draw, trick-shot artistry to defeat the robbers, though we understand his guns to be loaded with disabling but not lethal ammunition. It is a scene that Eastwood injected into the script, as the necessary setup for how Bronco Billy subjects himself later to humiliation before Sheriff Dix.[56] That humiliation would be considerably less if the film's audience did not understand how Billy would actually respond to a crisis by exploiting his quick-draw, surefire gun skills, where that was necessary and not gratuitous. He thus immediately becomes a local hero, surrounded by the local television news media. Bronco Billy answers queries humbly about his heroism and then leans into the camera repeatedly to advertise when and where his Wild West show is playing that evening. There is nothing phony on either side of this combination of heroism and showmanship. He responds spontaneously but deliberately to the urgent events in the bank and then just as deliberately and spontaneously to the opportunity for transferring attention to his deeds into a boon for the show. It is always for the sake of imparting what he stands for to all the "lil" pardners out there.

The interjection of Antoinette Lily into the story and into the troop provides Bronco Billy with the challenge of adjusting the easy script of both the show and the life he has rigidly become accustomed to. That shudder in his world exposes his proclivity to control those close to him, in the name of beneficence, and the chauvinism that lies just beneath the sublimely naive veneer of the Bronco Billy outlook. The resolution of her antagonism toward him comes at that point, which we guess he has crossed one by one with the other members of the troop before, when he explains how the show and his fabulated life began.

The New Jersey shoe salesman, that he once was, was bored with his life. He became violent with his wife's betrayal, which led to imprisonment, out of which he emerged with this invention of a life of his own design. The confession is without shame, secrecy, or pride. It is a simple explanation, one that applies to the rest of the troop—of having come through a rupture with a previous life to embrace this new one of pure invention. The Bronco Billy outlook comes to be all their freely chosen commitments, not an ideology to proselytize for, not an outlook that needs to be philosophically the right one, but an outlook that is livable, at least innocuous, good-hearted, and earnest.

Bronco Billy's costume is open to those who will choose it, without coercion or delusion, and thus who embrace the same opportunity for fabulation. His influence is mildly dispersed, and the troop he arranges around him is just enough to sustain and share in their mutually constructed marginal place in a social and economic world that functions on entirely different principles. At one point or another, all will utter the argot with the earnestness they see in Bronco Billy and thus choose that same fabulation as the nature of their life, a life they have constructed in place of the lives and behavior that came to them from the nature and nurture of their origins.

■ *Honkytonk Man*

"I'll try," the singer, the honky-tonk man, declares, sotto voce and unnecessarily, in response to the woman who owns the roadhouse. Warmly, she encourages him to sing well. She did not expect a response, and really it is only to himself that he directs this utterance as he moves toward the stage. His soft, breathy evocation of the simple sentence swallows the first word, the part of the sentence that declares the meaning to be his own, leaving just the "try" for even him to hear. He is relaxed, steady, reserved, confident—knowingly acknowledging what the world brings to his life as a honky-tonk man, and he would prefer no other. That soft breathiness hints at the tuberculosis that consumes him inexorably from within, against which this life of singing provides an escape—if not forestalling death, diminishing it by drawing up every ounce of purpose in his life into the voice in denial of death. He takes his place on a straight chair on the stage, with his guitar nestled in position in his lap. He pulls the microphone close to him and begins to sing—a song about not being able to express what he feels to the woman he loves, though it comes easily when he sings it. The figure he strikes is lit from the side and isolated in space on the stage in the roadhouse. He is hunkered over. The brim of his broad hat completes the encompassing of the space where the singer's mouth, guitar, and microphone are enclosed into a private capsule of personal presence. He is hardly cognizant of any impact he might have on the quiet crowd in the bar. He is, instead, thoroughly absorbed in the soft singing of the song that no one would guess speaks to his own self and to the loss that defines his despair. This scene comes after the initial scenes in the film that establish Stovall's itinerant, unhealthy life and how his sister welcomes what she knows can only be a brief stay with her family. But we see the singer in his own element in this self-preserved privacy on the stage of the honky-tonk. Here we see what even his sister may only vaguely perceive about him.

Red Stovall's guitar, his car, his hat, and his one suit of clothes are all that he owns, but they are his singular treasures, especially the guitar. Like him, the car, a large maroon convertible sedan, is modestly elegant and alluring. But, like him, it is afflicted with an engine that is perilously close to meltdown. He arrives drunk, in that car, at the home of his sister, her husband, and their children, in the midst of a dust storm, managing to temper their surprise and delight by happening to knock over the farm's windmill. That destruction does not compound the family's distress, since the excess of wind that the dust storm brings in combination with the drought has rendered the windmill useless—which ordinarily would serve vitally to convert wind into access to water. Red recuperates and prepares to travel cross-country, where an audition at the Grand Ole Opry awaits him in Nashville. Red wants his nephew, Whit, precocious in both talent for singing and coping, to be his driver—and enabler. The boy's grandpa wants to come along, to return to where he was born and raised, ostensibly to die there. The boy's father's bitterness at the hardness of his plight bears no succor for the boy's simple aspiration to have a life other than the misery of farming cotton. Resentful as he is himself about that life, the boy's father is more resentful of how his son could finagle a way out of that fate. The boy's mother sees the virtue of the escape, even as it means separation and exposure of the boy to the honky-tonk life that has been ruinous to her brother.

Red's joviality, his finagling, his thievery, and his ability—more from luck—to escape calamity earn the trust of the boy and the grandfather along the way. The girl who joins their journey shares dreams—though without the requisite talent—of the life of singing to enthusiastic audiences. As the hints of illness and death continue to evoke Red's overt aversion, the boy and the girl finally understand the nature of the travel—both of the adult men are traveling to where they will die, even as either would hardly be on the verge of confessing that. As they close in on the destination, that meaning becomes clear, and Red's compulsion to sing, to have his singing heard, becomes his sole meaningful response.

Sitting wanly in the window light that alone relieves the motel room of shadow, smoking a cigarette, sweating, weak, and pained, Red listens to the recording studio man as he irons out Red's last deal, the deal that firmly finalizes his life, his art, and his fate. Red capitulates. He has told the boy of the truth of that song in the roadhouse—there was a woman whom he stole from her husband, whom he had loved but then left, only to realize that he did love her, that she was the love of his life.

The weakness, the scoundrel's transgressions, the failure of the hero, and that he dies—these are aspects of the characterization that studio types warned Eastwood against—lest it lose him the following that eagerly anticipates the action hero.[57] But it is the honest story of the performer that interests Eastwood. It is a story without guarantee of happiness and, indeed, as predicated upon the tenuous importance of creativity and performance, in spite of the sacrifice of happiness. Since his films always make money, he can make them the way he prefers. Since he is a star, he can play against type whenever he pleases.

■ *White Hunter Black Heart*

A man rides a horse at full gallop through the fields of a vast country estate. The horse is powerful and fast, and the rider is hunched over the saddle, in full control of the animal even at breakneck speed. The ride is clearly for leisure, though the pleasure taken is in the challenge of meeting top possible speed, with its concomitant danger and thrill. The film begins with this extended image of John Wilson the filmmaker doing what gives him pleasure, and the ever-pressing need for life-challenging adventure is how we come to understand Wilson. He is a successful Hollywood director, with aristocratic friends in England who lend him the estate in which to while his time and who have fast horses for him to ride.

The character of John Wilson is based liberally upon John Huston.[58] A breakneck horse-riding scene of similar length and significance occurs in John Huston's *Reflections in a Golden Eye* (1967). That scene exhibits the overt struggle of the equestrian with his repressed homosexuality; he coaxes an uncontrollable gallop out of a thoroughbred stallion and then whips the horse viciously when he finally is able to halt its wild gallop by dragging himself along the ground. In contrast to that viciousness, the breakneck gallop at the beginning of Eastwood's film provides a potent image of a dangerous symbiosis of horse and rider. This is a man without apprehension about his life, about his sexuality, about his athleticism, or about his fearless encounter with natural danger.

Wilson is deeply in debt and delights in the thought of dying prematurely, thus to thwart his creditors. He is fond of sharing his jovial contemplations of his own demise, which betray a fixation with death that nevertheless is expressed with complete lack of trepidation. His thoughts for the script of his next project (which, deriving from the literary source

of the film, corresponds to John Huston's *African Queen* [1951]) contain an
ending that kills off the two principal characters along with their captors.[59]
He insists that this ending is honest, in contrast to the typical Hollywood,
happy ending, which would save the two. Wilson invests his integrity as
a writer and a filmmaker, insisting upon this variance from Hollywood
dramatic strictures, which he delights in as much as he delights in being
not wealthy but heavily in debt. That, too, bolsters his sense of personal
distance from the mainstream entertainment industry.

John Wilson debates the choice of ending with screenwriter Pete Verrill,
who sees the pragmatic virtue of box-office success and who also argues
philosophically against a gratuitously pessimistic ending. Wilson considers Verrill closely aligned with his own outlook. He smiles always, finding
the humor in all encounters, where the bemused irony in his indulgence of
the neurotic ordinary fixations in everyone he meets is made evident in the
sly glances he shares with Verrill but with no one else. He expects Verrill
to be equally enthusiastic about the opportunity that filming on location
will provide to go on safari and shoot an elephant. Wilson takes the same
delight in personally testing the dilapidated boat that will be the inani-
mate costar of the film by traversing the river rapids as will be required
in the story. His producer, Paul Landers, would rather shoot those scenes
with models or on more easily managed rivers in California, and Verrill is
indifferent to this choice. So, Wilson takes Landers and Verrill along as his
passengers on the test, laughing heartily at their abject fear. Their fear of
demise fuels his happy defiance of death. Hunting the elephant epitomizes
that need.

Eastwood's portrayal of Wilson incorporates emulation of the drawl
and cadence of John Huston's well-known speech, his full-bodied laugh
accentuated by bending forward nearly perpendicular at the waist, his
accommodation of his height in the presence of others by leaning forward
on a chair or other available prop, and his constant smile and wry delivery
of his witty, sardonic humor. Huston was the model for John Wilson in
Peter Viertel's novelized account, which became the basis for his screenplay. Viertel's novel derives, with some license, from his experiences in
Africa working with Huston on *African Queen*, with his own part as the
fictionalized Peter Verrill, though with license for dramatizing the events
and characters involved. Eastwood thought of the Wilson character as an
amalgam of different people, though with clear connection to Huston.[60]
Viertel's screenplay based on his novel served as the basis for Eastwood's

film. Eastwood claims to have sought to capture Huston's manner of thinking, not just his voice, and it is a way of thinking that is indeed evident in
the cadence and inflection of Huston's distinct speech.[61] One understands
Wilson's constant ironic, humorous distance in that cadence. The separation between the veneer of joviality and the constant, cynical delight is
strained in the severe invective he inflicts upon the anti-Semitic woman,
still couched in his regular polite repartee. That separation eventually
begins to erode from implied defiance as his responsibility for the production of the film becomes more than nominally jeopardized by his fixation on hunting the elephant. Verrill does not follow him in that trajectory.
Wilson is left alone in that fixation, with the sole exception of the man
Kivu, the African hunter and guide, whom Wilson gradually assumes as
his own genuine counterpart.

Wilson sports costumes—the borrowed equestrian outfit on the
English country estate, formal evening dress, the hunter's outfit in Africa,
and the amazing access to formal evening attire that he surprises the movie
company with upon their arrival at the hunting lodge on location. The
enormous joke of the elaborate formal dinner he has arranged for them
culminates in his pet monkey making off with the finished script, just as
Wilson hands it over to Landers, the film's anxious producer. The monkey
dashes all around the long dinner table, climbs into the rafters above, and
shows every indication that he may destroy the sheets in his paws and take
them away where they will be lost.

Bent over, but more curled into himself than simply bent at the waist,
Wilson remains upright but seized in uncontrollable laughter. He leans
against the wall, half-incapacitated by the combination of his chronic
coughing and his laughter and just barely sharing his impression that this
hilarity "almost makes it all worthwhile." The "it" that needs to be made
worthwhile is the business and responsibility of working in the movie
industry, the phoniness of the art that he is party to, the pain of that chronic
respiratory ailment, the pain of living, and the anguish in face of death that
he so heartily disguises in his sardonic humor and penchant for reckless
adventure.

As demonstrated in the testing of the old boat on the river, Wilson
finds vicarious solace in how he can disperse his passions and purposes by
enlisting others—Verrill, Landers, Kivu, the bush pilot, and white hunter
guides—into his contrived adventures. The film will be that adventure only
as he can jeopardize it—either by controlling its ending or by undermining

the production with his dalliance in the hunt for the elephant. His deep folly comes at the point of final confrontation with the bull elephant, the big tusker. As he looks down the barrel of his gun toward the massive angry animal, Wilson pauses, checks the safety trigger, and lowers his weapon. He has found grace in that visual communication with this enormous emanation of life and nature, one that dissolves all of his masked fascination with death. But he has tragically turned away much too late. His lack of expertise in hunting is a direct result of his fixation on the adventure of the hunt. Kivu intervenes to save Wilson, drawing the elephant's attention, but is then killed by the elephant.

Wilson has, in his existential folly, caused the pointless death of the man whom, alone, he considered nobler than himself. He has humiliated a woman for her anti-Semitism and challenged a man to a fistfight for his racism—and lost—and yet his own behavior results in travesty, one that betrays a failing of empathy that simple responsibility for the well-being of those around him would presuppose.[62] The affinity he thought to have gained with Kivu's people is dashed as the news spreads, more easily for the sake of how thin that affinity actually was compared with the horrifying loss of the man from their midst. That fact registers with how the news spreads, as Wilson is already known as "White Hunter Black Heart."

Wilson, speechless in his horror and in the realization of his folly, returns to the movie location. His chair awaits him, and the crew and cast are all in place to begin filming. Still speechless, he walks to that chair, moribund and slouched—so unlike his erect, vibrant natural gait. He slumps down in the chair, chin on his chest, facing away from our view, but with his broad-brimmed hunter's hat shielding his visage from those who would be able to see him from the other side. Told that everything is ready and awaiting his instruction, he pauses and then wanly gestures for it to start. But no one moves. Finally, he is reminded softly that he must say that one word, that it is incumbent upon him and him alone to indicate that the filming has now begun, simply by his saying, "Action!"

It is an example of what philosophers call a performative utterance, an utterance that constitutes an action just in its utterance, such as a justice of the peace pronouncing a couple married or a baseball umpire calling a base runner out.[63] Saying "Action!" is the film director's inalienable performative because it designates that what follows is now the *filming* of the planned film—a palpable part of the work of cinema that will be the result of the work of the company over a period of weeks and months. His saying it makes it so. Softly, barely audibly, Wilson intones, "Action." That performative, his first word after Kivu's death, inverts the solace of irony in which Wilson prefers to situate himself. It realizes the filmmaker's vicariousness in instructing action to happen, action that will depict only virtually the moving image that an audience will understand as existing only in a fictional narrative.

■ *Bird*

A boy leads a pony aimlessly around a family's yard, in and around the grazing chickens, along and behind the laundry hung up on the clothes-lines. A younger boy sits on the pony playing a pennywhistle. He toys with melodic flow, not sticking to the melody but pressing against each of the notes, finding ways to alter the tonality, to bend a note a quarter tone flat, to hear how that sounds next to other notes in time.

An older boy, a teenager, strolls up and down the porch of the same family home, with laundry again screening off the foreground of the image. He plays an alto saxophone, toying with a recognizable tune, a Christmas carol. He alters its flow, its rhythm, how it sounds with the tonality of this note changed, to be breathy or harsh, or with this note flatted. An older man sits at leisure on a chair on the porch, attentive to the boy's playing and understanding how the young musician is toying with melody.

A grown man, dressed in a dark suit, solos in front of a jazz ensemble before a receptive audience in a crowded and noisy jazz club. In the epitome of bebop, his solo is filled with long, fast runs and the occasional pause on a two- or three-note slower motif. His head pushes forward and back as far as the human neck will allow; his shoulders also fold forward and back; his eyes are closed. The concentration on performing through the alto sax is the center of the man's being, breathing, and thinking for the duration. There is enormous virtuosity in his playing, such as bebop demands, but no more exhibition of mechanical skill than is warranted by the expression of the playing.

In this opening sequence of the film, we see how since his childhood this man has toyed with the cogent, philosophical meaning of jazz improvisation for the performer and for his audience. There is no delight simply in playing what is difficult but, rather, profound exploration in playing what is deeply meaningful as could only be difficult to conceive and to perform. The inflection of virtuosity upon performance is entirely personal—this musician's own voice, and to have that voice, inimitable and expressive, is what it all means for the jazzman. To invoke what another saxophonist says in another film, there would be no worse humiliation and failure than for another musician to declare, "I do you better than you."[64]

These three performances, of the young boy, the older boy, and the mature musician, establish the origins of Charlie Parker's (Forest Whitaker) passion in the opening sequence of the film. Without needing to explain, Eastwood lets his audience assume a time lapse in the dissolves from one setting to the next, thus to trace quickly the genesis of the musician. In a film that uncharacteristically shows Eastwood's adeptness at a modestly fragmented temporal structure for the narrative, this opening uncued set of transitions is important for his audience to acclimate to the need to fill in themselves how succeeding scenes fit disparately into one encompassing time line.

Equally quickly we see Charlie Parker's physical addictions and moral afflictions. His anguish at not being able to command either nevertheless fathoms the depths of his love for those close to him, for it is how he harms them that drives that anguish deepest. A fear of the musician's humiliation becomes redundant in his improvisation. A womanizer's constant attraction to seduction makes his life impossible relative to the woman he adores and for whom his love is constant. His mercurial behavior and need to feed the addictions fail those who perform with him, who need him simply to show up on time. He neglects his children, though unbounded in his love for them when he is there to see them. His anguish is no deeper than when he learns of the death of one to illness, when he was thousands of miles away.

Charlie Parker enlists people into his traversals of life—musicians; his wife, Chan; the musician closest to him musically, Dizzy; agents; and producers. Their love for him abides beyond human endurance his tremendous failings and betrayals. What is present as philosophy in his music is also present in his compassion, in what makes someone want to love him. His life would have been emptier and with less depth to his pain and anguish, and to that of those close to him, had it not been for that compassion and the compassion it stirred in them.

He is, though, in his sole supreme element on the bandstand, a performer, but one who plumbs at truth, at what is genuine in life. He speaks through the alto sax, eyes closed to shut off all imposition of the world, to filter out all perception of anything but the music. The perigee opposite to that soaring height finds him trudging down a lonely, dark city street in the rain, coming from or going to where he would find his fix, the shuffling of his gait already or subsequently showing the effect, as if it mattered not when exactly the injection took place.

■ Dispersion, Performance, Rupture, Fabulation

Returning to the distinction Deleuze draws between organic and crystalline narrative, it would seem at first glance that with Eastwood's spare narrative, reserved style, and aversion to metaphor (particularly when an interviewer suggests one to him), there would be no filmmaker more entrenched in the mainstream, organic narrative than Eastwood. But it actually is not quite so simple as that. How Eastwood has carved out a sense of cinema ideal for the actor's yearning for nuanced, sophisticated portrayals and complex story relies upon being able to thrive within the culture industry by adhering to a small budget, always coming in under budget and on or before schedule, and always making a profit. But it is just that program of efficiency that allows dispensation from the usual studio imposition of inanity in the name of optimizing market appeal. If that inanity adheres religiously to the organic narrative, because it is never challenging, never confusing, then it will not be thoroughly surprising to see Eastwood, by virtue of that dispensation, taking liberties with that adherence.

First, organic descriptions fix images regularly with reference to objects in the real world understood to exist in the narrative diegesis. It is not metaphor that Deleuze means by the crystalline contrast, since the metaphoric depiction still refers to specifics in that diegesis, but only indirectly, as one image standing for what is not its indexical referent. The crystalline image is pure image—having significance independent of its placement in the diegetic.

We do find traces of crystalline images in these four Eastwood films. The slow-motion arc of the cymbal flying across the frame against a dark background in *Bird* is a crystalline image, and again as it is replaced later by a bottle of iodine. As well, the recurrent appearance of the pony or horse has meaning not as representing something other relative to Charlie Parker but as something in his life with which nothing else is associated. Parker in paradigmatic compositions—trudging through the rain or in his element in the spotlight, eyes closed and soloing onstage—likewise has meaning devoid of context and also nonmetaphorically. Here is Charlie Parker as he is in himself, with connection to nothing in the world in which we understand that character to traverse, interact, live, and suffer. The equestrian riding at breakneck speed at the opening of *White Hunter Black Heart* begins that film with this crystalline image. The man with the constant, ironic, delighting smile and the elephant—snorting, trumpeting, and ears flapping—likewise mean everything, not as interprctation of the rest but, rather, as an alternative "it" that is made worthwhile by the monkey's antics. The dust rising from the carefully tilled earth, blowing into a storm that then destroys the crop and chases away into hiding the farming family that has toiled marginally on that land, which opens *Honkytonk Man*, has that mode of significance as well—to impart everything that we need know about what the earth has done, in its full punishing paradox.

A car careens into the dust, its driver already impaired and never competent at managing a sure course on the road or in life. It comes to rest only as it knocks over the family's windmill, which, paradoxically, employs the wind to provide water that would be the sole antidote to the dust stirred up by the wind. That driver, Red Stovall, at once thoroughly reckless and also oblivious as to how his divergence from simple slavery to the earth renders him reckless to those who work it, likewise suffers from within from what will rob him of breath. The long-distant view of the Wild West show at the beginning and repeatedly in *Bronco Billy* shows the troop arriving at the carnival site, to embark upon the hard labor of unpacking and erecting the tent and thus to create that capsule of a world in which a gloriously imaginary rendition of life in the Old West, a century removed, will come to life and flourish for the duration of a show.

These depictions of all that one need know, all in a single complex image, are at once seated within the organic composition of the narrative and yet have a meaning independent of context, and thus the organic descriptions are stretched toward the crystalline. Similarly, the irrelevance of the differentiation between real and irreal obtains somewhat in these four Eastwood films, but in a terribly important way that connects these specific four films in Eastwood's corpus. These are Eastwood's films about creativity and performance. Eastwood went to considerable trouble in acquiring and preparing original recordings of Charlie Parker for the performance scenes in *Bird*, although the studio wanted to have the original performances rerecorded by a contemporary and presumably nameless musician.[65] Eastwood would pause to smile as he explained this discrepancy in understanding the importance of jazz performance. Without needing to explain, the smile betrays wonderment at how jazz performance could so easily be misconstrued and trivialized. The odd practice of training A-list actors to impersonate the singing of popular singers in Hollywood biopics rather than lip-sync original recordings perhaps better approximates the production values that ensure audience acceptance of the singing as real, but it also implicitly belittles the artistry of the subject of the biopic as easily equaled by an actor's crash-course emulation. Eastwood, who heard Charlie Parker play in 1946, esteemed his artistry immensely.[66] The repetition of Parker's performances in *Bird* is the unifying structure of the narrative. His playing needs to be original, since the music re-creates Charlie Parker better than any depiction of his life possibly could. These performances, replete with the musician's own musical voice—tonalities, inflections, phrasing, improvisations, and flukes—constitute what the voice imparts. It is the raspiness of the voice—its divergence from both neutrality and idealization—that delivers what is personal in the voice.

This importance of the *raspiness* of the personal voice is true for the musician, and particularly true for the jazz performer among musicians, but it also applies to actors. The sly genius of Eastwood's approach to handling actors—filming the "rehearsal" take and then printing it—captures that raspiness in the actor's performance, that moment in which the delivery is first being thought through, before it becomes polished, cleansed, perfected. It is in hearing that raspiness—just as surely as we can recognize the Charlie Parker recordings as original—that we hear the performer, both the musician and the actor.

So when Sondra Locke struggles with portraying a New York sophisticate in *Bronco Billy*, or Eastwood turns slightly to smile at us as he plays boogie-woogie piano with stiff fingering in *Honkytonk Man* (just as he had learned before ever thinking of acting as a career), or as we conjure up John Huston's actual voice in hearing Eastwood's emulation of Huston's cadence and drawl, though without attempting to impersonate Huston's voice fully, we attend to the performance, guided by the overt raspiness. That effect is as deliberate as Eastwood's management of acting on his set—get the fresh rendering before it becomes disguised, before it smoothes over the raspiness. And in the evident acting, the performer's presence stands forward, very much in contrast to the lacquered production values of Hollywood acting. It is in these moments when Eastwood's films, these four films, overtly erode the distinction between real and irreal in the organic diegesis.

In the initial moments of uncued narrative time line shifts in *Bird*, the image we see and hear stands out of time and space. At those moments before there is sufficient information revealed to place the action relative to what has transpired, the continuum of space and time is suspended, and thus for these moments, the organic narrative is forsaken. The scenes of Charlie Parker performing especially wander unfixed in time and location, with context supplied after the performance is concluded, and the music continues in overlap soundtrack as the scene shifts. The story of Parker's events of life trauma are all eventually captured in flashback—his confrontation with his likely fate as a junkie, the death of a child, and his humiliation as a young musician. Parker hints at his yearning for death repeatedly.

The parallel rupture in *Bronco Billy*—Billy's crime and imprisonment— is recounted in dialogue, and there is no hint of Bronco Billy having thoughts about his mortality. Similarly, it is only when Red Stovall tells Whit about his abandonment of the love of his life that the meaning of his songs and life becomes clear. Stovall shuns death and recoils from mention of his illness. The dramatic rupture for John Wilson comes at the very end of the film. Thus, though the narrative remains strictly comprehended in all four films, the import of dramatic rupture remains concealed. Wilson jokes about death, wondering how it would rile his creditors and how he will find it amusing when Hollywood finally reveres him only after his passing. These ruptures bend the narrative structure toward singular events, either literally or effectively independent of placement within a defined time and location. This, too, shows how Eastwood nudges his film's content toward the crystalline.

The rootedness of performance in the original Charlie Parker recordings in *Bird* and the displaced images in the interstices of the fragmented narrative demote the claim to truthfulness of the biographical account to a *telling* of the life of Parker. One witnesses renditions of scattered events in the life of the musician but hardly any promise of the truth of the whole of that life or any of its secrets. The preposterousness of the elephant killing Kivu grants *White Hunter Black Heart* a similar distancing from claims to biographical truthfulness about its indirect subject, John Huston. The vacillation between humor and downfall sustains *Honkytonk Man* in a similar ambivalence regarding plausibility. That humor is stronger in *Bronco Billy*, as is the improbability of the shoe salesman from New Jersey who shoots his unfaithful wife, serves time, and then refashions himself as a Wild West showman—the actual subject whom he portrays.[67] So, as with the other aspects of how Deleuze characterizes the divergence of crystalline narrative from the precise functionalism of the organic narrative that thrives in mainstream cinema, Eastwood's constructs wander away from those conservative traits, albeit not exotically far.

What interests Eastwood is that the principal character in each of these four films is a *fabulator* and, more specifically, a *self*-fabulator. Bronco Billy becomes the man whose life he fabulates out of pure will and just to have composed his life and himself as he wills them. Because there is no deception in that process, the creation is a fabulation but not a fabrication and not a delusion, either. In that difference we see authenticity on one side and lack of it on the other. Red Stovall, likewise, conceives of a life different from where he comes from in the world and preserves its deeper truths for what he sings about. John Wilson lives life with those he encounters always at arm's length, a distance that preserves his created role as ironic observer, until that moment when he looks the elephant in the eye and the distance dissipates, revealing that it never had been there. For Charlie Parker, the self-invention is entirely in the music, and his life and those he loves constitute points along the periphery of the music.

Understood in how Charlie Parker, John Wilson, Red Stovall, and Bronco Billy confront rupture, embrace performance, arrange those close to them to serve the dispersion of their creativity, and create a life fabulated out of whole cloth, these four characters are profoundly different on all four comparisons. The stories, development, and lighting are distinct in the four cases, but all bear out what Eastwood insists is what attracts him to scripts: characterizations that actors love to have as roles and an interesting, nontrivial story. Just in this, the stories of these films realize the fabulation that Deleuze identifies for literature: singularities and not generalities—and least of all variations on the same generality.

The worst error one can make in reading these films is to associate any of the protagonists with the outlook and sensibility of the filmmaker. As often as Eastwood has been able to quote the line about "eight million popcorn eaters" from *White Hunter Black Heart*, there is nothing to associate John Wilson with Clint Eastwood, particularly not in the issue of irresponsibility regarding the production of the movie project under way. There is, similarly, little to associate either Bronco Billy or Red Stovall with the filmmaker. There is unrestrained adulation of Charlie Parker, even as tempered by the frank depiction of addiction and betrayal, but clearly Eastwood does not imagine himself a sort of artistic genius of Parker's stature or as a man victimized by chemical dependency. If we look to how Eastwood manages filmmaking as an ongoing endeavor—to build a limited-budget project;

to conduct filming efficiency to capture fresh, spontaneous performances; to complete the filming and postproduction ahead of schedule and below budget—there is a correlation with Bronco Billy, whose careful management of the marginal operation keeps it alive and keeps his crew employed. The correlate character of protective responsibility in *Honkytonk Man* is the boy, Whit. In *White Hunter Black Heart*, it is Pete Verrill, and in *Bird*, it is Dizzy Gillespie. Always accompanying the story of the creative performer is the person from whose vantage point it can be feasible in the world of an entertainment industry and an audience. Though it hardly matters to Eastwood which actor gets this role, this is the consistent characterization in these four films that best echoes the filmmaker's worldview.

◼ Notes

1. Robert E. Kapsis and Kathie Coblentz, eds., *Clint Eastwood: Interviews* (Jackson: University of Mississippi Press, 1999), xvi.

2. Interview with Terri Gross, *Fresh Air*, WHYY, November 21, 1996.

3. Kapsis and Coblentz, *Clint Eastwood*, 73, 89; Michael Henry Wilson, *Eastwood on Eastwood*, rev. English ed. (Paris: Cahiers du Cinéma, 2010), 26.

4. Kapsis and Coblentz, *Clint Eastwood*, 57, 89, 191.

5. Ibid., 57.

6. Ibid., 52, 82, 155; Wilson, *Eastwood on Eastwood*, 159, 184, 186, 211.

7. Kapsis and Coblentz, *Clint Eastwood*, 19, 166, 173; Wilson, *Eastwood on Eastwood*, 27, 31, 39, 51, 187, 191.

8. Kapsis and Coblentz, *Clint Eastwood*, 56, 143; Wilson, *Eastwood on Eastwood*, 94–95, 188.

9. Kapsis and Coblentz, *Clint Eastwood*, 64, 90, 142, 166.

10. Ibid., 60; Wilson, *Eastwood on Eastwood*, 204–5, 210.

11. Kapsis and Coblentz, *Clint Eastwood*, 105, 149–50, 181, 191; Wilson, *Eastwood on Eastwood*, 39, 74, 80, 159.

12. Kapsis and Coblentz, *Clint Eastwood*, 48, 90, 98; Wilson, *Eastwood on Eastwood*, 39, 50.

13. Kapsis and Coblentz, *Clint Eastwood*, 53–54; Wilson, *Eastwood on Eastwood*, 137, 161.

14. Robert E. Kapsis and Kathie Coblentz, "Introduction," in *Clint Eastwood*, xvi; Wilson, *Eastwood on Eastwood*, 47.

15. Kapsis and Coblentz, *Clint Eastwood*, 122, 129, 133, 161, 183–84, 208, 228, 230; Wilson, *Eastwood on Eastwood*, 31, 46, 47, 74–75, 79, 132, 158.

16. Kapsis and Coblentz, *Clint Eastwood*, 201, 214; Wilson, *Eastwood on Eastwood*, 136–37.

17. See Bernard Benoliel, *Clint Eastwood*, rev. English ed. (Paris: Cahiers du Cinéma, 2010), 46.

18. Kapsis and Coblentz, *Clint Eastwood*, 36, 110–11, 132, 150, 154, 177–78; Wilson, *Eastwood on Eastwood*, 35, 43, 78, 94, 98.

19. Kapsis and Coblentz, *Clint Eastwood*, 32, 79, 158, 168, 220; Wilson, *Eastwood on Eastwood*, 47, 104, 169, 172.

20. Kapsis and Coblentz, *Clint Eastwood*, 176, 178; Wilson, *Eastwood on Eastwood*, 51, 71, 151, 160, 175, 198, 210, 215.

21. Kapsis and Coblentz, *Clint Eastwood*, 161, 164.

22. Ibid., 179, 184; Wilson, *Eastwood on Eastwood*, 42.

23. Kapsis and Coblentz, *Clint Eastwood*, 33, 87, 114, 118; Wilson, *Eastwood on Eastwood*, 51, 80, 137.

24. Kapsis and Coblentz, *Clint Eastwood*, 91–92, 96, 133–34, 200; Wilson, *Eastwood on Eastwood*, 62, 93, 125.

25. Kapsis and Coblentz, *Clint Eastwood*, 32–33, 79; Wilson, *Eastwood on Eastwood*, 126.

26. Wilson, *Eastwood on Eastwood*, 64.

27. Ibid., 52, 92.

28. Kapsis and Coblentz, *Clint Eastwood*, 212, 223; Wilson, *Eastwood on Eastwood*, 59, 174.

29. Kapsis and Coblentz, *Clint Eastwood*, 78, 92, 96, 180.

30. See Richard Schickel, *Clint: A Retrospective* (Bath: Palazzo Editions, 2010), 18.

31. See my "The Cowboy in the Shadows in John Ford's *My Darling Clementine*," in *Westerns: Paperback Novels and Movies from Hollywood*, ed. Paul Varner (Newcastle: Cambridge Scholars Press, 2007), 44–70.

32. Gerald Peary, ed., *John Ford: Interviews* (Jackson: University of Mississippi Press, 2001), 39, 50, 123.

33. Kapsis and Coblentz, *Clint Eastwood*, 72, 79.

34. See Howard Hughes, *Aim for the Heart: The Films of Clint Eastwood* (London: I. B. Taurus, 2009), 136; Wilson, *Eastwood on Eastwood*, 47.

35. Kapsis and Coblentz, *Clint Eastwood*, 164, 175, 179.

36. Ibid., 121.

37. Ibid., 108.

38. Ibid., 6, 28, 34, 125, 127, 154, 156, 180, 202, 211–12, 237.

39. Ibid., 211.

40. Schickel, *Clint*, 27.

41. Kapsis and Coblentz, *Clint Eastwood*, 218; Wilson, *Eastwood on Eastwood*, 168.

42. See Philippa Gates, "Acting His Age? The Resurrection of the 80s Action Heroes and Their Aging Stars," *Quarterly Review of Film and Video* 27, no. 4 (2010): 278.

43. Kapsis and Coblentz, *Clint Eastwood*, 226.

44. Ibid., 121.

45. Ibid., 214.

46. Ibid., 10, 25, 57, 73, 77, 79, 128, 135, 161, 166, 171, 183, 237; Wilson, *Eastwood on Eastwood*, 124–25.

47. Wilson, *Eastwood on Eastwood*, 46.

48. Gilles Deleuze, *Cinema 2: The Time-Image*, trans. Hugh Tomlinson and Robert Galeta (Minneapolis: University of Minnesota Press, 1989), 126–37.

49. See Hughes, *Aim for the Heart*, 30. See also Benoliel, *Clint Eastwood*, 83–88; and Michael Henry Wilson, "Prologue: The Maverick's Path," in *Eastwood on Eastwood*, 10; Wilson, *Eastwood on Eastwood*, 31, 58, 62, 103, 209. See also my "Mystical Moral Miasma in Mystic River," in *Clint Eastwood, Actor and Director: New Perspectives*, ed. Leonard Engel (Salt Lake City: University of Utah Press, 2007), 218–41.

50. Gilles Deleuze, *Essays Critical and Clinical*, trans. Daniel W. Smith and Michael A. Greco (Minneapolis: University of Minnesota Press, 1997), 3–4.

51. See Drucilla Cornell, *Clint Eastwood and Issues of Masculinity* (New York: Fordham University Press, 2009), vii–xi.

52. Peter Wollen, *Signs and Meaning in the Cinema*, 3rd ed. (Bloomington: Indiana University Press, 1972), 74–115.

53. Kapsis and Coblentz, *Clint Eastwood*, 77, 104, 109, 140, 154, 161, 163, 184.

54. Wilson, *Eastwood on Eastwood*, 42.

55. Kapsis and Coblentz, *Clint Eastwood*, 94, 105.

56. Ibid., 66.

57. Ibid., 94, 108.

58. Peter Viertel, *White Hunter Black Heart* (New York: McFadden Books, 1963).

59. John Huston had initially wanted to end *The African Queen* with Charlie and Rose married by the captain of the German gunboat and then hanged as spies, but the emergent humor of the film during filming led him eventually to agree to the ending of their miraculous reprise from the explosion and sinking of the German boat after its collision with the remnants of the *African Queen*. See Lawrence Grobel, *The Hustons* (New York: Charles Scribner's Sons, 1989), 377.

60. Kapsis and Coblentz, *Clint Eastwood*, 161.

61. Ibid., 162.

62. John Huston's obsession with hunting and killing "a big tusker" is recorded independently of Viertel's fictitious account of John Wilson in the novel and screenplay. There were no casualties in Huston's hunting forays, though Katherine Hepburn, after becoming fascinated with the hunt herself, did venture dangerously close to elephants and wild boar. That did not faze Hepburn, but it seriously perturbed Huston, his own penchant for danger notwithstanding. See Grobel, *Hustons*, 372–73.

63. J. L. Austin, *How to Do Things with Words* (Oxford: Clarendon Press, 1962), 5.

64. Dexter Gordon, as Dale Turner, gets to deliver this line in Bertrand Tavernier's *'Round Midnight* (1986), a film that Eastwood helped to make happen through a personal appeal to leadership at Warner Brothers. Kapsis and Coblentz, *Clint Eastwood*, 137.

65. Kapsis and Coblentz, *Clint Eastwood*, 138–39; Richard Schickel, *Clint Eastwood: A Biography* (New York: Vintage, 1996), 424–25.

66. Kapsis and Coblentz, *Clint Eastwood*, 139–40; Wilson, *Eastwood on Eastwood*, 85.

67. Richard Schickel names these aspects of the film as its flaws, that is, the ways in which it defies a plausible narrative (*Clint Eastwood*, 364–65).

Chapter 6

"YOU CAN'T HUNT ALONE": *WHITE HUNTER BLACK HEART*

Richard Hutson

*W*hite Hunter Black Heart (1990) dramatizes a number of themes
that can be seen in Clint Eastwood's films from the past, before
1990, and which he would use again in the future. The repetition of
themes and events is the mark of an artist who knows what he is interested in and is truly in charge of what he wants to do. As in *White Hunter
Black Heart*, the theme of the older man (John Wilson) with a younger
man (Peter Verrill) appears in a number of Eastwood's films. Another
theme is the story of the trials and tribulations of the artist—actor, film
director, musician, showman, journalist, photographer—a theme that
suggests reflexivity in a number of Eastwood's films, possibly even self-
reflection for the protagonists. Often entailed in the depiction of an artist is the theme of the character whose mysterious doubleness divides
him or her in such a way as to risk self-destruction or at least some
form of destructiveness. Instead of carrying out the duties one is con-
ventionally expected to perform, a character becomes obsessed with
some other idea, seemingly unrelated to the job at hand. Such a character, Eastwood notes, "fascinated me, as obsessive behavior always
does" (Ciment 1999, 160). Each new version of these themes is unique,
as Eastwood claims that he always wanted to do something different
in choosing another film to direct (Ciment 1999, 166). But as William
Beard has astutely noted, "Eastwood's films . . . combine relentless
restaging and repetition of persona—characteristics, narrative forms,
and individual tropes with a constant juggling and reconfiguring
of these same elements to see them in a different light" (2000, 13).
Eastwood might have identified with all of his film artists, but in
White Hunter, he plays Wilson, a relatively famous writer-director
of Hollywood films, a partner in a film production company, and a
prominent man in "show business," who insists that he is an "artist"

and pays little attention to anything other than the art of the film. It is as if his nonconcern with being $300,000 in debt (in 1950) proves that he is a genuine artist, not a businessman.

In *White Hunter Black Heart*, Eastwood is John Wilson, who is about to begin filming a movie in Africa. He has insisted that a film whose setting is Africa must be filmed in Africa, but his motive for going to Africa is always divided. "We're going on a safari, kid," he says to the young screenwriter and novelist, Peter Verrill, who has joined him to work on a draft of a script. Before Wilson shoots the film, he insists that he has to shoot an elephant, a "big tusker." And so Eastwood gets to merge his past themes into a narrative that is at once mediated by the fact that Wilson, a thinly disguised John Huston, is different from Huston and from Eastwood and also a version of Eastwood himself. As he said in an interview, "Because the character is called John Wilson, there is a fictional side" (Ciment 1999, 162). But he admits also that what guided him was "what I've felt in my own professional life." Wilson the character, Eastwood claims, "is an amalgam of several people" (Ciment 1999, 161). And so Eastwood makes a film that is a meditation about his own work as a film director and actor. And as *The African Queen* was something of a breakthrough for Huston, *White Hunter Black Heart* undoubtedly helped Eastwood to think about himself as a filmmaker, a moment that precipitated him into a higher level of critical reception, at least in the United States. Two years later, he would make the Academy Award–winner *Unforgiven*, and the rest is movie-making history.

Just as John Huston tended to use novels as first-draft screenplays, Eastwood and Peter Viertel used Viertel's novel as a first draft of the screenplay. The filmed version of the screenplay is a condensation and revision of the original, but the dialogue for the film and most of the major scenes are taken directly from the novel.[1] There is one difference: the bulk of Viertel's novel narrates the hunting trips. There is great detail about practicing shooting, flying over Africa to find hunting grounds, lots of talk about hunting, attempts to shoot various animals, constant efforts to get a proper hunting guide, and struggles to arrange transportation for hunting in different areas of Africa. As Viertel makes clear in his novel, one does not embark on a safari to hunt big game without the support of numerous guides and helpers of various kinds. Big-game hunting is a collaborative sport. The emphasis in Eastwood's film, however, is about the business of the many administrative and production issues in the preproduction planning for getting filming under way. As a consequence, Eastwood's version of John Wilson is a more intense narrative of Wilson's contradictory impulses, divided as he is between his responsibilities as a film director and as a partner in a film production company and his unaccountable will to risk his life and other lives hunting a dangerous, wild animal while neglecting all of the people involved in making the film. In utter exasperation at a dinner party, his producer Paul Landers hollers at him before a table of film people, "For God's sake, abandon your role of the great white hunter and become a movie director again." Wilson's response is that hunting is a sacred matter that has nothing to do with the film company, even though he is holding up everyone from beginning work on the film.

Thus, Wilson generates great frustration among the film people, especially his producer, because of his insistence on hunting, but Eastwood tends to perform this character as performing the bad and uncooperative director, a Hollywood outsider. Landers refers to him as a "monster," and his male star refers to him as "the ogre." As a hunter, he rather self-consciously imitates Ernest Hemingway in Africa, a writer who wants to be a man of action, risking his life. Wilson always insists on his sovereignty, on getting his way, even on choosing the location for the upcoming film he is supposed to direct, *The African Trader*. But he seems to be self-consciously playing a character, the willful, egotistical artist, as if trying to escape the stereotype of the Hollywood director in the service of the money people and, at the same time, playing the stereotype of the man of imagination and creativity who feels that he has to thumb his nose at the money power and other versions of authority. When he interferes with the racist African hotel manager in a fistfight and takes a beating (again, imitating Hemingway or John Huston as boxers), he still does not get serious about his responsibility for spending large amounts of money moving a film crew to a Congo wilderness where filming will always be challenging and expensive. Wilson's decision to go to Africa is, from the beginning, an act of bad faith, a divided focus between filming on location and going on safari.

In the beginning, this doubleness does not necessarily look like a problem even though his producer claims that he has almost killed the film project many times. Wilson can take the young screenwriter, Peter Verrill, with him, and they can scout for film locations and get a little hunting done before the producer, actors, and filming crew arrive. For instance, an intermingling of the two purposes leads Wilson to choose Kivu's village as "more authentic" than the village that the film crew has constructed. Since Kivu is the chief of the village and the "chief hunter" guide for Wilson, Wilson's choice is ambiguous, although plausible for filming. But soon the division becomes an unbearable problem for everyone, possibly even for Wilson, who, in his mean-spirited self-indulgence, ignores or insults people around him as he insists on moving out into the wilderness instead of preparing to film. This willfulness develops and intensifies into the "fever," as Peter names a passion or an obsession, and "it's destructive."

In Viertel's novel, John Wilson and Peter Verrill have a serious discussion about the script of the film that John is about to direct, *The Trader*. Once they begin the discussion, Peter says that John's "manner changed abruptly. The tone of half-serious mockery left him at once. There were no artificial gestures, no faces to be made. The clownish side of his nature had gone out of the house" (Viertel 1953, 50). In Eastwood's film, John stops playacting at certain moments, stops performing someone who is impossible to deal with. As Eastwood projects his character, we cannot tell whether he is trying to act like John Huston or whether he is just performing for performance's sake. For the most part, he performs the character of a cantankerous artist who tends to insult any position that he confronts. We cannot discern just what his position is on any topic because he is performing at being the impossible bad boy against everyone. One of the subtleties of the character is that many lines he speaks to others are improvisatory, basically meaningless and empty thrusts. Such a line is Wilson's claim to Pete that killing an elephant is not a "crime," as Pete accuses, but a "sin," as he confesses that he does not understand what he has just said.

What we can surmise from the discussion about the screenplay in Viertel's novel is that Wilson wants to go to Africa and live a dangerous life because the two characters in the filmscript undertake a life-and-death journey on a river in the heart of Africa. "There's death a thousand times over down that river," Charlie Allnutt says to Rosie Sayer in *The African Queen*. Wilson seems to be trying to understand his characters in real life. With Pete, the argument between them is about the script's ending, which Wilson has given him to make improvements. Pete argues that the script should allow the characters to live at the end, whereas the original script calls for them to be blown up in the end. Wilson claims that in writing the script and getting it filmed,

> We're gods, see, lousy little gods who control the lives of the people we've created. . . . I know the trader and I know the woman. . . . I've been off

in the jungle with the guy. I've slept with the dame over a dozen times.
I know they're both predestined to come to a bad end. I know *they* know it.
(Viertel 1953, 53)

The desire to kill an elephant develops into what Peter calls a "fever,"
and Wilson holds up the whole crew of movie people for days as he goes
into the wild with his native guide. His focus on what he is doing or supposed to be doing gets divided and distorted, while the whole company
lives in the anxiety that Wilson is going to ruin, if not destroy, the film
project.

I believe that this script was tempting to Eastwood because the sense
of contradiction in being a filmmaker and the roles that Eastwood special-
ized in up to this point all add up to this thorny character of John Wilson,
always thumbing his nose at the conventions and powers that be while also
defending those powers of compromise with artistic integrity. Eastwood
as Dirty Harry Callahan perpetually engaged in guerilla warfare against
his superiors in the police department is another version of this character.
With the character of Wilson, there is a sense that he has to engage in a
constant battle against the money powers, his superiors, in order to bring
about a work of art in which he can feel some pride. He wants to feel that
the story and its characters have been generated in an authentic, uncom-
promised commitment to the issues of human life and death. In Viertel's
novel, Wilson claims to be in Africa for artistic authenticity. In the screenplay, Wilson appears to be more deeply divided between his desire to make
an honest film and the sense that he wants to imitate Hemingway's heroes,
who face death in the bullring or in their big-game hunting excursions.
In shooting a film, he risks his moral integrity and artistic reputation; in
shooting an elephant, he risks his life, so to speak, but he needs this sup-
plemental risk to justify all of the compromises necessary to bring a film
into being.

People engaged in making films have to confront the need for compromise between money and art, "money or art" (Viertel 1953, 56). And
as Peter reflects about Wilson in the novel, "I felt that he was ashamed of
what he was, ashamed of his trade. Although no one in Hollywood had
done more to have movies taken seriously as an art form, no one in Hollywood really doubted them more than Wilson did" (Viertel 1953, 51). There
is an even more thorny issue for Wilson than a conflict between money
and art. It is that a film director can never be an artist as a pure, lonely,

creative individual, since filmmaking is so utterly collaborative. Laurence Knapp refers to Wilson's "pachydermatous ego and how it tramples everyone and everything in its path" (1996, 147). In the film, when Wilson confesses to Ralph Lockhart that he knows about Hollywood whoredom, since "I've done a little hustling in my time, more than I care to remember," he indicates that there is an anguish in wanting and needing something from somebody in the business, as we have already seen with Irene pitching her screenplay about a dog to Wilson. Irene offers sex to whoever shows an interest in her impossibly silly ideas for a screenplay.

There is a script of the film available somewhere when Pete Verrill arrives on the scene in London. It is possible that Wilson wrote the original draft, or maybe he has only dabbled with a draft, and Peter has been hired by the producer, Paul Landers, to improve upon the script, since no one likes the depressing ending in which the two leading characters die. Viertel's novel as well as Eastwood's film bring together a considerable number of people who are involved with the making of the film. The producer, British financial backers, director, writer, art designer, unit manager, cameraman, actor and actress, and other operatives are all important, necessary. When we watch a film, of course we never see all of these people, all of whom have a stake in the final product. Everybody and everything have to work in order for the whole to work. For Eastwood, the attraction of the novel is that it brings into the open many of the factors that create a successful film. The director, the "little god," may make the opening, ongoing, and final decisions, but such a work of art and entertainment depends upon all of the factors working together. Eastwood, as the producer, director, and actor (possibly torn between his complicated roles), could have enjoyed the opportunity to display the drama of multiple factors in which the producer is, in effect, tortured by the self-indulgent director who seems uninterested in the film. The opposition between the "desperate" producer and the irresponsible and carousing director makes for an intense, sometimes humorous, drama. Such a drama exposes the complexities and cross-purposes inevitable in filmmaking.

Eastwood might well have identified with John Huston as Huston was about to embark on filming *The African Queen* in 1951. Huston had gained fame as an uncompromising director whose early films had not been great financial successes, even as sophisticated film critics praised him. He had won an Academy Award for directing *The Treasure of the Sierra Madre* (1948), but his studio, Warner Brothers, wanted him to work on films that would make money: "At the end of 1951, John Huston was the darling of those in the intellectual world who detested Hollywood. His credentials were impeccable." Almost every one of his films "had avoided a happy ending, been spurned by the public, and thereby lost money at the box office. His work had proved by his unpopularity that he was no lowly hack pandering to popular tastes, but was indeed a 'serious artist'" (Hammen 1985, 61). John Wilson's diatribe to Peter about the "eight million popcorn eaters" might have come out of John Huston's mouth; Huston was considered to be a director of great artistic integrity, anti-Hollywood, antistudio, even as he worked within the studio system.

We can understand that Wilson's quest for a "big tusker" indicates his insecurity about being a Hollywood director. If he can risk his life hunting a dangerous animal, thereby gaining a mantle of authenticity, then he feels that he can also be a film director associated with what he calls the "product" of Hollywood rather than with the falsehood or whoredom of Hollywood. Risking one's life and risking one's artistic ability are both necessary and complement each other, in Wilson's mind.

In the end, this doubleness of Wilson's quest to kill an elephant and to make a film with the aura of authentic realism works together. The fact that a tribal chief sacrifices himself for the American Hollywood project is stunningly unexpected, collateral damage. Kivu's death on the tusks of an elephant is a trauma that generates a great film, that allows Wilson to understand that he is responsible for many people, even a movie audience, not just himself in his inauthentic individualism. In this film, the doubleness works out to be a kind of single-mindedness, allowing Wilson (Huston) to continue making the Hollywood product. Instead of achieving authenticity as the great white hunter, or as Lockwood refers to it, as a "Hollywood safari," Wilson's stereotyped, Hemingwayish quest for authentic masculinity ends in the tragic understanding that he is, after all, a director of films, the boss who generates and controls the action of multiple performances.

Beginning with *Bird* in 1988 and continuing for a little over a decade, until *True Crime* (1999), Eastwood seems to have been obsessed with characters deeply divided between wanting to do the right or proper thing and impulses that thwart this intention or purpose. *Bird* provides a powerful example of the brilliant saxophonist Charlie Parker, whose musical genius is always jeopardized by his drug addiction. *Unforgiven* (1992) presents a character loyal to his dead wife, on the one hand, but who reverts to a former, unreformed self, a drunk and brutal killer, as he oversees the killing for hire of a couple of cowboys who had cut up a prostitute's face. In *The Bridges of Madison County* (1995), we hear Francesca's voice-over reading from her diary, "I was acting like another woman. Yet I was more myself than ever before," as she has become passionately obsessed and potentially self-destructively involved with Robert Kincaid. What is an Italian immigrant woman who has been married to an Iowa farmer for twenty years doing, having a passionate four-day affair with a stranger? *White Hunter Black Heart* depicts a John Wilson who is about to begin making a film in Africa but is obsessed with big-game hunting to the point of having a self-destructive "fever."

We might ask, in retrospect, how such a figure as Wilson/Huston could have been tolerated in 1950, still a period in which studio executives and bankers controlled filmmaking. Huston had given the Warner Brothers studio a certain prestige with Academy Awards and nominations for earlier pictures. But the major studios were in irrecoverable trouble in 1950 as, for a number of reasons, they were breaking up (Schatz 1988, chap. 21). As a result, a figure like Huston was living on the cusp of a major transformation in the industry. Huston and other directors were no longer auteurs but could be considered "authors," gaining a certain prestige, authority, and independence now that they were out from under the strict and imposing thumb of studio bureaucracy. No matter, filmmaking is still an industry dependent upon a large community of people with various skills, including the ability to get financing.

Many reviewers wrote favorable reviews of *White Hunter Black Heart*, even though some had reservations about the way Eastwood invoked or played John Huston. Besides, the film was too downbeat for Eastwood audiences to accept and was not a moneymaker. "This was not the Clint his public loved," even as the film "forcefully foreshadowed the expansion of ambition" for Eastwood and the increasing respect he would gain in the United States (Schickel 1996, 450). Perhaps the intertextuality of the film did not allow viewers to feel that this was a human story as much as a Hollywood story. Filmic intertextuality had become important in film by 1990, and Eastwood had already exploited its rich possibilities in *Pale Rider* and *High Plains Drifter*. According to Robert Ray (1985, 263), from the 1960s to the 1980s, Hollywood's conservative commitment to sequels and parodies fostered the audience's ironic self-consciousness about the fictionality and intertextuality of film. The problem with Eastwood's deeply intertextual film is that no viewer today has to read it as intertextual. How many viewers in 1990 knew that Wilson is a version of John Huston or that the filmscript he is about to film is *The African Queen*? Even though Peter Viertel's novel was a *New York Times* best seller, that was in 1953, now long forgotten. Eastwood's film blends Viertel's novel, John Huston's film career, and Eastwood's own film career, not to mention references to Hemingway's hunting stories and Melville's novel about an obsessive hunter, *Moby-Dick*.

For Eastwood, a film like *White Hunter Black Heart*, which did not make money, was an important creative experiment, one that allowed him to think seriously about the issues of being an artist who produced, directed, and starred in films. Playing the character Wilson gave him maximum distance and proximity to his own creative enterprise. Such a laboratory of filmmaking in producing a downbeat and self-investigating film was a promise to all of us viewers of the great films to come.

■ Note

1. Ralph Lockhart (Alun Armstrong) and Hodkins (Timothy Spall) are given larger roles in the film than in the novel. Lockhart especially combines a number of characters from the novel, and we see him sink, under the ridicule and indifference of Wilson, into cynicism and drunkenness. Both the characters of Lockhart and Hodkins in the film are brilliant, as Eastwood shows his directorial power in presenting minor characters who steal some scenes.

■ Bibliography

Beard, William. 2000. *Persistence of Double Vision. Essays on Clint Eastwood*. Edmonton: University of Alberta Press.

Ciment, Michel. 1999. "Interview with Clint Eastwood/1990." In *Clint Eastwood, Interviews*, ed. Robert E. Kapsis and Kathie Coblentz, 160–71. Jackson: University Press of Mississippi.

Hammen, Scott. 1985. *John Huston*. Boston: Twayne Pub.

Knapp, Laurence F. 1996. *Directed by Clint Eastwood: Eighteen Films Analyzed*. Jefferson, N.C.: McFarland.

Ray, Robert B. 1985. *A Certain Tendency of the Hollywood Cinema, 1930–1980*. Princeton: Princeton University Press.

Schatz, Thomas. 1988. *The Genius of the System*. New York: Pantheon Books.

Schickel, Richard. 1996. *Clint Eastwood, a Biography*. New York: Vintage.

Viertel, Peter. 1953. *White Hunter, Black Heart*. Garden City, N.Y.: Doubleday and Co.

———. 1992. *Dangerous Friends: Hemingway, Huston and Others*. London: Viking.

CHAPTER 7

THE END OF HISTORY AND AMERICA FIRST:
HOW THE 1990S REVITALIZED CLINT EASTWOOD

Craig Rinne

Most Clint Eastwood fans are familiar with this narrative related to *Unforgiven* (1992): as the 1990s began, despite a measure of critical acclaim for directing *Bird* (1988) and *White Hunter Black Heart* (1990), Eastwood had not had a significant film, in terms of either box-office receipts or cultural influence, since his turn at directing himself as Dirty Harry in *Sudden Impact* (1983; most famous, perhaps, for President Reagan's appropriation of Harry's "Go ahead, make my day" line). *Pale Rider* (1985) was supposed to revitalize the Western, but, though it was moderately successful financially, it received mixed reviews and failed to strike the popular chord that may have reinvigorated the Western. However, once *Dances with Wolves* (1990) kicked off the Western mini-boom of the early 1990s, Eastwood soon followed with *Unforgiven*, his masterpiece, which established him as the most significant Western filmmaker and one of the most respected American directors.

There is nothing wrong with this narrative, but I would like to suggest a slightly different one: that the sociopolitical climate of the early 1990s is what made Eastwood, his changed star persona, and his films once again relevant. Paul Smith has suggested this direction with *Clint Eastwood: A Cultural Production* (1993), wherein he attempts to read Eastwood and his films as more than functions of a charismatic star and accomplished director. Focusing on the "tributary media" (interviews, news articles, etc.) as much as the films, Smith argues that both Eastwood's films and the mass media discourse that envelops, and often promotes, Eastwood's career inexorably moved him toward a role of "auteur-father," a parental director with his own small, homesteader-like production company, Malpaso, and a carefully protected family-man image. Eventually, Eastwood became a "guardian craftsman" of American popular genre cinema, culminating in *Unforgiven*'s genre-as-art status. This development is partially based on Eastwood's aging appearance on-screen (he was born in 1930), necessitating characters that differ from his youthful Man with No Name and Dirty Harry roles and leading to a reworked persona associated with redemption; as Walter Metz notes in his discussion of Eastwood's aging characters, his 1990s and later films "have invented a profound language of redemption surrounding questions of aging" (2007, 214).

Following Metz's insight and Smith's assertion that Eastwood can be considered a product of both his films and the discourses surrounding them, I argue that political and social developments in America during the 1990s meshed with the gradual reforming of Eastwood's persona, beginning in the 1980s, from loner action hero to fatherly figure atoning for his sins. This new persona needed the post–Cold War zeitgeist of the 1990s to truly resonate with American film audiences, and I will trace the development of Eastwood from Smith's "auteur-father" and "guardian craftsman," where he is defined primarily as a director and producer, to a popular star persona that incorporates his "auteur-father" status into his filmic characters. This new persona, which I will term his *senior persona*, consists of an aging, single, flawed, heroic character grappling with the sins of his youth and hoping to redeem them through a second opportunity, the winning of a violent, cathartic encounter. Additionally, the personal history of this character is explicitly tied to historical American events or period settings, suggesting that the film narratives with these characters serve as allegories for 1990s America.

To support the argument that Eastwood's senior persona resonated with 1990s audiences, I will examine five of his mainstream, commercial films, plus the Western genre in 1990s America—six long-range "bullet points," if you will, in reference to Eastwood's famous six-shooters, whether Colt or Smith & Wesson. I will begin each of these six sections with a key image that serves as an entry point into each film (or period) and then focus on the relation of Eastwood's senior persona to the visions of America the film represents. From the formation of his senior persona in the Cold War–influenced *Heartbreak Ridge* and the revealing misfire *The Rookie* to the changes in America that led to the 1990s Western boom and *Unforgiven*, *In the Line of Fire*, and *A Perfect World*, I intend to display that Clint Eastwood is, indeed, a sociopolitical production.

■ 1. *Heartbreak Ridge* (1986)

> KEY IMAGE: Gunnery Sergeant Tom Highway (Eastwood) has his
> Marine recruits of "Recon Platoon" out early, about to begin their first
> day of training under him. One of them puts on a pair of designer
> sunglasses and yawns. Highway asks his name, removes the sunglasses,
> and then . . .
>
> CLOSE-UP: Highway's traditional black leather boot crushes the glasses
> at the recruit's Nike-clad feet.

By 1986, Nike was already a billion-dollar corporation and had Michael
Jordan under contract—well on its way to becoming one of the most recognizable brands in the world. Eastwood, of course, can be considered a
brand in his own right, and many have noted that his production company,
Malpaso, means "bad step" and that Eastwood enjoyed the irony when
choosing the name for a company that would eventually become renowned
for its small, efficient, underbudget ethos. Considering Malpaso and
Eastwood's success, Highway's stepping on the sunglasses is yet another
symbolic "good step," wherein the traditional American work ethic and
frugality Malpaso represents stands before the excessive advertising of
consumer products, the Nikes or Ray-Bans of modern corporate America.
The stepping on the sunglasses is also a "good step" in that it exemplifies
the senior persona and Eastwood's move to it; he displays the discipline of
the father figure to the recruits, informing them that his traditional Marine
Corps values still trump those of modern America. For Highway, those
values grew out of a lifetime of service, beginning in the Korean War, and a
title sequence, consisting of Korean War documentary footage, introduces
Heartbreak Ridge.

The sequence begins with a military drum score and shows intensive,
mechanized warfare—large cannons firing, machine guns, and so on. Eventually, however, the music changes to Don Gibson singing "Sea of Heartbreak," and the images become more personalized, including wounded
soldiers and war orphans. This contrast neatly encapsulates the film, as
its plot of Korean/Vietnam War veteran Highway finding redemption in
Grenada is balanced by his attempts to reunite with his estranged ex-wife,
Aggie (a name similar to that of Eastwood's first wife, Maggie Johnson,
divorced in 1978). In both his husbandly and military roles, Gunny Highway is old-fashioned. He is nearing mandatory retirement from the Marine

Corps, and his traditional, gung ho style does not fit with the other two
options the film presents: the lax, self-absorbed soldier using the corps as
a job, symbolized by a supply sergeant offering bribes of Cuban cigars and
other benefits that Highway flatly refuses, or the modern rule of the corporate structure, epitomized by Highway's nemesis and commanding officer,
Major Powers, a straitlaced Annapolis graduate who began his service in
supply and logistics. But Highway's only home is the Marines; the narrative
opens with him in jail after a drunken fight, and he clearly has no place in
mainstream society.

Highway calls in a favor and is assigned to Powers's division to train
Recon Platoon. Powers instantly despises Highway, considering him a
"dinosaur" who is fit only for war—and whose career has been marked
by failures in Korea and Vietnam. The raw recruits of Recon seem uninterested in the Marines, epitomized by their leader, Stitch Jones (played
by Mario Van Peebles), and his obsession with a music career as the self-
described "Ayatollah of Rock-n-rolla." As Highway trains them and eventually gains their respect and admiration, he also attempts to win back
his ex-wife, Aggie, through his humorously portrayed study of women's
magazines.

As the renewed relationship with Aggie reaches a crucial point, Highway and the rest of the division are called away, to the invasion of Grenada.
With the help of the platoon he inspired, most notably Jones's ability to
repair a phone line and connect it using his credit cards so that a "cavalry to the rescue" air strike can be called in, Highway successfully guides
his platoon through several engagements as the U.S. forces take the island
(emphasizing the relevance of Highway's traditional character, the climactic battles occur in an ancient fort complete with relic cannons). Highway
returns to his role as warrior and achieves a measure of redemption for
past failures in Korea and Vietnam. Though somewhat ambiguously, the
film's ending suggests that after his success in Grenada, Highway can now
retire from the corps and devote his life to Aggie, who is waiting for him
upon his return, along with a celebratory band ("for the first time," Highway remarks to Jones, who is enjoying the celebration of his ascension to
true Marine status).

Though a modest box-office success, *Heartbreak Ridge* seemed out of
place during the muscular 1980s, ruled at the box office by Schwarzenegger
and Stallone. Perhaps tired of the interminable Cold War, the public's imagination was not captured by a film narrative dependent on a minor "police

action" like Grenada (unlike, for example, the fantasy of rewinning the Vietnam War in Stallone's *Rambo: First Blood Part II* [1985]; even the title is more exciting—and overblown). With Eastwood in his fifties, however, the film did prefigure the redemptive senior persona that perfectly meshed with his sixties and the 1990s: Highway is older, about to retire, estranged from his wife, and prone to drunkenness, a military hero who is haunted by overall failures in Korea and Vietnam; but ultimately he is able to justify and redeem his past via training and leading a new generation of Marine heroes to violent victory in Grenada. Certainly, the redemptive narrative is nothing new to Eastwood's characters (think of *The Outlaw Josey Wales*, 1976) or the Westerner in general, reflecting what Richard Slotkin (1992) calls "regeneration through violence," but the aged character played by Eastwood literally adds a new wrinkle to the story. And the incorporation of the Grenada invasion adds an allegorical layer; as Paul Smith (1993, 200) notes, the film suggests that the United States has, at least on a superficial level, regained a measure of post-Vietnam military might through Grenada and other 1980s military actions, such as Libya and Panama. Thus, as Eastwood's character is renewed by returning to military conflict, so is America regaining its public self-image as a military power, albeit with tentative steps against much smaller nations. While that militaristic message works for Tom Cruise in *Top Gun* (also 1986) and the aforementioned *Rambo: First Blood Part II*, Eastwood's character remains outdated; America was still locked in the lingering Cold War, and the sociopolitical climate had to change before Eastwood's senior persona could resonate.

- ### 2. Misfire: *The Rookie* (1990)

    KEY IMAGE: Long shot: At the end of the film, Nick Pulovski (Eastwood) sits behind the desk in his own office, now a lieutenant, assigning a new partner to his former partner, David Ackerman (Charlie Sheen), the former rookie. Dirty Harry has become the authority figure.

The Rookie tries to be a bit of Dirty Harry, a bit of *Lethal Weapon* (1987), and a bit of a 1980s action blockbuster. It never coheres, though, and Eastwood's first mainstream film of the new decade fizzles, despite many loud action scenes. Aspects of the Eastwood senior persona are present: Pulovski is not an invincible Dirty Harry, as he continually needs his partner to save him, and his motivation stems from his regret at always finishing second in his career, whether as an automobile racer or a cop. The exposition of

Pulovski's motive only lasts a few minutes on-screen, though, and is not developed further or strongly tied to the narrative, as the film focuses more on the Sheen character, Ackerman, and his back story (his brother died in a youthful accident, he became estranged from his wealthy parents, and he finally becomes his own man as a cop). And closing the film with Eastwood behind the desk as a mentor seems forced and out of character. Thus, without a strongly developed Eastwood redemptive character or any ties to American history, the film misfires as an attempt to cash in on the 1980s action cycle without tapping into the Eastwood senior persona, in contrast to the upcoming Eastwood successes. Tellingly, the climax of the film works a misfire into the plot, as Pulovski's second gun, taken from a security guard, only has five bullets in it instead of the expected six, causing him to be shot by the villain. *Unforgiven*, of course, also works a misfire into the climactic shoot-out, but before examining *Unforgiven*, a brief overview of the 1990s and the accompanying cycle of Westerns is needed, beginning with a historical climax, the fall of the Berlin Wall.

■ 3. The 1990s and the Western

   KEY IMAGE: The Berlin Wall falls.

Eastwood's senior persona needed the events of the 1990s to truly resonate. In *America between the Wars: From 11/9 to 9/11: The Misunderstood Years between the Fall of the Berlin Wall and the Start of the War on Terror*, Derek Chollet and James Goldgeier detail the political climate of the United States after the 1989 fall of the Berlin Wall and the end of the Cold War. They argue that while America had a sense of relief and cautious optimism after the Cold War, there was also anxiety concerning what the nation's path and purpose should be without the defining opposition of the communist Soviet bloc. In this context, Chollet and Goldgeier examine two influential thinkers of the moment, Francis Fukuyama and Patrick Buchanan, whose ideas suggested to many the possibility that America could retire, to a degree, from the international scene and turn more toward a self-examination of domestic issues. In 1989, Fukuyama proposed that the end of history, in terms of the now-inevitable ideological triumph of liberal democracy and equality over forms of totalitarianism and communism, had arrived; Chollet and Goldgeier explain that to many, Fukuyama seemed to say that "the big challenges were over and that the United States could move on to other things, especially at home" (2008, 23).

Similarly, although from a much more conservative viewpoint, Buchanan argued for "a new nationalism, a new patriotism, a new foreign policy that puts America first and, not only first, but second and third as well" (Chollet and Goldgeier 2008, 23). While the influence of Buchanan's political discourse was relatively brief compared with that of Fukuyama's better-developed and enduringly provocative arguments, Buchanan's flash of popularity (he won over 20 percent of the vote in the 1992 Republican primaries against the incumbent President Bush) exemplified a persistent American conservatism and nationalism that reacted to impending globalization. And although it would be a gross oversimplification to claim that America had become isolationist—for example, the most important "Clint" of the 1990s, President Clinton, certainly focused on domestic issues in his 1992 campaign, but he also argued that foreign and domestic policies were intimately tied—there was a certain sense in the public sphere that given the end of the Cold War, America's international interventions were no longer of utmost importance and internal issues were now more of a priority.

Oddly enough, the events surrounding the invasion of Kuwait and the first Gulf War seemed to confirm this, as President Bush saw America as part of an international coalition, not the heavyweight leader in the fight against communism:

> "No longer can a dictator count on East–West confrontation to stymie concerted United Nations action against aggression," Bush told a joint session of Congress in September 1990, just a month after Saddam invaded Kuwait. "A new partnership of nations has begun." He added, "We're now in sight of a United Nations that performs as envisioned by its founders." (Chollet and Goldgeier 2008, 7)

With most of the leading nations in seeming agreement, the United States would partner with many nations, as equals, in addressing foreign affairs, enabling America to focus on domestic issues. This turn inward assisted Bill Clinton's 1992 bid for the presidency; as noted, Clinton addressed foreign affairs, but he also realized that he could not match Bush's experience in the international and military arenas. Thus, Clinton stressed that the conflicts of the Cold War were over and instead looked forward to resolving domestic issues; as he said in a 1991 speech: "Having won the Cold War, we must not now lose the peace. . . . [W]hat we need to elect in 1992 is not the last president of the twentieth century, but the first president of the twenty-first century" (quoted in Chollet and Goldgeier 2008, 38). Clinton's subsequent victory indicated that American voters, for the moment, agreed.

Similarly examining the 1990s, but from a cultural studies and theoretical perspective, Phillip Wegner views the era as haunted by its Cold War past but also as a space "of openness and instability, of experimentation and opportunity, of conflict and insecurity—a place, in other words, wherein history might move in a number of very different directions" (2009, 9). Wegner could very well be describing the American frontier myth, the traditional history-centered vehicle of America's belief in the limitless possibilities of the future. Almost simultaneously with the beginning of what Wegner calls the "long nineties," the space where "history might move in a number of very different directions," representations of the historical frontier in film Westerns returned in force to Hollywood. In 1989, *Lonesome Dove*, about two aging Texas Rangers on one last adventure, became a television miniseries sensation; then, in 1990, *Dances with Wolves*, about a Civil War veteran heading to the closing frontier and interacting with the Lakota Sioux, was released and became an award-winning box-office success, and the film Western enjoyed a boom not seen since the 1970s. The return to the Western, ostensibly the most American of film genres, and its popular, mythic examination of ideological conflicts from both American history and contemporary culture and politics reflect Buchanan's call to consider "America first" and his emphasis on renewing nationalism and patriotism. Concurrently, the revisionist aspects of these new Westerns, which included relatively more complex representations of groups previously marginalized in Westerns, best exemplified by the more "politically correct" and improved portrayals of American Indians, coincided with Fukuyama's "end of history," the triumph of democracy and liberal equality. America needed a revised, inclusive history and relatively liberal ideology of equality to replace the paranoid and polarizing tendencies of the Cold War. Together, these approaches to the Western suggest some of the ideological hopes and the self-image of the post–Cold War United States through the Clinton era; the nation had survived decades of strife and war and now seemed ready to move on to new frontiers and away from the memories of a troubled past. The reopening of the frontier in the Western literalizes Wegner's point about the 1990s as an open, experimental space where "history might move in a number of very different directions"; the Western, a representation of history via the frontier myth, fills part of that open space and suggests revisions of American history by rewriting the Western, and thus American history, with frontier narratives that emphasize American Indians, women, African Americans, and other underrepresented groups and their stories. The history of the frontier is revised, not forgotten, and into this newly imagined frontier rides Eastwood with *Unforgiven*.

■ 4. *Unforgiven* (1992)

KEY IMAGE: Will Munny (Eastwood) has avenged Ned Logan (Freeman) by killing Little Bill Daggett (Hackman), his deputies, and Skinny Dubois, the owner of the bar and bordello where the narrative of the cut-up prostitute began. About to ride away into the pouring rain and the night, he stops in front of Ned's propped-up body and admonishes the townspeople of Big Whiskey, Wyoming, saying, "You better bury Ned right. You better not cut up nor otherwise harm no whores."

MEDIUM CLOSE-UP: "Or I'll come back and kill every one of you sons of bitches." Munny on horseback is on the left half of the screen, shot from a slight low angle; an American flag in the background is clearly visible on the right half of the screen.

Munny might come back, but Eastwood definitely had returned. All three previous historical Westerns (set in the late 1800s) directed by Eastwood employ the Westerner-as-avenger: In both *High Plains Drifter* (1973) and *Pale Rider*, Eastwood's character is a ghostlike figure who returns, in part, to avenge attempts at murdering him (or perhaps actual murder, depending on how one interprets the films), and in *The Outlaw Josey Wales* (1976), Eastwood/Wales first joins a band of post–Civil War raiders to avenge the murders of his wife and son and then continues to seek vengeance for a murderous betrayal of him and his fallen comrades.

Unforgiven, however, presents a slightly different scenario: A prostitute, Delilah, is cut up and scarred by two cowboys, the other prostitutes post a thousand-dollar bounty on the cowboys, and Munny (with Ned Logan and the Schofield Kid) set out to collect the bounty. In other words, they are motivated less by revenge than by profit. True, a certain avenging motive, to avenge the woman, does exist, and by the end of the film Munny is avenging both the murder of Logan and his own savage beating from Little Bill, but the initial motivation differs from that in his other self-directed Westerns. In fact, the "money"-driven "Munny" more resembles Eastwood's bounty-hunting "Man with No Name" from the Eastwood and

Sergio Leone collaborations—except that unlike the ahistorical and individual Man with No Name, Munny has a well-developed past, including being a widower with two children who gave up drinking, gunfighting, and other vices through the influence of his late wife, Claudia.

I emphasize this seemingly minor difference because it distinguishes the Eastwood senior persona characters from previous roles. Most well-written film narratives will have well-developed characters with back stories important to the narrative; even in *High Plains Drifter* and *Pale Rider*, where Eastwood's ghostlike characters initially seem to have no past, the films eventually reveal that the Eastwood characters have returned for personal revenge. In general, back-story motivation is usually tied directly into the action and conflicts within the main plotlines of the film (revenge, in the Eastwood-directed Westerns).

Unforgiven, however, by shifting the initial motivation from personal revenge to an impersonal bounty hunt, allows a more inner-directed, psychological motivation and back story to dominate the narrative; Munny grapples with his past as a mean, drunken killer, constantly repeating variations on "I ain't like that no more." The bounty on the cowboys serves as a plot device to release Munny's internal conflict; he has repressed his violent past, his personal history, but now he attempts to access it while controlling it, to use his capacity for violence for supposedly moral reasons (providing for his children and imposing justified punishment on the criminals, the cowboys who cut Delilah). Inexorably the release of his violence yields more violence and death. This obsession with the character's development away from a previous psychological state, as opposed to simply reacting to a past event, typifies Eastwood's senior persona. No longer an invincible killer or flawed-yet-dominant hero, he now becomes a vulnerable, near-elderly man wrestling with his past sins and denying the motivations behind them while seeking an opportunity to redeem them, to return to defining experiences and either reaffirm or overturn them.

In *Unforgiven*, despite his protests and all appearances to the contrary, Munny reaffirms that he still can be a cold-blooded killer. Eastwood even looks and sounds younger in the climactic scenes when he returns as an avenging killer; despite its deconstruction of gunfighting myths and critique of violence, the film ultimately reaffirms, and even glorifies, the climactic, heroic shoot-'em-up integral to the Western, wherein violent killing is legitimized. Granted, Munny was a murderer of women and children, but this time his violence is used justifiably.

This returns us to the key image and its overdetermined signifier of the American flag next to Munny/Eastwood's "or I'll come back . . ." warning. The allegory with America in *Unforgiven* is slightly more complicated, as Munny was not involved in an actual historical event, like Highway in Vietnam, that needs correcting. However, the flags are raised in Big Whiskey because the Fourth of July was only a few days earlier—the day when Little Bill savagely beat English Bob, who entered town discussing the July 2, 1881, shooting of President Garfield by Charles J. Guiteau. Furthermore, the film contains references to violent historical figures and settings glamorized in Westerns, such as William "Billy the Kid" Bonney and Dodge City. Thus, while the film is not about a specific event in America's past, it does address the American preoccupation with individual violence that persists throughout our nation's history, politics, and representations of history in frontier narratives.

Particularly in the wake of the stunningly efficient American-led military victory in Iraq (at least in the short term) with Desert Storm in 1991, Munny/Eastwood's struggle with returning to his violent ways throughout the film and his final pronouncement form a warning to the rest of the world: The Cold War is over; America wants to put behind its violent, military past; but if we have to, we can return to violence by sending our armies around the globe (note that Munny and Logan travel far, for the 1880s, from their Kansas home to Wyoming for the bounty). And considering how Munny's murders of Skinny, Little Bill, and the rest eliminate the immoral leaders of Big Whiskey while mirroring the assassination of Garfield, Munny's pronouncement also functions as a call to Americans to turn their individual abilities inward, to "clean up this town" and solve America's problems at any cost. Recalling the misfire in *The Rookie*, Munny's shotgun misfires during his showdown with Little Bill, but, unlike Pulovski, Munny easily overcomes that setback without aid and emerges victorious. Not only is the ultimately invincible Eastwood back (variations on "Eastwood is back in the saddle" permeated the media coverage of the film), but the Western and the frontier myth have also returned to help guide America and reestablish historical myths through a period of post–Cold War uncertainty and self-examination.

Unforgiven is arguably the most complex and most analyzed of Eastwood's films. David Webb Peoples's screenplay, one of the finest of all Western scripts, emphasizes reflexivity, irony, and genre deconstruction while sustaining contradictory ideological impulses, thus encouraging

multiple interpretations and rich analysis. No single reading can definitively encapsulate a film that spends nearly two hours critiquing violence
and demythologizing the Westerner hero—only to then present a climax
that stunningly reconfirms the hero's justified use of violence. My reading attempts to explain the popularity of the film at its initial release as
exemplifying the political moment of the early nineties; the critique of violence, the deconstruction of Western myths, and Munny's psychological
self-examination mirrored America reexamining its Cold War legacy and
searching for a new national identity, while Munny's triumphant gunfight
reaffirmed that America's legacy of violence has been justified (America
won the Cold War) and is still accessible in times of crisis (to maintain the
global peace), when self-examination can be conveniently set aside. With
its community of organized, angry prostitutes and the casual inclusion of
an African American cowboy as a primary character (who has an American Indian wife in a nonspeaking part), the film accepts the revisionist
view of the frontier as a potential site of limited liberal equality (following Fukuyama) while stressing that the hero who ensures that equality is
a conservative patriot, a white male capitalist espousing traditional family
values and notions of justice supported by violence (following Buchanan).
Unforgiven cloaks its climax in rain and darkness, much as the narrative
is permeated by ambiguity and deconstruction, but after Munny rides out
of Big Whiskey, the film visually ends with a sunset scene of Munny at
Claudia's grave; the hero has ridden gloriously into the sunset of innumer-
able other Western finales, triumphant in his use of violence and protection of democratic values.

■ 5. *In the Line of Fire* (1993)

> KEY IMAGE: Secret Service Agent Frank Horrigan (Eastwood) speaks
> on the phone with Mitch Leary (Malkovich), the would-be presidential
> assassin. Leary says to Horrigan, "I'm watching your movie"—a docu-
> mentary of the events in Dallas in November 1963. As Leary questions
> Horrigan about his role as an agent protecting President Kennedy on
> the day of his assassination, taunting him with statements like "JFK and
> Jackie and you, you looked so young and able, what did happen to you
> that day, Frank?"

> CLOSE-UP: Horrigan's face, looking pained as he remembers the tragedy,
> is superimposed over a montage of footage of the Kennedy assassination

(some of which has been altered to include images of a young Horrigan/
Eastwood). The camera slowly tracks in to an extreme close-up of
Horrigan's eyes, superimposed over the infamous Kennedy head shot.
The Horrigan close-up is a long take, over a minute, only interrupted by
an extreme close-up of Leary's eye for several seconds.

Although Eastwood did not direct or produce *In the Line of Fire* (Wolfgang
Petersen directed, Jeff Apple and Bob Rosenthal produced), the script
(by Jeff Maguire) seems tailor-made for Eastwood, and his performance
dominates the film, though balanced with a superb villainous turn by John
Malkovich. As the key image suggests, Horrigan was Kennedy's favorite
secret service agent, but he failed to react at his assassination, a failure he
has been haunted by for thirty years. Leary, an ex-CIA assassin who wants
to kill the current president as revenge against the government that he
believes betrayed him, provides Horrigan with a chance at atonement—
if he can prevent Leary from killing the president.

Eastwood's senior persona perfectly fits this plot. Horrigan's past failure permeates his life; after the assassination, he became an alcoholic, and
his wife and daughter left him, and now he lives alone and is considered a
borderline burnout at the service. While Eastwood cannot be an avenger
here—he cannot strike back at Kennedy's assassin—he can at least partially
redeem his failure by preventing Leary's assassination attempt (although,
by formula, some personal revenge motivation does enter the narrative, as
Leary kills Horrigan's partner). And despite the efforts of hundreds of Secret
Service agents, only the iconic, experienced Eastwood is a great enough
figure to prevent another tragedy. The film establishes that Eastwood is an
American monument; the president is only a peripheral character, often
in the far background while Eastwood/Horrigan looms in the foreground,
and at one point Horrigan explains that he does not like to get too close to
the First Family because "you might decide they're not worth taking a bullet for." The Washington, D.C., setting of much of the film allows Eastwood
to be framed with various monuments, most notably at the Lincoln Memorial when he turns to talk to Lincoln's statue, Eastwood's iconic face in
close-up, equaling the statue in the background, saying, "Damn . . . wish
I could have been there for you, pal."

Eastwood/Horrigan's monumental status inevitably leads to an allegorical reading. When fellow agent, and love interest, Lilly Raines argues that

Horrigan cared more about Kennedy's dignity than the current president's, they have the following exchange:

HORRIGAN: That was different. He [Kennedy] was different.

RAINES: Maybe you were different.

HORRIGAN: I was different. The whole damn country was different. Everything would be different right now too if I'd been half as paranoid as I am today, fuck.

While Horrigan cannot change history, the film suggests that it can be revised through its altered documentary footage that inserts images of a young Eastwood, thus implying that he is a key figure in American history, "JFK and Jackie and [Eastwood/Horrigan]." Leary, being a former CIA assassin presumably involved in Cold War international scandals (Horrigan asks a CIA man, "What the fuck did Leary do for you anyway? Run coke for the Contras? Sell arms to Iran?"), symbolizes the dark legacy of the Cold War. Horrigan represents the protection of presidents and, by extension, the nation; his defeating Leary and taking the bullet for the current president suggests that America has learned from, and overcome, its mistakes, putting the dirty but necessary illegal acts of the Cold War behind, even to the point of rewriting the tragedy of the JFK assassination, which can finally be forgotten as the nation moves toward a new future. Horrigan's role of preventing assassination seems opposed to Munny's role of bounty hunter and assassin, but, of course, the common link is that the true evildoers are punished, whether they be outlaws or leading citizens, at the hands of the Eastwood senior version of the Western hero, who has agonized over his own past but is ultimately not limited by it.

In the Line of Fire is clearly not an explicit Western or frontier narrative, but it arguably functions as a "disguised Western," as Robert Ray (1985) terms the structural affinity that many Hollywood films share with the Western. Horrigan is an in-between hero, "the man who knows Indians" (as described by Slotkin 1992, 14), with his near-psychic power to sense Leary's presence and his repeated line of "I know things about people." And, of course, Horrigan regenerates his life through violent conflict. Overall, like *Unforgiven, In the Line of Fire* looks back at and revises history but firmly moves into the symbolic frontier of an open future with "America first."

Leary's presence, and thus the past of the Cold War, does linger, however, as over Horrigan's denials, Leary points out that Horrigan never would
have been able to take the bullet if Leary had not taunted him and kept him
in "the game," as he calls it. Horrigan can only redeem himself by eliminating his doppelgänger, a federal agent who decided to rebel, implying that
America can only renew itself by purging itself of its checkered Cold War
past. When Horrigan and Raines return to his apartment, however, Leary's
ghost fills the room via a final message left on the answering machine
before his death. Horrigan seems to walk away from it and move on with
Lilly, but the voice plays on, haunting an otherwise happy Hollywood ending of Lilly and Frank cuddling on the steps of the Lincoln Memorial, shot
nearly from the Lincoln statue's point of view, the Washington Monument
rising in the background in front of the lovers, suggesting that Eastwood/
Horrigan's achievement has been similarly memorialized and America's
victorious status reaffirmed. But the tinge of unease left by Leary's recording, a counterhistory, leads to the tragedy and failures of Eastwood's next
film, *A Perfect World*.

■ *6. A Perfect World* (1993)

> KEY IMAGE: Red (Eastwood) has finally tracked down the escaped
> convict/killer Butch (Costner). Even though neither has a gun at this
> point, each advances toward the other in a Texas field, Butch holding
> the hand of Phillip, the young boy who was initially a hostage but is now
> his friend.

> EXTREME LONG SHOT: Red on the very left of the screen, Butch and
> Phillip on the right, in the classic showdown shot of hundreds of
> Westerns.

The plot of *A Perfect World* revolves around a manhunt; Butch escapes
from prison and takes a hostage (Phillip), and Red is the Texas Ranger
leading the chase. Although Butch kills two people (including his partner in the escape), he seems a sympathetic character whose goal is to find
his long-absent father, supposedly in Alaska. Similarly, Phillip's father is
gone, and Butch becomes a father figure to him. As the hunt progresses,
we discover that Red had convinced a judge friend of his to harshly sentence the young Butch, in effect causing him to become a career criminal. At the climax, Phillip shoots and wounds Butch to prevent him from

possibly killing a family that had taken them in. Meanwhile, Red and his crew finally catch up with them, so Phillip convinces Butch to surrender, and Red seems sympathetic to their plight. However, a trigger-happy FBI sniper fatally shoots Butch.

The key image, the Western-style shot, suggests that *A Perfect World* addresses the limitations of the return of the genre and the frontier myth in the 1990s. When the film was released in 1993, Clint Eastwood was the consensus last great Western star, but Kevin Costner, thanks to directing and starring in *Dances with Wolves* and an earlier, memorable support-ing role in *Silverado* (1985), was perhaps the only other A-list Hollywood star who could claim to be a Westerner. This film also marked the first time that Eastwood had directed a major star other than himself, result-ing in a film that features Costner, with Eastwood only in a supporting role—which, perhaps, is partly why the film was a box-office flop in the United States, grossing only $31 million, a very disappointing result for two major stars following up hit movies (*Unforgiven* and *In the Line of Fire* for Eastwood; *The Bodyguard*, *JFK*, *Robin Hood: Prince of Thieves*, and *Dances with Wolves* for Costner). The film was well reviewed, though, and made over $100 million in the foreign market (more than *Unforgiven* or *In the Line of Fire*), indicating that it was not the quality of the film as much as American audience expectations and preferences that caused its relative failure in the domestic market.

American audiences may have expected more interaction between the two stars (they only appear together on-screen at the very end of the film), or they may have been put off by Costner's somewhat dark turn as a convict and killer, despite his likable performance as a father figure to Phillip. Most obviously, the film's tragic ending, with Butch/Costner suddenly killed by an FBI sniper, may have left American audiences uneasy, with neither a clichéd happy ending nor at least a cathartic sense of purpose or meaning to Butch's death (unlike Eastwood's self-sacrifice at the end of *Gran Torino*, to cite a recent, relevant example).

I argue, however, that another significant factor, closely related to the tragic ending, in American audiences rejecting this film is that the opti-mistic expectations of Eastwood's senior persona are not met in *A Perfect World*, and the resulting tragedy fails to resonate with a nation uneasily excited about its present and future. While *Unforgiven* and *In the Line of Fire* both contain aspects that undercut the successes of the Eastwood char-acters, *A Perfect World* has Red explicitly failing on multiple levels without redemption: his unjustified punishment of the young Butch and his inability to atone by bringing in Butch alive, with the FBI agent out of his control. Similarly, Butch is unable to break away from his past by escaping to rejoin his father in the symbolic final frontier of Alaska. By denying the possibility of righting past wrongs and, instead, only bloodily eliminating them, the film rejects the redemptive appeal of Eastwood's senior persona.

At the allegorical level, this film also invokes the Kennedy assassination. The film is set in Texas prior to Kennedy's visiting Dallas; the custom trailer that Red appropriates for the manhunt is meant for the governor's use during the president's visit. In this context, the FBI sniper who kills Butch invokes Oswald, and, without dipping into conspiracy theories, the film suggests that the inability to prevent either shooting results from America's failure to address its institutionalized violence, whether carried out by a government agent or a lone gunman. Therefore, in the 1990s, American audiences declined to embrace a film that fails to optimistically heal the Cold War's legacy but, instead, suggests that the wounds of past violence remain open. While this message is partially mitigated by setting the film in the 1960s and having the young Phillip survive and be reunited with his family, audiences can only assume that Phillip has been scarred by these events, as the nation was post-JFK, without the possibility of escape to a new frontier.

Heartbreak Ridge begins with "Sea of Heartbreak," a song that is also played on Butch and Phillip's car radio in *A Perfect World*. With lyrics such as "lost love an' loneliness," "memories of your caress," and "I wish you were mine again," this melancholy love song matches Eastwood's senior persona and its obsession with recovering the past. But while the song is primarily nostalgic and regretful, Eastwood's senior persona films and characters of the early 1990s move beyond nostalgia, as those characters are able to revisit and redeem their past mistakes and continue forward into an uncertain, yet often hopeful, future, a trajectory that mirrors audience sensibilities and expectations in the United States after the Cold War. While variations on the senior persona persist in Eastwood's later films (such as *Space Cowboys* and *Million Dollar Baby*), those films lack the intertwined allusions to specific, grandiose historical events and frontier mythology that enabled an obvious, allegorical connection to post–Cold War America, a connection that makes the films of 1992 and 1993 among the most historically interesting and socially relevant of Eastwood's career.

■ Bibliography

Chollet, D. H., and J. M. Goldgeier. 2008. *America between the Wars: From 11/9 to 9/11: The Misunderstood Years between the Fall of the Berlin Wall and the Start of the War on Terror.* 1st ed. New York: BBS PublicAffairs.

Metz, Walter. 2007. "The Old Man and the C: Masculinity and Age in the Films of Clint Eastwood." In *Clint Eastwood, Actor and Director: New Perspectives*, ed. Leonard Engel, 204–17. Salt Lake City: University of Utah Press.

Ray, R. B. 1985. *A Certain Tendency of the Hollywood Cinema, 1930–1980.* Princeton: Princeton University Press.

Slotkin, R. 1992. *Gunfighter Nation: The Myth of the Frontier in Twentieth-Century America.* New York: Atheneum; and Toronto: Maxwell Macmillan.

Smith, P. 1993. *Clint Eastwood: A Cultural Production.* Minneapolis: University of Minnesota Press.

Wegner, P. E. 2009. *Life between Two Deaths, 1989–2001: U.S. Culture in the Long Nineties.* Durham: Duke University Press.

CHAPTER 8

"A MAN OF NOTORIOUSLY VICIOUS AND INTEMPERATE DISPOSITION": WESTERN NOIR AND THE TENDERFOOT'S REVENGE IN *UNFORGIVEN*

Stanley Orr

C lint Eastwood's *Unforgiven* (1992) may often be reckoned a noir Western,[1] but the film entertains a complicated and tendentious relationship with this well-known subgenre. Alain Silver and Elizabeth Ward point out that the wide-open spaces and polarized moralities of the Western seem at odds with the claustrophobia and ambiguity that lie at the dark heart of film noir.[2] And yet these critics concede what may be considered a "bête noire" that has trailed the Western since the early 1940s, when films such as *The Westerner* (William Wyler, 1940) and *The Outlaw* (Howard Hughes, 1943) began to infuse the convention-ally bright genre with low-key photography, "perverse sexuality," and "overt brutality" (Silver and Ward 1992, 325). Following World War II, noir pessimism came to pervade Westerns such as William Wellman's *The Ox-Bow Incident* (1943) and John Ford's *My Darling Clementine* (1946), giving way to productions all but indistinguishable from noir crime films; these include *Ramrod* (André de Toth, 1947), *Pursued* (Raoul Walsh, 1947), *Blood on the Moon* (Robert Wise, 1948), *Station West* (Sidney Lanfield, 1948), and *Yellow Sky* (William Wellman, 1948). Commenting on the production of *Blood on the Moon*, Wise reflects,

> Many of them [Westerns] are "bright"; this felt dark. And I told
> Nick Mursuraca, the cameraman, the kind of feeling I wanted.
> It was not your average Western, the story was not typical, and
> it needed a different approach photographically; so he gave it to
> me. . . . We knew it couldn't be lit like a normal Western, but that it

had to have a heaviness to it that matched the nature of the script. (in Silver 1999, 127)

Alongside *Blood on the Moon* and *Pursued*, the films of Anthony Mann persist as exemplary noir Westerns. A veteran director of crime noirs, Mann translated the integrated expressionism and realism endemic to noir thrillers such as *T-Men* (1947), *Railroaded!* (1947), and *Raw Deal* (1948) into his Westerns of the 1950s, most notably *Devil's Doorway* (1950), *Winchester '73* (1950), *The Naked Spur* (1953), *The Man from Laramie* (1955), and *Man of the West* (1958).[3] For Silver and Ward, these films "manipulate the environment to permit the fatalistic nature of his narrative to be echoed in the landscapes" (1992, 325–27).

Wise situates film noir on the periphery of the Western—a notion elaborated within Slavoj Žižek's theory of noir as a "logic" or "anamorphic distortion" that inflects various host genres, most especially the crime film.[4] As in John Ford's *My Darling Clementine*, however, the noir vision may centrally inform the Western. While eliding the larger tradition of Western noir, Sue Matheson describes the ways in which Westerns starring John Wayne often gravitate toward noir conventions, including expressionist treatments of the physical environment and thematics of pervasive corruption and sociopathy opposed to the moral individualism of existential thought. "Whether the Western is a romance, epic, or melodrama that offers definitions of masculinity," observes Matheson, "commentators agree that the plot is still resolved in terms of heroes and villains. Surprisingly, Wayne's characters do not—one may say inherently cannot—conform to this most fundamental convention of the Western genre because the Duke is hardboiled" (2005, 889). Wheeler W. Dixon finds an even bleaker story in the career of another Western icon: "Arguably the most authentically noir vision of the Western appears in an unlikely form; the films of one of the last undeniable stars of the genre, Audie Murphy" (2009, 66). As the most decorated Allied soldier of World War II, Murphy was thought to exemplify American values of courage and determination that drive conventional Westerns. According to Dixon, however, Murphy was a traumatized veteran plagued by depression, insomnia, compulsive behavior, and explosive rage. He fetishized guns, with which he was extremely proficient, and was notorious for tormenting costars. Saddled with a patriotic screen persona, Murphy only occasionally starred in downbeat films such as *No Name on the Bullet* (Jack Arnold, 1959)—movies that reflected his own tragic and truncated life (he died in a plane crash at the age of forty-six). Dixon concludes,

> The war and its aftermath had turned Audie Murphy into one of the walk-
> ing dead, even as Universal's publicity machine ground out fan magazine
> copy extolling him as the boy next door, the fresh-faced kid who'd come
> through the horror of war and beaten the odds to become a movie star.
> (2009, 69)

Inverting Murphy's fate, Clint Eastwood has emerged a celebrated actor/director whose success derives from innovations in Western noir. Eastwood's first major film, *A Fistful of Dollars* (Sergio Leone, 1964), owes much to Dashiell Hammett's *Red Harvest* (1929), which is widely recognized as the inaugural hard-boiled novel. In the midst of the film, the villainous Rojo brothers entertain themselves by ventilating an old suit of armor—a visual poem about Leone's demolition of the conventional chivalric hero (and, perhaps, an allusion to Philip Marlowe's pronouncement in *The Big Sleep* [1939], "Knights had no meaning in this game. It wasn't a game for knights" [Chandler 1992, 156]). Like Raymond Chandler, however, Leone recuperates the devastated cavalier. When Eastwood's Man with No Name finally confronts the Rojos, he slings dynamite and wears a breastplate hewn from scrap iron; in other words, this paladin deploys armaments suitable to the depredations of the modernist wasteland. *A Fistful of Dollars*, therefore, introduces a Western antihero possessed of ruthlessness and stoicism offset by a moral code: characteristics traditionally associated with the protagonists of hard-boiled fiction and film noir.[5] Throughout the 1960s and 1970s, Eastwood refined this frontier tough guy in Leone's *Dollars* trilogy as well as the American films *Hang 'Em High* (Ted Post, 1968), *Joe Kidd* (John Sturges, 1972), and his own *High Plains Drifter* (1973), which, according to Silver and Ward, turns upon the "noir-related method of dislocating the western milieu to create a quasi-metaphysical background for narratives of violence, greed, and, above all, indifference" (1992, 327). Don Siegel, who directed Eastwood in the hard-boiled Westerns *Coogan's Bluff* (1968) and *Two Mules for Sister Sara* (1970), dubbed his star "a tarnished super-hero, actually an anti-hero. . . . He's not a white knight rescuing the girl: he seduces her" (quoted in Lovell 1983, 58).[6] Dedicated to

"Don and Sergio," *Unforgiven*, on one hand, represents the apex of Western noir and, indeed, for some critics, the climax of the Western genre proper. In his study *More than Night: Film Noir in Its Contexts*, for example, James Naremore concludes that the "distinctly noirlike" film constitutes "the last important Western" (2008, 277). Evoking the noir Western in all its bathos, brutality, and claustrophobia, *Unforgiven* yet subordinates the realism of this dark vision to a postmodernist bricolage centered upon the dime novelist W. W. Beauchamp (Saul Rubinek). This city slicker represents the vengeful return of a much-maligned figure in the Western universe: the tenderfoot transmuted into a powerfully signifying confidence man.

Martin Rubin reminds us that "in the spectrum of thriller protagonists, the film-noir hero is one of the most profoundly vulnerable, with a passive or susceptible personality that combines with hostile outside forces to overwhelm him and sweep him away" (1999, 94). The vulnerability of the noir protagonist sets him apart from the mythic Western hero capable of mastering himself and his expansive physical environment.[7] From the outset of *Unforgiven*, Eastwood's William Munny recalls and deflates the actor's prior Western roles, which, though cynical, at least retain the Western's orientation toward competence. Whereas Josey Wales's vengeance quest commences with target practice that establishes his proficiency, Munny is unable to hit his mark with a revolver and must quickly resort to the clumsy scattergun, a bathetic moment that is immediately seconded when Munny fails to mount his horse.[8] As Janet Thumim (1998) argues, emasculating incompetence recurs throughout *Unforgiven* in the form of Will's clumsiness, the Schofield Kid's (Jaimz Woolvett) blindness, Ned Logan's (Morgan Freeman) squeamishness, and Bill Daggett's (Gene Hackman) poor carpentry. Indeed, the narrative is driven by Quick Mike's (David Mucci) sexual impotence, which triggers the violent assault on Delilah Fitzgerald (Anna Thomson).

Eastwood's depiction of violence is itself wholly consistent with the realism of the noir Western and of revisionist Westerns in general: if the apex of the classical Western is the bloodless, ritualized gunfight, then noir Westerns such as *Man of the West* set in motion a tradition of deglamorized violence that was amplified throughout the latter half of the twentieth century. *Unforgiven* extends the realism of the noir Western, promising to deliver a "real West" liberated from Hollywood artifice—we have only to recall the slashing of Delilah; the beatings of English Bob (Richard Harris), Munny, and Ned; the "gut-shooting" of Davey bunting (Rob Campbell);

or the climactic gunfight at Greely's.[9] Realism shades into naturalism as *Unforgiven* projects, in terms of both style and thematics, a claustrophobic world in which human agency, the philosophical cornerstone of the classical Western, is harshly conditioned and circumscribed.

Recalling Mann's Westerns, this frontier offers no horizon for self-reinvention: rather than riding, roping, shooting, and otherwise taming their environment, the cowboys of *Unforgiven* (like those of *Winchester '73*) are often found prone—crawling wounded through dark, cramped spaces, as when English Bob, Will, Davey, and Little Bill seek to evade their attackers. Indeed, contrary to the classical Western shoot-out, virtually every assault in the film is perpetrated against an unarmed and/or fleeing victim. Such moments contribute to the shocking violence of *Unforgiven* but also poetically underscore the film's naturalist thematics; consistent with films noirs such as *Out of the Past* (Jacques Tourneur, 1947), none of the principal characters are able to escape the consequences of their actions. Most obviously, Munny finds himself backslidden from the regeneration he has enjoyed with Claudia (his "angel in the house") into alcoholism and violence: his pathetic refrain, "I ain't like that no more," is finally replaced with the noirish lament, "We've all got it coming." After he learns of Ned's death, Will takes a pull from the Kid's whiskey bottle and prepares for the conclusive bloodbath.

If *Unforgiven* were simply the film described above, it would earn a place in the canon of the revisionist Western as a brilliant film noir. But Eastwood and screenwriter David Webb Peoples transcend such virtuosity by rendering in *Unforgiven* a reflexive film about contending modes of the cinematic Western. In order to appreciate this dimension of the film, we might continue our investigation of its realism. Eastwood's unflinching portrayal of a dark and bloody American West depends in part upon its deployment of irreverent dialogue. Citing Mel Brooks's use of flatulence in *Blazing Saddles* (1974), John Cawelti has suggested that humorous burlesque may invest

> a situation that we are ordinarily accustomed to seeing in rather romanticized terms . . . with a sense of reality. This is how the famous campfire scene in *Blazing Saddles* operates. The cowboys sit around a blazing campfire at night, a scene in which we are accustomed to hearing mournful and lyrical cowboy ballads performed by such groups as the Sons of the Pioneers. Instead we are treated to an escalating barrage of flatulence.

Anyone familiar with the usual digestive aftermath of canned wilderness fare is likely to be delighted at this sudden exposure of the sham involved in the traditional western campfire scene. (2004, 202)

Even as *Unforgiven* intertwines graphic violence with a Swiftian emphasis upon waste (we initially see Munny fouled in a pigpen; Quick Mike is later murdered in a reeking outhouse), the dialogue of the film is punctuated with vulgarities about shitting, farting, masturbation, and big and little "peckers." This is, after all, the real West, in which cowboys drink, gamble, fight, carouse, and talk dirty. Such uses of colloquial dialogue are also quite consistent with hard-boiled fiction and film noir. Admitting himself "an intellectual snob who happens to have a fondness for the American vernacular," Chandler praised Hammett's use of street argot.[10] And as Rubin and many others note, film noir persisted with the "caustic, ironic tone" and "colorful use of slang" that marks hard-boiled fiction (1999, 94).

In *Unforgiven*, the frontier vernacular is nowhere more poignant than in Little Bill's story of Two-Gun Corcoran:

Bob walked right into the bar and shot at Corky, only he misses, 'cause he was so damn drunk he couldn't see straight. Old Corky went for his gun and got in such a hurry that he shot his own toe off. Bob shot at Corky again, and he misses again, because he's still so damn drunk. . . . And now, the Duck of Death is as good as dead. Because this time, Corky does it right. He takes careful aim, slowly squeezes the trigger, and . . . BAM! That Walker Colt he was carrying blew up in his hand, a failing common to that model. See, what I'm trying to tell you is if Corky really had two guns instead of a big dick, he'd be alive today.

In one sense this moment offers an illuminating commentary on the revisionist Western. For William Beard, Little Bill's narrative "is an extended debunking of idealist attitudes." Countering W. W. Beauchamp's poetic license in *The Duke of Death*, Bill transforms the classical Western shootout into a drama at once comical and graphically violent: "a world of falling-down drunkenness, guns going off by accident or misfiring, and an absolute disregard on all sides for the principles of fair play" (Beard 2000, 60). Bill tells his tale in a frontier vernacular replete with profanity and grammatical contractions; indeed, his insistence upon "duck" over "duke" captures the wry, hard-bitten spirit of the story and the film at large. The sheriff finds an eager amanuensis in Beauchamp, whose enthusiastic reception of the tale implies the triumph of the noir Western over its romantic predecessor; but this conclusion is overturned in a gesture that might be described as "the tenderfoot's revenge."

"The cowboy as gunman," writes Scott Simmon,

> dominates the earliest Western fictional anecdotes, such as the twenty-second *A Bluff from a Tenderfoot* (1899), where the strawhatted tenderfoot proves a quicker two-gun draw than knife-wielding cowboys angry at their poker-table loss—the "bluff" revealed when the tenderfoot's "guns" turn out to be a pair of fans, useful in a visual punch line to cool the sweaty brow. (2007, 7)

This prototypical screen Western tells us as much about the tenderfoot as the cowboy gunman, for the fancy "dude" or Easterner recurs throughout the genre as a troubling figure paradoxically associated with incompetence and dangerous subterfuge. As in Owen Wister's 1902 novel *The Virginian: A Horseman of the Plains*, often considered the first full-fledged Western, the masculine prowess of the cowboy-hero is set off against the effete figure known as "the Tenderfoot."

Interestingly, Wister's dude is a writer-narrator, and although he exerts decisive control over the narrative universe, he yet emerges as a man whose natural vitalities have been sapped by "civilized" life in the East.[11] Figuring prominently in dozens of films, the tenderfoot figure appears in Ford's *Stagecoach* (1939) as Peacock (Donald Meek), the feeble whiskey-drummer who suffers his samples to be pilfered by Doc Boone (Thomas Mitchell) until he is shot through the shoulder by an Indian arrow. In *Cowboy* (Delmer Daves, 1958), as in *The Virginian*, the novice Frank Harris (Jack Lemmon) emerges as benign because, despite his inexperience, he submits himself to the tutelage of cowboy Tom Reece (Glenn Ford). *The Man Who Shot Liberty Valance* (1962) complicates this formula (John Ford, 1962). Variously dubbed "tenderfoot," "pilgrim," and "dude," Ransom Stoddard (James Stewart) refuses violent Western ways only to assume the heroic mythology that rightfully belongs to the cowboy Tom Doniphon (John Wayne). At once elegiac and cynical, *The Man Who Shot Liberty Valance* elicits a tenderfoot whose signifying powers may somehow threaten or displace the Western man of action.[12] *The Man Who Shot Liberty Valance* recalls the way in which noir Westerns, along with hard-boiled fiction and film noir as a whole, transmogrify the well-spoken dude into the even more vexing figure of the huckster or confidence man.[13]

One of the most despicable characters in Mann's *Winchester '73*, for example, is the Indian trader Joe Lamont (John McIntire), who gambles for the eponymous rifle at Riker's Saloon. Arrayed in cardsharp's finery, Lamont hustles Dutch Henry Brown (Stephen McNally) and his confederates, taking the sought-after Winchester. When he later attempts to sell shoddy rifles to insurgent Indians, Lamont is killed by Young Bull (Rock Hudson) and is later redundantly sniped by Dutch Henry. Lamont's inauspicious demise exemplifies the way in which other Westerns dispose of the tenderfoot-cum-huckster.

The famous opening sequence of Sam Peckinpah's *Ride the High Country* (1962) finds Western icon Randolph Scott devolved into a loquacious carny who parodies his own adventurous past. Sporting a garish Buffalo Bill wig and beard, Scott's character Gil Westrum proves as nefarious as Lamont in *Winchester '73*; he betrays the trust of his old friend Steve Judd (Joel McCrea) and redeems himself only at the conclusion of the film. Arthur Penn takes the huckster's perfidy to reflexive levels in *Little Big Man* (1970), in which Western picaro Jack Crabb (Dustin Hoffman) briefly joins the snake oil salesman Allardyce T. Merriwether (Martin Balsam).[14] Dismissing the sense of "moral order in the universe" that Jack has learned from Old Lodge Skins (Chief Dan George), Merriwether treats us to a meditation on the nihilist worldview that drives the confidence man figure:

> Those stars twinkle in a void dear boy, and the two-legged creature schemes and dreams beneath them, all in vain. . . . Men will believe anything, the more preposterous the better. Whales speak French at the bottom of the sea. The horses of Arabia have silver wings. Pygmies mate with elephants in darkest Africa. I have sold all those propositions. Well, maybe we're all fools and none of it matters.

Given his cynical outlook, it is little wonder that Merriwether suffers a humiliating reprisal as he and Jack are tarred and feathered by a mob of angry townspeople.

Eastwood himself joins this tradition with *High Plains Drifter*, which revolves around a battle royal between the spectral *pistolier* and a brace of lesser gunman, on one hand, and a township of real estate swindlers "hiding behind words like faith, peace, and trust," on the other. Such tensions also suffuse Eastwood's *The Outlaw Josey Wales* (1976), in which a dandi-fied patent-medicine salesman known only as "Mr. Carpetbagger" (Wood-row Parfrey) pesters Wales (Eastwood) and his unlikely band of refugees. In one memorable scene, he assures Wales that his product "can do most anything," only to have the outlaw spit on his white coat and query, "How is it with stains?" Although the Carpetbagger gets off easy—merely soiled with tobacco juice and mud—his comeuppance reads as a prime example of the anxiety that attends con artists throughout the Western genre as well as the hard-boiled/noir universe.

This apprehension stems in part from the Western's general elevation of action and experience, as articulated by Jane Tompkins in her study *West of Everything: The Inner Life of Westerns*:

> The Western is at heart anti-language. Doing, not talking, is what it val-ues. . . . For the men who are the Western's heroes don't have the large vocabularies an expensive education can buy. They don't have time to read many books. Westerns distrust language in part because language tends to be wielded most skillfully by people who possess a certain kind of power: class privilege, political clout, financial strength. (1992, 51)

Tompkins's remarks help us to better understand the opposition between populist Westerners and smooth talkers who may disdain the cowboy even as they depend upon his protection or forbearance. But the "power" repre-sented in the Eastern tenderfoot, and more particularly the huckster, goes beyond class tensions insofar as these garrulous characters portend the inextricable relationship between representation and reality. The snake oil peddler Merriwether, in Penn's *Little Big Man*, broaches this epistemologi-cal dimension of the huckster as he argues for a meaningless world of "pre-posterous propositions" in which "we're all fools and none of it matters." In this respect, the Western itself is a genre founded upon outrageous claims; as Tompkins goes on to suggest,

> The entire enterprise is based on a paradox. In order to exist, the Western has to use words or visual images, but these images are precisely what it fears. As a medium, the Western has to pretend that it doesn't exist at all, its words and pictures, just a window on the truth, not really there. (1992, 51)

Like the titular figure of Melville's 1857 novel *The Confidence Man, His Masquerade* (yet another patent-medicine salesman), the Western huckster signals a human subject that might "disappear out of sight behind the mechanisms of the fiction: everything inconsistent, changeable, shifting, identity-less" (Blair 1979, 139).

Although he initially suppresses the representational bind of the Western by enacting a harshly realistic film noir, Eastwood subverts this project through deft handling of W. W. Beauchamp, whom Brad Klypchak deems "an embodiment of the media" (2007, 165). The dime novelist's disciplining at the hands of Bill Daggett should represent a decisive moment in the opposition between frontiersman and tenderfoot. Beard all but names Beauchamp a tenderfoot with his observation that the writer's "iconic features—bowler hat, waistcoat, spectacles and sidewhiskers—signify civilization and education, as does his nervous bumbling when faced with the fact that his subject might actually involve him directly rather than remaining as passive narrative material" (2000, 59). Confronted, alongside English Bob, by Little Bill and his deputies, Beauchamp wets his fancy duds for an embarrassing spectacle followed by scenes in which the biographer ostensibly submits himself to Bill's revisionism. As such, Beauchamp appears a composite of the despised huckster (recalling *Little Big Man* and *The Outlaw Josey Wales*) and the submissive tenderfoot that harkens back to *The Virginian* and *Cowboy*. But this reading, which would edge *Unforgiven* toward the conventional Western, is circumscribed by moments that reveal Beauchamp as a wily con man who serially "ropes" and "takes" the film's gunfighters.

We are introduced to Beauchamp as he and English Bob make their way to Big Whiskey so that Bob might collect the bounty on Quick Mike and Davey. Herein lies one of the most thematically important shots of the film. We hear a conversation about the assassination of President Garfield, but our view of the speakers is obscured by the collage of passengers' newspapers.[15] The camera dollies down the aisle of the train, moving through the newspapers to the conversants at the head of the car. Here we meet English Bob, lecturing the group on politics as a smug Beauchamp smiles his approval. Although *Unforgiven*'s realist dimension primes us to read English Bob as the dangerous referential beneath the layers of mass cultural textuality, we find rather a pedant who talks down to his fellow passengers. And even when Bob does resort to gunplay, the action is wholly rhetorical: a pheasant-shooting contest in defense of his deadly reputation. *Unforgiven* hereby foregrounds, rather than suppresses, the representational status of the Western—with this scene, it becomes clear that there is no epistemological bedrock of violent praxis outside the mediation of newspapers, dime novels, and tall tales.

Although he plays the sycophant, Beauchamp ultimately emerges a much more potent figure. In a counterpoint to the jail scene in which he rewrites the story of Two-Gun Corcoran, Little Bill comes to demonstrate his deference to the biographer. Sitting in Bill's leaky house, Beauchamp records the sheriff's rough-and-ready memoirs: "I can't abide them kind . . . tramps an' drunk teamsters an' crazy miners . . . sportin' pistols like they was bad men but not having no sand nor character . . . not even bad character."

This exercise in Western realism falters, however, as Little Bill abandons his own idiolect for one he imagines more suited to Beauchamp's medium: "I do not like assassins," he solemnly intones, "or men of low character." We might recognize not only the humorless self-righteousness of this utterance but also its sudden bid for grammatical correctness—Bill leaves off contractions, along with the slang that has become a marker of realism in the film.[16] The implication of this dialogic shift is quite clear: Beauchamp exerts a hegemonic influence over Little Bill and English Bob before him. Given Ingrassia's interpretation of the Schofield Kid as an "uncritical reader" of dime novels (1998, 54), we might assume that Beauchamp has already taken this "mark."[17] In other words, the tenderfoot, whose conventional domain is language, comes into his own as a confidence man who manipulates the "doing" gunfighter.[18]

It might be tempting to read Munny as a noir protagonist impervious to Beauchamp's allure.[19] After all, Munny seems inimical to the romantic Western, capturing indeed the bathos, brutality, and naturalism of its revisionist counterparts. The conclusive showdown of *Unforgiven*, therefore, does not simply pit Munny against Little Bill but, rather, stages a confrontation between Munny and Beauchamp, an approach that accounts for the tonal disjunctions of this climactic sequence. On one hand, the shootout reasserts noir realism against the theatricality of Beauchamp and his recent convert, Little Bill. As Munny rides up to Greeley's Saloon, which has become an epicenter of signifying activity, he finds the morbid display of Ned's coffined body, torch-lit and captioned with a hand-painted sign that reads "This is what we do to assassins in Big Whiskey." The tableau sees the horribly real translated into Bill's violent rhetoric;[20] and it is a fitting epigraph for the scene transpiring within the saloon, where Bill performs for the crowd as Beauchamp looks on with the approving gaze that he had earlier reserved for English Bob.

Entering the saloon, Munny brings not only retribution but also a return to realism. "Who owns this shithole?" he asks, invoking the scatological frontier vernacular abandoned by Little Bill. After remorselessly shooting Skinny (Anthony James), Munny engages in an exchange with Bill that would almost seem a sparring of voices: to Bill's accusation, "You, sir, are a cowardly son of a bitch; you just shot an unarmed man," Munny replies, "Well, he shoulda armed himself, if he's gonna decorate his saloon with my friend Ned." Munny here realizes the Western's emphasis on praxis when he punctuates this terse, ironic statement with a hail of gunfire that decimates the Big Whiskey sheriff's office; as the deputies fumble their weapons before Munny's onslaught, they recapitulate the bathetic brutality critical to realism in *Unforgiven*. Munny enforces this realism throughout the course of the final sequence, maintaining a hard-boiled demeanor even into his nihilistic parting words to Bill ("Deserves has got nuthin' to do with it") and into his conversation with Beauchamp. To the writer's query about the order of killings in the shoot-out, Munny replies, "I can only tell you who's gonna be last." Under this reading, the final showdown of *Unforgiven*, at once mimetic and allegorical, fully realizes the central paradox in the Western between language and antilanguage.

Eastwood here again problematizes the obvious binaries of the sequence by suggesting that Munny himself is not wholly immune to Beauchamp's writerly wiles. Just before the shooting begins, Bill and Munny exchange barbs that sound quite consistent with Beauchamp's medium:

LITTLE BILL DAGGETT: You'd be William Munny out of Missouri. Killer of women and children.

WILLIAM MUNNY: That's right. I've killed women and children. I've killed just about everything that walks or crawls at one time or another. And I'm here to kill you, Little Bill, for what you did to Ned.

The exchange is intercut with a close-up of Beauchamp's delighted visage, suggesting not only that he intends to exploit the confrontation but that he is already exerting his hegemonic influence, already somehow directing the gunfighters' performances. Indeed, as Buscombe points out, "It's as though they are acting their parts, deliberately giving them weight and sonority" (2004, 18).

Upon leaving the devastated saloon, Munny pronounces a jeremiadic warning upon Big Whiskey:

> I'm coming out. Any man I see out there I'm gonna kill him. Any son of a bitch takes a shot at me, I'm not only going to kill him, I'm going to kill his wife and all his friends and burn his damn house down. Nobody better shoot. You better bury Ned right. You better not cut up nor otherwise harm no whores. Or I'll come back and kill every one of you sons of bitches!

Although Munny never becomes one of Beauchamp's creatures, as do Bob and Bill, he yet seems to have been persuaded by the writer's voice; Munny's warning is not only clearly performative but also reminiscent of the only line read aloud from Beauchamp's *The Duke of Death*:[21] "'You have insulted the honor of this beautiful woman, Corcoran,' said the duck. 'You must apologize.'"[22]

Taken together, the film's elegiac prologue and epilogue support this reading. In each instance, we are treated to the conventional mise-en-scène of the Western—the horizon at sunset—punctuated by intertitles that frame the narrative:

> She was a comely young woman and not without prospects. Therefore it was heartbreaking to her mother that she would enter into marriage with William Munny, a known thief and murderer, a man of notoriously vicious and intemperate disposition. When she died, it was not at his hands as her mother might have expected, but of smallpox. That was 1878.

> Some years later, Mrs. Ansonia Feathers made the arduous journey to Hodgeman County to visit the last resting place of her only daughter. William Munny had long since disappeared with the children. . . . [S]ome said to San Francisco where it was rumored he prospered in dry goods. And there was nothing on the marker to explain to Mrs. Feathers why her only daughter had married a known thief and murderer, a man of notoriously vicious and intemperate disposition.

Consistent with the Western's thematics of self-reinvention, this senti-
mental conclusion is, of course, at odds with the dark, claustrophobic film
in which "we've all got it comin." Imagination of a "forgiven" Munny is
here couched in a Latinate style that summons not only an "over-elaborate
Victorianism" (Buscombe 2004, 17) but, more specifically, the figure of
Beauchamp, to whom these lines may be attributed.[23] The telling phrase
"a man of notoriously vicious and intemperate disposition," derived from
a common construction in Victorian prose, underscores the way in which
Beauchamp has assimilated the antihero of Western noir into his novelistic
conventions.[24] Munny may not have been taken by the confidence man in
the same explicit fashion as English Bob and Little Bill, but he just as surely
disappears into Beauchamp's florid rhetoric—a turn perhaps suggested in
the final image of Munny riding into the darkness.

Unforgiven hereby shifts the emphasis away from noir realism and into
a world of depthless textuality; and the entity most at home in this milieu
is not the tough and practical cowboy/gunfighter but, rather, the voluble
tenderfoot-cum-confidence man. In this respect, *Unforgiven* joins a series
of 1990s crime films that dramatize the apotheosis of the con man, which
represents, in Calvin O. Schrag's phrase, "the self in discourse," a subject
"dispersed into a panorama of radically diversified and changing language
games" (1999, 27). Bryan Singer's *The Usual Suspects* (1995), for example,
foregrounds Verbal Kint (Kevin Spacey), a malleable bricoleur who, as his
name implies, spins a yarn that exploits the noir ethos alongside other narrative strategies, such as Orientalism and "the reality effect." In David Fincher's
Seven (1995), Spacey would reprise this role as John Doe, a homiletic serial
killer bent upon transcribing his victims into the exempla of a grisly sermon.
Memento (Chris Nolan, 2000) takes on an even more reflexive aspect, as the
amnesiac Leonard (Guy Pearce) contends with his manipulative "handler"
Teddy Gammell (John Pantoliagno) for narrative control of his own person.
Nolan's hapless isolato manages to free himself from the machinations of
the confidence man, but only in the sense that he must now "con" himself:
"I have to believe in a world outside my own mind," he concludes; "I have to
believe that my actions still have meaning even if I can't remember them."

This integration of agonistic noir hero with the signifying confidence
man likewise informs *The Man Who Wasn't There* (Joel and Ethan Coen,
2001), in which the Cainian protagonist Ed Crane (Billy Bob Thornton)
joins a parade of con men who liquidate self and world into a "Big Show."

Modernist humanism, therefore, gives way in these films to a vision of the self as protean textual construct, "Story A" and "Story B," as the Coens' philosophizing shyster Freddy Riedenschneider (Tony Shalhoub) has it.[25] Seducing hard-bitten gunfighters into his purple prose, W. W. Beauchamp joins postmodernist con men such as Verbal Kint and John Doe; indeed, *Unforgiven* may be recognized as an inaugural film in this series of revisionist noirs. So while *Unforgiven* undoubtedly represents the culmination of the noir Western, Eastwood's film achieves this status by subverting the subgenre's basic ideals.

■ Notes

1. Gary Hoppenstand, for example, affirms *Unforgiven* "a frontier noir masterpiece" (2004, 1); in *Horizons West: Directing the Western from John Ford to Clint Eastwood*, Jim Kitses likewise finds its "noir trajectory" commensurate with "an American society in which an appetite for . . . bloody justice persists" (2004, 310).

2. Edward Dimendberg similarly observes, "Unlike the contemporaneous conquests of the big sky and the open frontier by characters in the film genre of the western, the protagonists in film noir appear cursed by an inability to dwell comfortably anywhere" (2004, 7). See also Barr 2011, 165.

3. See Hirsch 2001, 53.

4. In *Tarrying with the Negative: Kant, Hegel, and the Critique of Ideology*, Žižek contends: "Cinema theory has for a long time been haunted by the question: is noir a genre of its own or a kind of anamorphic distortion affecting different genres? From the very beginning *film noir* was not limited to hard-boiled detective stories: reverberations of *film noir* motifs are easily discernable in comedies (*Arsenic and Old Lace*), in Westerns (*Pursued*), in political (*All the King's Men*) and social dramas (*Weekend's End*), etcetera. Do we have here the secondary impact of something that originally constitutes a genre of its own (the *noir* crime universe), or is the crime film only one of the possible fields of application of the *noir* logic, that is, is '*noir*' a predicate that entertains towards the crime universe the same relationship as towards a comedy or Western, a kind of logical operator introducing the same anamorphic distortion in every genre it is applied to, so that the fact that it found its strongest application in the crime film is ultimately a historical contingency? My thesis is that the 'proper,' detective *film noir* as it were *arrives at its truth—* in Hegelese: realizes its notion only by way of its fusion with another genre" (1993, 9).

5. See Moore 2006, 76. We should also bear in mind Rubin's qualification that the noir hero "whether a detective or not, is more of a victim and less in control than hard-boiled pros like Sam Spade or Philip Marlowe usually are" (1999, 94).

6. See also Tibbetts 1993, 12.

7. As Jane Tompkins points out in *West of Everything: The Inner Life of Westerns*, the Western hero is a capable figure whose "skills are roping cattle, shooting pistols, riding horses, and bossing hands" (1992, 142).

8. According to Beard, Munny's initial lack of proficiency with gun and horse—"the most important tokens of individual power in the Western"—distinguishes this antiheroic character from "Eastwood's prime persona" (2000, 46).

9. For discussions of violence in *Unforgiven*, see John Tibbetts's "Clint Eastwood and the Machinery of Violence" (1993) and Carl Plantinga's "Spectacles of Death: Clint Eastwood and Violence in *Unforgiven*" (1998).

10. Chandler (2002, 105) referred to himself as an "intellectual snob" in a 1949 letter to Alex Barris. For Chandler's appraisal of Hammett, see his essay "The Simple Art of Murder" (1944).

11. As Arthur G. Kimball notes, Zane Grey inherited and elaborated Wister's notion of the tenderfoot easterner as "a neophyte who needs to learn and adapt to western ways" (1993, 15–16).

12. See Cawelti 2004, 206.

13. According to Dixon, *The Man Who Shot Liberty Valance* "carr[ies] over the noir aesthetic to the world of 'manifest destiny' and national westward expansion" (2009, 66). See also Alan P. Barr's "*The Man Who Shot Liberty Valance* Inhabits Film Noir" (2011). In *Darkly Perfect World: Colonial Adventure, Postmodernism, and American Noir* (2010), I describe at length the ways in which writers such as Dashiell Hammett, Raymond Chandler, William Lindsay Gresham, and Jim Thompson recognize and respond to the confidence man as a figure for unchecked signification.

14. For a discussion of Jack Crabb as a picaresque antihero, see Richard Betts's article "Thomas Berger's *Little Big Man*: Contemporary Picaresque" (1981).

15. For more on the "uncommon lot of writing appearing on the screen in this picture," see Buscombe 2004, 25.

16. Buscombe notes, "Most of the principal characters in the film speak in this manner, slightly pedantic and self-conscious" (2004, 18). Even as English Bob loses his "plummy" accent along with his novelist, Bill is "becoming self-important now he's got a biographer, and eager to expatiate on his distinction between the respectable and the disreputable" (2004, 55).

17. For more on dime novel readers and writers in Western films, see Buscombe 2004, 50–51.

18. In "'I'm Not Kicking, I'm Talking': Discursive Economies in the Western," Ingrassia, following Jane Tompkins, argues, "Though the deeds of the men of action have some value, those actions must be articulated, narrated, transformed into a text that can circulate within the discursive community. The hero or the gunfighter must consistently negotiate his way between the textually constructed world which validates and perpetuates his existence and the material world from which that construction emerges and in which it actually exists" (1996, 5).

19. In "'I'm Not Kicking, I'm Talking,'" Ingrassia observes, "Munny, whose very name suggests the strength of his currency, resists participation in the circulation of alleged deeds, perhaps recognizing that his own silence only enhances his mystique. His value has increased because he has been 'hoarding' his cultural capital as it were" (1996, 11). See also Jeffords 1994, 187.

20. See Ingrassia 1996, 12.

21. In "'I'm Not Kicking, I'm Talking,'" Ingrassia argues that Munny here "prefaces his actions with the hyperbolic language that he has spent most of the film avoiding" (1996, 12).

22. As Fred Erisman has it, "The entire enterprise is driven by an increasingly distorted story of violence against a woman and its implications of chivalric revenge, and behind it all lies (in every sense of the word) the dime-novel, wild-west-show vision of the West" (2007, 188). See also Ingrassia's "Writing the West: Iconic and Literal Truth in *Unforgiven*" (1998).

23. See Beard 2000, 59–60.

24. For examples of similar expressions, see Arthur 1872, 155; Eddy 1852, 399; Semmes 1851, 33; Shaw 1922, 27; Swartz and Pearson 1835, 111.

25. I elaborate this reading of the confidence man in postmodernist films noir in chap. 6 of *Darkly Perfect World* (2010) and in "Razing Cain: Excess Signification in *Blood Simple* and *The Man Who Wasn't There*" (2008).

■ Bibliography

Armitage, Frederick S., dir. 1899. *A Bluff from a Tenderfoot*. American Mutoscope and Biograph.

Arthur, T. S. 1872. *Three Years in a Man-Trap*. Philadelphia: J. M. Stoddart and Co.

Arnold, Jack, dir. 1959. *No Name on the Bullet*. Perfs. Audie Murphy, Charles Drake, and Joan Evans. Universal International Pictures.

Bancroft, Hubert H. 1882. *The Works of Hubert Howe Bancroft*. San Francisco: A. L. Bancroft and Co.

Barr, Alan P. 2011. "*The Man Who Shot Liberty Valance* Inhabits Film Noir." *Western American Literature* 46, no. 2: 162–79.

Beard, William. 2000. *Persistence of Double Vision: Essays on Clint Eastwood*. Edmonton: University of Alberta Press.

Betts, Richard. 1981. "Thomas Berger's *Little Big Man*: Contemporary Picaresque." *Critique* 23: 85–96.

Blair, John G. 1979. *The Confidence Man in Modern Fiction: A Rogue's Gallery with Six Portraits*. New York: Barnes.

Brooks, Mel, dir. 1974. *Blazing Saddles*. Perfs. Cleavon Little, Gene Wilder, and Slim Pickens. Warner Bros./Crossbow Productions.

Buscombe, Edward. 2004. *Unforgiven*. London: BFI.

Cawelti, John. 2004. "Chinatown and Generic Transformation in Recent American Films." In *Mystery, Violence, and Popular Culture: Essays*, 193–209. Madison: University of Wisconsin Press/Popular Press.

Chandler, Raymond. 1944. "The Simple Art of Murder." *Atlantic Monthly* 174, no. 6: 53–59.

———. 1992. *The Big Sleep*. New York: Vintage.

———. 2002. "Letter to Alex Barris, 18 April 1949." In *The Raymond Chandler Papers: Selected Letters and Nonfiction, 1909–1950*, ed. Tom Hiney and Frank MacShane, 44–45. New York: Grove Press.

Coen, Joel, dir. 2001. *The Man Who Wasn't There*. Perfs. Billy Bob Thornton, Frances McDormand, and James Gandolfini. USA Films.

Daves, Delmer, dir. 1958. *Cowboy*. Perfs. Glenn Ford and Jack Lemmon. Columbia Pictures.

de Toth, André, dir. 1947. *Ramrod*. Perfs. Joel McCrea and Veronica Lake. United Artists.

Dimendberg, Edward. 2004. *Film Noir and the Spaces of Modernity*. Cambridge: Harvard University Press.

Dixon, Wheeler W. 2009. *Film Noir and the Cinema of Paranoia*. New Brunswick, N.J.: Rutgers University Press.

Eastwood, Clint, dir. 1973. *High Plains Drifter*. Perfs. Clint Eastwood, Verna Bloom, and Marianna Hill. Universal Pictures/Malpaso Co.

Eddy, Daniel C. 1852. *Europa, Or, Notes of a Recent Ramble*. Lowell: Nathaniel L. Dayton.

Erisman, Fred. 2007. "Clint Eastwood's Western Films and the Evolving Mythic Hero." In *Clint Eastwood, Actor and Director: New Perspectives*, ed. Leonard Engel, 181–94. Salt Lake City: University of Utah Press.

Fincher, David, dir. 1995. *Seven*. Perfs. Brad Pitt, Morgan Freeman, and Gwyneth Paltrow. New Line Cinema.

Ford, John, dir. 1939. *Stagecoach*. Perfs. John Wayne, Claire Trevor, and Andy Devine. Walter Wanger Productions.

———. 1946. *My Darling Clementine*. Perfs. Henry Fonda, Linda Darnell, Victor Mature, and Walter Brennan. Twentieth Century Fox Film Corp.

———. 1962. *The Man Who Shot Liberty Valance*. Perfs. John Wayne, James Stewart, and Lee Marvin. Paramount.

Hammett, Dashiell. 1929. *Red Harvest*. New York: Knopf.

Hirsch, Foster. 2001. *The Dark Side of the Screen: Film Noir*. New York: Da Capo Press.

Hoppenstand, Gary. 2004. "Editorial: Gone with the Western." *Journal of Popular Culture* 38, no. 1: 1–4.

Hughes, Howard, dir. 1943. *The Outlaw*. Perfs. Jack Buetel, Jane Russell, and Thomas Mitchell. Howard Hughes Productions.

Ingrassia, Catherine. 1996. "'I'm Not Kicking, I'm Talking': Discursive Economies in the Western." *Film Criticism* 20, no. 3: 4–14.

———. 1998. "Writing the West: Iconic and Literal Truth in *Unforgiven*." *Literature/Film Quarterly* 26: 53–59.

Jeffords, Susan. 1994. *Hard Bodies: Hollywood Masculinity in the Reagan Era*. New Brunswick, N.J.: Rutgers University Press.

Kimball, Arthur G. 1993. *Ace of Hearts: The Westerns of Zane Grey*. Fort Worth: Texas Christian University Press.

Kitses, Jim. 2004. *Horizons West: Directing the Western from John Ford to Clint Eastwood*. London: BFI.

Klypchak, Brad. 2007. "'All on Account of Pullin' a Trigger': Violence, the Media and the Historical Contextualization of Clint Eastwood's *Unforgiven*." In *Clint Eastwood, Actor and Director: New Perspectives*, ed. Leonard Engel, 157–70. Salt Lake City: University of Utah Press.

Lanfield, Sidney, dir. 1948. *Station West*. Perfs. Dick Powell, Jane Greer, and Agnes Moorhead. RKO Radio Pictures.

Leone, Sergio, dir. 1964. *A Fistful of Dollars*. Perfs. Clint Eastwood, Gian Maria Volonté, and Marianne Koch. MGM/UA.

Lovell, Alan. 1983. *Don Siegel: American Cinema*. London: British Film Institute.

Mann, Anthony, dir. 1947a. *Railroaded!* Perfs. John Ireland, Sheila Ryan, and Hugh Beau-
    mont. Producers Releasing Corp.

———. 1947b. *T-Men*. Perfs. Dennis O'Keefe, Mary Meade, and Alfred Ryder. Edward
    Small Productions.

———. 1948. *Raw Deal*. Perfs. Dennis O'Keefe, Claire Trevor, and Marsha Hunt. Edward
    Small Productions.

———. 1950a. *Devil's Doorway*. Perfs. Robert Taylor, Louis Calhern, and Paula Raymond.
    MGM.

———. 1950b. *Winchester '73*. Perfs. James Stewart, Shelly Winters, Stephen McNally, and
    Millard Mitchell. Universal International Pictures.

———. 1953. *The Naked Spur*. Perfs. James Stewart, Janet Leigh, Robert Ryan, Ralph
    Meeker, and Millard Mitchell. MGM.

———. 1955. *The Man from Laramie*. Perfs. James Stewart, Arthur Kennedy, and Donald
    Crisp. Columbia Pictures Corp.

———. 1958. *Man of the West*. Perfs. Gary Cooper, Julie London, and Lee J. Cobb. Ashton
    Productions.

Matheson, Sue. 2005. "The West—Hardboiled: Adaptations of Film Noir Elements, Exis-
    tentialism, and Ethics in John Wayne's Westerns." *Journal of Popular Culture* 38, no. 5:
    888–910.

Moore, Lewis D. 2006. *Cracking the Hard-Boiled Detective: A Critical History from the
    1920s to the Present*. Jefferson, N.C.: McFarland.

Naremore, James. 2008. *More than Night: Film Noir in Its Contexts*. Berkeley: University of
    California Press.

Nolan, Christopher, dir. 2000. *Memento*. Perfs. Guy Pearce, Carrie-Anne Moss, and Joe
    Pantoliano. Columbia/Tri-Star.

O'Donoghue, Alfred. 1869. "Thirty Months at the Dry Tortugas." *Galaxy Magazine* 7, no. 2
    (February): 282.

Orr, Stanley. 2008. "Razing Cain: Excess Signification in *Blood Simple* and *The Man Who
    Wasn't There*." *Post Script* 27, no. 2: 8–22.

———. 2010. *Darkly Perfect World: Colonial Adventure, Postmodernism, and American
    Noir*. Columbus: Ohio State University Press.

Peckinpah, Sam, dir. 1962. *Ride the High Country*. Perfs. Joel McCrea and Randolph Scott.
    MGM.

Penn, Arthur, dir. 1970. *Little Big Man*. Perfs. Dustin Hoffman, Faye Dunaway, and Chief
    Dan George. Twentieth Century Fox Film Corp.

Plantinga, Carl. 1998. "Spectacles of Death: Clint Eastwood and Violence in *Unforgiven*."
    Cinema Journal 37, no. 2: 65–83.

Post, Ted, dir. 1968. *Hang 'Em High*. Perfs. Clint Eastwood, Inger Stevens, and Pat Hingle.
    Leonard Freeman/Malpaso Co.

Rubin, Martin. 1999. *Thrillers*. Cambridge: Cambridge University Press.

Schrag, Calvin O. 1999. *The Self after Postmodernity*. New Haven: Yale University Press.

Semmes, Raphael. 1851. *Service Afloat and Ashore during the Mexican War*. Cincinnati:
    W. H. Moore.

Shaw, Bernard. 1922. *Man and Superman: A Comedy and a Philosophy*. New York: Brentano's.

Siegel, Don, dir. 1968. *Coogan's Bluff*. Perfs. Clint Eastwood, Lee J. Cobb, and Don Stroud. Malpaso Co.

———. 1970. *Two Mules for Sister Sara*. Perfs. Shirley MacLaine, Clint Eastwood, and Manuel Fábregas. Universal.

Silver, Alain. 1999. "Interview with Robert Wise." In *Film Noir Reader Three*, ed. Robert Porfirio, Alain Silver, and James Ursini, 121–34. New York: Limelight, 2002.

Silver, Alain, and Elizabeth Ward. 1992. *Film Noir: An Encyclopedic Reference to the American Style*. Woodstock, N.Y.: Overlook Press.

Simmon, Scott. 2007. *The Invention of the Western Film: A Cultural History of the Genre's First Half-Century*. Cambridge: Cambridge University Press.

Singer, Bryan, dir. 1995. *The Usual Suspects*. Perfs. Kevin Spacey, Gabriel Byrne, and Chazz Palminteri. Poly-Gram Filmed Entertainment.

Sturges, John, dir. 1972. *Joe Kidd*. Perfs. Clint Eastwood, John Saxon, and Robert Duvall. Universal Pictures.

Swartz, Christian F., and Hugh Pearson. 1835. *Memoirs of the Life and Correspondence of the Reverend Christian Frederick Swartz, to Which Is Prefixed a Sketch of the History of Christianity in India*. Boston: Perkins, Marvin.

Thumim, Janet. 1998. "Maybe He's Tough, but He Sure Ain't No Carpenter: Masculinity and In/Competence in *Unforgiven*." In *The Western Reader*, ed. Jim Kitses and Gregg Rickman, 341–54. New York: Limelight Editions.

Tibbetts, John C. 1993. "Clint Eastwood and the Machinery of Violence." *Literature Film Quarterly* 21, no. 1: 10–17.

Tompkins, Jane P. 1992. *West of Everything: The Inner Life of Westerns*. New York: Oxford University Press.

Tourneur, Jacques, dir. 1947. *Out of the Past*. Perfs. Robert Mitchum, Kirk Douglass, and Jane Greer. RKO Pictures.

Walsh, Raoul, dir. 1947. *Pursued*. Perfs. Robert Mitchum, Teresa Wright, and Judith Anderson. United States Pictures.

Wellman, Willman, dir. 1943. *The Ox-Bow Incident*. Perfs. Henry Fonda, Dana Andrews, and Mary Beth Hughes. Twentieth Century Fox Film Corp.

———. 1948. *Yellow Sky*. Perfs. Gregory Peck, Anne Baxter, and Richard Widmark. Twentieth Century Fox Film Corp.

Wise, Robert, dir. 1948. *Blood on the Moon*. Perfs. Robert Mitchum, Barbara Bel Geddes, and Robert Preston. RKO Radio Pictures.

Wister, Owen. 1902. *The Virginian: A Horseman of the Plains*. New York: Macmillan Co.

Wyler, William, dir. 1940. *The Westerner*. Perfs. Gary Cooper, Walter Brennan, and Doris Davenport. Samuel Goldwyn Co.

Žižek, Slavoj. 1993. *Tarrying with the Negative: Kant, Hegel, and the Critique of Ideology*. Durham: Duke University Press.

CHAPTER 9

A GOOD VINTAGE OR DAMAGED GOODS?:
CLINT EASTWOOD AND AGING IN HOLLYWOOD FILM

Philippa Gates

Clint Eastwood could be described as the epitome of tough American masculinity. As William Beard argues, "The Eastwood persona represents probably the single strongest icon of heroic masculinity in popular cinema over the past quarter-century" (2000, ix). Eastwood established himself playing vigilante heroes in Westerns in the 1950s and 1960s and then took the Western hero to the mean city streets of the 1970s and 1980s. With *Gran Torino* (2008), Eastwood was nearing eighty and still playing the leading role, surviving what is seen as the kiss of death in Hollywood—old age. Eastwood has remained a contemporary icon of American masculinity despite the fact that social conceptions of masculinity and heroism have undergone radical change since the 1960s—or, as this chapter will argue, *because* they have. In the late 1980s, Eastwood's final installment of the "Dirty Harry" series, *The Dead Pool* (1988), no longer seemed relevant—unlike the original film, *Dirty Harry* (1971), which had been so timely with its critical take on the justice system in the early 1970s—or even believable, as Dirty Harry, once able to take down the enemy with his famous .44 Magnum, resorts to a giant harpoon gun to exact justice. Just as it seemed that Hollywood had outgrown the type of masculinity his persona embodied, Eastwood reinvented himself as a respected actor and an acclaimed director of award-winning films, such as *Unforgiven* (1992) and *Million Dollar Baby* (2004).

In over fifty years on-screen, Eastwood has transformed from being an ideal for young viewers to emulate to being one for an older generation. From the tough guy to the tough guy with the heart of gold, Eastwood offers fantasies of the golden years, embodying masculinity that is tested—and proved to be vital and valued. And how did Eastwood beat the Hollywood clock? It was not by resisting the aging process, as Hollywood's leading ladies are expected to—but by embracing it. In Eastwood's films since the early 1990s—such as *Unforgiven* (1992), *In the Line of Fire* (1993), *Absolute Power* (1997), *Space Cowboys* (2000), *Blood Work* (2002), *Million Dollar Baby* (2004), and *Gran Torino* (2008)—much is made of Eastwood's age. His aged face and body are presented as a spectacle for the audience to behold; in doing so, his body's physical vulnerability is offered to, and read by, audiences as an emotional one. With this perceived vulnerability, Eastwood's tough-guy past is tempered, and his image is aligned with contemporary ideals of masculinity as physical and heroic but, simultaneously, sensitive and romantic. Thus, Eastwood is as much a hero for the early twenty-first century as he was once one of the mid-twentieth.

■ From the Wild West to the Mean Streets

Eastwood made his screen debut in small uncredited roles in monster movies like *Revenge of the Creature* (1955) and *Tarantula* (1955). As Peter Howell suggests, "He might never have risen above 'B' movies status—he was judged not handsome enough to play a leading man—but legend has it that a TV exec hired him to play *Rawhide* cattleman Rowdy Yates because 'he looked like a cowboy'" (2006, 19). Although this was not Eastwood's first time playing a man of the West (for example, he played a ranch hand in *Star in the Dust* [1956]), Yates was the role that established Eastwood's association with the Western—if only because it was in this role that he attracted the attention of Italian director Sergio Leone, who made him an icon of the Western. Eastwood starred in the three Leone "spaghetti Westerns"—*A Fistful of Dollars* (1964), *For a Few Dollars More* (1965), and *The Good, the Bad, and the Ugly* (1966)—as the strong and silent loner. By the 1970s, Eastwood brought his tough Western hero to the mean streets of the American city in Don Siegel's *Coogan's Bluff* (1968) and *Dirty Harry* (1971) to fight crime as a violent, vigilante hero.

As Rupert Wilkinson suggests, "Everybody knows the modern tough guy. . . . Writ large on the screen, he is most obviously a Bogart, a Wayne, an Eastwood" (1984, 3). According to Wilkinson, toughness was regarded as a quality that a man could acquire; in the 1940s and 1950s, it was demonstrated through cigar-chomping, jaw-working, squinting while smoking, and strutting (Wilkinson 1984, 11). These acts performed externally in order to suggest a natural identity internally of course evoke Judith Butler's notion of gender performativity: "Gender is the repeated stylization of the body, a set of repeated acts within a highly rigid regulatory frame that congeal over time to produce the appearance of substance, of a natural sort of being" (1990, 33). Eastwood became an icon of ideal masculinity through his performance of toughness on the screen: his tall stature, his cold and unreadable face, his famous squint against the sun, often a hat pulled low over his eyes and casting them into shadow, and his slow and calculated movements in the face of overwhelming danger. However, Eastwood's brand of tough heroism was an extreme one and not the standard; in fact, many found his representation of heroism not heroic at all—but brutal. Influential *New Yorker* critic Pauline Kael argues that Eastwood's Dirty Harry embodied a fascist attitude toward law and order and was "almost a machine for killing" (quoted in Boedeker 2000, 11). This was the image that Eastwood established as Leone's "Man with No Name" and cultivated as Dirty Harry—but by the end of the 1980s, this brand of heroism seemed to have lost its resonance with audiences.

■ Eastwood's "Big Switch"

The box-office success of *Dirty Harry* led to four more films starring the cop hero: *Magnum Force* (1973), *The Enforcer* (1976), *Sudden Impact* (1983), and *The Dead Pool* (1988).[1] However, by 1988, Harry Callahan and his cold and violent brand of justice seemed to have gone out of style, and newer, younger, and more comedic cop action heroes were in fashion, for example, Eddie Murphy's in *Beverly Hills Cop II* (1987), Mel Gibson's in *Lethal Weapon* (1987), and Bruce Willis's in *Die Hard* (1988). As Madison Dorval notes, the audience for Eastwood's movies had "fallen off steadily" in the late 1980s (1992, 24). This shift in audience taste was merely indicative of a broader change in social attitudes toward masculinity. By the late 1980s, there was a new concept in fashion culture—"The New Man." He was the product of feminism as a more sensitive kind of masculinity and also of a new consumerism as the male body became the center of male identity and sexuality. This incorporation of traditionally feminine characteristics—for example, being fashion-conscious and emotionally vulnerable—into masculinity could be read as an attempt to diffuse feminism. As Tania Modleski argues, "Male power is actually consolidated through cycles of crisis and resolution, whereby men ultimately deal with the threat of female power by incorporating it" (1991, 7). The New Man was, as a more feminized version of maleness, simultaneously a concession to female empowerment as well as a co-opting of it. Masculine ideals had changed before the late 1980s, and Eastwood was just lucky that they had tended to shift in a direction in keeping with his iconographic persona. Before the New Man appeared, the dominant kind of masculinity in the 1980s was what Jonathan Rutherford has referred to as "The Retributive Man," one that offered a destructive machismo as the solution for men's problems and confronted "a world gone soft, pacified by traitors and cowards, dishonourable feminized men" (1988, 28).

Dirty Harry was a destructive macho man who combated "a world gone soft," but by the early 1990s, a "Big Switch"—as Susan Jeffords (1993a, 200) has termed it—occurred in American culture: one from the valuation of hypermasculinity to that of sensitive masculinity. The muscle-bound, violent, vigilante hero of 1980s action films—most memorably embodied by Arnold Schwarzenegger as The Terminator and Sylvester Stallone as Rocky and Rambo—came to be replaced by heroes who were slimmer and smaller physically and more romantic and vulnerable emotionally.[2] While Gibson and Willis also embodied some aspects of the Retributive Man as action heroes whose most effective weapons were their muscled bodies, they were, however, emotionally damaged men (Riggs of *Lethal Weapon* is suicidal after losing his wife, and McClane of *Die Hard* attempts to woo his estranged wife)—unlike Eastwood's hero, who was emotionally indestructible. From the valuation of external muscular masculinity to a more internalized one, as Jeffords (1993b, 245) notes, film narratives placed a greater emphasis on the ethical dilemmas, emotional traumas, and psychological goals of the heroes than on their skill with lethal weapons. Indeed, Fred Pfeil describes 1991 as "the year of living sensitively" (1995, 37).[3]

It is not the case that Eastwood necessarily adapted to this new trend once it was initiated (i.e., jumping on the bandwagon), but he seems to have been responsive to the fact that ideals of masculinity were undergoing change. Indeed, his 1992 film *Unforgiven* marks the dramatic shift in his own persona—both public and on-screen. Although Eastwood had already moved behind the camera as a producer (he established the Malpaso production company in 1968) and as a director (beginning with *Play Misty for Me* in 1971), it is *Unforgiven* that raised him from the status of a star who dabbled in directing (to date, he has directed more than thirty feature films) to one who was a serious and accomplished artist. The film also marked the shift in his on-screen image from unstoppable action hero to a fallible and vulnerable man. Whereas Dirty Harry is perceived as the type who would shoot first and think later, Will Munny in *Unforgiven*, as Paul Baumann suggests, promoted Eastwood to "the status of the thinking man's gunslinger" (2000, 29). Chris Holmlund (2002, 148) suggests that Eastwood's career can be seen as a series of shifts in his persona from his days as the young vigilante (up to 1973), to middle age (up to 1985), to old age (1985 onward). I would argue, however, that while Eastwood himself may have been middle aged in his films of the mid-1970s to mid-1980s, the characters he played, and the narratives in which they starred, differed little from those of his first phase: those characters defied the label of older man by pursuing criminals and seeing "justice" served by the same means as those of his younger days—through violence, superior firepower, and unemotional exaction—and with little address to the issues or fears of aging or lack of competence. Dirty Harry does not blame an aging body or loss of self-confidence in his abilities (both qualities associated with advancing age) as the reason for his inability to exact justice; instead, it is the restriction imposed on law enforcers by liberal lawmakers (the institution of the Miranda rights in *Dirty Harry*) or the corruption that exists within America's law enforcement and justice systems (the law-defying lieutenant in *Magnum Force*) that impedes Harry from doing his job readily. Although Holmlund suggests that Eastwood's last (as of yet) phase of films—those that present him as "visibly old"—began in 1985, I would argue that it was not until *Unforgiven* that Eastwood's films offered narratives and themes related to advancing age or that Eastwood highlighted his aging body.

■ From a Man's Man to a "Ladies' Man"

Unforgiven is a revisionist Western in that it dispels the myths that classic Westerns perpetuated. The film begins a decade after a classic Western would have ended, with the tough hero hanging up his gun to settle down. Will Munny was a thief and a killer until his beloved Claudia tamed him and made him a family man before she died of smallpox; he returns to a life by the gun because—or so he says—he wishes to provide a better future for his two children than he can as a failing farmer and because the crime he will avenge was committed against a woman. These motivations define him as a humanized hero as opposed to a coldhearted criminal who kills for selfish reasons (as some of Eastwood's previous characters have been accused of being). Having said that, I would point out, however, that the film suggests that these are merely excuses and that Munny misses his old (exciting, masculine, violent) life.

As Richard Combs notes, Eastwood, the director, has a self-awareness of Eastwood, the actor, that he uses to an advantage; director-Eastwood has noted that actor-Eastwood's laconic persona from his spaghetti Western days has become a piece of film grammar, and his more recent roles are "preceded by all the men with no name, high plains drifters, and pale riders" (1996, 30). But that grammar is also changing. The types of camera shots most commonly associated with Eastwood as Dirty Harry include the extreme low-angle shot when he dispatches the bad guy and the silhouette shot when he is the hero arriving just in time. By the 1990s, however, director-Eastwood framed actor-Eastwood's body differently. This shift is most evident in *The Bridges of Madison County* (1995), based on the best-selling novel by Robert James Waller about a romance between a farmer's wife, Francesca (Meryl Streep), and a photographer, Robert Kincaid (Eastwood). The camera rarely displays Francesca as an erotic object for Robert to look at but, instead, rcpeatedly offers Francesca's point of view of Robert. While her naked body is hidden from the camera when she opens her dress to feel the night breeze, Robert/Eastwood's is put on display for her gaze as she watches him, stripped to his waist and washing at the pump in the yard. Thus, director-Eastwood shoots actor-Eastwood in ways more traditionally associated with filming the female body, making him stand still as the object of the camera and the female gaze—something that the Man with No Name or Dirty Harry would never have been "subjected" to. Similarly, in *Unforgiven*, there is a reversal of *Dirty Harry*'s heroic low angles; instead, our introduction to Munny/Eastwood is of him falling facedown in the muck as he chases a hog through its pen.

Indeed, the first third of the film sets up Munny as failing in his attempt to reclaim his past life, in effect, deconstructing Eastwood's own past as a mythic Western hero. As Munny prepares for his quest, he first practices shooting his old gun, which he has obviously not fired in years: he fails several times to hit a can. His handling of a gun is not the only skill he seems to have lost over the years; when he attempts to mount his horse, Munny trips, stumbles, and falls to the ground as he chases his horse in a circle with one foot in the stirrup. The horse defies mounting a second time when Munny stops to collect his old partner, Ned (Morgan Freeman), and Munny again falls. When Ned and Munny finally catch up to their new partner, the Kid (Jaimz Woolvett) mistakes them for enemies and fires on them. Both Ned and Munny leap/fall from their horses to take cover when Ned notices that Munny's face is bleeding. Ned is worried that Munny has been shot, but Munny answers somewhat sheepishly, "No, I bumped my head falling off my horse." Soon after their arrival in the town of Big Whiskey, Munny is beaten almost to death by the town's sheriff, Little Bill (Gene Hackman), and must be nursed back to health. He is also a kind man, respecting the prostitutes of the town, despite their marginalized social positions, and assisting them in their desire for justice when one of them is attacked by a knife-wielding john (notably, for giggling at the size of his diminutive manhood).

Initially, Eastwood presents Munny as not only out of practice but incapable of fulfilling the role of his younger days, but by the end of the film, Munny defies his failing body, recovers his previous skills, and exacts retribution against those who defy human justice—including the town's lawman. Munny represents a shift in Eastwood's career from playing the man's man—Dirty Harry—to playing a woman's man or even the new "sensitive man." This shift in Eastwood's on-screen persona is perhaps more obvious with his performance in the romantic drama *The Bridges of Madison County*. Robert is a traditional man's man in that he is independent and unfettered: He is a divorced photographer and journalist, and his travels around the world include visiting his many friends (including "women friends"). But he is very much the new sensitive man of the 1990s to Francesca—despite the story of their romance being set in 1965: He picks flowers for her, he offers to help her prepare and clean up after dinner, he does not slam the kitchen door as Francesca's son and husband always do, and he asks her about her dreams and desires. On their last day together, Francesca is angered at the thought that she has become just another of Robert's "women friends" and demands to know what "the routine" is now that he is leaving. Robert surprises her by telling her that she is much more to him than that and wants her to run away with him; however, Francesca feels obligated to stay behind for the sake of her children and husband. Even though Robert in *Bridges* is Eastwood's most obvious departure from his established roles, the character does not go entirely against type. As Streep discovered during filming, "Eastwood wouldn't cry for the camera because he said, 'People don't want to see me cry'" (Boedeker 2000, 19). However, it is not only in romantic dramas that Eastwood's heroes have become more sensitive, and my interest here is in how Eastwood altered his more "typical" action roles to deal with his age and shifting ideals of masculinity in traditionally male-centered genre films.

■ A Crack in the Mask/(qu)erade

Kathleen Murphy describes Eastwood's Man with No Name as "a masculine presence predicated on the strictest conservation of energy and emotion" (1996, 17). That conservation leads to an almost emotionless image: with nothing more than a squint and coldhearted stare half hidden in the shadow of his wide-brimmed hat, Eastwood's face has been described as "a mask" or "a face of marble" by critics. As Butler (1990, 47) argues, gender is performed, and that performance can be a false one—a masquerade—whereby individuals pretend to adhere to their gender while simultaneously being "other." In the 1980s, on-screen portrayals of the action hero negotiated changing social roles for men—mainly through disavowing them: with a focus on their muscled bodies as their most effective weapons to combat criminals, enacting a masquerade of hypermasculinity.[4] As Dirty Harry, Eastwood offered a similar masquerade of masculinity—although one that notably did not rely on his exposure of a muscled physique. Instead, Eastwood offered a different image of reassuring and empowered heroism through his composed carriage, his cool demeanor, his suit unruffled (although occasionally torn or stained), and his hardened face of marble. While in *Dirty Harry*, Eastwood's hero walks coolly through a seeming war zone, chewing a bite of hot dog as he slowly draws his .44 Magnum to dispatch the driver of a getaway car, in his films of the 1990s, his mask (or masquerade) started to crack.

While *Unforgiven* saw Eastwood literally fall down, *In the Line of Fire* (1993) similarly saw him struggle with the physicality of heroism. As Eastwood suggested in an interview regarding the film, "I'm playing vulnerability" (quoted in Spetalnick 1993). The Columbia Pictures Pressbook for the film explains, "It is also quite a reversal from the kinds of characters Eastwood has made a reputation portraying, most of whom were expert at delivering their share of bullets rather than receiving them" (1993). As W. C. Levin suggests, despite findings to the contrary, older members of the population are still judged to be of lower competence, activity, intelligence, attractiveness, and health (in Bazzini et al. 1997). This assumption is certainly supported by representations of older men and women in popular culture. According to Richard and James Davis, in prime-time television, the elderly tend to be depicted as more stubborn, eccentric, and foolish than younger characters (in Bazzini et al. 1997). Rather than defying this stereotype, however, Eastwood plays into it. Eastwood's characters are defined by their stubbornness and eccentricity, and this becomes the means by which his characters succeed where younger, and assumed more capable, characters fail. Eastwood's hero in *In the Line of Fire* is physically less competent than his younger colleagues; however, his years of experience and his conviction in his hunches mean that, ultimately, his hero is triumphant. *In the Line of Fire* takes *Unforgiven*'s visual exploration of Munny as struggling to embody heroic masculinity and makes it a central topic of conversation among the characters of the film.

When he discovers a plot to assassinate the president of the United States and hoping to redeem himself for his failure to protect his previous assignment from assassination (JFK), Secret Service Agent Frank Horrigan (Eastwood) requests reassignment. Secret Service Director Sam Campagna (John Mahoney) responds incredulously, "After all these years? Frank . . . Christ! You're a dinosaur!" While Frank is assigned to the president's detail, he immediately confirms that he is a dinosaur: he struggles to keep up with the motorcade, sweating and wheezing as the other (younger) agents jog easily along. Afterward, passed out in a chair from exhaustion, Frank is awakened by paramedics who have been called in by the other agents for a cardiac arrest (a joke to humiliate Frank). And Frank is impaired not just physically but emotionally too: the fallout from Kennedy's assassination included Frank's descent into alcoholism and his wife and daughter leaving him. Certainly, his reputation within the service is as "a borderline burnout with questionable social skills." When Frank embarrasses the president at a rally by mistaking a balloon popping for a gun firing, Sam implores Frank to retire: "Face it Frank! You're too old for this shit." However, Frank is able to prove his masculinity and legitimacy as a hero when he saves the president from assassination—and, importantly, he does so because of his age and experience. He "knows things about people," and his ability to get inside the head of the assassin (John Malkovich) leads to Frank's anticipating his next move. Old age may be a deficiency in the physical aspects of Frank's duty; on the other hand, in terms of tracking, identifying, and outsmarting a highly trained assassin, it is the ultimate weapon.

■ Myths of Golden Years

Steve Neale in "Masculinity as Spectacle" describes the young Eastwood of 1960s Westerns as an example of how male heroes engage spectators' "narcissistic phantasies . . . of the 'more perfect, more complete, more powerful ideal ego'" (1993, 12). Today, it could be argued, Eastwood still offers fantasies of masculine potency—this time to those audiences who have grown up along with him. Western society is ageist, but Hollywood is even more restrictive in terms of valuing age. With a good percentage of Hollywood's audiences being old, Andrew Blaikie (1999, 96) asks, why are there no representations of old people except in stereotyped negative roles?[5] Blaikie (1999, 86) argues that our society's obsession with youth is a result of our consumer culture: our bodies and appearance have come to reflect our morality and character. Mirroring the attitude of society at large, the world of film associates youth with beauty and age with ugliness and, by association, youth with goodness and old age with evil. As Karen Stoddard explains, images of older women in the media are conspicuous by their absence: "Rather, the media extoll the virtues of youth and the desirability of maintaining a youthful image as a measure of feminine fulfilment" (1983, 5).

No longer, however, is it just women who are the targets of the cultural war against aging; today, men are also told to consume anti-wrinkle cream, hair dye, and plastic surgery as the solution to the "problem" of—and the arsenal in the war against—aging. Eastwood also recognizes the pressure on older men. In a 1993 interview, Eastwood was asked what he thought about leading men who "when they get to a certain age, have facial surgery." Eastwood replied,

> I think men are foolish to do that. If you start not looking like yourself, the audience sees you've done a little something. I see a lot of this—I meet people who I don't even recognize as who they used to be. There's a great fear of aging ungracefully. I don't have that fear. (quoted in Thompson 1993, 28)

And film critics, for the most part, have noted that Eastwood—unlike his actor-director contemporaries—has accepted his aging gracefully in terms of his ability as a director to control his own image. For example, Todd McCarthy comments, "In nearly every film he's made at least since *In the Line of Fire*, Eastwood, far from ignoring his own advancing years *à la* Woody Allen, has incorporated some sort of commentary on getting old into his characterization" (2002, 19).

Eastwood, born in 1930, is a senior citizen and still making movies at an age when it is assumed most people would be retired. In his 1995 speech, "Reflections on Retirement," leadership authority Warren Bennis commented on the etymology of the word *retirement* (from the French verb *tirer*—to withdraw or to take back). Bennis prefers the term *transitioning* to *retiring*—evoking a new phase of life rather than the end of it. When asked once in an interview "who were [his] heroes or whom [did he] most respect about the whole aging phenomenon," he named Winston Churchill, Bertrand Russell, and Clint Eastwood because they never thought about retiring (1995, 752). In 2003, Eastwood joked, "I've thought about retiring for 30 years" (in Howell 2006, 20). For contemporary audiences living in a society in which old age is undervalued and associated with failing faculties, disease, and death, Eastwood, as Holmlund notes, presents "an encouragingly active, optimistic model of aging" (2002, 145). In *In the Line of Fire*, Lilly (Rene Russo) says to Frank when asked about her role as a female agent, "If I'm here to court the feminist vote, what demographics do you represent?" Frank replies, "Let's see. . . . White, piano-playing heterosexuals over the age of sixty. And there ain't a whole lot of us, but we do have a powerful army."

Certainly, Eastwood seems to be consciously aiming his films at an older demographic, as he explained in an interview:

> In my early days I did a lot of adventure stories, but at this stage of my life I want to make some sort of a statement, so for the last 15 years or so I've tried to make films for adult audiences hoping young people will come along too and appreciate the thoughts expressed in them. (quoted in Hiscock 2008, E4)

Although Scott Feschuk suggests that Eastwood's 2000 *Space Cowboys*, about four retired astronaut-hopefuls, was the "only film of summer 2000 to target the Queen Mum's demographic" (2000, B3), the success of the film would suggest that it—and Eastwood—had a broader appeal.[6] A. O. Scott argues that *Space Cowboys* was popular because, "without succumbing to bitterness or nostalgia or overstating the case for one generation's virtues, [Eastwood] and his cohorts mount a vigorous and funny defense of maturity" (2000, B16). Comedy, it would seem, is the politically correct way to explore social issues such as aging.

In *Space Cowboys*, Frank Corvin (Eastwood, seventy at the time of the film's release) collects together his old flying team—Hawk (Tommy Lee Jones, fifty-four), Jerry (Donald Sutherland, sixty-five), and Tank (James Garner, seventy-two)—for an adventure into space. But first they need to prove that they are physically competent to do so, and much fun is made of their age in the film as they struggle to run the required number of laps, as they cheat to pass their eye exam by memorizing the eye chart (although proving their excellent mental facilities in doing so), and as they strip for their physical exam and the audience is exposed to each "asymmetrical sagging ass." It is in space that the four men then prove their worth: They destroy the satellite that they discover houses nuclear missiles (whereas a younger colleague blindly follows her superior's erroneous orders and is killed in the process); Hawk sacrifices his life in order to save the mission, his teammates, and potentially the United States by sending the satellite off into space before it detonates; and Frank lands the damaged shuttle safely by using the manual skills he honed as a pilot in the 1950s, saving the lives of the remaining team members. Their successful completion of the mission is the result of their advanced experience in flying and related knowledge—in other words, because of their age. Last, but not least, the men also prove their sexual potency through their attractiveness to younger women: Jerry proves his physical prowess by having a girlfriend young enough to be mistaken for his daughter (Georgia Emelin, thirty-one at the time) and then later seducing a NASA medical examiner (Blair Brown, fifty-four); Frank, by seducing his wife (Barbara Babcock, sixty-three) in their garage when he accidentally locks them inside; and Hawk, by seducing NASA engineer Sara Holland (Marcia Gay Harden, forty). *Space Cowboys* could be accused of trivializing issues of age because it is a comedy and, at the same time, selling fantasies of an aging manhood. However, as Richard Corliss of *Time* magazine notes, "To be old in America is almost as uncool as being poor. That makes the recent films of Clint Eastwood a bracing, useful social corrective" (2000, 46). For that reason, whether or not they are the butt of a joke, the aging heroes of *Space Cowboys* do something that very few mainstream films do—give voice and space to older men and make age a central issue.

■ Acting His Age

The only film of Eastwood's in the last decade or so that critics have in general disliked is *True Crime* (1999). The main reason seems to be the fact that the hero, reporter Steve Everett (Eastwood), is the most cocky of Eastwood's recent heroes; indeed, critics—and audiences—seem to prefer an aging Eastwood only when he acknowledges that he is aging.[7] It appears that audiences like Eastwood as the underdog *because* he is old. Ironically,

Everett is failing and flawed: He is a recently recovered alcoholic; his career was floundering after he was fired from the *New York Tribune*; his career is now in trouble as his new boss knows that Everett is sleeping with his wife; Everett's wife is on the verge of kicking him out because she knows that he is sleeping around; and he has twenty-four hours to save an innocent man from the death chamber. Everett is struggling, but he is not vulnerable in the way that Will Munny (*Unforgiven*), Frank Corrigan (*In the Line of Fire*), and Frank Corvin (*Space Cowboys*) were. Everett—and, reviewers argue, Eastwood—denies that he is too old to be playing the womanizer. For example, Cameron Bailey suggests,

> You don't have to sit in the front row to notice that Clint Eastwood is old. Being old is now the subject of his movies. . . . And yet he consistently puts himself in stock situations that read virile young buck. He kicks up dust at the office. He neglects his infant daughter. He parades around bare-chested after a tryst with his boss's wife. This from a man with a neck like wet velvet. . . . But then, *True Crime* is fantasy. It's a fairy tale for alpha men. (1999, 63)

Reviewers complain that it is specifically Eastwood's age that makes *True Crime* unbelievable or unwatchable;[8] however, little such criticism arises regarding his other similar films, including *Absolute Power* (1997) and *Blood Work* (2002). Therefore, I would argue that it is less an issue of Eastwood's age and more the fact that he is playing a womanizer *at that age*.

One scene that incensed critics is the one in which Everett walks around wearing only a towel after sleeping with his boss's wife. He then reclines on the bed and nibbles on Patricia's thigh as he tells her the reason why he was fired from his last paper: he was caught seducing the owner's daughter, who, it turned out, was underage. In his defense, Everett insists, "She looked eighteen to me." She chastises him, "Bad man! First the owner's daughter, now the editor's wife!" The scene, however, that seemed to enrage critics more is an early scene at Everett's local bar in which he tries to seduce a fellow reporter. While critics despised Everett for his inflated sense of his own masculinity, hitting on a gorgeous twenty-three-year-old woman at a bar, they seemed to despise Eastwood more by having that gorgeous young woman receptive to Everett's advances.[9] As Patricia Hluchy says, unlike *Unforgiven*, *True Crime* is "unforgivable":

> Clint Eastwood must be going through his late-life crisis. How else are we
> to explain this 68-year-old actor and director casting himself as a swag-
> gering newspaper reporter and unrepentant womanizer, the kind of guy
> who goes on about his unfailing "nose" for a story while lunging at a
> 23-year-old damsel? And, shame on Clint, he actually has her respond-
> ing. (1999, 73)

Of course, the plot points of womanizing and infidelity come from Andrew
Clavan's novel on which the film is based—the protagonist of which is in
his mid-thirties. Eastwood's true crime, it would seem, was casting himself
in the role of Everett and not adapting the source material to something
more age appropriate. In other words, here Eastwood's aging hero is not
acting his age.

Although reviewers noted the age difference between seventy-
something Eastwood and his forty-something romantic interest (Wanda
de Jesus) in *Blood Work* (2002), none criticized the film as harshly as they
had *True Crime*. What was it about *Blood Work* that worked when *True
Crime* did not? Eastwood's films that seem most appealing to critics and
audiences are those in which he abandons his Dirty Harry associations
and presents himself as struggling and failing to be heroic—in other words,
when he acts his age in accordance with society's assumptions regarding
aging. For Eastwood's characters to be convincing as older, they must be
presented as physically flawed (i.e., the victims of aging) and emotionally flawed, failing to have good relationships with daughters and lovers
(i.e., the victim of his own machismo), especially as they are as mentally
capable as, and often superior to, younger characters in the film. In other
words, for audiences and critics to accept Eastwood in the leading role
(especially a romantic role), he must be, as Holmlund suggests, "visibly
old"—and of all of Eastwood's recent films, *Blood Work* is the one that calls
the most attention to the frailty of the hero/actor's body.

Blood Work begins with Terry McCaleb (Eastwood) chasing a serial
killer, nicknamed "the Code Killer," down an alley and over a wall, but
Terry has a heart attack and collapses against a fence as the killer gets away.
A couple of years later, we see Terry post–heart transplant, but his recovery
is placed in jeopardy, however, when the sister of his heart donor, Graciella
(de Jesus), wants Terry to investigate her sister's death. Doing so puts Terry
back on the trail of the Code Killer but also in the path of physical danger:

his aging body cannot take the stress of the investigation and may reject his new heart. There are a few key scenes in the film that display Terry's naked torso and the long, dark scar down the middle of his body from the transplant (including when Graciella seduces him by kissing the scar). His damaged body elicits sympathy: the audience sees that he is not so tough and needs the nurturing of a strong woman. His ill health, however, does not stop Terry from successfully cracking the case and dispatching the killer as well as winning the heart of a younger lover.

■ The "Eastwood Model"

Eastwood's model for reinventing himself has consisted of three key revisions: First, he has highlighted his age, encouraging audiences to read his physical vulnerability as an emotional one; second, he has established himself as an award-winning director; and, third, rather than focus on romantic relationships in his films, Eastwood has increasingly focused on the hero's problematic relationship with a child or substitute child. In other films, Eastwood has avoided the controversy of showing his heroes successfully seduce younger women by displacing the hero's role of lover to that of (substitute) father, as in films such as *Absolute Power* (1997), *Million Dollar Baby* (2004), and *Gran Torino* (2008). Beard argues that "Eastwood is concerned with 'the Good Father'—an idealization of the paternal and patriarchal role—and its contrasts with the weaker and more limited fatherhood or 'ordinary' or 'realistic' fathers" and that, mainly in his later films, the two functions—the Good Father and the Bad Father—exist in one character "to produce a doubled, self-contradictory, or deconstructed father-figure" (2000, 70–71). In *Absolute Power*, Luther Whitney (Eastwood) struggles to convince his daughter, Kate (Laura Linney), that they can have a meaningful relationship. While committing a robbery, Luther witnesses the president of the United States (Gene Hackman) beat, and his Secret Service men kill, the wife of the president's close friend; the president's chief of staff (Judy Davis) then attempts to pin the crime on Luther. At first, Kate is resistant to even speak to her father and does not necessarily believe him when he says that he is innocent. This changes when Kate visits her father's home, which she has never seen; inside are dozens of photos of her life from when she was a child, to her graduation, to the first case she tried. She had always resented her father because he was absent (always in trouble with the law) and assumed that he did not care about her; however, she comes to realize that he was, in his own way, always there for her. The film happily concludes with Luther clearing his name and seeing justice somewhat done (the president gets his comeuppance) but also having a new future with his daughter. Like *True Crime*, *Absolute Power* implies that its hero is successful at his career because he is a tough man but that his devotion to his work makes him a bad father. The films also suggest, however, that bad fathers desire to become good fathers when they get older and become less competent at their jobs; it is with age and the realization that their career cannot be their only focus in life that they mourn the loss of good relationships with their children.

Similarly, in *Million Dollar Baby*, hardened gym owner Frankie Dunn (Eastwood) reluctantly tries his hand at training a female boxer, Maggie (Hilary Swank). As his friend Scrap (Morgan Freeman) notes in voice-over, "Sometimes the best way to deliver a punch is step back. . . . But step back too far, you ain't fightin' at all." Indeed, Frankie seems to have stepped back too far; he holds his fighters back when they are ready to move forward, and this is why his star male fighter leaves him. Frankie holds back his students not because he does not want to see them succeed but because he made a mistake (as far as he is concerned) in the past: he feels responsible for Scrap losing his sight in one eye from letting him go back into the ring. The other failure that haunts Frankie is the loss of his daughter; he writes to her every week, but his letters are returned unopened. The mantra he teaches his students is "Protect yourself," and that is what he is trying to do—protect himself from getting hurt emotionally. However, Maggie opens up his heart again—first, by being a champion boxer and, second, by being a substitute daughter.

The film concludes with the revelation that Scrap's voice-over is, in fact, a letter he is writing to Frankie's daughter after Maggie dies and Frankie disappears. Scrap says, "I thought you should know what kind of a man your father was." Through her successes and her frequent defiance of him, Maggie teaches the old dog new tricks: he becomes a good man and a good father. Frankie allows Maggie to move forward when his fear tells him to hold her back, and she becomes an unstoppable fighter; however, her big fight for the championship with a boxer who fights dirty results in Maggie's being paralyzed. She cannot bear to live as a quadriplegic and pleads with Frankie to assist her in dying—to do as her father once did to their injured dog. It is only when faced with this decision that Frankie (and Eastwood) for the first time weeps. Sitting in a church pew, Frankie confesses his dilemma with tears streaming down his face: "Now she wants to die, and I just want to keep her with me. . . . It's committing a sin doing it—by keeping her alive, I'm killing her." As Amy Taubin suggests, "Age has clenched Clint Eastwood's face tight as a fist, but he has never been more tender, vulnerable, and heartbroken than in *Million Dollar Baby*" (2005, 26). Eastwood was wrong when he told Streep during the making of *Bridges*, "People don't want to see me cry." It turns out that that is exactly what the world was waiting for him to do, and he was given an Oscar nomination for the effort. When visibly old and visibly vulnerable, Eastwood is a hero whom audiences are happy to see succeed.

And this is perhaps why *Gran Torino* is such an important film: it was initially rumored to be resurrecting Eastwood's most famous hero, Dirty Harry.[10] And there are superficial similarities between *Torino*'s Walt Kowalski and Dirty Harry, from their association with (now) classic cars (a Gran Torino and a Ford Mustang, respectively) to their tough-as-nails attitude and antisocial personalities; however, Kowalski is a decidedly different model of masculinity as the product of the post-9/11 decade. As Eastwood explained in an interview, "*Gran Torino* had a role that was my age and seemed tailored for me" (quoted in Hiscock 2008, E1). Dirty Harry was a tough, independent, violent vigilante for the 1970s when President Nixon's hard-line politics on crime and the widespread loss of confidence in law enforcement were dominant in American society. Kowalski is similarly a vigilante who takes the law into his own hands when the law is proved ineffectual in the twenty-first-century fight against urban gangs. Telling of the post-9/11 era is that, while Harry would have broken the law—vigilante style—to blow away America's "yellow peril" invaders, *Gran Torino* surprises its audience by having Kowalski *use* the law to bring the criminals to justice—in effect, sacrificing himself to protect America's new multicultural generation. As reviewer Lisa Schwarzbaum suggests, "A different Eastwood in a different movie might have rasped 'Do you feel lucky?'" (2008, 40). While Kowalski does warn the gangbangers, "Ever notice how you come across somebody once in a while that you shouldn't have fucked with? That's me," ultimately his most telling line is "I finish things." Eastwood confirms that, in the twenty-first century, there is little room for outmoded heroes—even his own.

■ A Gran(d) Vintage

Eastwood explored the failure of excessive masculinity in his films of previous decades, but some of these attempts—such as 1971's *The Beguiled*—were better received than others—such as 1984's *Tightrope* (Schickel 1996).[11] However, it was not until the 1990s that Eastwood carved out a whole new phase of his career by portraying failing heroes through his own aging masculinity. It is Eastwood's aging body that has allowed his persona to coincide with his goals as a director, with his older image—and the vulnerability it implies—affording him new possibilities in terms of roles and themes to explore. After all, *In the Line of Fire* merely rehashes many action genre tropes—including the game of cat and mouse between the hero and villain, a hero whose abilities are doubted by his superiors, and a spectacular shoot-out as the climax; however, whereas Dirty Harry in *The Dead Pool* seemed to have lost resonance with the contemporaneous audience, struggling Frank Horrigan rang true. Allowing the face of marble to crack and reveal the emotions that Dirty Harry never demonstrated (and whose cold squint suggested did not exist), Eastwood, in his films of the last two decades, has offered audiences fantasies of old age in which the hero is presented initially as failing but eventually as valued. Through his aging appearance, Eastwood has tempered his past as a violent vigilante and may portray his characters as more mellow, restrained, and fragile.

Indeed, it would seem that the industry has recognized the success of the "Eastwood Model" with its recent backing of some other aging action stars and their 1980s heroes: from Bruce Willis in *Live Free or Die Hard* (2007) to Sylvester Stallone in *Rocky Balboa* (2006) and *Rambo* (2007) and Harrison Ford in *Indiana Jones and the Kingdom of the Crystal Skull* (2008).[12] While these films offer the return of characters popular twenty years ago, they do not necessarily bring the themes of the 1980s along with them. Following the example set by Eastwood over the past two decades, these films explore the problems that arise when the will is strong but the flesh not so much, when fathers have grown apart from their children, and when lone heroes can no longer fight evil on their own. Stallone has followed Eastwood one step further by also directing his latest films.[13]

Holmlund argues that "Clint has to date successfully managed to stay on the edge of the chasm dividing youth from old age" (2002, 148); however, I think that it is more a case of Eastwood choosing not only to accept his aging body but to exploit it as a means by which to remain relevant in the face of changing social expectations of masculinity. Eastwood's new image may be as much a masquerade as his original one; however, his shifting image reveals something about us and our changing social attitudes toward masculinity and—in Eastwood's case—age. As Eastwood said about his recent film *Flags of Our Fathers* (2006), "I think I've matured—that's a way of saying 'aging'—I've reached out to different sides of different stories" (quoted in King 2006, D1). Eastwood has managed to survive Hollywood by reinventing himself with his changing body and face to embody contemporary expectations of heroic masculinity. A good vintage or damaged goods? Clint Eastwood, as a senior citizen, is both—or the former *because of* the latter. Precisely because he has acted his age, Eastwood has transformed his image from a man's man to a woman's man—from tough guy to good father, from loner to lover—through highlighting his aging body.

▪ Notes

1. *Dirty Harry* earned $35.9 million at the box office; *Magnum Force*, $39.7 million; *The Enforcer*, $46.2 million; *Sudden Impact*, $67.6 million; and *The Dead Pool*, $37.9 million. Although *The Dead Pool*'s earnings seem in keeping with the performances of the previous films in the series, $37.9 million was not necessarily a strong performance in 1988 (as opposed to *Dirty Harry*'s similar performance in 1971). In fact, *Die Hard* (1988), starring Bruce Willis as a similar kind of cop action hero, earned $83 million the same year. See http://www.boxofficemojo.com and http://www.imdb.com.

2. For further discussion of the shift in 1990s film to sensitive heroes, see Gates 2006; Jeffords 1993a, 1993b; Pfeil 1995.

3. The year 1991 saw the release of films such as *City Slickers*, *Regarding Henry*, *The Doctor*, and *The Fisher King*, which all offer sensitive heroes.

4. Again note Gibson's role in *Lethal Weapon* and Willis's in *Die Hard*, which present the heroes as initially troubled but eventually triumphant. Their emotional vulnerability is disguised and transformed into heroic action, and their defeat of the villains reaffirms their masculine potency to their colleagues, themselves, and, in Willis's case, his wife.

5. The U.S. government estimated that 13.1 percent of the U.S. population was sixty-five or older in 2011 (https://www.cia.gov/library/publications/the-world-factbook/geos/us.html) and that, by 2050, people sixty-five and over will make up 21 percent of the U.S. population (http://usgovinfo.about.com/od/censusandstatistics/a/olderstats.htm).

6. Many reviewers were pleased to see *Space Cowboys* do well with audiences and suggested that it was a call to Hollywood to value aging stars *and* older audiences. For example, see Eller 2000 and Graham 2000.

7. *Unforgiven* earned $101.16 million and ranked eleventh as a top box-office earner for 1992; *In the Line of Fire* earned $102.31 million and ranked seventh for 1993; *The Bridges of Madison County* earned $71.52 million and ranked nineteenth for 1995; *Absolute Power* earned $50 million and was thirty-eighth for 1997; *True Crime* earned $16.64 million and ranked ninety-third for 1999; *Space Cowboys* earned $90.46 million and ranked twenty-fifth for 2000. See http://www.boxofficemojo.com.

8. See Bailey 1999; Cole 1999; Groen 1999; and Pevere 1999.

9. Although reviewers identified the character as twenty-three years old, Mary McCormack, who plays the reporter, was thirty years old at the time of the film's release.

Also, see Stein 1998 for an extensive list of older male stars and the ages of their youthful love interests over the course of their careers.

10. See Stephenson 2008.

11. Beard argues that Eastwood's persona was first constructed in a "deliberately exaggerated and 'impossible' way" and later appeared "in especially self-conscious, incongruous, or unexpected forms and contexts, commenting upon its essential self through exaggeration, ironization, or contradiction of existing traits" (2000, 2). While I agree with Beard that there is a self-consciousness and often self-parody in Eastwood's embodiment of his own persona starting with some of his films in the 1970s, what audiences and critics seem to take from (or at least recall in retrospect about) his films is the iconographic Eastwood persona—not its critique.

12. Achenbach comments in his review of *Poseidon* (2006) that Kurt Russell is also an "Aging Stud in Trouble" or "a macho guy who's rumored to be past his prime" (2006, W15)—as are Bruce Willis in *16 Blocks* (2006), Harrison Ford in *Firewall* (2006), and Kevin Costner in *The Guardian* (2006)—and, of course, they all have the opportunity to prove that they are not. As Achenbach suggests, although these aging action stars do still get the odd leading role, "their movies are rarely hits. You see their films on airplanes and can't recall them being in the theatre" (2006, W15).

13. For more on Willis, Stallone, and Ford adopting the "Eastwood Model," see Gates 2010.

■ Bibliography

Achenbach, Joel. 2006. "Falling Star: He's Hanging On for Dear Life. Finally, a Hero You Can Relate To." *Washington Post*, October 8, W15.

Bailey, Cameron. 1999. "Clint Eastwood Rebels by Aging Obviously" [review of *True Crime*]. *NOW*, March 18–24: 63.

Baumann, Paul. 2000. "The Wisdom of the Aged" [review of *Space Cowboys*]. *Commonweal* 127, no. 15: 28–29.

Bazzini, Doris G., William D. McIntosh, Stephen M. Smith, Sabrina Cook, and Caleigh Harris. 1997. "The Aging Woman in Popular Film: Underrepresented, Unattractive, Unfriendly, and Unintelligent." *Sex Roles* 36, nos. 7/8: 531–43.

Beard, William. 2000. *Persistence of Double Vision: Essays on Clint Eastwood*. Edmonton: University of Alberta Press.

Bennis, Warren. 1995. "Reflections on Retirement." *Vital Speeches of the Day* 61, no. 24: 752.

Blaikie, Andrew. 1999. *Ageing and Popular Culture*. Cambridge: Cambridge University Press.

Boedeker, Hal. 2000. "PBS Profile Falls on Its Knees before the Great Eastwood" [review of PBS *American Masters*: "Clint Eastwood"]. *Orlando Sentinel*, September 27, http://articles.orlandosentinel.com/2000-09-27/lifestyle/0009270040_1_clint-eastwood-american-masters-curtis-hanson, accessed March 30, 2012.

Butler, Judith. 1990. *Gender Trouble: Feminism and the Subversion of Identity*. London: Routledge.

Cole, Stephen. 1999. "Thirty-Six Years Ago, He Would Have Been Believable" [review of *True Crime*]. *National Post*, March 19, B4.

Columbia Pictures Pressbook. 1993. *In the Line of Fire.*

Combs, Richard. 1996. "Old Ghosts: *The Bridges of Madison County.*" *Film Comment* 32, no. 3: 25–32.

Corliss, Richard. 2000. "*Space Cowboys*" [review of *Space Cowboys*]. *Time,* August 14: 46.

Dorval, Madison. 1992. "Back in the Saddle Again." *Marquee,* July 1: 20–24.

Eller, Claudia. 2000. "'Cowboys' Guns Down Age Myth." *Los Angeles Times,* August 25, 1.

Feschuk, Scott. 2000. "Geezer Pleasers from Over the Hill" [review of *Space Cowboys*]. *National Post,* August 3, B3.

Gates, Philippa. 2006. *Detecting Men: Masculinity and the Hollywood Detective Film.* Albany: State University of New York Press.

———. 2010. "Acting His Age? The Resurrection of the 80s Action Heroes and Their Aging Stars." *Quarterly Review of Film and Video* 27, no. 4: 276–89.

Graham, Renee. 2000. "Aging 'Cowboys' Give Youth a Run." *Boston Globe,* August 8, C1.

Groen, Rick. 1999. "True Crime Is True Punishment" [review of *True Crime*]. *Globe and Mail,* March 19, D1.

Hiscock, John. 2008. "Interview: Clint Eastwood." *Toronto Star,* December 14, E1, E4.

Hluchy, Patricia. 1999. "Unforgivable Eastwood" [review of *True Crime*]. *Maclean's,* March 29: 73.

Holmlund, Chris. 2002. *Impossible Bodies: Femininity and Masculinity at the Movies.* London: Routledge.

Howell, Peter. 2006. "Winner and Still Champ." *Movie Entertainment,* January: 18–20.

Jeffords, Susan. 1993a. "The Big Switch: Hollywood Masculinity in the Nineties." In *Film Theory Goes to the Movies,* ed. Jim Collins, Hilary Radner, and Ava Preacher Collins, 196–208. New York: Routledge.

———. 1993b. "Can Masculinity be Terminated?" In *Screening the Male: Exploring Masculinities in Hollywood Cinema,* ed. Steven Cohan and Ina Rae Hark, 245–62. London: Routledge.

King, Randall. 2006. "Shades of Grey" [review of *Flags of Our Fathers*]. *Winnipeg Free Press,* October 20, D1.

Levin, W. C. 1988. "Age Stereotyping: College Student Evaluations." *Research on Aging* 10: 134–48.

McCarthy, Todd. 2002. "Clint's Still Got Heart" [review of *Blood Work*]. *Variety,* August 5–11: 19, 27.

Modleski, Tania. 1991. *Feminism without Women: Culture and Criticism in a "Post-Feminist" Age.* New York: Routledge.

Murphy, Kathleen. 1996. "The Good, the Bad and the Ugly: Clint Eastwood as Romantic Hero." *Film Comment* 32, no. 3: 16–22.

Neale, Steve. 1993. "Masculinity as Spectacle: Reflections on Men and Mainstream Cinema." In *Screening the Male: Exploring Masculinities in Hollywood Cinema,* ed. Steven Cohan and Ina Rae Hark, 9–20. London: Routledge.

Pevere, Geoff. 1999. "Too Bad Eastwood Won't Act His Age." *Toronto Star,* March 19.

Pfeil, Fred. 1995. *White Guys: Studies in Postmodern Domination and Difference.* London: Verso.

Rutherford, Jonathan. 1988. "Who's That Man?" In *Male Order: Unwrapping Masculinity*, ed. Rowena Chapman and Jonathan Rutherford, 21–67. London: Lawrence and Wishart.

Schwarzbaum, Lisa. 2008. "*Gran Torino*" [review of *Gran Torino*]. *Entertainment Weekly* 1026 (December 19): 40.

Schickel, Richard. 1996. "Clint on the Back Nine." *Film Comment* 32, no. 3: 10–12.

Scott, A. O. 2000. "Voices of Experience, Rocketing to the Rescue" [review of *Space Cowboys*]. *New York Times*, August 4, B16.

Spetalnick, Matt. 1993. "He'll Cry (and He Wants Us To)" [review of *In the Line of Fire*]. *Globe and Mail*, July 7.

Stein, Ruthe. 1998. "Act Your Age! As Male Stars Get On in Years, Their Leading Ladies Remain Remarkably Youthful." *San Francisco Chronicle*, June 17, E1.

Stephenson, Hunter. 2008. "Clint Eastwood's *Gran Torino* Is *Dirty Harry* 6?!" March 19, http://www.slashfilm.com/2008/03/19/clint-eastwoods-gran-torino-is-dirty-harry-6/, accessed April 3, 2010.

Stoddard, Karen M. 1983. *Saints and Shrews: Women and Aging in American Popular Film.* Westport, Conn.: Greenwood Press.

Taubin, Amy. 2005. "Staying Power." *Film Comment* 41, no. 1: 26–29.

Thompson, Anne. 1993. "Eastwood's World" [interview]. *Entertainment Weekly* 200 (December 10): 22–32.

Wilkinson, Rupert. 1984. *American Tough: The Tough-Guy Tradition and the American Character.* Westport, Conn.: Greenwood Press.

■ Filmography

Absolute Power. 1997. Dir. Clint Eastwood. Perfs. Clint Eastwood, Gene Hackman, and Ed Harris. Castle Rock Entertainment and Columbia Pictures.

Blood Work. 2002. Dir. Clint Eastwood. Perfs. Clint Eastwood and Jeff Daniels. Malpaso Productions and Warner Bros.

The Bridges of Madison County. 1995. Dir. Clint Eastwood. Perfs. Clint Eastwood and Meryl Streep. Amblin Entertainment and Malpaso Productions.

Gran Torino. 2008. Dir. Clint Eastwood. Perfs. Clint Eastwood and Bee Vang. Malpaso Productions et al.

In the Line of Fire. 1993. Dir. Wolfgang Petersen. Perfs. Clint Eastwood, John Malkovich, and Rene Russo. Castle Rock Entertainment and Columbia Pictures.

Million Dollar Baby. 2004. Dir. Clint Eastwood. Perfs. Clint Eastwood, Hilary Swank, and Morgan Freeman. Warner Bros. and Malpaso Productions.

Space Cowboys. 2000. Dir. Clint Eastwood. Perfs. Clint Eastwood, Tommy Lee Jones, Donald Sutherland, and James Garner. Malpaso Productions and Warner Bros.

True Crime. 1999. Dir. Clint Eastwood. Perfs. Clint Eastwood and Isaiah Washington. Zanuck Co. and Malpaso Productions.

Unforgiven. 1992. Dir. Clint Eastwood. Perfs. Clint Eastwood, Gene Hackman, and Morgan Freeman. Malpaso Productions and Warner Bros.

Chapter 10

SPACE, PACE, AND SOUTHERN GENTILITY
IN *MIDNIGHT IN THE GARDEN OF GOOD AND EVIL*

Brad Klypchak

For the cinematic adaptation (1997) of John Berendt's novel *Midnight in the Garden of Good and Evil* (1994), Clint Eastwood's choice to shoot on location in Savannah, Georgia, opportunistically draws upon a prevailing sense of the historic South. Be it the Spanish architecture, the garden squares and their statuary, or the richness of contrast between the green foliage and the drooping Spanish moss, Eastwood's film sets a mood fit for engaging the narrative's representation of Southern gentility. By using outdoor settings and allowing directorial choices of long tracking shots and limited cuts to move languidly through the travelogue-esque beauty the city emanates, Eastwood eases the viewer into the leisurely pace and privileged serenity of the Southern social elite.

From this introductory basis, Eastwood establishes juxtapositions that offer textures contrary to the seemingly idyllic Southern gentility. As actions move to interiors, an underlying sense of threat becomes evident as characters such as Jim Williams revel in both the beauty and the sordidness of society life. Contrast in composition highlights the divide of the outward portrayal of gentility and its thin veneer as the museum-like Mercer House becomes symbolic of ritual displays where hospitality and status expectancies are performed by rote. Further enhancing the contrast, Eastwood's treatments of seedier elements of Savannah including Williams's penchant for voodoo and the city's local drag circuit offer new facets to what otherwise might be perceived as Savannah's Southern charm. As a cumulative result, Eastwood's direction takes the Berendt novel and exemplifies the complexities represented by characters like Williams through manipulating space and pace. These choices invite the viewer to consider Southern gentility as well placed in the titular garden itself. Thus,

Eastwood's direction illustrates not only elements of what Sheldon Hackney terms the "molting South" but also the "double or bipolar identity" the contemporary South has come to represent (2004, 72, 65).

■ *Midnight in the Garden of Good and Evil*: A Brief Synopsis

Midnight opens with New York writer John Kelso (John Cusack) arriving in Savannah. Commissioned to cover a holiday party at the home of local antiques dealer Jim Williams (Kevin Spacey), Kelso is quickly introduced to the quirks of local culture, including the ubiquity of Savannah residents who already know Kelso, the curiosities of walking with imaginary and celebrity dogs, and distinct peculiarities such as attending an affluent dinner party hosted by a squatter and making a handshake agreement with the local lawyer, Sonny Seiler (Jack Thompson).

The night of the party, Williams shows off his home, his popularity within the community (despite being "nouveau riche"), and a hint of a sordid streak exemplified by his enthusiasm for the "deliciously evil" dagger used to castrate and murder Rasputin. Kelso leaves only to return once awakened by bustling police activity at Williams's home. There, he learns that Williams shot and killed Billy Hanson (Jude Law), an employee and lover of Williams. Claiming self-defense, Williams enlists Seiler, Kelso, and local voodoo priestess Minerva (Irma P. Hall) in helping substantiate his position, be it in terms of law or spirit.

Kelso's investigation further extends connections to aspects of local culture wherein class, race, and gender issues begin to emerge. As the trial continues, Kelso becomes disillusioned when Williams foregoes truth to capitalize on favorable legal technicalities. Nonetheless, Kelso becomes more attracted to life in Savannah, particularly after developing a romantic relationship with local songstress/florist Mandy (Alison Eastwood) and a friendship with drag queen Lady Chablis (played by herself). Cleared of all charges, Williams is released, yet soon thereafter he dies of a heart attack or, as claimed by Minerva, of Hanson's lingering vengeance and unwillingness to accept the court's decision. Kelso, now fully enamored by Savannah and its residents, becomes one of them as he relocates there permanently.

■ The Critical Response to *Midnight*

With kindness, one might term the critical response to *Midnight* as middling, if not mildly disappointing. Predictably, the old "the book was better than the movie" cliché resounded from the critics, perhaps best exemplified by Roger Ebert, who suggests that "something ineffable is lost just by turning on the camera: Nothing we see can be as amazing as what we've imagined" (1997). The ongoing comparison between Berendt's nonfiction account and its adaptation, John Lee Hancock's fictionalized screenplay, proved common. Kenneth Turan laments that the cinematic version lost the vibrancy of the original text, the experience of feeling as "lifelong local residents" having been turned into "tourists, on the outside looking in" (1997). Most harshly, Charles Taylor claims, "Eastwood's 'Garden' is one scrubby, sorry-ass patch of land, denuded of beauty and largely untended" (1997).

While some critics praised the performance of Kevin Spacey (for example, Guthmann 1997b; Howe 1997; McCarthy 1997; Savlov 1997; Sragow 1997) and noted how well the film communicated the pristine beauty of Savannah (Kempley 1997; Maslin 1997; Shulgasser 1997), many found the film flawed in both its artistic conception and its execution. Introducing Mandy as a romantic subplot (Ebert 1997; Maslin 1997; Shulgasser 1997; Turan 1997) or emphasizing a Perry Mason–esque courtroom drama (Ansen 1997; Freer 1997) weakens the structure, and with a running time of over 150 minutes, the film has been described as "meandering" (Turan 1997), with "sprawling, languid storytelling" (Freer 1997) that is "all exposition" (Sragow 1997) and "never reaches takeoff speed" (Ebert 1997).

■ *Midnight's* Directorial Choices as Southern Representation

In contrast to the critics, I offer that many of the seemingly extraneous moments of *Midnight* serve as consciously framing a sense of Savannah's own Southern representation. The very essence of languid meandering deemed problematic by the film's reviewers illustrates a pace unique to Savannah life as culturally connected to the ways of Southern culture, a quality that reflects Henri Lefebvre's claim that "each society offers up its own peculiar space, as it were, as an 'object' for analysis" (1991, 31). Through directorial choices, Eastwood, particularly in the opening third of the film, manipulates space and the actions taking place within those spaces, thereby fostering a mood representative of Southern gentility yet also highlighting the performative plasticity embedded within that very persona.

In the introduction to *Spaces of the Modern City*, Gyan Prakash claims that it is "in the space of the everyday that the familiar is defamiliarized, where the routine can be made strange." He adds that "through the construction and consumption of public culture, such as cinema," such an examination can take place (2008, 12). Similarly, Christine Geraghty notes, "In terms of production design, the building and dressing of the set and location is intended both to create an imagined world for the narrative and to provide ways to make it meaningful" (2008, 168). Following in the same vein as Geraghty in deconstructing film adaptations of historic New York, or as Rajani Mazumdar (2008) explores differing cinematic portrayals of Bombay, I engage Eastwood's *Midnight* and its depiction of Savannah's spaces, as both interiors and exteriors, as providing insight to where the familiar and the strange coexist.

From the film's opening sequences, Eastwood introduces the viewer to Savannah in systematic steps, each previewing an additional layer of the coming narrative while simultaneously creating a characterization of the town and its residents. Scenic slow-moving pans successively fade into the next, coastline to moss-laden trees to Bonaventure Cemetery to a circling of the iconic "Bird Girl" statue. The first definitive cut opens in Forsyth Park: a mounted policeman in the most casual of walks exiting the shot to reveal Minerva at rest on a park bench. Be it the subsequent conversation between Minerva and a squirrel, her recognition of the overhead noise of a jet plane, or, following a cut, the jet's actual landing, Eastwood lets each action proceed at its own leisure, resisting the choice to shorten the reaction shot of Minerva in favor of continuing the same, paced pans established earlier. In doing so, he captures the relative tempo of Savannah life—the preferred deliberate ease of motion versus a stressful, time-crunched rush.

With no cab readily available (a contrast to the expectations of urban haste), Kelso elects to take a double-decker bus tour to enter the city. Two specific landmark sites that never recur through the course of the film are specifically noted. The conductor's narration first highlights the historic Pirate House for "scalawags and ne'er-do-wells" dividing up "booty," inviting a connection to the wealthy in the current city. The tour continues to the second site, the Green Meldrim House, where Sherman resided during the Savannah portion of his infamous march to the sea. At this residence, the conductor notes, the exceptional hospitality of Savannahians "drowning [Sherman] in Chatham Artillery punch and fancy parties" was the only thing that saved the city from the devastation Sherman visited upon Atlanta.

Following a walk through Forsyth Park, Kelso arrives at Mercer House, where the famed Savannah hospitality is immediately displayed. Drink in hand, Kelso is escorted through the grounds to the carriage house, each shot highlighting the scenic beauty of the architecture and landscaping and indicating the significant wealth necessary to maintain such pristine conditions. A scene change finds the lone Kelso rushing to a meeting, his entrance immediately welcomed (and slowed) by the Savannahians with their practiced, formal manners. Here, Eastwood uses both the setting and the actions inside Sonny Seiler's law office to establish simultaneously the qualities of the Southern gentleman working in the New South.

After Eastwood slowly pans a series of pictures of Uga, the iconic bull-dog mascot of the University of Georgia, he has Seiler stiffly propose a con-fidentiality agreement to Kelso. Kelso's first questions regarding *Town and Country*'s stance on the matter are rebuked by Seiler—"wanting your word than some New York lawyer." Based on professional ethics, Kelso refuses, prompting Seiler to exclaim, "Damn, how come? It's just a little ol' party rider." As Seiler foregoes his lawyer persona for that of the good ol' boy, his demeanor changes to something far more comfortable in posture and tone. In effect, Seiler offers a gentleman's agreement of fairness between the two, as the chivalrous Southerner, taken at his word and gallantly represent-ing his honor. Seiler, as lawyer, must function within the newer order but inevitably prefers to retain the manner of traditional Southern practice and protocol.

For the Yankee to be afforded further access to Southern society, Kelso must pass Seiler's inspection, a form of "border crossing," which Susan Mains argues reinforces traditional Southern stereotypes as "conservative, locked in the past . . . [ensuring] insularity" (2004, 260). Though Kelso remains the outsider throughout the film and serves as the ongoing reminder of his Northern, white masculinity, he is still allowed entry largely because he shows a willingness to accommodate to Southern ways of etiquette and promises to be fair and to represent his own form of gentlemanly honor. This is what ultimately earns the formal introduction of the outsider to the Southern aristocrat Jim Williams.

In the last component of the expositional sequence, Eastwood intro-duces the Williams character and elements of his membership in the gen-tility. We first see his back, and then he makes a slow, clockwise turn toward camera. Mustached, smoking a cigar, and wearing a topcoat of Confederate gray, Williams immediately seeks refuge from his law office for a stroll out-side in Forsyth Park. The walk is shot primarily head on, with no change in distance from actors to camera, and, again, Eastwood allows the action to take place without haste. As the conversation progresses, Eastwood subtly reveals Williams's attention to manners through his speech and his tales of local history.

The arrival at Mercer House draws attention to two points of divergence between Williams and Kelso. A question regarding Johnny Mercer songs reveals a generation gap between the two men; Kelso answers by way of alluding to his mother. Immediately following this exchange, Williams shows his first inhospitable moment, denying Kelso's request to cover the "gentlemen-only" party: "I'm sorry, it's private. Reporters aren't allowed." By answering Williams's initial invitation to attend with business, Kelso's breach of etiquette excludes him from a gentleman's standing. No sooner does this moment pass than Williams returns to the role of cordial host and invites Kelso to see his antique-restoration workshop.

Marie Liénard-Yeterian draws a connection between Williams and the Southern gothic of Flannery O'Connor, in that good manners serve as "a condition of survival" (2009, 46). To Liénard-Yeterian, the Savannahians Kelso encounters represent the grotesque in such a way as to expose the underlying tensions within the South. I apply this notion to the ways in which social etiquette becomes a means of avoiding confrontation. Throughout the film, proper manners serve as a ritualized script to be adhered to. Deviating from the script produces social tensions wherein the presumptions of status hierarchies become exposed. Whether it is a resistance to Northern infringement (such as the reactions Kelso receives when being too forward in his vocational pursuits) or the denial of the existing prejudices in Savannahian society (particularly racial), Eastwood's *Midnight* illustrates those moments of protocol whereby protecting the status quo is preferred to addressing unpleasant realities directly. The grotesque becomes evident when looking beyond the surface's refinement, where the complexities of Southern identities hidden by etiquette begin to emerge.

■ Society Life in Savannah: Appearances and Deeper Issues

Kelso first encounters the interior of Mercer House at the public Christmas party, where he is greeted by the evening's caterer, an elderly black woman. Predictably, the house is immaculate, filled with antique finery recalling images of the antebellum past. Clad in a servant's uniform, the woman declares that "Mr. Williams insists on ol' country cooking for his parties," which prompts an association of her with a house slave. Kelso and the party's photographer, both tuxedoed white men, are markedly differentiated from the caterer by both race and dress. Thus, Kelso gains another form of border access, similar to that of privileged Southern aristocrats.

Eastwood captures the superficial performances of this privileged group with a series of shots following Williams as he makes his way through the crowd, stopping to say hello, kiss women's cheeks, and extend holiday wishes. There is no evidence of deeper connection or actual enjoyment on Williams's part. Upon entering, Kelso observes and then duplicates this ritual with his fellow party guests.

The first conversation of substance occurs when the flamboyant and flirtatious Serena Dawes arrives. Dawes, an elderly diva, initiates a discussion on handguns, prompting one of the guests to display his small pistol, "loaded, of course." Another guest unabashedly and unapologetically recounts her husband's suicide—"Everybody knew our marriage was a disaster. If I had so much touched that gun, they'd have charged me with murder." Kelso's reaction contrasts sharply. While the locals look on with bemused faces, suggesting that such an attitude is relatively commonplace, Kelso visibly squirms and cradles his mouth and chin in an attempt to hide his shocked discomfort. Eastwood further highlights the perversity of priorities as Dawes haphazardly waves her own pistol around while adamantly declaring her enthusiastic willingness to kill a man.

Eastwood's choice to frame Dawes in such atypical extroversion reveals her as being simultaneously within and apart from Southern gentility. In this case, Kelso gains further access behind the curtain of etiquette and discovers sordid secrets that fuel gossip circles but are rarely addressed openly. While Liénard-Yeterian interprets Dawes in this scene as representing the South's underlying potential for violence, taken in conjunction with a later scene, the sexual proclivities, obscured by the performance of Southern gentility, become exposed as well. Kelso's shocked reactions (so prevalent that many critics condemned Cusack and Eastwood) to the grotesque in these scenes draw explicit attention to such volatile moments.

Similar to his treatment of Dawes, Eastwood's treatment of Jim Williams emphasizes all the outer markings of Southern gentility in appearance and action but demonstrates Williams's difference as well. Williams's lavishly decorated mansion is always pristine, and the contrast of antique furniture with colorful pastel walls gives the feeling of a museum or showroom rather than a home. Throughout the party, a claustrophobic unease comes through the cinematography, particularly in comparison with the open qualities of the previous outdoor scenes; people and objects crowd each room, leaving little space to act outside the ritual of meeting and greeting. As each new trinket of Williams's collection is noted, his persona is similarly displayed. Williams revels in his membership in the social elite, as if to compensate for being both "nouveau riche" and gay. He delights in the power of determining his party's guest list, in moments where he holds knowledge others lack, or when he subtly, yet demonstratively, displays his wealth.

Through juxtaposing Williams with the youthful hustler Billy Hanson and the voodoo priestess Minerva, Eastwood establishes additional borders, distancing the perception of Southern gentility. Hanson, the archetypal, misspent youth, sneers, yells, and seeks to either fight or "get fucked up." Williams views Hanson condescendingly throughout the film, often citing Hanson's penchant for marijuana cigarettes as a primary reason for scorn and, in turn, revealing a moral supremacy. Though acknowledging "their special bond" during the murder trial, Williams never shows remorse or guilt over Hanson's death. Rather, one gets the impression that Hanson is another piece of Williams's collection of pretty things, all the more valuable because of his dangerous background yet readily disposable if necessary. The sense of privilege and possession highlights Williams's status.

Similarly, Williams respects and employs Minerva for her voodoo skills but hardly recognizes her when outside the social scene—to greet her while passing in Forsyth Park would violate status protocol. He is only willing to engage the stratum of the working-class black woman solely when his need demands, and even then, he contacts her under cover of night in the isolation of the black cemetery at the outskirts of town. Though this meeting includes Kelso also, Kelso is similarly subject to Williams's manipulations. Here again, the grotesque underside of Southern gentility becomes evident. The propriety and ritual of good manners and societal seclusion are postponed as the outsider, regardless of his position, proves useful. As Kelso shares greater connection to the gentility through race and cultural capital, he is afforded preferential access. Since Minerva is "the other," social distance is maintained. The journalist, though defined as Northerner, can be understood through the ways and means of the New South. The voodoo priestess, however, retains too close a connection to the Old South's constructs of segregation and racial hierarchy to merit the same begrudging acceptance as Kelso.

- Generational Difference as Representing
  Old and New Southern Identities

The contrast between the lingering remnants of the Old South and the New may also be considered through contrasting Jim Williams's elderly societal circuit with that of Mandy, Joe Odom, and their younger crowd. With Kelso as symbolic juxtaposition, each respective generation offers its version of the white Southerner, yet specific actions highlight what Marie Liénard-Yeterian terms "the bipolar nature of the South" (2009, 41). For Liénard-Yeterian, a Derridean supplementary occurs throughout *Midnight* wherein the South as a whole is caught among ongoing contradictions such as those of negotiating the historic and the present, be it of white and black, old money and new, or, as fittingly represented by Kelso, *town* and *country*. Both generations become better characterized by noting where overlaps and divides take place.

While there is still a degree of the chivalrous attention to present manners, the younger generation is far less committed to the formalized rituals that are strictly adhered to by the elders. As an example, the squatter party sequence opens as Mandy rouses Kelso from sleep, enters his room without knocking, and asks for ice—indifferent to any possible rejection. Despite such brusque forwardness, Mandy's charm also connotes a sense of comfort and casualness that befits the laissez-faire ethos of Savannah's spirit. Kelso must attend the party so that he can observe the city as it is, a welcoming and cavalier host appreciating life's pleasures and readily sharing them with all. At the Williams party, a formal menu is featured, and the evening's music is steeped in native son Johnny Mercer chestnuts while attendees stiffly congregate in small clusters.

In contrast, Odom's party resounds with youthful energy as smiles abound among the mingling revelers, no doubt aided by the Chatham Artillery punch: "three parts fruit, seven parts liquor, whatever's available on both accounts." Odom ignores the sheet music for "Piano Literature" in favor of the upbeat boogie-woogie blues of "Dumpster Love." Despite the more modern differences, elements of the past still resound: formal toasts, the recurrence of proper introductions, and the jazzy rendition of a Mercer tune that follows Odom's musical performance.

Relations across sex and race mark another form of generational distinction between Old and New Savannah. Among the younger generation, no one harbors any outward resistance or hesitance toward gayness. Two scenes, one at Odom's party and one occurring later as Kelso conducts his background interviews, specifically highlight the local hairdresser as a gay man welcomed into the youthful social circle. For the Williams crowd, Jim's homosexuality goes unspoken yet seems understood. In Sonny's words, "Proper folks don't discuss such things." However, Mandy notes of the older generation, "Jim's friends knew he was gay. Secretly, they congratulated themselves for being so cosmopolitan. But if they knew he was so open with his sexuality, they would have shunned him." Prominence in local standing, reflected by the clamor for invitations to Williams's parties, can occur provided there is no explicit display of his stigmatized sexuality. Once Hanson is killed, the story is far too prominent to ignore and infiltrates the social circle, thus needing explanation in order to preserve the status quo.

Eastwood illustrates this accounting with the stylized treatment of Kelso's attendance of the Married Women's Card Club. Underscored by a bright, yet reserved, waltz, the scene opens as women emerge from cars filling the entire block with doors opening in synchronization, as if ritually choreographed. The women, all white and all dressed in anachronistically prim dresses, congregate on the steps of a majestic home. Kelso, already an outsider by being the lone male, further transgresses by asking why no one has rung the doorbell. After a pair of ladies explain, "Oh heaven's no," "We have very strict rules. The door opens precisely at 4:00," Kelso redeems himself by returning to etiquette: "You all look lovely."

Inside, the hostess welcomes Kelso on behalf of Williams yet asks that Kelso not mention her role as intermediary to the ladies of the club. She explains: "Most of these ladies are trying to decide how they'll respond to this current predicament . . . you know, the incident." Two immediate impressions are communicated. First, etiquette protocol is used to distance the hostess from confronting the grotesque; the selective language of *predicament* and *incident* obfuscates the realities of a potential murder. Second, there is an underlying fear of being associated with the now-stigmatized Williams, not so much because of the shooting but because it was, as described by one of the cardplayers, "a *crime passionelle*, a lover's quarrel."

Shortly thereafter, an interview scene with Serena Dawes gives further evidence of the societal circuit's seedier side. She was previously established as Savannah's most flirtatious socialite, and Dawes's testimony declares the illicit sexual proclivities within Savannahian society; the death of Hanson, "an accomplished hustler . . . very much appreciated by men and women," is lamented as "a good time not yet had by all." Homosexuality exists and is surreptitiously known, if not practiced, within Savannahian society, yet it must remain unspoken, recalling Sonny's declaration that "proper folks don't discuss such things."

The culmination of sexual, generational, and societal differences becomes best exemplified in scenes featuring Lady Chablis. Transgendered, sexualized, and black, Chablis marks the separation, yet attraction, of those outside Southern gentility. Once again, Kelso, Mandy, and Joe Odom engage Chablis with no hesitation, readily accepting what the drag queen calls her "t" (truth). A spectacle commanding attention, Chablis's club routine plays to an audience made up of Kelso's generation, and when Chablis crashes the all-black cotillion, her provocative actions please the debutantes far more than their stunned, yet entranced, parents. Grimaced faces and shocked expressions from the jury box greet Chablis when she takes the stand, and the elderly white judge admonishes her stringently, raising questions of whether his reaction stems from judicial integrity or disgust at Chablis's persona.

Worth noting here is that Eastwood made the specific choice to cast Sonny Seiler, the Savannahian lawyer from Berendt's nonfiction account, in the role of the judge. At the time, Seiler was an untrained actor, and the emotion shown by Seiler in the scene suggests greater intention on Eastwood's part to emphasize racial and sexual dynamics. Seiler's volatile reactions to Chablis, the patriarchal white man silencing Chablis's voice and commanding her—"If I tell you to stop, you stop. If I tell you to sit, you sit"—illustrate the tensions separating the Old South from the New. The past archetypal divisions historically linger, yet the emergence of new, postmodern disruptions creates anxieties wherein the well-learned scripts of hierarchical social roles and manners fall short. For Luis Garcia Mainar, *Midnight* reflects its contextual climate as it "reflects the pressure placed . . . on traditional models . . . deeply revised at the hands of civil rights, feminist, homosexual and ecological movements" (2007, 32). Similarly, exchanges like those between the judge and Chablis extend to the complex negotiations between historical and contemporary versions of the South.

Along with portraying the generational divide between the Jim Williams socialites and the younger cohort of Mandy and Joe Odom, depicting issues of sexuality and race historically left unspoken, or constructing moments where past and present simultaneously meld yet fragment, Eastwood's treatment of Savannah is similarly divided. The city's beauty captures the attention, and its investment in the past envelopes all that one encounters. Yet Eastwood's outsider status, much like Kelso's in the narrative itself, affords perspective where local practices invite deeper examination, as do Savannahians and their ongoing negotiations of Southern identity.

■ *Midnight* and the Contemporary South

During the time of *Midnight*'s theatrical release, a feature article in *The Advocate* raised the question as to why the straight Eastwood would be the right choice to direct this film (Guthmann 1997a). Arguably, a parallel version of Eastwood's positioning of sexuality is exactly what allows *Midnight* to reflect notions of the contemporary South; Eastwood, the non-Southerner, becomes the border crosser of geographic culture as well. Much as Kelso, juxtaposed to the Savannahian locals, serves as a narrative device to cross the borders of Southern culture, Eastwood as director affords a similar distance for engaging the complexities of the South. As Sonny explains to Kelso in the film, "Saving face in light of unpleasant circumstances, it's the Savannah way"; Eastwood, as outsider, is free of the compulsions to save face here. Savannah can be celebrated for its beauty, its historic majesty, and its collection of colorful characters but also can be considered for what lies beneath.

Sheldon Hackney describes the South as "molting" (2004, 72), with the contradictory connections of Southern identity emerging from the antebellum pastoral as well as the technologically modern. The ongoing cycle of regeneration emphasizes the prior form so readily that the new developments can only be seen and understood through comparisons with that past. *Midnight*, set in the mid-1980s yet released in 1997, captures that sense of competing duality.

In the most direct example, Jim Williams complicates the previously established archetypes of the Southern gentleman. The chivalrous aristocrat of wealth, refined manners, and reserved composure fits the archetype, yet a gay man having earned his wealth over the previous decade also contrasts with it. At the same time, the generational distinctions (and similarities) between those of the gentility and those of Mandy and Joe's cohort account for elements of transition between Old and New Southern practices—When and where do the rituals of etiquette still apply? This film's presentation of Savannah, a metropolitan city dramatized through pastoral settings, indulges the past in a way that, as Susan Mains notes, "becomes symbolic of small town life in 'The South'" (2004, 261) yet also highlights the New South's infringing upon the stereotypical assumptions of that past; Mercer House is still an attraction, but so is the club where Chablis's drag show takes place.

Film critic Todd McCarthy calls *Midnight* "an outstanding lean film trapped in a fat film's body" (1997). Yet it is the "fatness" that Eastwood indulges that extends Savannah and its residents beyond the narrative. Whether it be in choices to include sequences like those of the black cotillion ball, the assorted walks around Forsyth Park, or the many seemingly innocuous conversations between Kelso and the locals, those potentially extraneous moments are exactly where the richness of space and pace illustrate Savannah, which, in turn, exemplifies the complexities embedded within the contemporary South and the conflicting tug between past and present.

■ Acknowledgments

Special thanks go to Erin Reeser for her translation help with the Liénard-Yeterian article.

■ Bibliography

Ansen, David. 1997. "*Midnight in the Garden of Good and Evil.*" *Newsweek*, December 1: 87.

Berardinelli, James. 1997. "*Midnight in the Garden of Good and Evil*: A Film Review." *Reel-Views.net*, http://www.reelviews.net/movies/m/midnight.html, accessed July 14, 2010.

Ebert, Roger. 1997. "*Midnight in the Garden of Good and Evil.*" *Chicago Sun Times*, November 21, http://rogerebert.suntimes.com/apps/pbcs.dll/article?AID=/19971121/REVIEWS/711210303/1023, accessed July 12, 2010.

Freer, Ian. 1997. "Review of *Midnight in the Garden of Good and Evil.*" *Empire Online*, http://www.empireonline.com/reviews/reviewcomplete.asp?FID=1856, accessed July 14, 2010.

García Mainar, Luis. 2007. "Authorship and Identity in the Cinema of Clint Eastwood." *Atlantis* 29, no. 2 (December): 27–37.

Geraghty, Christine. 2008. *Now a Major Motion Picture: Film Adaptations of Drama and Literature*. Lanham, Md.: Rowman and Littlefield.

Glieberman, Owen. 1997. "Movie Review: *Midnight in the Garden of Good and Evil.*" *Entertainment Weekly/EW.com*, November 28, http://www.ew.com/ew/article/0,,290436,00.html, accessed July 14, 2010.

Guthmann, Edward. 1997a. "In Like Clint." *Advocate*, November 11: 25–35.

———. 1997b. "Midnight Rambler: Eastwood Lets Stretched-Out Mystery Go Slack." *San Francisco Chronicle*, November 21, http://www.sfgate.com/cgi-bin/article.cgi?f=/c/a/1997/11/21/DD60702.DTL, accessed July 14, 2010.

Hackney, Sheldon. 2004. "The Contradictory South." *Southern Cultures*, Winter: 64–80.

Howe, Desson. 1997. "Too Much of a 'Good and Evil' Thing." *Washington Post*, November 21, http://www.washingtonpost.com/wp-srv/style/longterm/movies/videos/midnightinthegardenofgoodandevilhowe.htm, accessed July 14, 2010.

Kempley, Rita. 1997. "'Midnight in the Garden': Savannah When It Slumbers." *Washington Post*, November 21, http://www.washingtonpost.com/wp-srv/style/longterm/movies/videos/midnightinthegardenofgoodandevilkempley.htm, accessed July 14, 2010.

Lefebvre, Henri. 1991. *The Production of Space*. Trans. Donald Nicholson-Smith. Malden, Mass.: Blackwell.

Liénard-Yeterian, Marie. 2009. "*Midnight in the Garden of Good and Evil*: Parcours et détours du Sud." *Revue Française d'Études Américaines* 120, no. 2: 37–53.

Mains, Susan P. 2004. "Imagining the Border and Southern Spaces: Cinematic Explorations of Race and Gender." *GeoJournal* 59: 253–64.

Maslin, Janet. 1997. "*Midnight in the Garden of Good and Evil*: Conjuring Up Eccentricities amid the Oaks and Azaleas." *New York Times on the Web*, November 21, http://movies.nytimes.com/movie/review?res=9C06E2DD153BF932A15752C1A961958260, accessed July 14, 2010.

Mazumdar, Rajani. 2008. "Spectacle and Death in the City of Bombay Cinema." In *The Spaces of the Modern City: Imaginaries, Politics, and Everyday Life*, ed. Gyan Prakash and Kevin Michael Kruse, 401–34. Princeton: Princeton University Press.

McCarthy, Todd. 1997. "*Midnight in the Garden of Good and Evil* Review." *Variety*, November 21, http://www.variety.com/review/VE1117906595?categoryid=31&cs=1, accessed July 14, 2010.

Osborne, Lisa. 1997. "*Midnight in the Garden of Good and Evil*." *Box Office Magazine*, November 21, http://www.boxoffice.com/reviews/theatrical/2008-08-midnight-in-the-garden-of-good, accessed July 14, 2010.

Prakash, Gyan. 2008. "Introduction." In *The Spaces of the Modern City: Imaginaries, Politics, and Everyday Life*, ed. Gyan Prakash and Kevin Michael Kruse, 1–18. Princeton: Princeton University Press.

Savlov, Marc. 1997. "Film Review: *Midnight in the Garden of Good and Evil*." *Austin Chronicle*, November 21, http://www.austinchronicle.com/gyrobase/Calendar/Film?Film=oid%3a140840, accessed July 14, 2010.

Shulgasser, Barbara. 1997. "Eastwood Leads Us Down the Garden Path." *San Francisco Examiner*, November 21, http://www.sfgate.com/cgi-bin/article.cgi?f=/e/a/1997/11/21/WEEKEND2734.dtl, accessed July 14, 2010.

Sragow, Michael. 1997. "Wilted Garden." *Dallas Observer*, November 21, http://www.dallasobserver.com/content/printVersion/272806, accessed July 14, 2010.

Taylor, Charles. 1997. "Cement Garden." *Salon.com*, November 21, http://www.salon.com/entertainment/movies/1997/11/cov_21midnight.html, accessed July 14, 2010.

Turan, Kenneth. 1997. "Tending to the Garden." *Los Angeles Times*, November 21, http://www.calendarlive.com/movies/reviews/cl-movie971120-6,2,7608959.story, accessed July 14, 2010.

Chapter 11

MYSTIC RIVER AS A TRAGIC ACTION

Robert Merrill and John L. Simons

[*Mystic River*] is a tragedy, a street opera.
    —DENNIS LEHANE, in *"Mystic River*: From Page to Screen"

"Mystic River" is as close as we are likely to come on the screen
to the spirit of Greek tragedy.
    —DAVID DENBY, "Dead Reckoning: *Mystic River* and *Kill Bill-Vol. 1*"

This film is about how you can't get away from your own past.
    —CLINT EASTWOOD, quoted in Erica Abeel, "Clint
    Eastwood Explores Haunted Lives in *Mystic River*"

Our epigraphs are meant to suggest that the author of the novel *Mystic River* (Lehane 2001), one of the subsequent film's best critics, and the film's director all agree that *Mystic River* is a formal tragedy. Clint Eastwood does not use the term *tragedy*, but he has said that he followed Lehane's book very closely, and Lehane has characterized his novel as "classically structured tragedy" (quoted in Rothermel 2007, 241n16). Dennis Rothermel has objected that Eastwood's *Mystic River* (2003) does not offer "the relief of completeness, reversal and recognition of the classical model of tragedy" (2007, 218), effectively invoking the Aristotelian concepts of completeness, *peripetia* (reversal), and *anagnorisis* (recognition) to argue that *Mystic River* departs from the "classical" structure elucidated in Aristotle's *Poetics*. We agree that Lehane's novel and Eastwood's film do not represent the recognition of error and reversal of conduct that we (and Aristotle) associate with Oedipus and other Greek protagonists, but we think that there are elements of these classical features in Eastwood's tragic action and that, in any case, this action is as "complete," indeed, as satisfying, as any to be found in modern film. Our goal will be to define the film's tragic structure, one in which the characters' failure to recognize their mistakes and reverse course is as essential to Eastwood's tragic world as it was, say, to Faulkner's *The Sound and the Fury*.

We think that it is important to recognize that *Mystic River* is virtually the only film in which Eastwood strives for tragic effects, classical or otherwise.[1] Eastwood's reluctance to make tragic films is especially evident in the genres for which he is best known, the Western and the crime film. We have argued elsewhere that the major Western directors other than Sam Peckinpah—John Ford, Anthony Mann, Howard Hawks, Budd Boetticher, Fred Zinnemann, George Stevens, Sergio Leone, and Eastwood—all embraced nontragic forms in which their protagonists may be flawed and suffer greatly but survive their ordeals morally and physically intact.[2] Eastwood's Westerns, the six in which he only stars and the four in which he stars and directs, all resolutely avoid tragic outcomes, with the possible exception of *Unforgiven* (1992). Moreover, Eastwood has been only slightly more inclined to work toward tragic or near-tragic effects in his crime films. The five Dirty Harry films might be called many things, but tragic is not one of them, and even very good films such as *Play Misty for Me* (1971), *Thunderbolt and Lightfoot* (1974), and *In the Line of Fire* (1993) would never be mistaken for tragedies (though the somber conclusion to *Thunderbolt and Lightfoot* hints at later developments).

Unforgiven is the Eastwood film prior to *Mystic River* often characterized as tragic. The story line of *Unforgiven* strikingly anticipates that of *Mystic River*. Like the latter's Jimmy Markum (Sean Penn), William Munny (Clint Eastwood) has retired from a life of crime to become a family man, Munny working a small Western farm, Jimmy operating a small neighborhood grocery store in contemporary Boston. Both men return to their violent ways, Munny to make the money he needs to keep his farm after the death of his wife, Jimmy to avenge the murder of his nineteen-year old daughter, Katie (Emmy Rossum). The apparent difference in motivation narrows when Munny seeks revenge against Sheriff Little Bill Daggett (Gene Hackman) for the brutal slaying of Munny's friend and partner Ned Logan (Morgan Freeman). Each quest for vengeance embodies a form of tragic error (*hamartia*), as Munny kills more or less innocent bystanders and Jimmy willfully executes the wrong man for his daughter's murder.

Unforgiven and *Mystic River* are powerful evidence that Eastwood's later films effectively revise his earlier ones on the subject of revenge. Nevertheless, the two films are quite different formally. Though both Munny and Jimmy seem to shrug off the guilt each should feel, Munny's happy new life with his children in San Francisco (described in the film's quite believable epilogue) constitutes an ironic but hardly tragic conclusion to an action filled with rich but largely unfulfilled tragic possibilities; whereas Jimmy's failure to confront the moral implications of his misdeeds dovetails with the tragic fates of the other major characters to create the collective, one might say communal, tragic effect so powerfully achieved at the end of *Mystic River*.

Mystic River is sometimes denied tragic status because of its generic connections with such films as *Absolute Power* (1997) and *Blood Work* (2002). Even an admirer of *Mystic River* such as David Denby remarks pejoratively that "you can still see some genre conventions at work" (2010, 58), a comment that seems to presume that *Mystic River* succeeds only to the extent that it sheds the "genre conventions" of the detective novel and, in fact, transcends its origins in this popular form. We ourselves think that *Mystic River* succeeds as a tragic film precisely to the extent that it follows Lehane's almost uniquely tragic detective novel. Indeed, Eastwood's fidelity to his source novel is unprecedented in his career as a director, as Rothermel (2007, 218) has noted and as Eastwood acknowledged in an interview with Charley Rose ("*Mystic River*: From Page to Screen" 2003). We would speculate that Eastwood remains almost totally faithful to Lehane's novel because he wants to make a tragic detective film, one that does not aspire to transcend its generic origins but, rather, to render them as fully as possible in the medium of film.[3]

To flesh out these claims about *Mystic River*, we will focus, in turn, on the film's three central characters, Dave Boyle (Tim Robbins), Jimmy Markum, and Sean Devine (Kevin Bacon), an approach that will establish how closely Eastwood follows the structure and spirit of Lehane's novel and honor the fact that *Mystic River*, much like *The Oresteia*, is a collective tragedy rather than one that highlights a single tragic protagonist. We also intend to emphasize the changes Eastwood made in Brian Helgeland's script, alterations that either revert to Lehane's original story or embody Eastwood's attempt to do justice to the dark implications of Lehane's novel through the language of film.

■ I

Denmark's a prison.
—*Hamlet* II.ii.238

Like Lehane's novel, Eastwood's film begins with the scene of three eleven-year-old boys huddled together outside Jimmy Markum's house in the East Buckingham section of Boston. Scenarist Brian Helgeland adds the game of street hockey they are playing, but the scene unfolds much as in Lehane's book, with two men driving up who represent themselves as police detectives and who order one of the boys, Dave Boyle, to get into their car so that they can drive him home to his mother. The two men are in fact pedophiles who abduct Dave for four days until he manages to escape. The driver of the car refers to the boys as "a pack of punks" (see Lehane 2001, 14), but it is the men who prove a vicious "pack," predators Dave will come to think of as wolves. Eastwood captures something of Dave's experience here by taking two flashbacks from Helgeland's script and moving them forward to their chronological position in Dave's ordeal, one a brief shot of Dave's captors descending the stairs to a basement where Dave cowers on a battered sleeping bag, the other a shot of the terrified Dave escaping through the woods while fearing the pursuit of his unforgivable "wolves."

Dave then returns to his home in a scene that Helgeland almost totally excised but which Eastwood restores in order to represent Dave in the midst of an ambiguous celebration in which he is almost totally isolated, standing by himself looking down from his second-story apartment to the neighborhood streets where those assembled think of him as "damaged goods" and Dave is effectively excluded. We next see the three young boys twenty-five years later, the one who got into that car (Dave) and the two who did not (Jimmy and Sean). As the subsequent action makes abundantly clear, the effects of this appalling episode still manifest themselves in the lives of the middle-aged men we will follow for the rest of the film.[4]

The scene of the young Dave fleeing through the woods recurs through the film, strongly suggesting that the adult Dave Boyle remains haunted by his traumatic experience as a boy. The man we first meet seems to have survived his hellish initiation into the worst human behavior, however, especially as played by the towering (6'5") Tim Robbins. We first see him dealing warmly and intelligently with his young son, Michael (Cayden Boyd), who wants to be a baseball player like his father, who became an all-star shortstop for his high school team. Dave has gone on to sustain a marriage of eight years (see Lehane 2001, 269) and to support his family of three in inelegant but perfectly respectable circumstances. His dealings with his wife, Celeste (Marcia Gay Harden), are loving and sensitive throughout the film, even as she comes to suspect that Dave has murdered Jimmy Markum's daughter; and he even proves capable of dealing shrewdly (if only once) with the pressure of experienced police detectives who also suspect that he is a murderer, a scene in which we observe, as Helgeland puts it in his script, "a cooler, tougher Dave than we've seen before" (2002, 88).[5] The crucial scene in which Dave visits with Jimmy on Jimmy's porch in the aftermath of Katie's murder is dominated by Sean Penn's unforgettable depiction of naked grief, but it also reveals Dave's intelligence, tact, and genuine compassion for a boyhood friend he has hardly seen over the years.

Unfortunately, this scene with Jimmy also reveals Dave's fundamental incompetence, his inability to deal with life with anything but fantasies and outright lies, in this case his story about how he came to have a damaged right hand. In the course of the film we see this fumbling, maladroit Dave repeatedly: when he tells his patently unconvincing story to Celeste about how he came to be covered with blood when he returns home at 3:00 a.m. the night Katie is murdered; when he stumbles through his first two interviews with Sean Devine and his partner, Whitey Powers (Laurence Fishburne), again lying about his hand and telling a different tale from the one he told Jimmy; when he tries to persuade Jimmy that he killed a child molester and not Jimmy's daughter. The adult Dave is not damaged goods in a moral sense, but rather in his inability to deal with life's complexities.

If Dave, Jimmy, and Sean are held together by "a bond of shame and contempt," as Denby (2010, 59) puts it, it is Dave who experiences this "shame" in what turns out to be an ineradicable form. The depth of his sickness is suggested by the weird story he tells his sleeping son, the tale of a man who as a boy escaped from wolves and came to live in a private world he shares only with the fireflies. (The link to Dave's boyhood experience is reinforced at this point by repeating his memory of fleeing through the woods, the cry of wolves pursuing him.) Subsequently, Celeste returns to their apartment to find Dave watching a film about vampires, whom Dave seems to envy: "They're undead, but I think maybe there's something beautiful about it. Maybe one day you wake up and you forget what it's like to be human. Maybe then it's okay." This speech reveals Dave's acute understanding of the terrible pain of being human, even as it convinces Celeste that her husband is unstable and fully capable of murdering Katie. Here Dave tries for the first time to explain how he feels, invoking Henry and George (the wolfish pedophiles) as vampires as well as wolves, a crucial identification because, as Dave tells Celeste, "once it's in you, it stays," a vampirish fate Dave fears he is experiencing, with the dreadful implication that he is himself becoming a wolf/vampire. At this point Eastwood has Helgeland add a speech not in Lehane, Dave's question to Celeste, "Did you know there were child prostitutes in Rome Basin?"[6] The reference is to the child prostitute Dave "protected" the night Katie was killed by beating to death the boy's client in a parking lot, which explains the blood all over Dave when he returns home and offers crucial evidence of Dave's obsessive fear that Henry and George have left their brutish poison in his own blood.

Dave's fear is that he is about to become a werewolf, which means he suffers from lycanthropy, "the delusion that one was capable of such transformations [from human form to wolf], whether this delusion was the result of madness, melancholy, hallucinogenic drugs, illness, or the diabolic exacerbation of any number of these causes" (Hirsch 2005, 1). Clinically speaking, Dave is the victim of the melancholy, indeed, the deep depression, he has lived inside since the day he was abducted. Ironically, his attack on the child molester is meant to free him from this crippling disease, as he fights back against the abuser(s) who violated him in the first place, but he effectively becomes the werewolf he loathes with his deadly assault. At the end of the film, as we shall see, Dave tries to extricate himself from this vicious cycle, but it is far too late to escape again from the new wolves who stalk him, Jimmy Markum and his brothers-in-law, the aptly named Savages.

It is important that we appreciate the savagery that everywhere surrounds Dave in *Mystic River*, from the child abuse of his youth to the violence that ends his life at film's end, for Dave's horrific condition is anything but unique in Eastwood's tragic world. Violence and confinement are pervasive in this dark film, in specifics such as Pen Park, the former penitentiary grounds where Katie's body is found in a sunken bear cage (a naturalistic detail Eastwood added to the depictions in Lehane's novel and Helgeland's script); in the several porch railings, which recall prison bars; in the many small, dimly lit rooms, much like Jimmy Markum's claustrophobic office; in the general "landscape of enclosure" Len Engel describes so well in noting East Buckingham's narrow streets, which "seem to have no outlet and to lead relentlessly back to the same houses and neighbor-hoods" (2007, 120); and most especially in the murderous actions of Jimmy and the Savages. If Hamlet's Denmark is a prison, so, too, is the world Katie Markum and Brendan Harris (Thomas Guiry) were planning to abandon for the glittering lights of Las Vegas the day after Katie was murdered.

In this regard, one of the film's most telling moments is when Dave accepts a ride from Val and Nick Savage (Kevin Chapman, Adam Nelson) near the conclusion. "For the second time in his life, Dave gets inside a car he shouldn't," as Helgeland (2001, 98; 2002, 104) remarks, and Eastwood captures the parallel by having two Savages pick up Dave instead of Val alone in Lehane and Helgeland and by having Dave look back through the rear window almost precisely as he looked back at Jimmy and Sean when the "cops" drove away with him at the beginning of the film. Eastwood continues his incisive depiction of Jimmy and the Savages when he first has Val Savage answer Dave's query about their criminal ways, "We're like a couple of bats. We like the night too much. Days are just good for sleeping through," and then has Jimmy gut Dave with a violence almost shocking in a film filled with scenes of violence. Val's vampirish reference to bats and the zeal with which Jimmy stabs Dave before shooting him are Eastwood's additions to the already grim materials he found in Lehane's novel and Helgeland's script, confirming that the film's director understood perfectly the dark environment in which Dave struggles to avoid his descent into bestiality.

The execution of Dave is the film's most obvious confirmation that you can't get away from your own past, as Eastwood has said. Whereas Lehane includes many passages in which Dave reflects on his attack on the child molester and Helgeland (2001, 37; 2002, 40) includes a scene in which Dave sees the boy prostitute he has tried to protect and unsuccess-fully attempts to talk with him, Eastwood reveals Dave's futile effort to escape from his past only at the end of the film, with the initial flashback of Dave assaulting the child molester, a scene in which the sound of the pedophile unsheathing his knife exactly reproduces the sound of the were-wolves pursuing Dave in his escape through the woods. Now, of course, Dave is the attacking wolf, the brutal instrument from which he suffered so unjustly, and so his attempt to liberate himself from his painful demons only deepens his traumatic malaise. Helgeland's screenplay has been criti-cized because it supposedly "shies away from grappling with Dave's nascent pedophilia" (Hendrickson 2004, 73), but we think that Helgeland's script and Eastwood's film do full justice to this important topic, with the crucial assistance of Tim Robbins's Oscar-winning performance. Eastwood captures as well Dave's belated attempt to turn things around by having Dave speak aloud to Jimmy the thoughts he cannot utter in Lehane's novel, even though they might help save his life (Lehane 2001, 405): "I thought I was turning into him [the pedophile]." At this last moment, Dave is able to acknowledge his need to exorcise this unacceptable possibility, though his means are equally unacceptable and might even be seen as justifying his execution.[7] It is of course typical of the world Dave inhabits that his audience, Jimmy Markum, responds to Dave's first honest self-analysis by gutting him like a deer. From one form of abuse to another, Dave's sorry fate is realized in his terrible death.

■ ‖

> As a rule, I always shy away from exposition.
> —CLINT EASTWOOD, quoted in Richard Thompson and Tim Hunter,
> "Eastwood Direction"

Eastwood's well-known disdain for "exposition" figures prominently in his depiction of Jimmy Markum, the work's protagonist according to Dennis Lehane and the most celebrated of the three central characters developed by Eastwood.[8] Throughout his novel Lehane provides abundant information concerning Jimmy's past and motives, information Eastwood largely excludes from his film. The man we meet now owns a neighborhood store but was in prison for two years sixteen years ago, the price he paid for leading an advanced gang of thieves at the precocious age of nineteen. So far as we can tell, he has not resumed his career in crime after leaving prison, devoting his time instead to his business and his family: his daughter Katie with his first wife, Marita, who died from skin cancer while he was in prison; his second wife, Annabeth (Laura Linney); and his two daughters with Annabeth.

  Not everyone has seen Jimmy as a retired criminal, however. Charlene P. E. Burns refers to Jimmy as "the ring-leader of a gang of petty criminals" (2004, 2), for example, and Nancy Hendrickson speaks of Jimmy's "ongoing criminal associations" (2004, 72). Moreover, Adrian Wootton characterizes Jimmy as "a one-time career criminal and sometime single parent now gone straight for the sake of his second family" (2003, 12). It is easy to smile at these errors, for we know that Jimmy retired from crime even before meeting and marrying Annabeth and that he went "straight" for his first daughter, Katie, and not his second family. We only come to know such things very late in the film, however, when Val Savage tells Dave that Jimmy went straight because of Katie one hour and forty-seven minutes into the film. And even then we are not told Jimmy's reasoning (fully expressed in Lehane's novel), that the five-year-old girl he returned to after leaving prison had been left alone, effectively abandoned with the death of her mother, and Jimmy cannot stand thinking of what would happen to her if he continued his life of crime and was sent back to prison (see Lehane 2001, 108).

It would have been fairly easy for Eastwood to insert Katie as the reason for Jimmy's retirement into his speech about his love for Katie on the porch with Dave. Eastwood could also have retained Val's reply when Jimmy asks him whether he still has bolt cutters in his trunk, "Guy's gotta make a living, Jim" (Helgeland 2001, 28; 2002, 30), a remark that establishes that Jimmy is no longer familiar with the Savages' daily activities. Instead, Eastwood declines to clarify Jimmy's history through traditional exposition, trusting that his audience will be able to put the situation together from the details we are given (as when Whitey asks Jimmy about his stint in prison) and especially the fact Jimmy seems totally absorbed in the life of his family and business, a citizen of his neighborhood who seems to know everyone and commands the respect of almost everyone we meet (the major exception being Brendan Harris's mother [Jenny O'Hara], an older woman who dismisses Jimmy as a thief and a "scumbag burglar").

What is ultimately at issue here is what we are to make of Jimmy's conversion to family life and the customs of the community, especially its religious customs. Eastwood's disdain for "exposition" allows even a critic as sensitive to the film as Rothermel to argue that providing Katie with "a permanent home and love" has in turn "provided [Jimmy] with salvation and a purpose to sustain him in enduring the loss of her mother" (2007, 219). We think that this view is no more persuasive than Allen Redmon's suggestion that after leaving prison Jimmy has "forsaken violence" (presumably doing so immediately after he kills Just Ray Harris, the man who sent Jimmy to prison by informing on him) (2004, 324). Indeed, Rothermel's argument that Jimmy achieves salvation and purpose in renouncing crime strikes us as fundamentally untrue to Eastwood's understanding of the action and Sean Penn's powerful performance.

This is not to argue that Penn's Jimmy is incapable of moral commitments and distinctions. Helgeland and Eastwood suggest otherwise by including a brief scene drawn from Lehane's novel (2001, 262) in which Jimmy stares out from the stoop of his house and whispers, "I know in my soul I contributed to my child's death, but I don't know how." Moreover, as we shall see, Jimmy understands the enormity of what he has done in killing Dave and expresses what seems genuine remorse for his mistake. But we think that it is clear that Jimmy never does see how he is fundamentally responsible for what happens to Katie, and his misgivings about killing Dave are for killing the wrong man, not for pursuing vigilante justice, and in any case he is all too easily convinced by his wife, Annabeth, that his action against Dave is not really a moral fault at all. These later moral failures on Jimmy's part suggest that we should be careful not to give Jimmy too much moral or spiritual credit for renouncing his criminal past. Indeed, the film everywhere suggests that Jimmy and his neighbors enact familial and religious conventions that have little spiritual content. As Burns says of their religious pretensions, "For these people the church is nothing more than a social institution" (2004, 4). This is confirmed in Lehane's novel (2001, 129) when we are told that Jimmy has not attended church for ten years prior to Katie's baptism and in Eastwood's film when Jimmy teases his daughter Nadine (Celine Du Tertre) during her First Communion with no apparent concern for the event's spiritual content. Jimmy engages in the religious rituals of East Buckingham with no grasp of their spiritual implications, much as he and his surviving family attend the neighborhood parade at the end of the film because it is expected, even though there is no obvious moral or spiritual dimension to the parade.

Eastwood's critique of Jimmy's spiritual pretensions climaxes with the odd Irish Catholic tattoo we observe on Jimmy's back during his encounter with Annabeth after Dave's execution. This tattoo is in the form of a cross, with a traditionally Trinitarian shamrock at its center (each of the three leaves shaped like a heart), the final instance in a film (and a society) filled with such crosses, from the "gold ring decorated with a cross" (Burns 2004, 3) on the right hand of the second pedophile at the scene of Dave's abduction, to the more traditional crosses we observe in almost every neighborhood home we enter, to the cross of light on the wall at the morgue, the cross behind Jimmy and the Savages at the stonecutter's (where the religiously indifferent Jimmy chooses a rather generic gravestone instead of a circular

Celtic cross and gravestone for Katie's grave), the prominent cross in the vampire movie Dave watches, and Jimmy's physical gestures as he walks away from Sean near the end of the film. Eastwood provides all of these crosses, as none appear in Lehane's novel or Helgeland's script, presumably to bear witness to the religious symbolism that pervades this Boston neighborhood even if there is scant evidence of genuine Roman Catholic belief. Jimmy's tattoo is especially incongruous, for nothing in his life suggests that he strives for spiritual redemption or in fact seeks such redemption through a cross or religious icon on his back, as actually occurs in one of Flannery O'Connor's finest stories, "Parker's Back," where the image of a "flat, stern, Byzantine Christ with all-demanding eyes" (1971, 522) glares judgmentally out of O. E. Parker's tortured back.[9] As Len Engel says about Jimmy's cross, "To me, the tattoo on Jimmy suggests his own crucifixation. It is the cross of vengeance and guilt, now permanently fixed on his back" (2007, 122). We would add that whatever guilt Jimmy finally feels is on his back and nowhere else, for the final thrust of his late scene with Annabeth (for Lehane, and perhaps for Eastwood, the most important scene in *Mystic River* [see "*Mystic River*: From Page to Screen" 2003]) is that Jimmy is "cured" of any guilt he has experienced for killing Dave (and before Dave, Just Ray Harris) and has a "haht" big enough to support his whole family.

The interesting thing about Jimmy Markum, especially as played by the mercurial Sean Penn, is that his virtues are as credible as his moral limitations. His lifelong concern for Katie is intensely represented, not so much in his reasons for leaving the world of crime (as in Lehane) as in his obvious affection for her on the day of her murder, rendered nicely in a scene at Jimmy's store that turns out to be a truly final farewell, as well as his unspeakable grief at her loss, expressed variously at the park in which Katie's body is found, in the morgue where he promises Katie's body that he will catch and kill her murderer, on the porch of his house where he tells Dave that he always loved Katie more than anyone else in his life, and perversely enough in the rage he brings to the execution of the man he wrongly thinks guilty of Katie's murder. This rage is perfectly understandable, even sympathetic, and there seems to be a good case for seeing Jimmy as tragically unlucky in the several circumstances that lead him (like Sean's partner, Whitey Powers) to conclude that Dave is Katie's murderer. Like Oedipus and other Greek protagonists, Jimmy seems the benighted victim of coincidences that point him in the wrong direction and which culminate in Dave's tragic death.

In Eastwood's film, however, we are encouraged to take a more critical view of Jimmy's role in the death of his daughter and his violent reaction to it. However we read Oedipus's culpability in the events that lead to his undoing, we must finally see that Jimmy *Markum* is a "marked" man, the one who "contributed" to his child's death, as he himself puts it. Like Dave Boyle, Jimmy cannot run away from his past, specifically his retaliation against Just Ray Harris. Even his seemingly guilt-ridden gesture of sending $500 each month to the Harris family contributes to the catastrophe, for the monthly check encourages Mrs. Harris to stay in East Buckingham rather than to make a new life elsewhere. There is a perverse justice to what ensues, the romantic attachment between Jimmy's daughter Katie and Just Ray Harris's son Brendan and the senseless murder of Katie by Harris's other son, Ray Jr. (Spencer Treat Clark), and Silent Ray's companion John O'Shea (Andrew Mackin), two thirteen-year-old boys who visit upon Katie a form of violence not entirely unlike what happened to Dave Boyle twenty-five years earlier. Though Jimmy tells Sean and Whitey that everything turns on seemingly random choices that lead to unintended consequences, he cannot see Katie's death as a grim confirmation of his own theory, one in which the sins of the father are visited on his offspring. The *hubris* Jimmy displays in executing the wrong man should remind us that he has killed before to satisfy his sense of personal grievance against another, violent acts meant to deflect, respectively, Jimmy's own responsibility for his imprisonment and, much more horribly, his own role in the death of the person he values most in his life.

Jimmy expresses what we have acknowledged to be genuine remorse for killing the wrong man, but he is all too easily persuaded by his wife, Annabeth, that his "mistake" was no more than a show of strength on the part of a man who loves his family and will defend it fiercely against the "weak" Others who put his loved ones at risk. Annabeth's remarkable rationalization of Jimmy's violence has rightly provoked comparisons to Lady Macbeth, but we need to see that Jimmy's acceptance of her views is self-serving and morally obtuse, ultimately nothing like Macbeth's tormented acknowledgment of the evil he has done and continues to do. Jimmy's own rationalization of his behavior is most conspicuous when he prepares to execute Dave near the Mystic River. "We bury our sins here, Dave. We wash 'em clean," Jimmy says in what amounts to an appalling parody of the rite of baptism, an appropriate climax to Eastwood's depiction of East Buckingham's hollow religiosity. Like Macbeth, Jimmy says that he cannot "undo" his fatal mistake, but in fact he seems prepared at the end to set it aside and go forward (or backward) to the life of crime he thought he had abandoned years ago. "You could rule this town," Annabeth whispers to Jimmy, whom she labels a "king" whose heart is large enough to beat for his wife and children, and Jimmy proves all too willing to take up the perverse challenge of defending his family by dominating others as a kind of benevolent Godfather for this crime-ridden neighborhood.

Jimmy's rejection of the guilt he should feel is fully on display in the film's finale, where King Jimmy stands with his putative queen and his courtiers, the Savage brothers, while he oversees *his* parade in *his* neighborhood. Effectively hidden behind the dark sunglasses that mark his new role, Jimmy seems fully prepared to come out of retirement now that Marita and Katie are gone forever. His dismissive gesture in response to Sean's reminder that Jimmy is himself the guilty party in the disastrous events of the last few days signals Jimmy's complete moral degradation as the film ends, an outcome that richly embodies the tragedy of a man who has sought survival (if not "salvation") in a conventional life but who returns with a kind of tragic inevitability to what he sees as his appropriate role as a Nietzschean warrior who will impose his beneficent will on his world. Though Jimmy does not literally die, as we have come to expect of Shakespearean tragic heroes, he suffers the kind of spiritual death we encounter at the end of modern tragedies such as *The Godfather* (1972) and *The Godfather II* (1974).

■ III

> Jesus, I can't do this tonight. I can't do it.
> —SEAN DEVINE to his wife, Lauren (Tori Davis), in *Mystic River*

> There are stories a river can tell and truths it cannot hide. There are ways it brings us together that we may never see, connecting us with places we never expected, places like fear, like betrayal, like murder.
> —CLINT EASTWOOD, in "*Mystic River*: Beneath the Surface"

Rothermel includes a very interesting section on the film's "detectives," a term that refers not only to the official detectives, Sean and Whitey, but to the other characters who "search for the truth," as Rothermel (2007, 226) puts it: Jimmy, Celeste, Dave, Brendan, and Sean. We do not think that Dave should be on this list, but Rothermel rightly reminds us that many of the characters try to penetrate the film's mystery, often with disastrous results. Jimmy is the prime example of a "detective" who commits himself to a difficult task, assembles evidence of various kinds (rumors for the most part, but also Dave's unreliable account of his actions on the night Katie was killed and Celeste's virtual accusation against Dave), and then reaches the wrong conclusion. Celeste's "analysis" of the case against Dave seems almost paranoid, but her suspicions are more or less the same as Whitey's, and while Brendan reaches the right conclusion about Silent Ray and John O'Shea, his immediate reaction is to confront his brother and threaten to kill him if he does not speak up, an investigative "method" all too reminiscent of Jimmy's approach with Dave. Indeed, we think that it is likely that Brendan would have beaten Silent Ray and John O'Shea to death if Sean and Whitey had not interrupted his investigation/attack. Rothermel points to the "floundering" of the film's several detectives as evidence of "the collapse of the standard suppositions of the mystery-thriller genre" (2007, 227), presumably referring to the common pattern of the commanding detective who restores order to a world in chaos by identifying the culprit, who will subsequently be dealt with by institutions now restored to their proper place in an orderly society. As Rothermel points out, virtually nothing like this conventional pattern works itself out in *Mystic River*.

The problem with this otherwise excellent analysis of the film's use of detective conventions is the inclusion of Sean as someone who "flounders" in his pursuit of Katie's murderer. Though Kevin Bacon has referred to his character as "flawed" both as a detective and as a man ("*Mystic River*: From Page to Screen" 2003), we trust that he would not agree that Sean flounders professionally, even though the term aptly describes his personal life. In fact, we think that Sean's handling of this case confirms his reputation as an up-and-coming detective explicitly remarked in Lehane's novel and implicit in Eastwood's film. After all, Sean manages to solve this murder within three days despite having to deal with Whitey's suspicions about Dave, Jimmy's parallel investigation, and Brendan's refusal to level with him about the crucial evidence in the case, the murder weapon, which belonged to Brendan's father. Sean constantly asks the right questions and draws the right conclusions, whether questioning Dave's motive for killing Katie, remarking that Brendan seems genuinely to have loved Katie, or insisting that the key to the case is the murder gun, used in the past by Just Ray Harris. Sean is not Sherlock Holmes or Hercule Poirot (as Kevin Bacon may have meant to point out), but his pursuit of the truth *contrasts* with the floundering of everyone around him.

We would suggest that it is very much to Eastwood's point (following Lehane) that even the most exemplary pursuit of truth or justice is likely to fail in a world such as the one we encounter in *Mystic River*. Even "success" in such an inquiry is of limited value; Sean cannot explain why Katie was murdered, and he is confident that the killers do not know why they did what they did. The solution to the murder casts ironic light on Jimmy's search for an evil culprit on whom he will exact the appropriate vengeance. Sean himself tries to explain the problem here to his estranged (and silent) wife, Lauren, during one of their phone "conversations": "Tired of wishing things made sense. Tired of caring about some dead girl, and there's just going to be another one after her. Sending killers to jail is just sending them home, to the place they've been headed all their dumb, pathetic lives. And the dead are still dead." Sean utters these disillusioned lines just before he tells Lauren that he cannot do this tonight. He is, of course, referring to *talking* about the hopeless cycle of victim and victimizer, but we should not forget that Sean *can* continue to try to do something about life's most senseless injustices, as the film documents even as it acknowledges that apparently successful investigations often fail to forestall the ugly consequences of human misdeeds. Sean ultimately comes to seem a kind of Sisyphean detective, rolling his rock up the same hill again and again, a tragic pattern that weighs on him heavily, as we see in his speech to Lauren, but which does not lead Sean to abandon what may seem to us his tragic quest.[10]

If this account of Sean's situation is at all accurate, it would explain why Eastwood rejected Helgeland's original conclusion to his script and instead restored the ending from Lehane's novel. Helgeland punctuates his original script with actual conversations between Sean and a woman never named in which Sean invokes the hopelessness he expresses in the phone call with Lauren still in the film. For Helgeland, these conversations apparently pointed to Sean's disillusionment with the whole process, especially after Jimmy kills Dave before Sean can reveal the true solution to Katie's murder; so he had Sean call his wife at the end and announce that he is going to quit his job, which so impresses his wife that she asks him to get on a plane and reunite with her elsewhere (see Helgeland 2001, 115). Eastwood's Sean is very much Lehane's character, someone who does not plan to quit trying to do what he can even though he knows that it will always be next to impossible, in this case because he knows that Jimmy is too smart to have left clues of his guilt. But Sean's indignation at the end is intact, as when he asks Jimmy, "You gonna send Celeste Boyle five hundred a month, too?" This judgmental spirit informs his gesture toward Jimmy at the final parade, his "finger gun," as Helgeland (2002, 127) calls it, directed at Jimmy even as Sean drops his thumb on the imaginary hammer.

Lehane has Sean explicitly tell Celeste that he knows Jimmy killed Dave and that he will try to prove it ("I'll try, Celeste. I swear to God" [2001, 446]), but Eastwood eschews this expository directness and relies instead on Kevin Bacon's performance at the end to assure us that he is not giving up, just as he decides to apologize to his estranged wife. Earlier, Eastwood inserts a conversation between Sean and Whitey in which it becomes apparent that Sean has told his partner about his separation from Lauren and the fact that she periodically calls him but then declines to speak until she finally hangs up. "Maybe she's waiting for you to say something," Whitey suggests. Whitey proves prophetic when Lauren calls Sean just after he talks to Jimmy about the resolution of Katie's case. Sean begins by saying, "I'm sorry . . . I need you to know that. I pushed you away," presumably referring to his immersion in the horrors of his job, which have so overwhelmed him that he has had no time or space for his wife (or the child she bears while they are separated). As Whitey effectively predicted, Lauren responds by speaking for the first time, "I'm sorry, too. Things have been so messed up. Loving you, hating you." Sean asks her to come back, and she not only does not decline but tells him for the first time that his daughter's name is Nora. We will see Lauren and Nora with Sean at the parade that concludes the film.

Eastwood's version of these final scenes, drawn scrupulously from Lehane, offers what may seem a kind of happy ending, one in which Sean persists in his professional and personal lives rather than restoring his marriage by abandoning his career. Certainly Sean is the most positive character in this film, and we are clearly led to suppose that his future is not hopeless, unlike the very different but equally chilling conclusions to the stories of Dave Boyle and Jimmy Markum. Even so, Sean's story is cautionary as well, the most positive feature in a dark narrative that nonetheless suggests the terrible odds we face in confronting our pasts or even dealing with them, as Sean tries to do throughout the final scenes. Sean may well succeed with Lauren and his new child, though Sean and Lauren agree that they can only "try," but he has been unable to assist Dave or Jimmy in dealing with the problems that afflict all of the characters, men and women alike; so the conclusion to his story only partially qualifies the almost Shakespearean darkness that descends on these people by the end of the film.

Indeed, just as Shakespearean tragedies, such as *Hamlet*, *King Lear*, and *Macbeth*, conclude with characters who have survived their play's disasters, so, too, *Mystic River* ends with one less-than-catastrophic outcome that highlights by contrast the fates of all the other characters. This somber conclusion includes the missing Dave Boyle and the man who has killed him, but also Jimmy's wife, Annabeth, whose eerie composure and condescending gaze at Celeste Boyle capture her frightening descent into moral indifference; and the frantic Celeste, whose frenzied search for the husband she has betrayed to Jimmy and concern for her morose son offer the most authentic emotions in this final scene but confirm as well that Celeste has been effectively destroyed by her role in Dave's death. The Aeschylean fates of Annabeth and Celeste, the most prominent women in *Mystic River*, mirror those of their husbands and complete the film's unrelenting depiction of a tragic world almost entirely defined by its victims and victimizers.

As if to underscore the film's entrapping circularity, the present invariably repeating the past, Eastwood returns at the end to the scene of the original crime. The camera rises above the fading sounds of the parade and then slowly zooms and circles down upon the forlorn cement slab where twenty-five years ago each of the boys first indelibly inscribed his name in wet cement (Dave's name, like his identity, forever incomplete) just moments before Dave was abducted. The imprisoning cement now resembles a gravestone more than a sidewalk. Eastwood's camera holds on that stone for several seconds, as a light wind seems to blow across it, gently ruffling three small leaves (one slightly larger, separated from the other two). A single leaf quivers and falls over in the faint breeze, but finally the leaves do not move. Slowly the frame dissolves from this mournful moment to a last iconic long shot of the bridge off in the distance. Next there is a crane down to *Mystic River*'s most recurring image, the camera moving swiftly in close-up over the dark, despairing waters of the Mystic. The screen then fades to total blackness, and the film is over.

■ Notes

1. We say "virtually" because we believe that *Letters from Iwo Jima* (2006) is "a tragic rather than heroic inquiry into the nature of leadership," as A. O. Scott (2009, 2) has remarked. Though *Million Dollar Baby* (2004) is one of Eastwood's most powerful films, we do not think that it is a tragedy.

2. Our treatment of the major Western directors is in chapter 1 of our *Peckinpah's Tragic Westerns: A Critical Study* (Simons and Merrill 2011). Interestingly, Clint Eastwood

has several times added Raoul Walsh to his own short list of the great Western directors (see Cahill 1999, 127; Champlin 1999, 79; Roberts 1999, 225).

3. In addition to the critics previously cited, A. O. Scott (2003, 1), Len Engel (2007, 119), and Al Collins (2004, 68) have remarked on the tragic form of *Mystic River*, especially its parallels with Greek tragedy.

4. Eastwood's film does not date these events, but in Lehane the opening scene occurs in 1975 and the subsequent action is set in 2000. The idea of young boys not getting into a predator's van is first introduced in an earlier Lehane novel, *Darkness, Take My Hand* (1996, 245).

5. We quote from what we take to be the shooting script of *Mystic River*. This undated script (which we cite as 2002), taken from the Internet, is labeled "Final Draft" and includes various materials not to be found in the "early" script Dennis Rothermel discusses in his excellent essay on *Mystic River* (see 2007, 220–23). We will be noting the more important scenes altered or restored in the later version of the script from which we quote. The early script is, indeed, early, as it is dated July 30, 2001, not too long after Lehane's novel first appeared and over a year before the film was shot on location in Boston. Erica Abeel reports that Eastwood gave Helgeland a synopsis of the story, somewhat simplifying Lehane's novel, and Helgeland produced a first draft in two weeks that Eastwood thought "a terrific interpretation" (2003, 2), even though he worked with Helgeland to restore the last two scenes of the film. We take the script Rothermel cites and graciously shared with us to be Helgeland's first draft.

6. We say that Eastwood had Helgeland add this speech because the line first appears in the shooting script (Helgeland 2002, 82), and we take the alterations and additions of the shooting script to be dictated by Eastwood though presumably written by Helgeland.

7. In Lehane's novel, Jimmy Marcus (Markum in the film) does come to think of Dave's murder of the child molester as justification for what he did to Dave for the wrong reason. See Lehane 2001, 441.

8. We attribute this view to Lehane because in "*Mystic River*: From Page to Screen" (2003) he suggests that Jimmy's scene with Annabeth at the end is the most important in the work, the scene everything else was leading up to.

9. Since there is no mention of a cross tattoo on Jimmy's back in Lehane's novel, and Eastwood offers no explanation for it, we are left to speculate about its origin and meaning. It seems likely that Jimmy first got the tattoo while in prison (surprisingly, no one else in the film seems to have a tattoo, not even the Savages). The cross would then make sense as a punishment Jimmy inflicted upon himself for his first wife's death and for deserting his baby daughter by taking the rap for a robbery and being sent to prison for two years. Another late example of this pervasive pattern of empty religious symbolism occurs at the Black Emerald, the bar by the river where dark-hearted Jimmy kills first Just Ray and then, later, Dave Boyle. Here the Christian symbol of the Irish cross with its trinity of three shamrock leaves is depicted in neon green, beneath an equally green illuminated Budweiser sign.

We would also note that the Irish cross is not the only tattoo on Jimmy's body. On his right bicep there is a sort of circular band-like design that is difficult to discern. On his left bicep there is a large tattoo of a crab. The crab has many symbolic meanings including that of the Zodiacal feminine moon. The crab reminds us of Marita's cancer (Cancer is the crab symbol in the Zodiac) but also and more obviously of the sea and the victims whom bottom-feeding Jimmy, a killer without conscience, sends rolling out into the ocean from the Mystic.

10. Robert Merrill has previously used the image of Sisyphus to describe the efforts of another fictional detective, Dave Robicheaux, in the novels of James Lee Burke. See Merrill 2009, 153.

■ Bibliography

Abeel, Erica. 2003. "Clint Eastwood Explores Haunted Lives in *Mystic River.*" *Film Journal International* 106, no. 10 (October), http://www.filmjournal.com/filmjournal/esearch/article_display.jsp?vnu_content_id=1000692751.

Burns, Charlene P. E. 2004. "*Mystic River*: A Parable of Christianity's Dark Side." *Journal of Religion and Film* 8 (April): 1–5, http://www.unomaha.edu/~jrf/Vol8No1/MysticBody.htm.

Cahill, Tim. 1999. "Clint Eastwood: The *Rolling Stone* Interview." In *Clint Eastwood: Interviews*, ed. Robert E. Kapsis and Kathie Coblentz, 117–29. Jackson: University of Mississippi Press.

Champlin, Charles. 1999. "Eastwood: An Auteur to Reckon With." In *Clint Eastwood: Interviews*, ed. Robert E. Kapsis and Kathie Coblentz, 76–80. Jackson: University of Mississippi Press.

Collins, Al. 2004. "Outside the Walls: Men's Quest in the Films of Clint Eastwood." *San Francisco Jung Institute Library Journal* 23: 62–73.

Denby, David. 2003. "Dead Reckoning: *Mystic River* and *Kill Bill-Vol. 1.*" *New Yorker*, October 13, http://www.newyorker.com/archive/2003/10/13/031013crci_cinema.

———. 2010. "Out of the West: Clint Eastwood's Shifting Landscape." *New Yorker*, March 8: 52–59, http://www.newyorker.com/reporting/2010/03/08/100308fa_fact_denby.

Engel, Len. 2007. "To Avenge or Not to Avenge: Violence, Vengeance, and Vigilantism in Clint Eastwood's Westerns and in *Mystic River.*" In *Westerns: Paperback Novels and Movies from Hollywood*, ed. Paul Varner, 112–24. Newcastle upon Tyne: Cambridge Scholars.

Helgeland, Brian. 2001. *Mystic River*. Original screenplay, July 30.

———. 2002. *Mystic River*. Final draft.

Hendrickson, Nancy. 2004. "*Mystic River.*" *Creative Screenwriting* 11 (January–February): 72–74.

Hirsch, Brett D. 2005. "An Italian Werewolf in London: Lycanthropy and *The Duchess of Malfi.*" *Early Modern Literary Studies* 11 (September): 1–22, http://extra.shu.ac.uk/emls/11—2/hirswere.htm.

Lehane, Dennis. 1996. *Darkness, Take My Hand*. New York: HarperTorch, 2000.

———. 2001. *Mystic River*. New York: HarperTorch, 2002.

Merrill, Robert. 2009. "James Lee Burke and the American Detective Novel." *Explorations* 11: 133–59.

"*Mystic River*: Beneath the Surface." 2003. Documentary short. *Mystic River*, 3 Disc Deluxe Edition. DVD. Warner Bros.

"*Mystic River*: From Page to Screen." 2003. Documentary short. *Mystic River*, 3 Disc Deluxe Edition. DVD. Warner Bros.

O'Connor, Flannery. 1971. "Parker's Back." In *The Complete Stories of Flannery O'Connor*, 510–30. New York: Farrar, Strauss and Giroux.

Redmon, Allen. 2004. "Mechanisms of Violence in Clint Eastwood's *Unforgiven* and *Mystic River*." *Journal of American Culture* 27 (September): 315–28.

Roberts, Jerry. 1999. "Q&A with a Western Icon." In *Clint Eastwood: Interviews*, ed. Robert E. Kapsis and Kathie Coblentz, 222–26. Jackson: University of Mississippi Press.

Rothermel, Dennis. 2007. "Mystical Moral Miasma in *Mystic River*." In *Clint Eastwood, Actor and Director: New Perspectives*, ed. Leonard Engel, 218–41. Salt Lake City: University of Utah Press.

Scott, A. O. 2003. "Ms. Macbeth and Her Cousin: The Women of *Mystic River*." *New York Times*, October 12, http://www.nytimes.com/2003/10/12/movies/film-ms-macbeth-and-her-cousin-the-women-of-mystic-river.html.

———. 2009. "Final Score: Future 1, Past 0." *New York Times*, December 11, http://movies.nytimes.com/2009/12/11/movies/11invictus.html.

Simons, John L., and Robert Merrill. 2011. *Peckinpah's Tragic Westerns: A Critical Study*. Jefferson, N.C.: McFarland and Co.

Wootton, Adrian. 2003. "Play Madigan for Me." *Sight and Sound* 13: 12–14.

Chapter 12

LIES OF OUR FATHERS: MYTHOLOGY AND
ARTIFICE IN EASTWOOD'S CINEMA

William Beard

Flags of Our Fathers (2006) is the most extended and articulate itera-tion of a theme that has been a central distinguishing feature of Clint Eastwood's cinema for many years. Eastwood, as an actor probably the biggest and most powerful heroic persona in American film in the last third of the twentieth century, has (as I have argued elsewhere) almost always accompanied his representations of heroic and superheroic char-acter and action with indications of their impossibility and/or their arti-fice.[1] These indications have perhaps a status of confession (conveying Eastwood's own sense of nonheroism), or perhaps simply of a kind of two-mindedness, but in any event they have formed an insistent shad-owy presence in Eastwood's films right from his Leone days to the pres-ent. In this essay I would like to illustrate the operation of this aspect of Eastwood's cinema as it expresses itself particularly in a handful of films where the phenomenon has not simply a heroic or genre-related basis but expands to take on a wider social application. *Bronco Billy* (1980), *Heartbreak Ridge* (1986), and *Unforgiven* (1992) are three films that particularly embody this tendency, and I will look at them as a prelude to a more extended examination of *Flags of Our Fathers* from the same perspective.

■ Bronco Billy

In *Bronco Billy*, Eastwood's eponymous hero is the owner-operator-star of a tiny contemporary Wild West show, touring small towns and presenting its leading performer as a late—a very late—avatar of the clean-living, dude-ranch-costumed, naive cowboy hero of the Roy Rogers sort.[2] Bronco Billy is ridiculous (and the film is a comedy, at times even a farce), but he also turns out to be a model of the personally and nationally salvational qualities of belief in an ideal. The film advances this idea in a heartwarming Capraesque or Spielbergian way even as it is pointing out first the impossible obsoleteness of its mythic style and then its status as total fabrication (the Eastwood character is revealed to have been a New Jersey shoe salesman ex-convict who has simply reinvented himself as a cowboy). At the end of the 1970s—a particularly harrowing decade in America, what with Vietnam, assassinations, ghetto riots, vicious culture wars, Watergate, oil embargos, stagflation, Japanese cars, Iranian hostages, and so on and so forth—and as an uncannily clear harbinger of the imminent arrival of Ronald Reagan in the White House, *Bronco Billy* addresses the ideological problem of a loss of faith in America and in American ideals.

Eastwood himself had appeared in some important death-of-ideology films, notably Sergio Leone's cynical Westerns of the late 1960s, which had nailed down the coffin lid on the entire genre by recasting the cowboy hero as an entirely self-interested money-grubber possessing a killing power that came not from virtue but from some transcendent, unaccountable, and amoral myth-space. The Dirty Harry movies, though they definitely had an ideological axe to grind, were essentially depictions of a dysfunctional social wasteland where the only positive refuge was a regressive anger at everything that rendered America ugly: an infestation of criminal scum at street level and a plague of cowardly, prevaricating, self-serving apparatchiks in charge of all the institutions. In this climate, just killing people becomes a socially useful act; and probably the only regret Harry's fans had was that he did not move on from blowing away all the perps to blowing away all the bureaucrats and politicians too. But this kind of scorched-earth environment was never a very pleasant place to live or even a tolerable one in the long run; and during the decade Eastwood began painfully to construct for himself a heroic character who could once again be pro-social. The key film here is *The Outlaw Josey Wales* (1976), where the hero actually makes the same journey—from whole and happy to horribly scarred and violent to nascently hopeful and strong—that American ideology itself wants to make.

But a movie in which the transcendently violent hero is gradually coaxed into pro-sociality is quite a distance from what goes on in *Bronco Billy*. For Billy is not a transcendently violent hero or even extraordinarily gifted in any way but one: his ability to substitute an imagined version of himself for his real history. The world is full of Walter Mittys, but Bronco

Billy has taken that crucial extra step of actually realizing the new myth of himself in his life's work and social position. An East Coast shoe sales-man imprisoned for shooting his wife has actively reinvented himself as the cowboy hero he has always wanted to be, learning the skills of quick-draw, sharpshooting, knife-throwing, and trick riding. The most striking thing about the film is that the cowboy hero that Billy wants to be is not just outdated in the way that all cowboy heroes are but *ludicrously* out-dated, a parody of all the mythical idealizations that ever inhered in the form. In other words, he is not a realist cowboy (think of some of Cormac McCarthy's contemporary examples), and not even an attempt to bring cowboy qualities into an urbanized present-day world (as in Don Siegel's 1968 cop film *Coogan's Bluff*, starring Eastwood), but an unreconstructed version of B-Western cowboy characters whose drastically flattened quali-ties of virtue and knightly prowess constitute their own pastiche and who are intended basically for children—or, as they say, for children of all ages. There is no authenticity whatever in this model; it is always completely, and flimsily, artificial. The movie spends a lot of time poking fun at this artifici-ality and its simplemindedness, in Billy's land-boat car with steer horns on the hood and six-shooters for door handles; his solemn pronouncements to children to mind their parents, say their prayers, keep away from tobacco and hard liquor, and stay in school ("at least until the eighth grade"); and most surreally in a horseback attempt to rob a transcontinental passenger train that rushes by heedlessly. His ragtag company includes an ex–con man emcee, a marksman who has blown off his hand in a shotgun mishap, an Indian who keeps getting bitten by his own rattlesnakes, and a draft dodger. But all of these people, and also eventually the spoiled-heiress-on-the-run descended from *It Happened One Night* who represents Billy's love interest, are existentially redeemed and reborn through their surrender to Billy's absurd code of the West. The truth value and social functional-ity of their new personae are 100 percent irrelevant, and the ridiculous outmodedness of their chosen model is merely a way of clearly illustrat-ing that fact. All that is important is wholehearted *belief*. The message that individuals in America, or the nation itself, need to recover their faith is completely endemic in Hollywood cinema; but the message that they need to invent their faith, and attach it even to something laughably impossible, is far more radical and, of course, not nearly so widespread. The ending of *Bronco Billy* is quite astonishing. The company has just lost its big tent in a fire and is bunking in a mental asylum where the troupe has given free performances over the years and the head doctor is taking fast-draw lessons from Billy. The whole company's faith in Billy is at an all-time high following the conversion of the heiress, and the asylum director is able to help Billy by converting the patients' workroom activity of sewing flags for the government into the material for a new tent—now constructed exclusively of dozens of large, stitched-together Stars and Stripes. This provides the movie's grand finale not only with the amazing visual tour de force of an all-flags environment but with the potentially devastating caveat that this heavily symbolic performing venue has been produced by madmen and -women for the purpose of selling a faith based on nothing but self-hypnosis. Here is Eastwood's double vision at its most unmistakable: the symbolic activity, the act of belief, is from one standpoint fake in every direction but from another truly beneficial in its ability to confer happiness and purpose on people.

■ *Heartbreak Ridge*

In *Heartbreak Ridge*, Eastwood plays an aging Marine sergeant haunted by memories of American quasi failure in Korea and outright failure in Vietnam ("We're 0-1-1"), who, like the nation, has to look all the way back to World War II for properly warm and heartening feelings of military/national virtue and victory. The film is massively distracted from this question into other narrative strands (Eastwood trying to regain the affections of his estranged wife, Eastwood trying to whip a platoon of comical slackers into proper soldiers), but when it resolves its national self-doubt, it does so in a fashion that betrays its artificial and even pastiche qualities all too clearly: in the popgun invasion of the tiny island of Grenada, which the Eastwood character holds up as an actual makeweight to the wounds of Korea and Vietnam ("Now we're 1-1-1"). Of course the blatant inadequacy of this mythmaking scheme directly echoes that of the actual historical event and its architect, Ronald Reagan; but in Eastwood's hands the make-believe and playacting aspects of the process are highly visible.

Heartbreak Ridge is not exactly a good movie. Its training camp high jinks make it look almost like *The Phil Silvers Show* at times. Eastwood's hand with comedy is very often uncertain or just crude, and such is the case here; and the transformation of *Animal House* goof-off recruits into semper-fi Marines is surreal as a proposition and painfully unconvincing in the event. Meanwhile, the getting-back-together-with-Marsha-Mason strand, which attracted by far the most attention upon the film's initial release and has continued to do so since, is an important stage in Eastwood's self-reconstitution as a person actually suffering from the emotional isolation entailed by being a heroic man's man, yearning for comfort and love in a way that it is hard to imagine the Man with No Name or Dirty Harry doing, and moreover bearing a history of failure in this relationship and a consciousness of unworthiness. So his wooing process, conducted as a fifty-six-year-old man only recently acquainted with cultural changes in women's status and aspirations, is marked by an endearing clumsiness and such romantic-comedy activities as reading women's magazines to find out what his wife might actually want. The third strand, and the one I am mostly concerned with here, is the character's, and the film's, profoundly mixed attitudes toward warrior mythology in America and in particular to the interface between combat results in Korea and Vietnam and the idea of national honor. Nobody remembers Korea anymore, and nobody remembered it in 1986, either—except for Eastwood, whose war this was. Too young for World War II, he was drafted to go to Korea, but after surviving a plane crash off San Francisco and swimming four miles to shore, he was kept Stateside to testify about the accident while his fellow draftees were sent off to combat,[3] and then he ended up as a lifeguard and swimming instructor at Fort Ord for the duration. Eastwood's character in *Heartbreak Ridge*, Gunnery Sergeant Tom Highway, dwells almost obsessively with other old-timer veterans on the original "Heartbreak Ridge" in Korea, a place of carnage and heroism, but especially carnage. A sense of honor and duty fulfilled is certainly part of this recollection, but even stronger is a sense of sorrow and ongoing pain. This character, with his Congressional Medal of Honor and his searing memory of the death of others, will be emphatically recalled in *Gran Torino* (2008), where—in a way that is entirely in keeping with Eastwood's constantly revised and constantly darkening cinema—another decorated Korean War veteran will obsessively recall his experience there with a mixture of pride and horror that is now far more horror than pride. Korea was no joke, and no victory, but it was also no Vietnam, where the American experience was even worse, and the blows to national ideology were very serious indeed.

So *Heartbreak Ridge* presents a national heritage of military pride that has suffered stains and compromises and in 1986 is difficult to see as nothing but a pageant of glorious victory. The country's Vietnam sickness was profound and, like malaria, always ready to come back just when you thought you were over it. The invasion of Grenada on October 25, 1983, inaugurated a minuscule Potemkin war that comprehensively addressed many U.S. worries about loss of invincibility: not only Vietnam but the four-year-old memory of the Iranian hostage crisis and the two-day-old memory of the suicide bombing attack on the U.S. Marine base in Beirut, which killed 241 American troops. Every aspect of this teensy war (whose more than usually comical official designation was "Operation Urgent Fury") was rooted in misapprehensions, overreactions, and transparently false claims, even if much of the country, and perhaps even of the government and the military, may actually have believed the administration's propaganda. Its putative aim was to "restore order" (code for removing a Marxist regime that might turn out to be more unfriendly to the United States than the Marxist regime it had replaced) and to "rescue" the roughly five hundred U.S. citizens on the island, including about four hundred medical students attending the university there. It was conducted by elite units with over three-to-one numerical superiority and overwhelming technological advantage against an island of about eight by twenty miles in extent and with a population of one hundred thousand, despite strong objections not just from the United Nations but from important allies such as the United Kingdom and Canada. Clearly, the will to a symbolic victory, no matter how absurdly minor and one-sided, was very strong. Then the actual campaign contained such events as the U.S. bombing of a mental hospital and a naval air raid that hit a Ranger command post rather than Grenadian snipers.[4]

Heartbreak Ridge takes the ridiculous exaggerations and "toy" aspects of this military operation and just inserts them with a straight face into the larger narrative of American ideological crisis, out-Reaganing Reagan with its presentation of Grenada as having a stature equivalent to that of Korea or Vietnam. It unleashes on this from-one-viewpoint risible war a platoon of Spring-Break-movie recruits whose transformation into "real Marines" is exactly parallel to the transformation of Grenada into a "real war." In both cases the process of transformation is clichéd, theatrical, unconvincing, and completely *fictional*. On the other hand, even if Highway's hard-drinking, bar-fighting, recruit-abusing figure is also a cliché, his grieving over Heartbreak Ridge is not, and neither is his emotional isolation and repursuit of his ex-wife, whatever its conventional romantic-comedy affinities. Underneath the farce of recruit training and the farce of Grenada as something big and serious are genuine pain and real regret. Formally speaking, the movie is a mess—not so much narratively chaotic as thematically chaotic—but, as is so often the case in Eastwood's oeuvre, its mess is more interesting and suggestive than many another film's conventional coherence. Cultural studies scholars spend entire careers quarrying hidden contradiction from mainstream Hollywood movies; but in Eastwood's cinema he does most of the work himself. The way that *Heartbreak Ridge* allows its theatricalities, its fictionalities, and its incommensurables to show, rather than covering them over through a process of "well-made" repression and disavowal, makes it into a film that simply blurts out the truth about its ideological impossibility, just as *Bronco Billy* does.

For me two details in the film encapsulate its multivalent activity in small visual gestures. The first is Eastwood's combat face camouflage—a lurid black-brown-and-three-shades-of-green concoction that makes him look like a jungle-warfare circus clown and perfectly expresses the movie's nested layers of fictionality and theatricality, where we now see the film's star and creator *made up* and *performing* as a warrior in a movie in which he is made up and performing as a warrior and which is itself the performance of a performance (the invasion of Grenada). The second occurs in the final scene, when the troops are deplaning after the successful conclusion of their mission accompanied by a brass band and in front of an assembly of cheering family members and spectators arrayed in *bleachers* erected for their attendance at *this* performance. There, among the band and the officers in their dress blues and the big flags rippling against a bright blue sky, is Marsha Mason, decked out in a rather 1950s-ish outfit of flouncy dress with immaculate little white gloves. As Eastwood looks toward her, she gives him a wonderfully complicit little sideways smile, and she waves her tiny Stars and Stripes in tiny symbolic support of both his mission and him (she will be welcoming him back into a renewed relationship now). Everything is recuperated here—American military glory, Eastwood's regret-filled career, and his regret-filled relationship—but it is recuperated in staged, toy, playacted terms. As Mason through her costume carries us back to a period of putative ideological wholeness, her little flag signals the homuncular and voodooistic nature of this rebirth of values, and her smile implies, in a very charming recasting of Reagan's own pitch, that everybody knows that all this isn't real, but doesn't it make us feel good? And isn't it fun? And when the reunion of Mason and Eastwood is followed by a shot of a very large Stars and Stripes, that, too, has these qualities transferred to it. Like *Bronco Billy*, then, *Heartbreak Ridge* is both reassuring and redemptive, on the one hand, and highly visible in its portrayal of the process of artifice and fakery that enables that reassurance and redemption.

- ■ *Unforgiven*

Bronco Billy is about the myth of the cowboy, and so is *Unforgiven*. *Bronco Billy*'s cowboy hero is absurdly naive, and he has no authenticity or solid foundation at all, yet faith in this ridiculous figure can rescue Americans from hopelessness in their lives. *Unforgiven*'s cowboy hero is the diametrical opposite of naive: he is the ultimate descendant of the hard men of the genre, the most deadly combatant, the final winner of all the masculinity-measuring lethal showdowns whose history stretches from the beginning of the Western to the latest examples. In particular, he represents the very last stage in the evolution of the cowboy hero from the naive hero of which Bronco Billy is a pastiche through the ever darkening, ever more ethically compromised succession of figures to be seen in 1950s Westerns such as *The Naked Spur* and *The Searchers*, through Leone's cynical bounty hunters and killers, and through Peckinpah's carnage-dealing antiheroes. In *Unforgiven*, the equivalent of the admiration of little kids, asylum directors, and nuns for Bronco Billy is the reputation of William Munny as a pure, pitiless, stone-cold killer who is a figure of charismatic attraction to the novice would-be killer the Schofield Kid and also, ultimately, to the writer of cheap popular Westerns W. W. Beauchamp. The movie devotes itself seriously to an inquiry into this set of questions: What constitutes cowboy heroism? What is its relationship, if any, to morality and justice? What kinds of narratives does it provoke? Indeed, it recapitulates that evolution of the genre I just referred to, in the successive theories expounded by English Bob (the chivalrous "Duke of Death" who avenges the honor of fair women), by Little Bill Daggett (who comprehensively destroys the idealisms of English Bob's accounts and presents an exposition of his own "grit" as a necessary element in community building in the town of Big Whiskey and who represents the violent pro-social hero), and finally by William Munny, retransformed into his awesomely death-dealing former self, as he shoots down Little Bill, all his deputies, and a few other people in Greeley's Saloon without the slightest form of rationale but vengeance and blind rage. Beauchamp, an actual professional narrativizer, gives this whole schema an unmistakably reflexive quality, repeating in an even more emphatic and articulate way the reflexive strategies of *Bronco Billy* and *Heartbreak Ridge*. Moreover the evolutionary-end-point cowboy whom

Eastwood finally reembodies in the film is first and foremost the cowboy originally embodied most powerfully in Eastwood's own Western roles of the 1960s and 1970s.[5] For Eastwood was the first definitive American anticowboy: divorced or nearly divorced from pro-social projects, a long way from being an iteration of the Western's traditional magical solution to the conflict between violence-endowed individuals and the community that needs defending (cf. *Shane* for a late textbook example). There is no community worth defending anymore in *For a Few Dollars More* (1965) or Eastwood's own *High Plains Drifter* (1971): Society is a mere aggregation of vices, and to prey upon it is a form of rational behavior. Under those circumstances the only yardstick left for heroism is the amount of effective violence a protagonist can bring to bear, and Eastwood's brand of violence is taking place on an entirely new level, a place never inhabited or imagined by John Wayne and Gary Cooper.[6] Its source is occult and unaccountable, its exercise transcendentally invincible; it is on this account more purely *mythic* than that of any earlier, more realist forms. This investment of a pagan, godlike power is Sergio Leone's doing, that of a European who instantly sees the Western's connection to traditional mythology and is uninterested in its connection to American nation building and, moreover, an Italian with a jaundiced view of the morality of human behavior in general. And so the Western ends up (in the 1970s) in a place where sheer killing power, a fantasy-like extreme of superhuman invincibility, is invested in the cowboy hero, specifically in Clint Eastwood (even as the physical environment becomes increasingly dirty and chaotic as a marker of its anti-idealism). Twenty years later, in *Unforgiven*, Eastwood revisits this territory and this character. Instead of being anonymous and unaccountable, Munny is given a psyche and a personal history. Earlier avatars of this character had needed no reason to be violent: It was their nature, and there were no competing values. Munny's violence, however, is marked as coming from some deep psychic pit filled with pain, hatred, and oblivion. It is a place of torment, and it gives rise to atrocities. It is very hard for viewers to maintain this character in the role of a hero, or if they do, it will be at the cost of sacrificing every possible moral and ethical basis for that heroism and for their admiration—a rather extreme step when Munny begins the film as a responsible single father trying to provide for his children. Moreover, the excavation of this Eastwood protagonist creates a disturbing set of retrospective shadows falling over all of Eastwood's earlier cowboy heroes.

Unforgiven fits into the pattern I am trying to establish here of *artificial mythologies* in Eastwood's cinema through its very self-conscious discourse about the legend of William Munny, charismatic badman, and his place within the schemata of heroism in the Old West. As I just remarked, the film obliterates the whole edifice of the violent Western hero by demonstrating how inadequate Little Bill's account of virtuous toughness is and substituting instead a kind of pure bloodlust without rationale or method. When Munny is questioned by Beauchamp about the strategy that allowed him to win the battle of Greeley's Saloon, he just remarks: "I was lucky . . . but then I've always been lucky when it comes to killing folks."[7] That is a very heavy blow to the moral underpinnings of the genre. The distillation of Eastwood's heroism then simply becomes killing power pure and simple. But insofar as that in itself might be a charismatic quality—and it certainly might be for fans of the Man with No Name, Dirty Harry, and the heroes of *High Plains Drifter* and *Pale Rider*—it, too, is strongly undercut by the film. The Schofield Kid is drawn to track Munny down to his home by the former outlaw's reputation as a "meaner-than-hell cold-blooded damn killer" and "the meanest goddamned son of a bitch alive"—qualities that the Kid holds in the highest esteem. (So Munny's reputation is what inaugurates the action, so to speak.) How debased, and how false, such criteria for admiration are becomes apparent when the figuratively and literally myopic Kid actually gets to see some killing close-up and quickly decides to pursue a quiet life instead of a charismatic one.

In the end, then, *Unforgiven* has attacked every theory and practice of heroic mastery in the Western and also Eastwood's own history as a violent screen hero. All of these stories about the Old West, about the cowboy hero, about heroic violence, and about Eastwood are shown to be false or ugly or both. But like all of the Eastwood films we are considering, *Unforgiven* also is two-edged. Eastwood does mow down a building full of bad guys (though their bad-guy status is actually debatable) at the end of the movie, his project of revenge for the unjust killing of his friend Ned accomplished in a complete and total way (no matter that Ned's involvement and death were Munny's responsibility), and he even manages (though in a heavily compromised way) to avenge the young prostitute whose mutilation sets the action in motion. As difficult as it is for me personally to believe, many of the film's viewers were able simply to accept this as just one more case of Clint Eastwood shooting down everyone in sight. Eastwood does not die, is not required to back down in the face of another authority (as he does before the town sheriff in *Bronco Billy*). So *Unforgiven* must finally be described as schizophrenically both the triumph of the Eastwood character and the total compromise of the Eastwood character simultaneously. And in this, it replicates the action of *Bronco Billy* and *Heartbreak Ridge*, where the protagonists, and the films, are both true and false.

One last point. We have seen how both *Bronco Billy* and *Heartbreak Ridge* have deployed the Stars and Stripes in strategic ways to connect the protagonists' projects with that of the nation and how in both cases there was a strong ironic undercurrent to those deployments (flags sewn by lunatics formed into a circus tent, a toy flag for a toy war). In *Unforgiven* there are two scenes in which the flag figures prominently. The first is on the Fourth of July in Big Whiskey. With a large flag flying very visibly, English Bob starts discoursing on the superiority of monarchy to democracy as a political system, and then Little Bill proceeds to administer to him a disturbingly severe beating—partly as an exercise in no-nonsense preventative law enforcement and partly out of patriotic annoyance. This America is a place where you get beaten half to death by a law officer with no warrant or charges if you say something unpatriotic. The second notable appearance of the flag is during Munny's last exit from the town. After the bloodbath in the saloon, he makes his way into the torrential rain, thunder, and lightning in the torch-lit street, and with the flag waving dimly but quite visibly behind his head in a low-angle shot, he shouts hoarsely:

> Any man I see out there I'm gonna kill him. If he takes a shot at me not only am I gonna kill him I'm gonna kill his wife and all his friends, burn his damn house down. Nobody better shoot. You better bury Ned right. You better not cut up nor otherwise harm no whores. Or I'll come back and kill every one of you sons of bitches!

The notion that America might preside over this scene and these sentiments is chilling; the implications are sweeping—and shocking.

■ *Flags of Our Fathers*

Flags of Our Fathers, alone in this selection as a film without Eastwood's presence as an actor, then becomes an almost didactic exposition of the gulf between truth and fiction in the realm of a national heroic narrative. The film's source is a work of historical nonfiction, James Bradley's book of the same name, which details the author's quest to discover the details of his father's story as one of the three surviving men from the famous flag-raising photograph and to investigate the histories of the other men in the photograph as well.[8] But Eastwood's version goes beyond the realm of historical exposé by virtue of its vivid illustration, its perfect expression, of this nagging aspect of his own artistic oeuvre; and whereas Bradley's book spends a good deal of its length on the men's early years and the battle on Iwo Jima, the film is more interested in the after-story—in the nature of that image and its propagation and reception. Truth is a very early casualty in this narrative of an actual series of events that were not short of genuine heroism and inspiring deeds but whose most immediately striking mythic image was an entirely inauthentic one.

The story is fascinating even in outline. On February 19, 1945, the United States invaded the Japanese island of Iwo Jima with a force of about thirty thousand Marines (another forty thousand would follow). The island was defended by eighteen to twenty thousand Japanese. After five days of intense fighting, the fortress of Mount Suribachi was on the point of suppression, and the American flag was raised on its summit. The detachment sent to raise the flag had encountered no resistance, although it had expected to come under heavy fire (apparently Suribachi had fallen even though nobody quite knew it). The event was photographed. On seeing the flag, U.S. units on the beach and at sea raised a great cry of celebration. At this very inaugural moment, the distorting factors of politics and claims to narrative ownership immediately raised their heads. Secretary of the Navy James Forrestal had accompanied the invasion and seeing the flag raised, exclaimed that it ensured the survival of the Marine Corps "for the next five hundred years" and expressed the wish to obtain the flag as a personal souvenir. When this message reached Battalion Commander Chandler Johnson, he muttered, "The hell with that!" and made arrangements to requisition the flag himself as a memento for the battalion. He instructed the raising of a second, larger flag to take its place. That flag—also delivered to the top of the mountain without any Japanese resistance—was erected by five Marines and a Navy corpsman who were conducting various duties. The event was captured by photographer Joe Rosenthal, who was caught by surprise when the flag was actually raised and did not even look through the viewfinder when he got what turned out to be the most famous of American war images. Rosenthal's film roll was sent back to Guam without annotation or explanation, and when it was developed the picture was seized on in short order for its iconic resonance.

Meanwhile, the fighting on Iwo Jima continued for another brutal thirty-five days before it was completely subdued, with over 95 percent of the Japanese defenders being killed, together with 6,821 American dead and another 21,000-odd wounded.[9] In that fighting, three of the six men who had raised the second flag were killed also.

Then began the extraordinary afterlife of these events. The power of "The Photograph" (as James Bradley calls it) was so strong that it was instantly reprinted on the front pages of newspapers and achieved universal recognition.[10] It prompted the Post Office to issue a stamp bearing its image. And it prompted President Roosevelt to order the three flag-raising survivors brought back home to boost home front morale. They became the centerpiece of the Seventh, and last, Bond Tour, which raised money for the war from the sale of government bonds to citizens whose contributions were solicited amid the most garish theatrical hoopla imaginable. Earlier bond tours had featured major Hollywood stars (as they had already done during World War I); but the presence of the actual heroes of Iwo Jima boosted the seventh tour so much that it broke all records and all expectations. The three survivors of the second flag raising—PFC Rene Gagnon, PFC Ira Hayes, and Navy Corpsman John Bradley—were whisked from city to city and event to event, trotted out and made to say a few words, several times required to inhabit symbolic representations of the flag raising, and at the final event at Soldier Field stadium in Chicago actually made to storm a papier-mâché mountain and plant the flag, amid the glare and racket of exploding fireworks. At most of these events the three survivors were accompanied by the "Gold Star Mothers" of their three dead comrades. This gesture, somewhat distasteful in itself, carried its own special flaw, since one of the celebrated dead men had not actually been there at all (but by a wonderful irony had actually been part of the *first* flag-raising party), with the true participant in the photograph recognized only by his mother on the basis of his buttocks. In other words, one of the three was the "wrong" mother. The bond tour experience was not good for any of the three servicemen. Native American Ira Hayes developed a serious drinking and behavior problem during the tour and had to be sent back to the Pacific against his will, and then he had an ill-starred postwar life as a farm laborer in and out of drunk tanks until he died of exposure in a field at the age of thirty-two in 1955. Rene Gagnon took to heart the promises of dozens of backslapping businessmen during the tour that they would give him rewarding and well-compensated work after the war and was very discouraged when none of them followed through. He ended his life working as a janitor. John Bradley did in fact lead an exemplary life as a fine, prosperous family man and pillar of the community in his small Wisconsin town, but it is rather thought-provoking that he expressed the profound wish that the photo had never been taken and not only refused to speak about his wartime experience to anyone but, according to his son, tried hard to literally forget as much of it as he could.

The most remarkable thing about this story is its stark and repeated demonstration of how simple-narrative and image-driven patriotic enthusiasm is, how much more powerful exalted visual rhetoric is than anything that the mere truth can inspire. The Photograph was instantly misinterpreted, and that more or less honest initial mistake was very quickly amplified into a big, viral lie. Though the participants (including the photographer) were quite forthright in their protestations that what had been captured in its image was a completely routine activity of raising a replacement flag, nobody was interested, nobody wanted to hear it. At a certain point a spurious question did arise as to whether the photo had been staged; but although this accusation was completely groundless, it, too, had its basis in the emotional potency of the image. It boggles the mind to consider how many lies were piled up over The Photograph: the primary level of what was occurring in the photo and who the participants were and then the subsequent levels of the suppression of the truth, the crassest hucksterism in refashioning the mendacious event for lowest-common-denominator public consumption, and the crowbarring of the three servicemen into a sickening series of boosterish pageants regardless of the psychological effect on these actual combatants. The fact that all these crimes against truth and decency paid off in an avalanche of bond purchases demonstrates that an uplifting fiction is the most effective selling tool there is, certainly better than complicated and messy actual events. Lies, indeed, are the only thing that the public *will* buy.

An analysis of the picture shows its value as a symbolic representation. The servicemen are battered and battle-worn, none of their faces are visible, and they act as one: They are the allegorical essence of democratic effort, to raise aloft the symbol of America and everything it stands for; their grouping is dynamic yet balanced, and the composition is perfect. The Photograph was almost accidental, its pro-filmic content banal, and the emergence, as if by magic, of this immensely powerful image is very much akin to the mysterious origins of the power of the transcendent

Eastwood hero of yore: Its nature is irrational and impenetrable, it comes from nowhere, its name is nobody. The infinite proliferation of the image into every level of American life, high and low, culminates in the gigantic bronze statuary group at the Marine Corps War Memorial in Arlington, Virginia, where the Brobdingnagian flag raisers create the same effect as a gargantuan statue of Comrade Stalin in some Russian city in 1950 commemorating his leadership in the Great Patriotic War, and is the result of something like the same cultural process.[11]

The crucial point here is that, although there was true heroism aplenty on Iwo Jima, from virtually every combatant on the island, such merely "true" heroism was unmarketable for propaganda purposes and indeed even now needs to be massaged into some form that allows the preservation of those uplifting feelings of piety and pride that are the essence of the patriotic impulse at its most intoxicating. The three survivors repeated over and over that "the real heroes of Iwo Jima are the men who didn't come back" and that they themselves did nothing whatever that was special (this was taken as a highly becoming modesty and simply added to their heroic stature). Every serious account of conditions of intense combat shows something like the same story: of terrible, unspeakable experiences gone through collectively. Some soldiers may have behaved with more than ordinary bravery, others with less, but basically there was nothing to choose between them. One is reminded of the remark of the French legionnaire in Georges Bernanos's 1936 novel *Diary of a Country Priest* and repeated in Robert Bresson's 1951 film: "Si le bon Dieu ne sauve pas les soldats, tous les soldats, parce que soldats, inutile d'insister." [If God doesn't save soldiers, all soldiers, just because they're soldiers, what's the use?]. But again a sentiment like this is of very limited usefulness in the effort to stoke patriotic pride. (It is, in fact, especially the sentiment of Eastwood's two Iwo Jima films taken as a matched pair.) It is notable that although *Flags of Our Fathers* is relentless in its focus on factual distortion and the seemingly endless trail of phoniness, the documentary extras accompanying the DVD issue, the A&E documentary *Heroes of Iwo Jima* that covers the same events, and even to an extent also Bradley's original book all cannot remain aloof from the compelling patriotic emotions arising from the spectacle of Marine heroism on Iwo Jima, as from all spectacles of military sacrifice. We must honor their sacrifice, we must shed a tear, we must feel humbled and holy. And this is very arguably not a response that is wholly appropriate to the horrors of Iwo Jima, however universal it seems to be in practice.

As *Bronco Billy* and *Heartbreak Ridge* enter into and engage with the ideological landscapes of their time, so does *Flags of Our Fathers* intervene in contemporary ideologies of military patriotism, especially the increasingly pervasive iterations of reverential pride surrounding the U.S. participation in World War II. This attitude to World War II has always been present, but in the past decade or so there has been a fat thread of revival and escalation. America's troubles during these years have undoubtedly provided a crucial spur to this revival. Vietnam never ceased to be a bad dream, a handful of "ragheads" with box cutters brought down the World Trade Center, Iraq was a mess, domestic politics had never been more viciously quarrelsome, and the achievements of contemporary American bellicosity were fractured and unsuitable for framing. The dream of a golden past where Americans were united, where they stepped in to restore order and goodness and gave the world a living example of the superiority of their ideology and unique national gifts, where they inevitably defeated the enemy in combat not in the guise of hypermasculine action heroes but as regular guys played by movie stars, is immensely consoling.[12]

Perhaps it was Ken Burns who first struck the soft, almost voluptuous, quasi-Lincolnian note of nobility and sorrow in his *Civil War* series back in 1990. Then he struck it again and again, notably in *Baseball* (1994) and *Jazz* (2001) and *The War* (2007), spreading out vast tracts of American history and culture with aching nostalgia. The instantly recognizable tone of all these powerful series proclaims that they are conveying exactly the same meaning: a melancholy recognition that the past is the past and our heroes are all dead, together with a wonderfully warm pride that they are ours and ours alone. America's past is beautiful—and gone. The quality of sweet, sacred memorialization was taken up and applied to World War II by Steven Spielberg and DreamWorks in *Saving Private Ryan* (1998). Clearly, Spielberg felt a kinship with these powerful, melting, uplifting emotions, connected both with an awful loss and with a sense of redemption and transfiguration. In particular, Tom Hanks's almost unbearable death is transmuted into something beautiful, and the agent of transmutation is this man's sacrifice of his life for America, for the *idea* of America as encapsulated in the mission to retrieve Private Ryan; and the result is an upwelling of piety and a belief in national self-worth.

From *Saving Private Ryan* came *Band of Brothers* (2001), based on Stephen Ambrose's historical account of the experiences of a single company of U.S. soldiers from Normandy to the German surrender—another

DreamWorks production (with HBO) among whose executive producers were Spielberg and Tom Hanks. While never approaching the wrenching loss and beatific consolation of *Saving Private Ryan*, it offers the reassuring spectacle of buddies risking their lives for one another; a benevolent commanding officer who nurtures them, writes their families when they are killed, and agonizes about his worthiness; and a basically triumphant progress from boot camp to armistice with numerous instances of the dangers of battle. Next up was Burns's *The War* (2007), a 680-minute documentary with a special emphasis on the small-town home front and manifesting, again, a hypnotized desiring gaze at these people, places, and attitudes nested in the common past. Its unwillingness to gloss over racial discrimination drew complaints that the film was "leftist," but the overwhelming themes are those of sacrifice and common effort.[13] Yet another Dream-Works Spielberg–Hanks production followed: *The Pacific* (2010), seemingly intended as an "other theater" bookend to *Band of Brothers*. The first episode glows with piety, as the boys from beautiful period neighborhoods rush to enlist, while their anxious but nonetheless admiring parents look on. Later on, the series becomes much less comfortable, and its explicit depictions of combat horrors go a lot further than anything else in this category (including both Eastwood Iwo Jima films), so that its efforts at the end to reach that safe haven of ideological affirmation can only be partly successful.[14] But whatever momentary difficulties this collection of films may encounter in their ideological mission, their overwhelming effect is one of reassurance, an encapsulation of reverent national pride in a bubble of time past where nobody can get at it anymore to besmirch it or temper it with the caveats and confusion that contemporary national pride has been compelled to endure.

It is precisely this safety of the past that *Flags of Our Fathers* refuses. Indeed its principal mission seems to be exactly to breach that bubble. It is odd that both it and *Letters from Iwo Jima* (2006) are also DreamWorks productions and that Steven Spielberg was the one who bought the screen rights to Bradley's book. Certainly the finished film has not much of a Spielbergian feeling to it (unless it is of an anti-Spielberg Spielberg movie, such as *Munich*). Spielberg did offer it unhesitatingly to Eastwood, possibly recognizing that Eastwood's affinity with a double-faced project of this kind was a lot greater than his own.[15] *Flags* was a large-scale production for Eastwood, but it was a big subject, and there were hopes for a big box-office success (hopes that one look at a film this complicated and emotionally difficult ought to have dispelled). But although the movie was not a flop, its performance in theaters was disappointing,[16] and many viewers plainly did not know quite what to do with it. Roger Friedman, reviewing *Letters* for Fox News the following year, comments: "But what I think will make the difference for *Iwo Jima* is that it arrives just at the right time politically in this country. *Flags of Our Fathers* had a hard time finding an audience because people thought it was rah-rah patriotic."[17] *Flags of Our Fathers* did not perform well at the box office because people thought it was *too patriotic*? A myopia this dense is difficult to fathom; but if this really is the case, the presence of a number of key signifiers—bravery in battle, a sympathetic depiction of soldiers, the very presence of the flag—must have prevented viewers from seeing anything in the movie *but* patriotism, despite the extended, explicit demolition of the process of patriotic celebration taking place. And that fact is an illustration of what the movie is addressing. No wonder the film was often characterized as "confusing." This "confusion" is, in fact, the same as that to be found in *Bronco Billy* or (in a different way) *Unforgiven*: it arises from the activity of trying to read as harmonious the subliminal cacophony of conflicting imperatives.[18]

There are only two small moments in *Flags* where the solemn patriotism of those other World War II films raises its head for just an instant. They coincide with the unfolding of the two flags brought to the summit of Mount Suribachi, before they are actually raised. At these moments, the music (Eastwood's own) briefly enters very quietly to mark these flags as the bearers of American ideals—so briefly and quietly that it is scarcely perceptible. Nothing of the sort accompanies the actual flag raising on Suribachi, and when giant Stars and Stripes are plastered all over the bond tour events, with brass bands in abundance, the effect is actually repellant. We are reminded of how complexly, and counterintuitively, Eastwood has always used the flag—particularly in the three films already discussed (and also in the recent *Gran Torino*). There is even a return of Marsha Mason's little toy flag from *Heartbreak Ridge* in the form of the tiny Stars and Stripes that Ira Hayes excruciatingly brandishes to gawking tourists who seek him out where he works in the fields. Is there anyone else in mainstream American culture who has treated the flag with such ambivalence? The automatic uplifting emotional response prompted by its very appearance is held in abeyance in Eastwood's films, and in its place is a detached, almost Brechtian, recognition of how freighted with conflicting meanings that image is. *Flags of Our Fathers*, then, signifies exactly that ambivalence, and it is no wonder if the place of the flag itself in the narrative lent it a particular attraction for the director. The idea that the flag is a mindless hot button, and is exploited by every salesman, circulation-seeking newspaper, and politician, is just inescapable in the film. But is the film then saying that these vulgarizations are a traducing of the flag and what it stands for? Is it saying—and in this it would be the opposite of original—that America is not worthy of its heroes, that these brave boys suffered and died to preserve our freedom and our shallow celebrations of them are more about us than about them? Well, to a degree, perhaps. But that conclusion is neither conflicted nor troubling. By contrast, the film's final assessment is quite a bit more complex.

When the three boys first arrive in Washington, they are brought in to meet the Treasury Department official, Bud Gerber, who is in charge of the tour's presentation and who will now explain everything that is going to happen. In a sublime piece of casting serendipity, he is played by John Slattery, who would show up again on TV the following year in *Mad Men* as Roger Sterling, the irresistibly cynical senior executive at the Sterling Cooper advertising agency. Gerber does present everything to the three heroes exactly in the shallow and infuriating way you would expect a Madison Avenue guy working for the government to do. When Bradley, looking at the itinerary, asks who these "Gold Star Mothers" are, Gerber replies: "That's what we're calling the mothers of the dead flag raisers. You present each mother with a flag. They say a few words. People will shit money. It'll be so moving." Immediately, things start unraveling, as it becomes clear that one of the men in the picture has been misidentified and then that this was not the first flag raising. Gerber starts to have a tantrum, and Hayes quietly asks Bradley if he can hit him. Eventually, Hayes says that the whole thing is a farce. At this point, Gerber delivers a long speech that is perhaps the best piece of writing in the film:

> You know what they're calling this bond drive? The Mighty 7th. They might have called it The We're Flat Fucking Broke And We Can't Even Afford Bullets So We're Begging For Your Pennies Bond Drive, but it didn't have quite the ring. They could've called it that, though, because the last four bond drives came up so short we just printed money instead. Ask any smart boy on Wall Street, he'll tell you—our dollar's next to worthless. We borrowed so much. And nobody is lending any more. Ships aren't being built. Tanks aren't being built. Machine guns, bazookas, hand

grenades, zip. . . . If we don't raise 14 billion dollars—and that's million with a "b"—this war's over by the end of the month. . . . 14 billion! The last three drives didn't make that altogether. [*He pauses, wipes his face, gestures at the flag-raising poster.*] People on the street corner, they looked at this picture, and they took hope. Don't ask me why, I think it's a crappy picture myself, you can't even see your faces. But it said, "We can win this war—*are* winning this war, we just need you to dig a little deeper." They want to give us that money. No, they want to give it to *you*. But you, you don't want to ask for it, you don't want to give them hope. You want to explain about this person and that flag. Well, that's your choice. Because if we admit we made a mistake, that's all anybody will talk about, and that will be that.

Suddenly the perspective shifts. Gerber, instead of being some huckster you love to hate, turns into one more person—an important one—doing his job to win the war. It is not his job to feel the pain of Marines on Iwo Jima or their grieving parents; it is his job to raise money. It takes all kinds of people to win a war, the film shows us. Not all the contributors are the people fighting and dying: You need people like Gerber, and you need the millions contributing their "pennies." It is a complex and inspiring perspective, showing the mixture of calculation and populist feeling on the home front that is actually required. The bond drives themselves seem like a strategy particularly suited to America: The government does not just raise taxes or commandeer property to finance the war; it asks its people, democratically, and they contribute. At the same time, it is this consultative and popular-inclusive aspect of the project that calls for the stirring populist imagery and the inspiring populist rituals (such as the presentation of actual heroes). They want the personal connection. And so, from this perspective, the corners cut and the airbrushing of facts and images are completely justified. They are all part of a great cause.

Yes and no. The longer one looks at anything in this film, the more it shifts its shape. Gerber's speech is also full of lies. The war will not end by the end of the month if the results of the bond drive are disappointing. The United States had at this point incomparably greater financial resources than any other combatant—than any other nation, for that matter—and now that the Great Depression had been snuffed out like a candle precisely by this massive infusion of borrowed government money into the war effort, the nation was set for an unprecedented period of widespread social prosperity. As for the war itself, the enemy—Japan especially—was defeated not so much by the excellent fighting qualities of the American armed services as by an avalanche of resources. Far from running out of bullets, by 1945 the United States had an astounding quantity of war matériel to shower liberally onto every aspect of the Pacific campaign. The Manhattan Project, with its associated crash development project of the B-29 bomber, had cost $5 billion in itself. The Seventh Bond Drive took in an amazing $26 billion, almost twice its target sum, but before the money could be spent on ending the war, the war had ended: the Japanese surrender took place a mere six weeks after the conclusion of the tour. Doubtless the $26 billion went toward some other worthy government priority,[19] but the fact remains that the Seventh Drive, with its attendant lies, distortions, cheapening, and collateral psychological damage, did not really help win the war in any substantial way. Of course, nobody could have known that, not Roosevelt or Truman or the Treasury people and not the citizens who bought the bonds. Nevertheless, the end result is to move the entire effort into the realm of the virtual: the money raised *would have* helped win the war if the war had continued. But now the sacrificial contribution of the three servicemen, the strenuous efforts of Gerber and company, and the generosity of all the Capraesque "little people" who ponied up share in that same virtuality, that artifice or fictionality, that informs the movie's whole project.

The image of The Photograph, reproduced at the time of the drive on 5,000 large billboards and in 15,000 banks, 16,000 movie theaters, 30,000 railroad stations, 200,000 factories, and one million retail store windows, simply rises above any of its causes, including the actual fighting on Iwo Jima.[20] It has the power to move millions, but that power comes not from its resemblance to anything factual or real but from its *distance* from anything factual or real. Instead, it accesses the transcendent and transfigured realm of myth. One sees this process over and over again in the daily life of the culture, where the public (and its pimp, the media) seizes on any actual happening that superficially resembles something in the realm of fiction and pursues that fiction-that-is-really-happening with insatiable hunger. Eventually, enough facts emerge to destroy or seriously weaken the appetite, or else the story simply passes into the realm of the narrative archive, and the culture is ready for the next frenzied feeding. Obviously, the tremendous seriousness of the war for the American people in 1945 is not on a level with the tabloid and talk show scandals-of-the-week today. The crucial point, though, is that The Photograph *is* fiction, it *is* myth, and was from the first moment somebody looked at it and jumped a foot in recognition of its dramatic power. Does it really represent the experience or even the achievement of American forces on Iwo Jima? No: it is not a recognizable representation to anyone who was there. What actually happened on Iwo Jima was immensely more terrible and moving than anything indicated in The Photograph but will never move anybody to those transports of pure enthusiasm and pride that are the essence of bond drives in 1945 or Good War narratives today. Reality can never do this—only fiction.

This is a difficult idea, especially in America, where feelings are never wrong and the fundamental idea of America must always be something authentic. For almost its whole history, Hollywood has devoted itself to stitching together incommensurables and smoothing over the joints to create a seamless fabric of feeling for viewers. In this respect *Saving Private Ryan* is just another movie (and, indeed, Spielberg has made a career out of his special realization of how movies work in this way). But *Flags of Our Fathers* is not just another movie. It insists on pointing out how antifactual the story of Iwo Jima as conveyed by The Photograph is and exploring in excruciating detail how the sausage of charismatic patriotism is made. In doing this, it blows a rather large hole in the prevailing narrative of the Good War and takes at least a step in the direction of making that ideological landscape as difficult for comfortable mythology as Vietnam or Iraq. (*Gran Torino*, meanwhile, is doing something similar with the Korean War.) Again we must remind ourselves that it is *Clint Eastwood* doing this, not some revisionist historian or cultural studies scholar.

As I remarked at the beginning of this essay, Eastwood has spent his whole creative life embodying myths and simultaneously commenting on them in a deconstructive way. Principally his theme has been the impossibility, the unreality, of heroic character and action as incarnated in his own persona, in a context where the fundamental quality of that persona was its charismatic attraction. Earlier in his career, it was possible for these films to be consumed mostly in an unproblematic way, for the deconstructive activity did not insist on being overtly recognized, and the heroic persona itself covered its status in a cloud of mystery or presented itself as simply an exaggeration of existing realist action-genre stereotypes of the power hero. But beginning in the 1990s, Eastwood started to make films in this vein that were more openly problematic, films such as *White Hunter Black Heart* (1990), *A Perfect World* (1993), and, of course, *Unforgiven*. In these films, the charismatic hero retained his charisma, but its basis and constitution were uncovered to reveal something profoundly unacceptable. In the four films that I have concentrated on here, Eastwood has addressed himself to issues that attach heroic character to something broader—something social or cultural. In *Bronco Billy* and *Heartbreak Ridge* the hero's heroic activity has been seen as something necessary to save or preserve the nation, while in *Unforgiven* it is placed, reflexively, at the absolute center of a whole genre of narrative important to America as mythic expression of its character and abilities. And in all of these films, the heroic activity is simultaneously seen to lack authenticity or desirability or both. *Flags of Our Fathers* is certainly Eastwood's most detailed, intricate, and self-conscious project of this kind. Now the heroic activity—combat on Iwo Jima—is depicted in a plain and unadorned way. But, as when William Munny's heroic activity is presented "naked" at the end of *Unforgiven*, that unedited, unretouched picture is useless to any kind of positive mythology. Only some distortion and fictionalization, some re-presentation in the form of myth, will give it the power to inspire. Where *Unforgiven* leaves offscreen the process whereby William Munny's reputation, circulated through the culture by word of mouth, can inspire a Schofield Kid to emulate that model of a pitiless killer until he himself can see it truly, *Flags* devotes the greater part of its length exactly to a naked depiction of the process of mythmaking. Its mythic subject is not the ambiguous figure of the fearsome gunfighter of the Old West but, rather, something absolutely sacred and unambiguous: the bravery and sacrifice of American fighting men in the Good War, the wonderful unity and enthusiasm of the American people in their support for that war, and the most revered single image in the history of American warfare. Yes, that myth cluster is something truly heartening: The pride that arises from it is something that constitutes and sustains the nation; selling The Photograph and the survivors of the flag raising both helps the national budget and stages an act of collective affirmation that manifestly helps public belief in the cause and the nation. But the same thing might be said about the fictionalization of the death of Pat Tillman. Eastwood recognizes the positive effects, is willing probably to concede their necessity, even. But the main mission of his film is to show the roots of this mythical activity in untruths. It definitely revisits this thematic activity in a more discouraged way than *Bronco Billy* or *Heartbreak Ridge* does—more, even, than *Unforgiven* does. Like almost all of Eastwood's recent films, *Flags of Our Fathers* is sad and reflective. It may even be the most radical of all those films because its target is the idea of America itself.

■ Notes

1. See William Beard, *Persistence of Double Vision: Essays on Clint Eastwood* (Edmonton: University of Alberta Press, 2000).

2. It seems likely that the hero's name derives from Broncho Billy Anderson (1880–1971), the first movie cowboy star.

3. Shades of his real-life swim for survival can be seen in the Don Siegel/Malpaso *Escape from Alcatraz* (1979), where Eastwood's character does something similar.

4. These details come from the official account of the action, Ronald H. Cole's "Operation Urgent Fury: The Planning and Execution of Joint Operations in Grenada 12 October–2 November 1983" (Joint History Office of the Chairman of the Joint Chiefs of Staff, Washington, D.C., 1997).

5. This is to omit *Pale Rider* (1985) from the list—though, of course, that film, with its quasi-supernatural hero and transcendental violence, fits perfectly into the general picture.

6. The coming of the comic book or quasi–comic book superhero did attain this level—pioneered by Arnold Schwarzenegger and now the province of every computer-generated fantasy action hero. But all these figures pay a very stiff price in terms of gravity and authenticity and are always constituted on a ground of hyperartifice.

7. This scene revisits a conversation from *The Outlaw Josey Wales*, where Lone Watie asks Josey how he managed to shoot down a whole group of men. There, Josey answers with a technical analysis of who was likely the most dangerous, who looked afraid, and so on. In *Unforgiven* all this has now—as in the Leone films—been brutally reduced to something irrational and impenetrable.

8. James Bradley and Ron Powers, *Flags of Our Fathers* (New York: Bantam, 2000).

9. See http://www.ibiblio.org/hyperwar/PTO/Iwo/Casualties.html. Owing to the mostly island-hopping nature of the Pacific campaign, the numbers of combatants on both sides were quite small by the standards of other theaters. Indeed, the total number of American deaths in all services throughout the whole of the Pacific War (around one hundred thousand) was less than the number of civilian deaths in Tokyo in one large U.S. bombing raid (March 9–10, 1945). On the other hand, the casualty *rates* on Iwo Jima were very high—obviously on the Japanese side but also, relatively speaking, on the American—and the conditions of battle were terrible.

10. Color newsreel footage of the same event was taken from almost the same vantage point as Rosenthal's photograph, and it is possible to find the frame that almost exactly reproduces its content. But the moving picture footage never achieved anything like the same acclaim. It was the freezing of the image into a sculptural form that carried the power.

11. At one point the 2001 A&E documentary *Heroes of Iwo Jima* (written and directed by Lauren Lexton) explores an Iwo Jima memorabilia collection consisting of dozens and dozens of commemorative plates, mugs, plastic action figures, miniature lead or bronze statuary, plaques, special-edition photographs, spam advertisements, and many, many other items, while the collector, Fran Manucci, tells us that it was "reproduced on hats, T-shirts, statues, key chains, silver and gold coins, posters . . . almost anything you

could think of." And Iwo Jima veteran Tedd Thomey remarks that "it's been carved in ice, it's been made out of hamburger."

12. The unity of the American nation during World War II and its contrast to present-day social disunity are points explicitly made by Ryan Philippe (the actor playing Jack Bradley in *Flags of Our Fathers*) in the disk-length documentary accompanying the DVD issue of the film.

13. It is interesting to note that all of these Burns/Spielberg/DreamWorks offerings come from what the political Right has labeled "liberal Hollywood"; and this reminds us that Democrats are just as eager as Republicans to wrap themselves in the flag—and that this particular strain (the sweet, sorrowing, heartfelt variety) seems the particular property of liberal ideology.

14. It is noteworthy that at one point (Episode 7) in the series we are shown John Basilone, hero of Guadalcanal, brought back home to be paraded at fund drives until he becomes so sickened by the horrific banality and fakery of the process that he requests to go back overseas, where he promptly dies a gung ho death on the battlefield like the hero he is (on Iwo Jima during the first day of the assault, actually). Both this and the events of the Seventh Bond Tour are factually based, but one suspects that this particular aspect of *The Pacific* derives from *Flags of Our Fathers*.

15. If this was indeed the case, it would recall the production history of one of Spielberg's very best films, *A.I.*, which was handed to him to direct by Stanley Kubrick, who had bought the project for himself but in the end recognized that Spielberg was better fitted for it. Details about Spielberg's involvement in the project, and Eastwood's co-option to it, may be found in John H. Foote, *Clint Eastwood: Evolution of a Filmmaker* (Westport, Conn.: Praeger, 2009), 164–65.

16. The final production budget was $53 million; the domestic box office, $33.6 million; the foreign box office, $28.3 million; and DVD sales (to date), $45.1 million. Factoring in publicity and marketing costs, the production has not done much better than break even. See http://www.the-numbers.com/movies/2006/FLAGS.php.

17. Roger Friedman, "Clint Eastwood Makes a Huge Anti-war Statement with 'Iwo Jima,'" December 11, 2006, http://www.foxnews.com/story/0,2933,235805,00.html.

18. In her thoughtful appreciation of the film, Drucilla Cornell says that this reaction to the film is the result of its deconstruction of the notion of heroism and deglamorization of war: "The thematic point here is that war itself breaks up any possibility of narrative coherence. . . . The film can have no overarching coherence because the very real themes with which it engages have no coherence of their own" (*Clint Eastwood and Issues of American Masculinity* [New York: Fordham University Press, 2009], 153–54).

19. And indeed it was followed by a postwar bond drive, the so-called Victory drive, which netted another $9 billion (though falling short of its $11 billion target). See http://library.duke.edu/digitalcollections/adaccess/warbonds.html#victory.

20. See http://www.iwojima.com/bond/index.htm.

CHAPTER 13

EASTWOOD'S *FLAGS OF OUR FATHERS* AND *LETTERS FROM IWO JIMA*: THE SILENCE OF HEROES AND THE VOICE OF HISTORY

John M. Gourlie

Challenging our conventional historical understanding, Clint Eastwood offers in *Flags of Our Fathers* and *Letters from Iwo Jima* (both 2006) two very different cinematic "takes" on one of the most reverenced battles of World War II. The first such take, *Flags of Our Fathers*, gives us a multifaceted portrayal of the human encounter with a searing and overwhelmingly traumatic experience of war—specifically from the perspective of the U.S. Marines who fought at Iwo Jima in 1945. The film itself is complexly structured. On one level, it is structured so that the fighting retains a primacy and an immediacy. It is as though the fierce intensity of the fighting occurred at such a cataclysmically white-hot heat that the battle continues to exist and replay itself, even though the calendar time of history has moved on to other events in other places. Another level of the film's structure captures this truth. For it shows us—in terms of memory, nightmare, and PTSD flashback—the battle as it lives on in the minds of the Marines who experienced it.

A third aspect of the film's structure is the framing narrative in which John Bradley reconstructs the personal history of Iwo Jima that his father, John "Doc" Bradley, sealed off behind an impenetrable wall of silence during his lifetime. Intrinsic to the son's recovery of his father's wartime past is an exploration of why the public values and meanings that history has assigned to the actions of Doc and his fellow Marines—heroism, victory, patriotism—do not encompass the Marines' own sense of what these experiences mean to them. The son's search leads him to understand more deeply what "heroism" means, especially to the men who were the "heroes." It is a lived definition—inseparable from the human bonds that were forged by

their friendships, their shared traumas, and their sacrificial dedication to
one another. Like the book upon which it is based, Eastwood's film portrays
a vulnerable, wounded, and immeasurably valuable humanity. The book and
film equally portray how history inevitably plasters over this lived human
substratum with a fresco that simplifies and distorts even as it offers those
shapes and colors that create our public understanding of such events.[1]

The film opens in a dream, a nightmare really, and it ends with the
memory of a joyful swim in the Pacific Ocean, a moment snatched from
the ongoing rigors of the battle on Iwo Jima. Between this beginning and
ending, the film weaves together a complex series of memories, narrations,
and flashbacks to tell the story of the Marines who fought and died on Iwo
Jima. Eastwood's cinematic effects combine to render the characters and
their actions on a human scale—and to maintain them there. Any imagery
of glorification or lingering of shots for emotional heightening is avoided.
Instead, the imagery and editing move at a rapid pace, at times almost too
quickly for us to grasp what is happening. The lighting is somber, with
shadows cast upon characters much of the time. The color is desaturated,
drained of any vibrancy. In addition, the consistent use of narration, flashback, and dream underlines how much the experience of battle has been
deeply internalized. While the film graphically portrays the physical chaos,
brutality, and trauma of the battle, it emphasizes even more the inner landscape of emotional disfiguration and psychic wounds that such violence
creates.

In avoiding glorification, the film follows the book by James Bradley.
Both depict the lives of those Marines who participated in raising the
American flag above Mount Suribachi after its Japanese defenders had
been partially subdued. These Marines were captured in the act of raising
the flag by AP photographer Joseph Rosenthal. The book calls Rosenthal's
photo "the most famous image in the history of photography" (Bradley
2000, 282). As Bradley describes the impact of the photograph during the
Seventh Bond Tour in which it was featured together with the surviving
Marine flag raisers:

> The photograph's mystical hold on the nation continued to deepen.
> Detached—liberated—even from the merely factual circumstances
> that produced it, the photograph had become a receptacle for America's
> emotions; it stood for everything good that Americans wanted to stand

for; it had begun to act as a great prism, drawing the light of all America's values into its facets, and giving off a brilliant rainbow of feeling and thoughts. (2000, 282)

. . . The Photograph had transported many thousands of anxious, grieving, and war-weary Americans into a radiant state of mind: a kind of sacred realm, where faith, patriotism, mythic history, and the simple capacity to hope all intermingled. (2000, 292)

To reclaim Doc Bradley's personal past, his son's book and Eastwood's film need to somehow dismantle the fame, glory, and heroism that the photograph, military victory, and national history have wrapped around the flag raisers. Part of Eastwood's task, in particular, is to depict the flag raising itself without adding to the heroic imagery that is historically associated with it. Eastwood's task is especially difficult because he is handling visual images, and one such image is Rosenthal's own image, which has blazed its path to glory.

The primary basis for avoiding a depiction that features heroism and glory is that the Marines did not see themselves or their own actions that way. In the film, the Marines'-eye view is developed through three soldiers. They are John "Doc" Bradley, Ira Hayes, and Rene Gagnon. After being photographed by Rosenthal as they and their companions raised the replacement flag, they survived the fighting on Iwo Jima long enough to be recalled to the United States to participate in a bond tour. Bond tours raised the money necessary to fund the war effort. In the current era of mass media and unfunded wars, it is perhaps difficult for many of us to imagine the power and importance of the bond tours. As James Bradley describes them:

National in scope, local in flavor, Bond Tours combined the old fashioned elements of vaudeville, the country fair, the Fourth of July parade. And they anticipated some of the flash and crowd-pleasing fervor that would accrue . . . to Elvis, the Beatles, and the Rolling Stones. . . .

This was the ponderous challenge—and incomparable excitement—of reaching a mass public in an age before television: a great roving road show that would personify the war's realities and deliver them to Americans' home precincts. An effort by the government to communicate

almost face-to-face with as many of its citizens as possible, and to make
its case for voluntary sacrifices, rather than simply confiscate the needed
money through taxes. A gargantuan feat of popular democracy, the likes
of which have since vanished from the culture.

     . . . The Mighty 7th would have as its emblem the most famous image
in the history of photography. And the 7th would exhibit, for public view,
three of the six figures from that almost-holy frieze. (2000, 282)

The Mighty 7th Bond Tour was colossally successful. The money it raised
almost doubled its goal. To put this in perspective, "Americans had pledged
$26.3 billion. . . . Equal to almost half of the 1946 total U.S. government
budget of $56 billion" (Bradley 2000, 294).

    Very early in the film, a narrator is explaining the power of Rosenthal's
photograph of the flag raising. The narrator says, "The right picture can
win or lose a war." He goes on to explain that the country was bankrupt, the
mood had turned cynical, and the people were tired of the war. "One photo
turned all that around"—there is a quick flash to a bond tour reenactment
of the flag raising in a stadium, and interrupting that is a quick flash to Doc
attending a wounded man on Iwo Jima. A Japanese soldier attacks Doc,
and Doc kills the attacker with his knife. Upon returning to his foxhole,
Doc cannot find his buddy Iggy. In another flash, we are returned to the
flag being raised in the stadium reenactment. The film then traces the history of the Marines' preparation for the Iwo Jima invasion beginning with
training at Camp Tarawa in 1944 and ending with Ira Hayes reluctantly
being flown home from Eniwetok in 1945 after having been taken out of the
battle itself. Clearly, Eastwood is offering rapidly edited, complexly layered
imagery as a counterweight to Rosenthal's single mythic image.

    Far more than in prior eras, we recognize the posttraumatic stress
syndrome that the three soldiers are suffering from in varying degrees.
In Doc's case, it is his frantic worry over his friend Iggy's disappearance
that recurs in flashbacks. In a different vein, Ira's drinking represents his
effort to cope with the haunting inner images of war. But on top of the
inner battle trauma, the bond tour imposes immense additional stresses.
Some of these have to do with confusions and falsehoods that grate against
the truth as the three men know it. Not understanding the circumstances
of the replacement flag raising, the press has picked up rumors that the
photo of the Marines was staged. Even more intense and emotionally painful are the issues of who is actually in the photo. These issues surface in the

meeting with the Gold Star Mothers. Hank Hansen has been mistakenly identified as one of the figures, and Doc confirms that it is, indeed, him to Hank's mother, compassionately sacrificing the "truth" to give some import to her son's death and to offer whatever consolation that might bring. But Doc and the others know that the figure is actually Harlon Block. Likewise, they know that their flag raising is a second act to replace the original flag that other Marines raised over Mount Suribachi. While not posed or in any way "staged," their flag raising is nonetheless not the one the soldiers fighting at Iwo Jima actually cheered as the initial sign of victory.

At the Gold Star Mothers ceremony, in a mixture of all of these emotions and more, Ira collapses in sobs into the arms of Mrs. Strank, the mother of Mike Strank, who is now dead. Sergeant Strank was the leader of the flag raisers' platoon and is one of the figures in the famous photograph. All Ira can utter is, "He was the best Marine I ever knew." Both Ira and Doc are acutely aware that the label of "hero," automatically extended and genuinely meant by the public, is not a label they would apply to themselves. But whatever the "truth" is, the three surviving flag raisers have a public role to play and a public image to enact. They must play the hero. Given this function in the bond tour, Rene looks forward to profiting from the public acclaim. At the other end of the spectrum, Ira feels that "this whole damn thing is a farce." Ira and Doc deeply sense the difference between the brass-band CELEBRITY and HEROISM of the bond tour and their actual experience on Iwo Jima. They deeply feel the difference between the authentic actions of the Marines in battle and the photographic images and staged reenactments of such actions. In the book, James Bradley comments directly on these issues in discussing his father:

> Hero. In that misunderstood and corrupted word, I think, lay the final reason for John Bradley's silence.
>
> Today the word "hero" has been diminished, confused with "celebrity." But in my father's generation the word meant something.
>
> Celebrities seek fame. They take actions to get attention. Most often, the actions they take have no particular moral content. Heroes are heroes because they have risked something to help others. Their actions involve courage. Often, those heroes have been indifferent to the public's attention. But at least, the hero could understand the focus of emotion. However he valued or devalued his own achievement, it did stand as an accomplishment. (2000, 260)

James comes to see that his father "understood that this image of heroism was not the real thing."

Silence, heroism, and celebrity—interestingly, such issues are deeply embedded in the act of filmmaking as well as in the bond tour. Although these issues are not as openly discussed in the film as in the book, it is hard to think that the film does not, in some measure, also include Eastwood's own artistic response to precisely these issues and that they might have been one of the elements that drew Eastwood to the story of the flag raisers. Like the flag raisers, Eastwood has enjoyed enormous celebrity. Like them, Eastwood's celebrity has been created by photographic images, that is, those images we have seen of Eastwood throughout his film career. Like those of the soldiers on Iwo Jima, the actions Eastwood has been associated with have often been violent actions during which he has performed heroically as understood by conventional standards. The Man with No Name and Dirty Harry probably provide the most iconic of these images, but there have been many more. Clearly, Clint Eastwood, the human being, is none of these cinematic characters. But he enjoys a celebrity and an image as a "hero" that have been created by the photographic imagery that gives us his characters on the screen. So it ultimately becomes an issue of identity— a "silent" actual personal identity and a "created" persona photographed and put on-screen to receive the public's acclaim. The Hollywood stars who have survived for many years as "stars" have all found some solution to maintaining a strong sense of their personal "identity" as the core of their being apart from the roles—the public images—that have brought them fame. So a photographic image that makes one famous is something that Eastwood has lifelong experience with himself—as well as all the accompanying issues of identity, self-worth, and the virtues ascribed to a staged public persona. A major purpose of the film, following Bradley's book, is to discover and honor the actual personal experience of the Marines. One would imagine that Eastwood himself would be especially sensitive to the weight heroic status and mythic stories place upon the person whose life has given rise to them. And one can see how freeing that person's life of its mythic veneer would represent the search for a certain deeper, more authentic truth—the very human truth of a man simply living through experiences as life presents them.

So the film searches for the truth of the human being that lies beneath the mythic image of the flag raising. Thus, during the bond tour, we see the flag raisers fighting to maintain their hold on their personal truth of self. Accordingly, Doc, Ira, and Rene struggle with their own sense of personally defined identity in the face of an overwhelmingly powerful public identity accorded them. Indeed, the photograph of the flag raising on Iwo Jima generates an irresistible force of publicity that assigns the identity of "hero" to each of the flag raisers. But the men are aware that the "heroism" belongs to a collective identity they share as U.S. Marines. It is the Marines as a unified whole who have behaved heroically and to whom the designation "hero" rightly belongs. "Heroism" is not a personal attribute they possess as individuals. Each Marine may recognize that the designation applies to his comrades, but he declines it as inappropriate for himself. Thus, when they are introduced as "the Heroes of Iwo Jima," Doc replies to the audience, "The real heroes are dead on that island, and we'd appreciate it if you bought bonds in their honor."

In real life, Doc Bradley's "silence" about his experiences on Iwo Jima and his avoidance of any fame for being one of the flag raisers provide the occasion for the story of *Flags of Our Fathers* as both the book and the film. In both, after his father's death, the son James must seek out the story of his father's war experience. Both book and film consist of the reconstruction of the father's experience through interviews with survivors from World War II. As the film's narrative reconstructs the story of Iwo Jima and the flag raisers, Eastwood essentially honors the view of collective heroism while avoiding a Hollywood glorification of individual heroism or even of military victory itself. The rapid editing, the dark lighting of much of the battle action, and the relative anonymity of the narrators as characters all conspire to render the story one of a collective valor rather than of individual heroic feats. Although the film is in "color," it is so darkened and drained of vivid hues that the impression is far more that of seeing a film in black and white; thus any potential celebration of its action as heroic is muted. The rapidity of the action and the editing further deny any single characters or set of characters the prolonged focus necessary to emerge as individual heroes.

Indeed, the film ultimately portrays the battle as taking place in a nightmare realm where conventional conceptions of "heroism" lose all meaning. The action descends into a netherworld of violent brutality, maiming, and death so profound that the very structures of civilized consciousness collapse into terrifying nightmare and agonizing flashback. Those who survive physically prove to have been wounded emotionally and psychologically. Their civilized consciousness, where concepts like "heroism" might exist, has been broken apart. The memories that surface in reconstructing the past include nightmares, flashbacks to horror, and shattered minds. The ordinary consciousness of the men has blocked this past and its memories simply to survive in a relatively coherent state. But even when remembered, the experiences are so beyond words that they have produced an intense gravity of "silence"—a nightmarish black hole that swallows up all ordinary conversation and communication about them, all the shared exchanges of dialogue upon which our daily civilized lives are normally based.

As James Bradley and Clint Eastwood dredge this black hole to reconstruct its memories in word and image, a certain reassessment of history takes place. The mythic history of "The Photograph" of the flag raising is placed in a more complicated, less grand, human context. And the traditional meanings of "heroism" are redefined. We are reminded that "history" is, in the actuality of its happening, a far more complex and multilayered reality than the simplified linear narrative customarily instilled—close to indelibly—in our minds as children in school. It is usually a narrative that serves to explain, legitimize, and celebrate the actions, practices, and values of the nation. In this vein, the mythic photograph of the Marines raising the flag on top of Mount Suribachi serves the national purposes of the United States and of its populace as a whole quite well. The extraordinary success of the Mighty 7th Bond Tour stands witness to that. That the perspective of those individual Marines who fought at Iwo Jima is so different comes as something of a shock in the face of this mythic national history. It is especially a shock because the mythic history grows precisely from their image as captured in the photograph. Indeed, Eastwood's nonlinear, multilayered narrative cuts beneath the unified history of the single mythic image. His narrative suggests the presence of multiple perspectives with differing angles of perceived truth. And to the degree that the film emphasizes the perspectives of Doc, Ira, and Rene, our sympathies lie with their truths, truths seen from the angles of their experiences.

From their perspective—at least from Doc's and Ira's—the country fair/ Fourth of July parade hoopla of the bond tour entailed continual indignities and emotional pain. But given the importance of the Mighty 7th in financing the war effort, one can make a case for the Marines' heroism in enduring the flag-raising reenactments on papier-mâché Mount Suribachis and the miniature Mount Suribachi desserts served with strawberry topping at the sit-down banquets. One can even argue that their participation in the bond tour with its mythic imagery made a far more important contribution to the war effort than their actions in combat could ever have achieved. The perspective of the film, however, aligns with that of the individual experiences of Doc, Ira, and Rene. And from their point of view, the bond tour inflicts its own cruelties and entails its own brand of meaningless chaos. Creating and promulgating a mythic history might well be necessary to sustain certain fundamental values of the nation, but the film reveals the additional sacrifice of their personal truth that the Marines must make to this process.

At its ending, the film offers an insight into the necessity we feel to create heroes. At the same time, it honors Doc's view of his experience rather than sacrificing it. Such differences are reconciled through the voice of Doc's son as he articulates the new understanding of "heroism" accorded him by his search for his dad's missing past:

> I finally came to the conclusion that maybe he was right. Maybe there is no such thing as heroes. Maybe there are just people like my Dad. I finally came to understand why they were so uncomfortable being called "heroes." Heroes are something we create, something we need. It's a way for us to understand what is almost incomprehensible. How people could sacrifice so much for us. But for my Dad and these men, the risks they took, the wounds they suffered, they did that for their buddies. They may have fought for their country, but they died for their friends—for the man in front, for the man beside him. And if we wish to truly honor these men, we should remember them the way they really were. The way my Dad remembered them.

And in the ordering of its narrated memories, the film saves for its ending the episode where the Marines who took Mount Suribachi are permitted to swim in the ocean. The image of their frolicking in the water acts as a sort of final blessing upon the lives of the men who are now dead. It somehow reminds us that they were boys, most of them around nineteen years old, that they had the capacity to enjoy the simple pleasures of life, and that it is as valid to remember them swimming in the ocean as to recall their intense suffering. It is perhaps necessary for us to have such a memory so that a peace of some order might settle upon our knowledge of what the participants in the battle went through. We are granted this somber peace as the camera withdraws into the heavens above the island.

■ ■ ■

Clint Eastwood's companion film *Letters from Iwo Jima* presents the island battle from the perspective of the Japanese soldiers who fought it. Unlike *Flags of Our Fathers*, the story is told in a straightforward, flashback narrative. When the film opens in something close to our present time, Japanese researchers in white overalls are unearthing a cache of letters. The letters were written by the Japanese soldiers defending Iwo Jima, and they were buried in the floor of their cave when defeat seemed a certainty. As the researchers dig out the packet of letters, the film flashes back to Japanese soldiers digging trenches near the beach in preparation for the American invasion. From that point to its ending, the narrative follows the preparation and the battle from the perspective of several officers and several ordinary soldiers. Chief among the officers are General Kuribayashi and Baron Nishi. The central soldiers are Saigo, formerly a baker; Shimizu, a disgraced military police trainee; and Nozaki, Saigo's buddy who fears that Shimizu is there to report on their unpatriotic griping. These characters—especially General Kuribayashi and Saigo—are the anchor points around which the host of other characters unites as the overall narrative of Iwo Jima's defense unfolds.

Just as *Flags* offers an extended exploration of the meaning of "heroism," *Letters* presents an extended exploration of "honor." To a man, the issue of personal honor is at stake as each fighter undertakes his allotted actions in defense of the Japanese homeland, for the defenders are keenly aware that Iwo Jima is that part of Japanese soil first threatened with American invasion. In accordance with Japanese conceptions of military honor at the time, the soldiers do acquit themselves "honorably." Many die in the battle itself. Others, who have held out as long as is humanly possible, commit suicide—an honorable death to be preferred to the disgrace of capture by the enemy. So we see many officers and soldiers blowing themselves up with hand grenades. A few, such as Baron Nishi and General Kuribayashi, shoot themselves. General Kuribayashi's suicide occurs when he is wounded while leading the remaining defenders in a final charge against the American forces. A few who do surrender are callously shot by their Marine guards, for the prisoners simply provide an inconvenience their guards are unwilling to accept. Of those characters we follow, only Saigo survives in the end.

Eastwood's film puts a human face on "the enemy." On one level, for instance, the film's treatment of honor appears to be a respectful portrayal of traditional Japanese cultural values. But beyond the respect for differences in culture, the film presents its characters in such profoundly human ways that the viewer, particularly the American viewer, is led to see the human being in the "enemy's" guise. We see the humanity in General Kuribayashi's letters to his son Taro. We see it in Baron Nishi's grief over his dead horse. We see it in Shimizu's refusal to shoot a barking dog. Within the film itself, we see such a recognition occur most pointedly in the interactions among the Japanese and the captured American Marine named Sam. Nishi orders that his wounds be treated and that he be given some of the last remaining morphine. Nishi then converses in English with him about his friendship with Douglas Fairbanks and Mary Pickford, about his participation in the 1932 Olympics in Los Angeles, and about where the American is from. At the end of the conversation, both men shake hands as they exchange names. They have become "friends" in some odd but natural sense that contradicts the role of "enemy" their countries have defined for them. After Sam expires from his wounds, Nishi translates aloud from a letter found on him. Saigo and his fellow soldiers realize that Sam's mother has written exactly the same thing to her son as their mothers had written to them: "Do the right thing because it is right." They realize that they have been taught false beliefs about American soldiers being weak and cowardly. Saigo realizes that his American opponents fight bravely and intensely. Throughout the film, the American viewer is offered the same opportunity to recognize the humanity of the Japanese defenders of Iwo Jima.

Referring to the captured American, Baron Nishi asks the key question, "Son, have you ever met one?" His question ends the argument over whether or not to give medical treatment to the wounded American. A Japanese soldier has argued, "An American wouldn't treat a [wounded] Japanese soldier." But the import of Nishi's question is that the Americans would indeed offer such medical treatment. Like Baron Nishi, General Kuribayashi has also met Americans; in fact, he has lived as a diplomatic military attaché for a number of years in America. In one remembered scene, we see Kuribayashi receiving the gift of a 1911 Colt .45 pistol upon his departure from America for Japan. In the ceremony's dinner conversation, when the issue of a possible war between Japan and the United States is raised, Kuribayashi confirms that, if so, his nation's convictions and his own convictions would be the same. Indeed, General Kuribayashi's brilliant defense of Iwo Jima would bear out how identical the convictions are.

In a way, the Colt .45 is a subtle reminder of how little such national convictions are questioned or challenged. Men like General Kuribayashi and Baron Nishi both have international experience. In fact, both men have spent time in the United States. Throughout the film, we see General Kuribayashi bearing the pearl-handled Colt .45 in its holster, even though we only learn in a scene toward the film's end of its significance as a gift from American colleagues who honor and admire him. When Kuribayashi and Nishi meet on Iwo Jima, they toast one another with Johnny Walker scotch. Kuribayashi has fond memories of American automobiles and its car culture. Yet the men's experience of and affection for America do not elevate them beyond their nation's "convictions," which have led to a state of war. Knowing America, these men recognize the tragic mistake of engaging in such a war. As loyal officers, however, they are honor-bound to carry out the policies and convictions of their nation. The constant presence of the Colt .45 on General Kuribayashi's person is perhaps the ironic reminder of how the traditions of honor among Japan's officer class—even at its educated and internationally experienced best—compel them to follow "national convictions." The tragic consequence is the death of noble, good, and humane men like Nishi and Kuribayashi in a battle that can only be lost. Perhaps this loss is further underscored in Kuribayashi's death. General Kuribayashi seeks an honorable samurai death in a beheading with his own sword. He has asked and learned that Iwo Jima is still Japanese soil. But just as his junior officer is poised to swing the sword, he is shot. So Kuribayashi must shoot himself. He does so with his Colt .45. Perhaps such plot details suggest, however subtly, the collapse of traditional samurai codes and control as both the emblems and the brute fact of American power come into play.

The deepest motive of Eastwood's film is to humanize the battle and, in particular, the Japanese soldiers. Eastwood succeeds in conveying the humane and noble bearing of Baron Nishi and General Kuribayashi. But his greatest success is the character of Saigo. Saigo is the quintessential civilian. Unlike that of the officer class, his commitment is not to national "convictions" or even to some sense of traditional personal honor. His commitment is to his family in the most elemental and immediate ways. This commitment emerges in the scenes depicting Saigo's drafting into the army and its aftermath for his family. With great poignancy, Saigo utters his acceptance of the "honor" of serving in the military when the draft officer announces the order at his door: "I am happy to serve my country." Later at dinner, his pregnant wife, Hanako, grieves over her husband's certain death: "What am I to do when you die?" She observes that no Japanese soldier ever returns home alive from service. After comforting her, Saigo puts his ear to her stomach and then speaks a promise to his unborn baby: "Your dad is going to come home for you."

Throughout the flow of the action, Saigo embodies unobtrusively those values that most fundamentally question the national convictions. The least of soldiers—a poor shot, suitable mostly for digging, latrine duty, and running messages—Saigo is the one most interested in surviving the battle. Having overheard General Kuribayashi's order to fight on rather than engage in a suicide charge, he speaks up for strategic retreat. Later, he is the one who explores the possibility of surrender with his fellow soldiers. He is the focus of General Kuribayashi's mercies throughout the film, being spared three times from suffering or death—from exhaustion in the digging of trenches on the beach, from beheading for supposed dereliction of duty, and from the final suicide charge by his assignment to a destruction-of-documents detail instead. The deepening bond between the general and the soldier reflects the humanity of both men in each encounter. Movingly, Saigo's simple ability to use a shovel permits him to render a final crucial service to his commanding officer. He is the one who buries Kuribayashi after he commits suicide. In a rage at seeing General Kuribayashi's Colt .45 stuck in the belt of a Marine, Saigo flails his shovel against the surrounding American soldiers, who ultimately subdue him. So the film never portrays Saigo's actions or his commitment to survival as cowardice. He is as brave as the next man in all his endeavors. Somehow through his luck and his commitment, he survives, presumably to return to mainland Japan, home, and his family. Such a return is suggested in the final image of him lying on a stretcher on the beach at Iwo Jima when he props himself up and looks across the sea to the rising sun.

The shot of Saigo lying on a stretcher lined up with all the other stretchers of wounded American Marines conveys certain larger implications of "family." For ultimately, this is a shot of the "family of mankind." There is no distinction between Japanese or American. There is simply a line of wounded men, a common humanity whatever the cultural differences or the national affiliation. The scene is cinematically understated, glorified neither by swelling music nor by special lighting and held only briefly. Moreover, it weighs against a complex presentation of the issues throughout the film. At this stage of the war, Japan is poised for an all-out effort to defend the homeland, and Iwo Jima is the first stage of that defense. Even the children of Japan are mustered into the effort, as a song sung by the children's choir of Nagano is broadcast to the Iwo Jima defenders. In a final letter, General Kuribayashi expresses one of his few doubts as he vows to "fight to the death for my family." But the very thought of his family makes it hard for him to accept that he best serves them by dying. The film itself has been a continuous set of parallel deaths—deaths in battle, deaths in honorable suicide. Most of the deaths we witness are of Japanese soldiers, but the anonymous deaths of American Marines are also part of the overall action. Emerging from the carnage is Saigo, a lone Japanese Odysseus, surviving and longing to return home. Aligned with the other wounded soldiers lying on stretchers, he bespeaks a larger brotherhood of mankind, no matter how much it has been denied or brutalized by the extended battle for Iwo Jima.

One further image lends weight to the value of family. That is the slow-motion image of the buried letters, now discovered and floating to the ground in a collective "delivery." While the film has depicted General Kuribayashi and Saigo as the chief correspondents, clearly their letters represent similar letters written by all the soldiers. And of course, these are letters to families back home. In some sense, the recounting of the battle that we view has been evoked by the search for exactly such surviving documents. The tale itself seems to emerge from an energy attached to the letters, buried with them and unleashed by their discovery. So it is in the quiet, human moments of writing letters home where the universal human family might best be recognized. Indeed, this recognition of common humanity occurs when Baron Nishi reads the letter from Sam's mother to the Japanese soldiers. The humble details of everyday life—dogs escaping to chase roosters, the repair of a kitchen floor, advice to the children, the love of mothers, fathers, and wives—speak a universal language. The title of the film, *Letters from Iwo Jima*, and the structuring of the story around these letters thus emphasize the membership of all nationalities and all peoples in the universal family of mankind.

Indeed, we might see Eastwood's film itself as one last "letter" from Iwo Jima. It is a surprising one and perhaps even a shocking one. For an American audience, it involves the willingness to look through the eyes of a onetime "enemy" and see "yourself," or at least your military self as the "enemy." For Americans like Eastwood, those old enough to remember World War II, it is a shock of a certain kind. For the attitudes of those war years—often driven home in films about the war—tend to remain buried in our minds, too little questioned and too infrequently updated. That Eastwood's film may still be a shock when we have been friends and allies of Japan for over sixty years indicates how our minds remain imprinted with old animosities and even the racial or national stereotypes of wartime that supported them. The history we tell ourselves in our own national narratives—in this case of the "good" war, as World War II has come to be seen—often preserves these or fails to challenge them thoroughly enough to completely dislodge them.

According to James Bradley's summation of the Battle of Iwo Jima, there was a lot of blood, death, and trauma for Americans to forgive:

> [Captain] Severance was the only one of six Easy Company officers to walk off the island. Of his 3rd Platoon, the one that first scaled Suribachi, only Harold Keller, Jim Michaels, Phil Ward, and Grady Dyce came through the battle untouched. Easy Company had suffered eighty-four percent casualties. Of the eighteen triumphant boys in Joe Rosenthal's "gung-ho" flag-raising photograph, fourteen were casualties.
>
> The hard statistics show the sacrifice made by Colonel Johnson's 2nd Battalion: 1,400 boys landed on D-Day; 288 replacements were provided as the battle went on, a total of 1,688. Of these, 1,511 had been killed or wounded. Only 177 walked off the island. And of the final 177, 91 had been wounded at least once and returned to battle.
>
> American boys had killed about 21,000 Japanese, but suffered more than 26,000 casualties doing so. This would be the only battle in the Pacific where the invaders suffered higher casualties than the defenders.
>
> The Marines fought in World War II for forty-three months. Yet in one month on Iwo Jima, one third of their total deaths occurred.
>
> . . . [During all of World War II] only 353 Americans were awarded Medals of Honor, the nation's highest decoration for valor. Marines accounted for eighty-four of these decorations, with an astonishing twenty-seven awarded for just one month's actions on Iwo Jima, a record unsurpassed by any battle in U.S. history. Iwo Jima stands as America's most heroic battle. (2000, 246–47)

This is a formidable, marble monument moment of history. It is one that is difficult to view from a perspective other than the established conventional one—a view reinforced by The Photograph, the Marine monument based on this image, and films like John Wayne's *Sands of Iwo Jima*. And probably only the passage of more than sixty years makes any renewed perspective possible at all. But Eastwood's ambition is, indeed, to recount the battle from "the enemy's" point of view. Perhaps the lesser goal in this is to address our historical understanding as such. His larger goal is one of storytelling. And that is to tell the tale so that the range of human compassion and shared understanding is extended. The power of *Letters from Iwo Jima* lies in Eastwood's success in doing so. He does so not through a philosophical abstraction but through the vivid imaginative experience in which the battle springs to life on the screen before us. The result of viewing such action is not simply a lesson in history, then, but a lived experience of deepened compassion.

■ ■ ■

Taken together, Eastwood's two films on Iwo Jima create a panoramic perspective that explicitly encompasses views from both sides of the battle. Such a complex perspective extends the mission of compassion more fully. While the films are about a specific and searing moment of the past, they engage history as something more than a record of facts. In the context of active wars in Iraq and Afghanistan, Eastwood's films are the reminders of a storyteller about the human costs of war and the neglected brotherhood of our common humanity. They are a reminder of the possibilities for historical change along the axis of a shared humanity. During World War II, we fought all-out war against Germany and Japan. Each side barely saw "the enemy" as human. Today, Germany and Japan are among our major friends and allies. Later during the Cold War, we feared that Russia or China would launch a nuclear attack against us, even as we threatened them with the same. Today, China is our largest trading partner, and Russia is sought after as an ally in world affairs. Surely, there is some lesson in this segment of history if we but have the insight to see it and the wisdom to heed it. *Flags of Our Fathers* and *Letters from Iwo Jima* serve as the kinds of stories that reshape how we see our history. Insofar as they help us to think and feel in more compassionate ways about the history we already have, such stories lead us toward that understanding and that wisdom necessary to create a new history—a history where the accolades of "hero" and "honor," at the very least, no longer signify that the blood of the world's youth has been spilled. And at their best, such stories impel us to hammer upon the swords of our national histories until they become the plowshares of those mythic tales whereby we truly recognize the common humanity from which we all spring.

■ Note

1. My discussion of Eastwood's *Flags* and *Letters* derives primarily from a close viewing of the films. I have found that reading *Flags of Our Fathers*, James Bradley's (2000) extraordinary book about his father and his fellow Marines, greatly illuminates Eastwood's approach in the film. I have also benefited from Drucilla Cornell's fine discussion of both films in the chapter "Militarized Manhood" (2009, 151–68).

■ Bibliography

Bradley, James, with Ron Powers. 2000. *Flags of Our Fathers*. New York: Bantam/ Random House.

Cornell, Drucilla. 2009. *Clint Eastwood and Issues of American Masculinity*. New York: Fordham University Press.

Eastwood, Clint, dir. 2006a. *Flags of Our Fathers*. Malpaso/Amblin DVD. DreamWorks Pictures and Warner Bros. Pictures.

———. 2006b. *Letters from Iwo Jima*. Malpaso/Amblin Entertainment DVD. Warner Bros. Pictures and DreamWorks Pictures.

Eliot, Marc. 2009. *American Rebel: The Life of Clint Eastwood*. New York: Harmony Books/ Random House.

Foote, John H. 2009. *Clint Eastwood: Evolution of a Filmmaker*. New York: Praeger.

Chapter 14

GRAN TORINO: SHOWDOWN IN DETROIT, SHRIMP COWBOYS, AND A NEW MYTHOLOGY

John M. Gourlie and Leonard Engel

To fully appreciate Eastwood's accomplishment in *Gran Torino* (2008), it is important to recognize the central role "family" plays in the drama. For, ultimately, both the meaning and the emotional power of *Gran Torino* spring from Eastwood's handling of Walt Kowalski and his adopted Hmong family. As a storyteller, Eastwood has built the family into a dramatic center of meaning in recent films, such as *Mystic River* and *Million Dollar Baby*, and *Gran Torino* falls into this pattern. It is a pattern that enables Eastwood to create films of far greater significance and emotional depth than he was able to in the past. Indeed, as a cinematic storyteller, Eastwood's greatest artistic achievements evolve from and are rooted in his use of family as the central dramatic structure of his films.[1]

It was not always the case. A brief reminder of Eastwood's treatment of family in several earlier films may provide a helpful context. Think, for example, of Eastwood's film with Sergio Leone *A Fistful of Dollars* (1964; U.S. 1967), the first of what have become known as the spaghetti Westerns. Eastwood plays the Man with No Name, a loner, who appears to have no guiding ideals, acting for the most part out of pure self-interest and self-preservation. As a peripheral consequence, his actions save the Mexican woman Marisol and unite her with her husband, Julian, and their child, Jesus—perhaps a glancing reference to the Holy Family. Later, in *The Outlaw Josie Wales* (1976), Josie's wife and son are brutally murdered in the first few minutes of the action, and for the majority of the film, Wales is the loner seeking revenge. But in the course of his wanderings, he collects around him a motley group of people, a communal family, as it were, and in the final scene, he appears to be returning to them. As Preacher in *Pale Rider*

(1985), likewise, Eastwood unites another family at the end, in addition to preserving the small community of mining families, by killing the hired thugs of the brutal mining company in a final shoot-out. In *Unforgiven* (1992), Eastwood plays William Munny, another loner, who tries to break the pattern of his gunfighter past by marrying a good woman and raising a family. When the film opens, however, his wife has died, but in his devotion to her, he vows to continue on the reformed path she laid out for him and to keep the family together. He presumably succeeds in the latter but fails in the former. The following year, in *A Perfect World* (1993), the good bad-guy Butch Haynes (Kevin Costner), before he is shot to death at the end of the film, creates an alternative, though fleeting, loving family with the boy he has abducted.

In all these earlier films, the protagonist is essentially a loner, a man without family and often without a past. But by *Mystic River* (2003), even though Eastwood does not appear in the film, family issues have become central to the tragic drama, where both the perpetrators of violence and the survivors are heavy with feelings of suffering, guilt, and the knowledge of major mistakes because of their family ties. Unlike the deaths in earlier films, in *Mystic River* we *see* only *one* of the actual killings, for the emphasis is not upon the killings themselves but upon the devastating effects they have on the families involved. As in a Thomas Hardy novel, circumstances are confused, misinformation is taken as fact, and events are misinterpreted. The initial murder of Jimmy Markum's (Sean Penn) daughter sets events in motion that bring hidden emotional layers to the surface with volcanic force. These events and their emotional lava flow with the inevitability of naturalistic tragedy. In his passion to find the murderer, Jimmy takes the law into his own hands and kills the wrong person, brutally ruining that family, while Jimmy's wife (a modernized Lady Macbeth) justifies her husband's action with claims about the necessity of family unity and praise for Jimmy's fierce protection of its sanctity.

In the closing scene, Eastwood takes us to the narrow city streets, filled now with the assembled families watching a parade amid the surrounding crowd—suggestive perhaps of the grand parade of humanity. With most of the principal characters present, the camera comes to rest on the destroyed families. First, we see the depressed son and distraught wife of Dave Boyle (Tim Robbins). They are juxtaposed to Jimmy Markum's family. Initially destroyed by the death of the daughter, the Markum family is brazenly restored by the wife's justification of murder in the name of primitive family values. Directly across the narrow street, we see the detective Sean (Kevin Bacon) reunited with his wife and new baby. He knows that Jimmy is a killer but, of course, cannot prove it and probably never will. The murder becomes a secret shared by a number of families, somehow forming a society that closes in around them as the parade of life flows on—a mystic river.

In *Million Dollar Baby* (2004), director Eastwood transforms the conventional parameters of a boxing film into a deeply engaging, emotionally powerful, multilayered drama that achieves a tragic dimension surpassing even that of *Mystic River*. The film quickly introduces its characters: the crusty, world-weary former trainer and current manager of a run-down gym, Frankie Dunn (Eastwood); the narrator, his one-eyed, wise and loyal sidekick, "Scrap" Dupris (Morgan Freeman), a has-been fighter who now cleans the gym; and, most important, a tough, determined, young fighter, Maggie Fitzgerald (Hilary Swank). Eastwood depicts the growth of what essentially becomes a father–daughter relationship between Frankie and Maggie. The poignancy of the relationship is beautifully captured in the Gaelic phrase "Macushla" embroidered on Maggie's boxing robe. In the phrase, Frankie declares Maggie to be his daughter, for it means "My blood, my kin." However, in gaining this new daughter, the sorrow is that he suddenly and without warning loses her. We do not know how he has estranged his biological daughter, but we do know that he feels the loss deeply, as evidenced by his continually writing letters despite her returning them unopened. But Maggie's loss is even more tragic for Frankie because he has chosen to end her life, killing the one thing that has come to mean more to him than anything else. A boxing film on the surface, *Million Dollar Baby* is really the story of the bonding of a father and a daughter to one another to create a true and loving family, whatever the biological lineage—and then the tragic loss of that family.

As in *Million Dollar Baby*, Eastwood grounds *Gran Torino* in family drama, but from the beginning, he boldly sets the film in the context of the larger issues of life and death. These issues enter the film explicitly through the sermons the priest preaches at the opening funeral service for Walt's wife and the closing funeral service for Walt himself. By raising the issue of the meaning of our lives and deaths, the character of the priest serves to greatly expand the context in which we see the film's actions. While it is the film as a whole rather than the priest that provides a response to these questions, the priest's character is essential to our understanding that the film is undertaking the sacred artistic mission of addressing the deepest values of our existence. So when Eastwood employs Christian iconography in the film's denouement, it is to suggest the mythic universality at work in the human drama of *Gran Torino*—a drama that works itself out through the prism of the family.

Thus Eastwood roots the film's deep issues in the small rituals of daily living, especially those centered on the family home in a neighborhood whose ethnic composition has changed drastically. Such rituals include getting to know your neighbors, celebrating family meals, and a man teaching a boy the ways of manhood as well as protecting the womenfolk. These rituals become complicated because they are extended from one culture to another as well as from one generation to another, but as they play out, we see the universals of life that unite us beyond our differences. We also see the types of differences that so often divide us. But in the film's drama, these differences are overcome in ways that offer warmhearted comedy before its tragic finale.

At the center is Walt Kowalski, who possesses a proud command of these rituals. He is equally adept at the traditional male rituals of domestic home life and at the warrior rituals of violence. So he becomes the film's center—its focus for addressing the larger framework against which these rituals play out, namely, the questions of life and the questions of death that are evoked by the priest in his sermons and in his conversations with Walt.

What gives *Gran Torino* its appeal is the degree to which its action depicts the growth of compassion in Walt's seemingly hardened heart. His teenage neighbors—Sue and Thao—are the key elements in the gradual change of heart Walt experiences. In most of the film's earlier scenes, Walt appears locked in postures of self-defense against multiple assaults: the death of his wife, the fractured relationships with his sons and their families, the unwanted outreach of the priest, and—perhaps most in his face— the invasion of his neighborhood by the Hmong newcomers. But over the course of the film, surprisingly, Walt's Hmong neighbors are transferred from their initial status as alien invaders to a place in his heart as his newly adopted family.

The first few scenes of *Gran Torino* portray Walt as a man with a hardened heart. Walt is a crusty, old geezer, who has spent a half century working for Ford. He is also a Korean War vet carrying unresolved issues from that conflict. Now retired, he lives alone with his anger and prejudices; his beloved wife has just died, and his appearance and demeanor suggest that he wants to join her. He is partially estranged from his two sons and their families; pride, intransigence, and misunderstandings outweigh affection on either side. The sons seem ambitious in middle-class ways, and they make little time for their father beyond surface duty or considerations of how he might benefit them and their kids. The opening scenes, showing the funeral of Walt's wife and the family gathering at his house afterward, reveal the grandchildren slyly eyeing things they hope to inherit when Walt dies. Especially prominent is Walt's prized possession, a 1973 vintage Gran Torino, which he keeps in mint condition. The granddaughter, who is soon to begin college, makes no secret of her desire to possess it. When Walt finds her in his garage eyeing the car while smoking, his disgust spews forth in snarls and growls, especially as he notices the rings in her pierced ears and stomach. His anger spills out at his sons too. In the later scene showing Walt's birthday, when the older son and his wife bring a garishly decorated cake and presents, one of which is a telephone with enlarged numbers for the elderly who are visually challenged, Walt's outrage is palpable. But Walt's anger truly boils over when they suggest that he move into senior housing; he will have none of it, and he virtually throws them out of his house.

Later, in one poignant scene, Walt tries to confide to the older son a seriously disturbing medical diagnosis he has just received, but the son is too occupied with his own affairs to hear him out. Apparently, there was never good communication between Walt and the sons. It seems that Walt's wife provided the glue that held the family together, and she also generated whatever family feeling existed. But with her passing, that, too, has dissipated.

In addition to the estrangement from his sons, Walt is also isolated from, and contemptuous of, his neighbors. Hmong immigrants have recently moved into the neighborhood, and simply by being Asian, they remind Walt of the North Koreans he fought in the war. In unspecified ways that would probably count as posttraumatic stress disorder, Walt bears a heavy burden of guilt and inner pain from his war experience in Korea. Although undefined, these memories grip his mind and come spewing out in stress-ful moments when his anger explodes. Such anger nearly proves fatal when he catches Thao attempting to steal his Gran Torino. Pointing a gun at Thao after catching him in his garage, Walt says, "I used to stash guys like you five feet high in Korea. Used 'em for sandbags." He is "not at peace," as an elder tells Walt during one of the Hmong family functions. Walt's not being "at peace" takes on a further edge in the light of his worsening medical condition. He coughs up blood during much of the film, and the implication is that he has a fatal illness, probably lung cancer, though the illness is not named. Walt's time to find peace is limited, even, it would seem, as is his desire to find it.

Cracks in the armor around Walt's heart begin to appear when he saves first Thao and then Sue from gang violence. He unintentionally saves Thao when the Hmong gang attempts to press-gang him into its ranks. A scuffle results as Thao's women defenders pull him back, and the tug-of-war spills over onto Walt's front lawn. Walt ends the fight by pointing his rifle at the gang members and ordering them, "Get off my lawn." Later, Walt intentionally saves Sue from a gang of black teenagers who waylay her and her Anglo boyfriend Trey as they walk home through the gang's territory. Walt has been driving by, spots Sue being accosted, and intervenes. Again at gunpoint—Walt has pulled a .45 pistol from under his jacket—he saves Sue from whatever further assault might be coming her way. As Walt gives Sue a ride home in his pickup truck, the warmth of a certain bond kindles. Walt has taken opening steps in what develops into a larger role of fostering and protecting both Thao and Sue.

During this ride, Sue tellingly states the dilemma the Hmong youth face, "The girls go to college; the boys go to jail." In the breakdown of traditional patterns of Hmong social and family order, the gangs create an alternative pattern of disorder and violence. During his failed rite of initiation into his cousin's gang, Thao risks becoming a thief, and, indeed, he is lucky to escape with his life. Thao's aborted attempt to steal Walt's Gran Torino, however, becomes the basis for Thao's formal apology to Walt. The apology entails a period of personal labor meant to offer restitution and thereby to remove the blot upon the family's honor his attempted theft has caused. Over these days of penance, Walt uses Thao as a one-man workforce to clean up the eyesores on properties in the immediate neighborhood. Reluctantly, Walt develops a sense of responsibility for Thao, and, eventually, he takes on the mission of instructing Thao in the ways of manhood.

A good deal of the film's comedy of manners derives from Walt's efforts, especially the scenes in which Walt teaches Thao how to talk to other men, as practiced at the barbershop. Thao comes up against the barber Martin's rifle when his attempts at a language of male camaraderie come across as a language of insult. Indeed, his words seem identical to those Walt utters to Martin. The comedy in Thao's case makes the dramatic irony of the language of insult clear. The language of ethnic insult disguises the friendship and its emotions, which cannot be openly acknowledged by Walt and Martin according to the male codes of their day. That they accept the surface insults in good humor offers proof of the deeper friendship that underlies their words. The power of this deeper friendship transforms the surface insults into carriers of a male affection that cannot be spoken of openly. Once mastered, such instruction helps Thao enter the manly world of construction as a laborer.

Without seeking it, Walt has earned the status of hero among his Hmong neighbors by besting the gang. Although annoyed and unwilling at first, Walt allows himself to be drawn increasingly into the Hmong culture around him. Much of this occurs at Sue's urging and under her tutelage. Sue serves as Walt's Sacajawea. Her quick wit, sharp tongue, and spirited ways provide the starch required to face Walt down at the same time she offers a warmhearted embrace of his presence in her family. Sue provides the feminine center he misses after the death of his wife. In turn, Walt supplies the masculine presence and material help that Sue's family needs after the death of her father. Aligning wobbly dryers, repairing broken sinks and ceiling fans, offering up his old freezer, and cooking barbeques, Walt asserts a role he defines as: "I fix things." And although he denies it, Walt seems to respond to Sue's affection and endorsement, "You're a good man, Wally."

As the Hmong family increasingly becomes Walt's own adopted family, the course of Walt's life and the lives of Sue and Thao would seemingly be on opposite trajectories as old age declines and youth rises. But the Hmong gang and the escalating levels of violence as Walt seeks to defend his "family" from the gang's depredations complicate and entwine the natural course of their lives. In terms of dramatic gesture, a good deal of this is worked out around Walt's cigarette smoking. Walt's character is defined by a number of repeated acts. One of these is his incessant cigarette smoking. Presumably, a lifetime of heavy smoking has left him suffering from a debilitating cough that now brings up blood. Both Thao and Sue witness such episodes, and their concern for Walt's health is justly awakened. Walt lights his cigarettes with his 1951 lighter, which bears the emblem of his Korean War outfit, the First Cavalry. The cigarette lighter links Walt's current peacetime self sitting on his porch drinking beer and smoking cigarettes with his previous warrior self as a soldier in Korea. And, of course, the cigarette lighter ultimately figures as a central element in the film's dramatic climax.

So when the Hmong gang attacks Thao on a back road as he is returning home after working at his construction job, it is significant that they burn a cigarette into his cheek. It is as though they are symbolically challenging Walt, perhaps implying that Thao's association with Walt will only bring Thao pain and injury. Earlier, in seeing the Hmong gang drive by, Walt has recognized that "this kid doesn't have a chance." His response to their drive-by is a pantomime, hand gesture of a pistol firing, a gesture he also made to warn off the gang accosting Sue. But after Thao is beaten up, Walt forms his hands into fists and assaults the most guilty member of the Hmong gang. While Walt most likely is seeking both to punish the offenders and to prevent them from attacking in the future, he fails. For the gang badly shoots up Thao's home, slightly wounding Thao in the neck. Even worse, the gang members abduct Sue and brutally beat and rape her. Walt has not expected such violence and blames himself. He returns to his home to punch his fists through the cupboards, both in rage and in self-punishment, it would seem.

In his ensuing conversation with the priest, Walt recognizes that "Thao and Sue are not going to find peace in the world as long as that gang is around." His own achievement of personal peace is inextricably connected to his efforts to bring peace to Thao and Sue. After Walt has decided how he will proceed, he prepares for death—buys a new suit, mows his lawn, and, most important, goes to confession to receive absolution. As he is leaving the church, the priest makes the sign of the cross and says, "Go in peace." This is a significant moment, for Walt has not been at peace previously. He could not, at any earlier point, look the priest in the eye and say from his heart, as he does now, "I am at peace."

Walt's peace plan requires the elimination of the Hmong gang. The suspense of how Walt is to achieve their elimination underlies the last segment of the film. Walt's goal of saving Thao and Sue requires that the plan not include Thao himself. Walt is keenly aware of his own internal guilt over those he has killed in Korea, and he does not want to make the price of justice a similar burden Thao must carry within himself. So in locking Thao in the basement, Walt keeps him from the showdown. But in pinning his Korean War medal on Thao, Walt recognizes his bravery and anoints him as his heir. In these actions, Walt assumes his final self-definition: "Me, I finish things. And I'm going it alone"—the Handyman Warrior.

Walt's showdown with the gang has all the old-time appearance of a sheriff in a Western calling out the bad guys for a final shoot-out. Set against our expectations and this imagery, the denouement contains a good deal of irony. Walt calls the gang out with a string of insulting epithets—"shrimp dicks, midgets like you, miniature cowboys"—and he repeats his hand pantomime of firing a pistol, further suggesting that he has a shoot-out in mind. Saying, "I've got a light" and "Hail, Mary, full of grace," Walt reaches inside his jacket, just as he did earlier when he pulled a .45 on the gang troubling Sue. Walt is then gunned down in a hail of bullets. His arms and hands spread out in a crucifixion pose as he hits the ground, blood trickling down one wrist, and his military cigarette lighter slipping from his open hand. Not the result we were expecting. And, strikingly, the iconography of Walt's death aligns the Warrior and his self-sacrifice with the imagery of Christianity's Prince of Peace.

Walt's death is coupled with the scene of his funeral and the reading of his will as a rounding out of whatever by way of the meaning of life and death the story of Walt Kowalski can teach us. Sue and Thao's arrival in full Hmong ceremonial dress is quite moving, for they have become Walt's true children by virtue of the heart's bonds. Likewise, Walt's previous hostility to the priest has been resolved in their recent "Want a beer? Call me Walt" conversation. The priest has come to feel that he has learned a great deal about life and death from Walt. In turn, Walt feels freed to leave his house to the church because his wife would like it. But, most significant, he leaves his Gran Torino to Thao. This gift is the surest sign that Thao is Walt's chosen son and heir—deemed the one most worthy to continue the lineage of Walt's spiritual essence and conception of true manhood.

Beyond Walt as an individual, the Gran Torino seems to symbolize a whole generation of Americans, indeed, a whole way of life that is passing. This is a generation that may have installed steering wheels in cars in an industrialized America. This is a generation that may have fought Asian foes in distant lands like Korea and Vietnam. But as this generation passes away, the America that remains is increasingly characterized by the multicultural neighborhoods in Detroit where your neighbors are more likely to be Hmongs or members of other ethnic groups different from those largely European groups that preceded them. As the keys of Walt's classic Gran Torino pass to his Hmong "son," the film suggests a new mythology to replace the increasingly outmoded ones of the cinematic past—even Clint Eastwood's own cinematic past.

Thus, the price of the new mythology of American manhood involves the sacrifice of an older conception. When Walt sacrifices himself, he embodies an old conception of American manhood—war hero, craftsman, middle-class homeowner. And because Clint Eastwood portrays Walt, by extension, perhaps he also embodies the ethos of the Western gunman and hero through all the ghostly, remembered cinematic past that trails after the screen image of Eastwood as an icon. We are perhaps reminded of Eastwood's earlier characters: the Man with No Name, the Stranger, Dirty Harry, Preacher, and Will Munny, among others. Their ghostly cinematic images are hovering around Eastwood's face, whose image collects and embodies them all. We feel their presence, especially in Walt's slow but purposeful movements, in his mutterings and silences, and in his fixed jaw and steely, glinting eyes. To the degree that such powerful memories are etched in the lines of Eastwood's leathery face, they offer Walt as an amalgam of Eastwood's previous incarnations, a summation of his heroic, cinematic past.

When Walt is shot down in a hail of bullets, it is a far more distant and pronounced "Death of the West" than when Butch Cassidy and the Sundance Kid are mowed down or when the Wild Bunch is massacred. Walt is not the nineteenth-century cowboy riding a horse and battling outlaws or Indians on the plains or corrupt lawmen in the towns. He is a city dweller who rides in a pickup truck, and he is caught not in the closing of the West but in the closing of an era of industrialized manufacturing. He lives in Detroit, the capital of the American automotive industry, symbolic of American industrial might, now, increasingly, a strength and way of life that seem to be slipping, as did the cowboy, into the days of yore.

If the film is suggesting it, what might this new mythology embody? The story seems to suggest that a man's true family may be larger than his bloodline kin. It might not even be among his own race or ethnicity, and it might include those of other races and ethnicities, such as the barber, the construction boss, and the Hmong neighbors. In passing the keys of American manhood to immigrant sons of another race, Eastwood seems to be laying out a narrative that embraces all of humanity. In this mythology, the principle that "All Men Are Created Equal" would truly embrace all men and all women—of whatever race or ethnicity—in an American family and community. In this mythology, the crucifixion pose of Walt's death is not an image meant simply to reinforce the older orthodoxies of religion and state. Instead, his death is to make us rethink those very orthodoxies, perhaps reconciling what is best in the traditional with what is most promising in the new—and like the priest, to come to a new understanding of what death teaches us and of what life means because we have known Walt Kowalski. If this is so, perhaps it is as Walt says, "I've got a light."[2]

■ Notes

1. The thematic progression of Eastwood's use of family in his films invites comparison with his own extended family, which, until his marriage to Dina Ruiz in 1996, had been anything but peaceful. As Marc Eliot notes, concerning the recent past, "Clint's personal life had settled down. Dina regularly organized huge weekend outings for all the Eastwoods. She had performed the mighty task of bringing the entire Eastwood clan together, the mothers, the sons, the daughters, even some of the ex-girlfriends, give or take an unforgiving one or two. Even Maggie, who lives in the same area and remains Clint's business partner, often attends. Today the Eastwood ranch feels like a vast homestead" (*American Rebel: The Life of Clint Eastwood* [New York: Harmony Books, 2009], 331–32). If the conclusion of *Gran Torino* puts to rest many of the disturbing family issues Eastwood dramatizes in earlier films and attempts to construct a new mythology built around family, there might be more than a passing resemblance to the current, extended family Dina and Clint have created.

2. In the last scenes of *Gran Torino*, Thao drives the car along the waterways of Detroit. It is interesting to note that one of the waterways thus evoked is Lake St. Clair, *clair* being the French word for "light," hence "Lake of Holy Light."

Chapter 15

INVICTUS: THE MASTER CRAFTSMAN AS HAGIOGRAPHER

Raymond Foery

Clint Eastwood is as much a product of the age of the antihero (an age that I, for one, feel is now probably over) as is any other "modern" or "postmodern" director. Indeed, Eastwood might have been seen as an exemplar of the zeitgeist of the age even before he had directed his first film. After all, "Clint Eastwood" made his early reputation as an actor, and the character he played—the man with no name—established him as perhaps the most universal persona of the antihero. One could argue that he literally came to own the role in the Sergio Leone trilogy often referred to as "the Dollars films": *A Fistful of Dollars* (1964), *For a Few Dollars More* (1965), and *The Good, the Bad, and the Ugly* (1966). Other titles can be cited, of course, and other characters mentioned, but had Eastwood played in no other films than those of this trilogy, his contribution to the cult of the antihero would have remained strong.

In the opening chapter of his wide-ranging 1999 study, *In Praise of Antiheroes*, Victor Brombert notes that "the lines of demarcation separating the heroic from the unheroic have become blurred."[1] While Brombert's study examines European literature extending back through the 1830s, his commentary upon the nature of the antihero remains intriguingly applicable to the cinematic model. "The negative hero," Brombert observes, "more keenly perhaps than the traditional hero, challenges our assumptions, raising anew the question of how we see or wish to see ourselves."[2] Brombert could be describing any number of characters played by the actor Clint Eastwood, and he could also be describing any number of the characters directed by Eastwood the auteur. Whether we go as far back in Eastwood's directorial career as *High Plains Drifter* (1973) or look at a work as recent as *Gran Torino* (2008), the case can be made that Eastwood creates and directs characters who certainly challenge our assumptions and who often provoke personal musings on "how we see or wish to see ourselves."

A change has occurred in the twenty-first century. I would argue that the mature Eastwood—the director of every film he has been involved with since *Mystic River* (2003)—has emerged as an artist far more interested in exploring what it might mean to be a good, old-fashioned (premodern, pre-postmodern) "hero" and that his work can be seen as a kind of gradual shift from the previous age to the one (not yet labeled) in which we now live. This can certainly account for his dedicated interest in the World War II era; his twin films on the subject—*Flags of Our Fathers* and *Letters from Iwo Jima* (both 2006)—can almost be seen as illustrations of the qualities so earnestly described by journalist Tom Brokaw in his best-selling *The Greatest Generation*. Genuine heroes inhabit the landscapes of both of these films; antiheroes are in short supply (as they are in the Brokaw text).

With *Invictus* (2009), Eastwood has proceeded to an unabashed elaboration upon the very definition of the contemporary (as opposed to modern or postmodern) hero, a meditation upon the possibility that there can exist among us genuine saviors—or at least, unifiers. With Nelson Mandela as his subject, Eastwood has found a character as far removed as possible from a high plains drifter; Mandela, indeed, could hardly have drifted through any plain, high or low, incarcerated as he was for twenty-seven years. With Mandela, Eastwood has a genuine hero, one might even say a saint. That is the premise of the film, and that is the approach that Eastwood takes toward constructing the narrative. *Invictus* is a kind of cinematic hagiography, or at least one chapter in the story of the life of this particular saintly individual, a man so revered that he provokes responses like the one Matt Damon's character gives to the question of what the great man might be like: "He's not like anyone I've ever met before."[3]

Eastwood takes this observation of Mandela as a given, and he then arranges his visual treatment around that presupposition. Every scene is carefully designed and every camera movement precisely orchestrated toward this end. Within a structure that appears at first viewing to be that of merely an extended documentary, Eastwood manages, subtly yet expertly, to arrange visual motifs to emphasize the hagiographic nature of his approach.

This is evident from the opening scene. After the simple titles—white letters on a black background accompanied on the soundtrack by a melodic choral chant—the scene opens to the sound of a whistle, and we see a group of white schoolboys practicing on a well-manicured field. At this point we do not know who they are, of course, or even what they are practicing. The man blowing the whistle is obviously in charge, and play begins as he retreats from the immediate area. It is obvious that we are watching an organized team—they are all in the same green and white jerseys—and it becomes clear that they are playing a game that involves passing a ball around. The camera has followed the play with a slow right-to-left traveling movement. The camera glides past the edge of the playing field and continues across a country road that separates this field from a scruffy pasture on the other side of the road. (Indeed, there are fences around each field; a stately iron one fronts the manicured field, and a run-down utility fence surrounds the other.) At this moment, the traveling shot pauses, and a title card is superimposed over the background: "South Africa, February 11, 1990." In the background—and therefore across the road from the field we have just seen—is the pasture. Playing there are two dozen or so young black kids. It is not clear to us what game they are playing, either, but the difference in the topographical conditions must register in at least some subliminal way as the scene cuts immediately back to the previous (well-manicured) field. A short series of "comparison shots" contrasts the two games: one we soon ascertain to be rugby being played by an all-white group, the other is soccer being played by the all-black group.

After a couple of shots comparing the two groups, an overhead shows us a motorcade proceeding down the road that separates the fields. We hear a siren and are thereby alerted to the importance of the procession. More cuts between the two groups continue the comparison: while the black kids run ecstatically toward the wire fence to get a look at the motorcade, the white kids stand stiffly by their iron fence and simply stare. A few of them display obvious expressions of disdain. Then a cut to the white coach of the white team concludes the sequence as he answers the query of one of his players ("Who is it sir?") with, "It's that terrorist Mandela. They let him out. Remember this day, boys. This is the day our country went to the dogs."

With these seventeen shots, Eastwood has set the scene for his hero's entrance. He has also provided a brief summary of the recent history of the state of South Africa as it entered a period of monumental change in the 1990s. The two societies, one white and privileged, the other black and subjugated, were now to enter into a period of enormous political and social upheaval. The task of managing such a transition fell to the "terrorist," and the ploy he was to use to unify the two sides was to engage them in an

appreciation of the same sport, indeed the same team. Eastwood's opening, then, quite succinctly presents the players and the plan. And while
his use of the moving camera suggests the approach of a documentarian,
it is obvious from an examination of the rhythm of the editing and the
actual setups of the camera placement that this was a well-composed, well-
orchestrated narrative sequence, hardly the serendipitous result of documentary coverage.

This is the strategic narrative approach that Eastwood uses throughout
Invictus. He quite often makes the film *appear* to be a documentary when
in fact it is a carefully composed, precisely shaped drama in the classic,
Aristotelian sense. It only *looks* as if the camera happens to be in place
during crucial moments, and this ruse is aided by the careful intermixing
of stock news footage to make the material seem to have been shaped by a
journalist rather than by a dramatist.

This "pseudo-documentary" approach is especially evident in the
rugby sequences. The fact is that South Africa won the 1995 Rugby World
Cup with a team that was not expected to even make the finals. During
the progress of the film, the audience sees rugby practices, rugby team
meetings, professional rugby players (virtually all white) tutoring amateur
younger players (virtually all black), and rugby sports commentators. Various parts of at least four matches are shown, with Matt Damon giving a
credible impersonation of someone who actually can play the game. Much
of this material looks as if it could have been shot by a television news
team. The odd thing is that the rugby material actually slows down the
film, as ironic as this might seem, in that whatever sports fans usually find
in the give-and-take of a game that they so passionately follow is oddly
missing here. Rugby is certainly as exciting a game as American football.
Eastwood simply fails to show us that. The rugby material seems somehow
flat, lacking in any narrative arc, failing to engage the viewer in the actual
match on the pitch. This observation may seem to be a damning one, given
the precision that I would argue Eastwood brings to the rest of the film.
Yet the fact is, of course, that *Invictus* is not a film about rugby, nor is the
progress of any individual match the subject of this news-like "coverage."

The subject is leadership, and it is obvious from the way Eastwood
shapes the film that this is what he wishes to emphasize. Take, for example,
the first meeting between Mandela (Morgan Freeman), now the president
of the country, and François Pienaar, the captain of the rugby team (Matt
Damon). President Mandela has invited Pienaar for tea. The scene between

the two of them opens in the president's outer office as Pienaar is greeted by an assistant. The clock on the wall tells us that it is precisely four o'clock. (The British colonial habits die hard.) The first shot of the two together is taken from behind the president's desk. Mandela rises to greet his guest. Then Eastwood cuts to an overhead as Pienaar moves toward Mandela. The overhead shot is rarely used in this film (with the exception of the obvious ones from the stands toward the playing field), and when it is, it punctuates a moment that might otherwise slip by unnoticed. Here it announces the significance of the meeting and serves at the same time to indicate that the two protagonists are to be seen as equals. During their conversation before sitting down, the exchange of pleasantries is shot with matching over-the-shoulder reverses, once again emphasizing that we are in the presence of equals and that Mandela feels as privileged to be meeting the famous rugby player as Pienaar is to be meeting the president of his country.

When they sit, the editing strategy used is the principle of separation: each character occupies a single frame as the camera cuts between them. The height of the camera placement and the shooting angle upon each protagonist remain precisely the same, once again saluting their equal status. And it is during this exchange that the essential meaning of the film, its raison d'être really, emerges. "Tell me, François," asks Mandela, occupying his own cinematic frame, "what is your philosophy on leadership?" The cut to Pienaar reveals him within his own frame as he answers: "By example. I've always thought to lead by example, sir." The conversation continues as Mandela presses Pienaar: "But how to get them to be better than they think they can be; that is very difficult I find." At this moment, a subtle movement of the camera closes in on Mandela. He is now in a slightly magnified position on the screen compared with his position in the previous shot. It is almost as if Pienaar has leaned forward a bit to make sure that he hears what is being said. The camera movement suggests that we, too, are leaning in, that this moment is worth our full attention.

Indeed it is, for Mandela goes on to speak of the importance of "inspiration" ("How do we inspire ourselves to greatness when nothing less will do?") and relates to Pienaar the story of a Victorian poem that served to inspire him during his years of incarceration. After a quick cut back to Pienaar, who is simply listening attentively (as are we at this point, Eastwood having guided us into the conversation), the reverse shot is much more of a close-up on Mandela. He makes the point that we often rely on the words of others for such inspiration. The reaction shot to Pienaar follows, and it, too, is more of a close-up. Once again, Eastwood keeps his players in balance and makes the point that this is a conversation between two captains, each sharing a personal anecdote about the nature of leadership itself. The conversation ends with Mandela leaning even further forward, directly into the camera, as he tells Pienaar that "we must all exceed our own expectations."

Mandela is, of course, speaking of the political unification of South Africa; Pienaar takes it as his inspiration to succeed in the World Cup. Indeed, this is how Mandela wishes Pienaar to take it, for he has decided that victory in the Rugby World Cup is essential to his vision of a unified South Africa, a vision that could only be exemplified by a country where both blacks and whites might celebrate such a success together.

Most of the middle part of the film reveals the progress of Mandela's charmingly Machiavellian scheme. At one point he is told that the World Cup finals will be broadcast to over a billion people. Astonished by this, he simply acknowledges to his aide that "this is a great opportunity." Eastwood intercuts between scenes like that and various scenes showing the team preparing for its matches. As part of its preparation, though, the team has been asked by the president to conduct some clinics around the country. Here is where the brilliance of Mandela's vision emerges. We see an enormous, brightly painted, seemingly brand-new bus pull into a dusty school yard. The players get off the bus and engage the local children in a teaching clinic, showing them how rugby is played. In this way the opening scene of the film is amplified as we see the two societies—the whites who play rugby and the blacks who play soccer—come together. As the bus pulls out of the yard at the conclusion of the clinic, Eastwood's camera reveals a sign that announces Mandela's bold scheme; on it is written "One team, one country."

Eastwood proceeds to tell the sports story rather straightforwardly, again returning often to a pseudo-documentary approach. Match by match, the South African team grows in stature not only among its traditional supporters—the country's white population—but also now among its newly converted black followers. Eastwood even goes so far as to intercut between two groups watching the matches on television, one from the den or living room of an extended white family, the other from a bar or tavern filled with black fans. Mandela's seemingly quixotic scheme appears to be working.

Just before the beginning of the finals match against New Zealand's team (ironically called the All Blacks, a reference only to the team colors),

Eastwood introduces the only moment of pure melodrama into the proceedings. It has to do with Mandela's security detail, a group made up of black supporters of Mandela (who had been his bodyguards for years) and white members of the national security force that traditionally guards the president of South Africa. There has been tension between the two groups throughout the film, and one of the running tropes has been the gradual easing of this tension as the members come to know each other as fellow professionals and not as mere representatives of their respective races. Here on the morning of the big match, the security detail has met to discuss strategy and to prepare for the fact that "all it takes is one idiot trying to make a statement" and an assassination attempt can occur. Meanwhile, we are introduced in just two brief shots to a white man with binoculars who appears to be "casing" the stadium. Since we have not seen him before, we quite naturally view this as ominous. Eastwood then returns to the buildup to the match, with crowds entering the stadium, fans cheering, athletes in their locker room preparing, and a journalist doing a stand-up to set the scene for the millions of television viewers.

With the stadium now filled, we cut to a shot of a jet plane over the city. This seems quite incongruous until the next cut reveals that the pilot of the plane is the young man we had just seen with the binoculars. He tells his copilot to let it be noted that he is taking over control of the plane and that he will take full responsibility for what now happens. This clearly has been shot in such a way as to lead the viewer into fearing the worst—certainly any viewer who had lived through the 9/11 attack on New York City. Indeed, the plane dips down and appears to be heading directly toward the stadium. A cut to the interior of the stadium reveals that the security detail has also noticed the oncoming plane. The black man in charge of security asks his (white) second-in-command if permission had been given for a flyover and is told that it had not been. He immediately orders another of his assistants to keep the president out of the stadium. It is too late. Unable to do anything, he simply stares as the plane descends almost into the stadium and then pulls up and reveals a "Good Luck" sign painted on its bottom. The crowd cheers wildly, and the tension has dissolved.

Eastwood orchestrated this sequence brilliantly. It is worthy of comparison to one of Hitchcock's signature scenes, for it creates the kind of cinematic tension that only a master can realize. Yet, as with so much of his work, the achievement of this moment seems almost effortless. Eastwood does not waste a shot. He knows exactly what he needs to do to produce this kind of moment, and he efficiently produces it. It is Hitchcockian without the Hitchcockian ego. That is to say, the seeming effortlessness of the buildup and then release of tension appears understated compared with so many examples one could cite from Hitchcock's oeuvre. Effortless yet effective: this is Eastwood as a director. He is like a great athlete or ballet dancer, in that the moves he makes seem to require no real exertion; rather, they seem to arise gracefully from his polished cinematic memory. This, of course, is the sign of a pure professional, of someone who has mastered his craft.

The rest of the film deals with the rugby matches and the eventual success of Mandela's unorthodox scheme. "This country hungers for greatness," he says at one point, and his remarkable equation of success in international sport with recognition on the world stage seems by the end of the film to be obvious to all. The title match itself consumes over fifteen minutes of film time. This is considerable, given my claim that the film is not really about rugby. Nevertheless, Eastwood makes certain concessions here to the "sports documentary" genre, and we watch various aspects of the game as if we were watching television coverage of it. In a final concession to the form, Eastwood underscores the dramatic ending, the winning goal being made as the ball sails through the uprights in slow motion. Euphoria swirls through the stands, and whites are seen embracing blacks, even (or especially) those members of the security detail we have been following throughout the film.

After the match (South Africa has defeated New Zealand's All Blacks in overtime), we see Mandela being driven away from the stadium in his official car. Pandemonium surrounds him. The car creeps through the ecstatic crowd—made up, Eastwood's wandering camera reveals, of blacks and whites cheering together and congratulating each other. In the car, very little is said. Mandela recalls the words to the Victorian poem as a voice-over on the soundtrack shares them with us: "I am the master of my fate; I am the captain of my soul." A slow fade-out brings us to the end credits, the first one reading "Directed and Produced by Clint Eastwood."

At one point in the film, just as Mandela's plan is being implemented, he finds that he must address a group of his followers in order to convince them to change a policy that they had just moments before voted to accept. "In this instance the people are wrong," he declares to his assistant as he makes his way to the meeting, "and as their elected leader, it is my job to show them that." In a film that has as its central philosophical theme the nature of leadership, this statement serves as a summation of the argument. Mandela is a leader, and he recognizes another leader in Pienaar. Eastwood recognizes them both, and his cinematic strategy carefully and unfailingly reveals the equation. Yet it is not the athletic hero Pienaar who resides at the heart of this film. It is, of course, Mandela, the unorthodox hero, the man who is said by one of his black bodyguards to be "not a saint" but a "man with a man's problems." During this very scene, Mandela reveals to the bodyguard that he has a family of "forty-two million." His problem is that he must save them, and he must save them by uniting them.

For Eastwood, this mission of salvation makes Mandela a kind of saint, a contemporary hero with the classical virtues that have traditionally been described by hagiographers. Clint Eastwood, the master director, has joined these hagiographers with this film. For with the Nelson Mandela of *Invictus*, he has chosen a subject worthy of his full cinematic powers, and he has used them precisely, effortlessly, and wisely.

■ Notes

1. Victor Brombert, *In Praise of Antiheroes* (Chicago: University of Chicago Press, 1999), 2.

2. Ibid.

3. For a standard resource on hagiography, see David Farmer, *The Oxford Dictionary of Saints*, rev. ed. (Oxford: Oxford University Press, 1997).

CHAPTER 16

HEREAFTER: DREAMING BEYOND OUR PHILOSOPHIES

John M. Gourlie

Eastwood has said, "There's a rebel lying deep in my soul."[1] In Eastwood's later films—*Mystic River* (2003), *Million Dollar Baby* (2004), *Flags of Our Fathers* (2006), *Letters from Iwo Jima* (2006), *Gran Torino* (2008), and *Invictus* (2009)—the rebellion is not simply against villains, the failures of frontier law, or the blunderings of big-city corruption. The rebellion is against an injustice at the very heart of life itself and in all the stuff of which life is made—its conditions, its circumstances, its events. In these later films, Eastwood's rebel soul increasingly becomes the rebel soul in us all.

In *Hereafter* (2010), Eastwood addresses that ultimate "injustice" of life—violent and sudden death through sheer accident or natural calamity and, more generally, the injustice that life seemingly ends in death. But in a major departure for Eastwood, the film's approach is more mystical than tragic. In portraying the near-death experience (NDE) of French journalist Marie Lelay (Celine de France), Eastwood explores the possibility that the soul survives and that life continues beyond death.[2] In depicting the film's psychic hero George Lonegan (Matt Damon), Eastwood presents the possibility of communicating across the boundaries between life and death. Lonegan has the intuitive gift of reaching beyond the seemingly final barriers drawn by death, usually by holding the hands of the bereaved. The drama of the film centers on the acute isolation the main characters endure because of the charged nature of their unique experiences. The French journalist and the psychic are isolated by their insight into "the hereafter." Like other bereaved characters in the film, the young boy Marcus (Frankie McLaren), who has lost his twin brother, Jason (George McLaren), is isolated by the sheer intensity of his grief and loss.

While subject matter such as "near-death experiences" and psychic mediums may be unusual terrain for Eastwood, the theme of human isolation and the painful toll of its silences is familiar ground. We see the isolation occur for each of the three main characters. In Paris, Marie Lelay is basically furloughed from her job as a television journalist to recover from the lingering effects of nearly drowning in the Indonesian tsunami. During the hiatus, she writes the book *Hereafter*, a study of NDEs such as she has had and the research done on them. But her altered state of consciousness and her preoccupation with NDEs fray her relations with her book editors, who expected a political exposé, and with her television producer/lover Didier (Thierry Neuvic) to the breaking point. After several months, Marie is shuttled off to another publisher, she is dropped as the star of her news program, and her producer/lover Didier admits over dinner that he is sleeping with the show's new star.

Likewise, George Lonegan's life in San Francisco pitches him into a state of isolation. In some of the most tender scenes in all of Eastwood's films, we see George and Melanie (Bryce Dallas Howard) feeding one another in a cooking class as they try to identify flavors and ingredients blindfolded. But the incipient relationship fails when, later in George's apartment, Melanie pushes him into doing a reading for her. Her father's sexual abuse of her as a child surfaces. Melanie cannot handle the revelation, and she flees from George's apartment in deep turmoil. At the same time, George is laid off from his warehouse job. Despite deep reservations, George seems on the verge of accepting his brother's plans to reestablish him in a business as a psychic communicating with departed loved ones for paying clientele. But, instead, George flees to London hoping to escape the psychic "gift" that he feels is more truly a personal curse.

Even more painfully, Marcus's life falls apart when his twin brother, Jason, is killed by a car on a neighborhood street in London. Jason and Marcus have been holding their family together by propping up their addicted mother so that Social Services does not take them off to foster homes. The twins have just given their mother a photographic portrait of them as a birthday present. While on an errand to the drugstore to fill a prescription for his mother, Jason is killed running away from a gang of bullies. Marcus's life is shattered. His mother goes into rehab, Marcus is sent to a foster home, and his dearest companion in life has been torn from him—leaving only his baseball cap.

The synchronicities whereby Marie, George, and Marcus meet in London suggest that, contrary to all appearances, benevolent forces beyond chance and human agency play a hand in shaping our destinies. Meeting as if by chance at a book fair, George glimpses the light images of Marie's NDE when their hands touch briefly as she autographs her book *Hereafter* for him. But Marie slips away into the crowd when Marcus recognizes George as a psychic and pursues him. Marcus, nonetheless, proves to be the catalyst who breaks through the isolation, his own and that of the other chief characters. Compassion for Marcus, who stands cold vigil on the sidewalk outside George's hotel room, ultimately compels the psychic to use his gifts to contact the soul of Jason, Marcus's dead twin. In turn, Marcus opens the door for the psychic to unite with the French journalist Marie, for he knows which hotel she is staying at. In the plaza café at the film's end, we see the flash-forward of George and Marie kissing. It promises that Marie is a woman whose journey into the land of light beyond death will allow her to understand and appreciate George and his gift. George need no longer fear the touch of another. Just as Marcus must set aside his brother's baseball cap, George must remove the gloves that shield him from contact with others. For in each other, Marie and George have found a partner whose unique knowledge and sympathy will end their isolation.

The film itself is carefully set above the levels of either sensational commercial exploitation or commitment to theological doctrines. In his search for closure, the boy Marcus runs through a gamut of these on the Internet and in person. Without much theory or doctrine, then, the film portrays the psychic, the journalist, and the young boy uniting as they come to terms with their direct experiences of death, the soul, and "the hereafter." In their experiences of life's sometimes permeable boundaries, this nonbiological "family"—man, woman, and child—becomes, it would seem, emblematic of the human family. Moreover, their lives are set against global events, such as the Indonesian tsunami and the terrorist bombings of the London subways. At the same time, they are equally set amid the personal pain of life's bereavements, such as the slow dying of patients in hospice and the sudden revelation of a dead father's sexual abuse of a daughter. Ranging from the personal to the global, then, this background context strengthens the suggestion that the truths of the film exist for us all.

In the case of its heroes, the film supports the genuineness of the near-death experience and psychic communication, even as it does not define these in any very clear or specific manner. Indeed, the images of the World of Light are blurry and indistinct. But, we must assume, the film pushes the door open as far as it feels comfortable into visualizing the Light of the Beyond. Like the French journalist Marie, the film has pushed beyond the limits of the world of journalism, with its cynicisms and the tangible, usually corrupt or sordid, realities journalism investigates. In the "Here," through its heroes Marie, George, and Marcus, the film suggests that love and compassion exist sufficiently to free us from our personal isolations. In the "Hereafter," it suggests that death is not the absolute boundary or extinction it appears to be—that undiscovered country from whose bourn no traveler returns. Instead, the film encourages us to believe that we continue in a spiritual existence and that love, compassion, forgiveness, and communication remain the central values between beings.

In the sweetness and the promise of the closing embrace George and Marie share, we see the triumph of love over isolation, of illuminated personal truth over the lesser "realities" of mass consciousness, of individual courage over all that would deny the integrity of the heart's chosen path, however unconventional that might be. Though they shade off into intangible realms, the film implies that the psychic communication of holding hands and the loving embrace of a kiss better indicate the ultimate realities of existence than the dying flesh of our too, too solid world does. In the final kiss and in the film *Hereafter* as a whole, Eastwood has himself chosen daring subject matter to affirm such truths to the degree that they challenge the very boundaries of the "reality" we think we know so well. Though it takes place in the valley of the shadow of Death, this kiss leads the rebel soul to the still waters of an inner land where the heart runneth over with joy and Love affirms its transcendence of death's sting.

■ Notes

1. Richard Schickel, *Clint Eastwood: A Biography* (New York: Vintage, a Division of Random House, 1996), 16.

2. A substantial literature exists in support of the validity of the near-death experience phenomenon. Scientific researchers, such as Elisabeth Kubler-Ross, Raymond Moody, and Kenneth Ring, have explored the subject and published numerous volumes on the NDE and its implications. For those wishing to venture further, an equally credentialed researcher such as Brian Weiss explores the continuity of the soul after life—in fact, through many lives—in *Many Lives, Many Masters* (New York: Simon and Schuster, 1988) and his other works. And like George Lonegan in the film, the medium James Van Praagh, among others, seemingly has the ability to contact departed beings in meaningful ways for the benefit of the bereaved. For those of an even more metaphysical bent, the most extended spiritual discussion of the nature of death is the last volume of Neale Donald Walsch's *Conversations with God* series: *Home with God in a Life that Never Ends* (New York: Atria Books, 2006).

CHAPTER 17

CITIZEN HOOVER: CLINT EASTWOOD'S *J. EDGAR*

Kathleen Moran and Richard Hutson

U nlike the obsessively and destructively divided characters in films such as *Bird* (1988) and *White Hunter Black Heart* (1990), *J. Edgar* (2011) presents a character so obsessively single-minded in his view of the world that it seems impossible for him to imagine simple matters of humanity. In a number of films, Eastwood created interesting characters with deeply divided commitments, oppositions within the protagonists that can lead to destruction, and oppositional loyalties that frustrate the greatest features of their genius. Eastwood's Hoover, in contrast, seems almost pathologically focused. He has difficulty thinking about anything other than his job as the chief law officer of the land. Throughout his career Eastwood (as character and/or as director) has emphasized the outsider, the maverick, the guy who refuses to play by the ordinary rules of being a cop or being an artist of one sort or another. At first glance, J. Edgar is the ultimate insider, a man in a highly important administrative post who wields unprecedented power over others, including U.S. presidents. Advances in forensics and surveillance technology account for part of J. Edgar's control, but it is his pathological sense of the connection between private sex and public crime that funds his various campaigns to undermine anyone with unconventional ideas. Eastwood makes a few weak references to some of Hoover's most vile tactics: we see J. Edgar send his minions out to collect damaging sexual information about Eleanor Roosevelt, JFK, and Martin Luther King Jr. But it is not Hoover's assaults on democracy and civil rights that interest Eastwood, even though those assaults may resonate with viewers. Rather, we see the psychological damage and pathos in Hoover that generate these paranoid actions.

In the end, J. Edgar works so completely as an insider, he operates so completely inside a "closet" of power, so to speak, that he is finally an outsider. He is America's chief lawman, who almost always works outside the laws of the land. To a surprising extent, he ends up a geriatric, pop psychology version of Dirty Harry: the lonely enforcer of the nation's morals, even as he is constantly breaking her most basic laws. Hoover's status as insider/outsider is presented throughout, but especially in two scenes when we see Edgar stepping onto the balcony of his office to observe presidential inauguration parades, of FDR and Nixon. He is literally physically elevated, reminding us that he insists on people "looking up to me" (as he says to his secretary Helen Gandy, who places a podium for his office chair), observing the street and its crowds as if he were a pope offering a gesture of blessing to those below. But the shot also makes Edgar's isolation clear, as well as his delusions of grandeur. The president below is in the position of real power, with the blessing of the nation's people, and Edgar actually goes unnoticed in his self-created elevation.

A number of film critics and bloggers have noted that *J. Edgar* alludes to one of the greatest films ever made—namely, *Citizen Kane*, 1941. Not only does Eastwood include visual quotes of Welles's masterpiece and rely on a flashback structure to narrate the story, but Eastwood's film, like Welles's, is a tale about a powerful and ruthless man who is secretive, complicated, and, in the end, tragic. In both films, mothers are presented as lying behind the emotional deprivations that create the main characters' need for power and control. Not surprisingly, J. Edgar's obsessive paranoia, like Kane's self-defeating megalomania, appears to be the result of maternal abandonment and/or emotional abuse. Edgar's mother tells him (commands him?) at the beginning of his career as a law officer, "You will rise to become the most powerful man in the country," so that his unremitting quest for greater power is his mother speaking inside of him. The scene immediately after his mother's death, when Edgar goes into her room and puts on her necklace and pulls one of her dresses over him, reveals the inner mother. In full drag, Edgar speaks to himself as his mother and answers her as Edgar. The film suggests that Edgar's extreme interest in the sexual irregularities of various people he wants to control owes a great deal to his mother's statement, after the discovery of the skeleton of Lindberg's kidnapped son, that "the nation is sinful. We all have blood on our hands." That is, it is private sin that ultimately puts the whole nation in danger. The single-mindedness of Edgar's need to uncover hidden corruption is that of his internalized mother whose presence never leaves him, at least not until after her death, when he can relax a bit and take up drinking and going to racetracks.

J. Edgar narrates the life of J. Edgar Hoover in flashbacks, though in a much more simplified form than those used by Welles. Whereas Kane is presented through multiple flashbacks narrated by a number of his acquaintances, Edgar is dictating his life story to a couple of agents at a typewriter. He insists on telling "my side of the story," and his is the presumed point of view throughout the film except for the scenes in the present, of Hoover as an elderly man, presumably shortly before his death in 1972. (Leonardo DiCaprio in his makeup as an old man closely resembles the made-up Orson Welles as Kane in his middle and old age.) This self-serving feature of the narrative, a story that has disappeared with the loss, probably destruction, of the actual manuscript of Hoover's memoirs, is obviously a cleaned-up version of a life that was often controversial and in danger of imploding.

In all fairness, 2011 is not 1940. The current recession, for all its pain, is not the Great Depression. And if there is a culture of paranoia today, it is not being played out in secrecy—but, rather, in blatant partisan hysteria. More to the point, movies are no longer the powerful social media they were at the end of the 1940s when it was possible to think of Chaplin and Capra as credible and even potent answers to Hitler. And Eastwood is eighty-one, not twenty-five. If Eastwood humanizes Hoover, and I believe that he is trying to do that, it is not because he is interested in exploring some horrific psychic split that doomed a life but, rather, because he is interested in forgiving the mistakes and flaws of a man at the end of his career. When Welles shot his fictionalized biography of William Randolph Hearst, he was twenty-five years old and had never made a movie before. Welles put the explanation for his cinematic experimentation in the mouth of his protagonist: As Thatcher sputters his outrage on the young and appealing Charles Foster Kane (played by young and appealing Orson Welles), he asks, "Is this your idea of how to run a newspaper?" Kane replies, "I have no idea how to run a newspaper, Mr. Thatcher. I just try everything I can think of." Far from not knowing how to run a film, Clint Eastwood does not try everything he can think of in *J. Edgar*. Rather, he employs the consummate skill of a filmmaker who knows how to move, cut, color, and form every scene. But to what end? Welles was in the business of making an anti-Hollywood film. All of his technical invention was in the service of making the experience of watching a movie "strange," of calling the dream machine to account and focusing attention on the very experience of film. Eastwood is in the business of making a Hollywood film, insistently, even as "Hollywood" is no longer a coherent concept. Eastwood can still make films that display the artistry and deft of classic studio efforts.

Hoover's total commitment to seeing others as criminals and hunting them down or trying to ruin their careers is presented in rather classic Freudian terms. Hoover sees himself as the embodiment of law and order as a way to deny some hidden corruption—in theory, his own repressed homosexuality. There is a scene in which he is talking to his constant assistant and companion, Clyde Tolson, wondering to this confidant whether he should propose marriage to Dorothy Lamour. Tolson bursts out with anger, feeling that Hoover has betrayed him, is making a fool of him, since he has assumed, on the basis of their long relationship, that Hoover is at least a Platonic lover even if the two of them have never actually engaged in sex. This outburst ends up with the two men physically fighting each other, ending with Tolson kissing Hoover, both men with bloody mouths. *J. Edgar* trots out this rather standard psychology equation, suggesting that Hoover sublimated any expression of eroticism into his paranoia about criminals endangering the country, especially about sexual irregularity as "anti-American activity" and, thus, legitimate action for governmental surveillance.

J. Edgar hints that repressed homosexuality is central, and it makes sense that the mystery about Hoover's sexual behavior with Tolson (did they actually sleep together?) has been the focus of much reviewer commentary. But this is not really the most interesting question. In fact, I would argue that it amounts to a barely disguised sleight of hand, almost a distraction. The real question is not about a closeted gay man but about a closeted power-monger. In his paranoia (and, one might say, his cultural acumen about how sexual irregularities have played historically in the United States right up to today), which leads to his illegal surveillance, he dared not let anyone in any position of power suspect his spying and wiretapping. Exposure of these activities could have brought about the destruction of Hoover, even the FBI, since the actions were highly illegal, unconstitutional. Like Charles Foster Kane, who believed that he was the only person in the country who could stand up for the common "people" against corrupt politicians, J. Edgar believed that he was the only person in the United States looking out for the safety (and purity) of the nation. So what if Hoover was sexually repressed? What gay man was not closeted in Hoover's lifetime? What Eastwood and screenwriter Dustin Lance Black seem most engaged by is the link between the exercise of power and sexual irregularities. Eastwood offers a narrative that connects the possibilities for enhanced power with sexual "perversity" and explores the way a man was astutely able to take advantage of events as they fell into his purview by using them to enhance his power. Sexual irregularity is one of the basic events of human history, and Hoover knows that he will always find it if he just keeps his focus on people in power.

Eastwood and Black appear to have their own sense of Hoover the man, perhaps somewhat unique in the tradition of Hoover studies and biographies. Nixon's homage to the dead Hoover in the final scene of the film is, I think, a devastating critique of Hoover (as well as of Nixon, of course). All his life Hoover had been seeking power and recognition. To have the president of the United States offer a statement about his long friendship with Hoover (false) and about Hoover's many accomplishments, even as Edgar predicted that Nixon would bypass the FBI with his own illegal and secret group of surveillance men (foretelling Watergate), is a recognition of Hoover's self-aggrandizement with the deepest irony. The summation of the man that Edgar himself would have liked to have made is given here in the most fraudulent way imaginable, as if Nixon is channeling Hoover's own assessment of his importance. Eastwood and Black are more interested in subtle and devastating ironies than in explosive action.

In this brief statement about *J. Edgar*, one cannot do justice to the richness and thoughtfulness of the film. But the more we think about this film in relationship to Eastwood's oeuvre and his knowledge of American film history and American history in general, the more we will be able to appreciate his accomplishment. Early in the film, Edgar tells his associates that "it's important that we leave the audiences with some mystery." Eastwood and Black have opened up the life of J. Edgar Hoover in a dramatic fashion, perhaps forgiving him for a lot of damage to individuals and the country, both endorsing and countering Clyde Tolson's outburst that "you're a scared, little heartless man."

■ Note

We and Carol Clover have been going to films together for thirty years. After the film, we spend a couple hours discussing it. Our remarks here are indebted to our discussion of *J. Edgar*. There are a great number of books on Edgar Hoover. One that is useful, in contrast to the film, is a defense of Hoover against rumors about his homosexuality: Athan Theoharis, *J. Edgar Hoover, Sex and Crime: An Historical Antidote* (Chicago: Ivan R. Dee, 1995). There is another interesting study of Hoover written and published just before his death in 1972: Jay Robert Nash, *Citizen Hoover: A Critical Study of the Life and Time of J. Edgar Hoover and His FBI* (Chicago: Nelson-Hall, 1972). It does not mention *Citizen Kane*.

FILMOGRAPHY

■ Eastwood as Actor (1955–2011)

Francis in the Navy (1955)
Tarantula (1955)
Revenge of the Creature (1955)
Away All Boats (1956)
The First Traveling Saleslady (1956)
Never Say Goodbye (1956)
Star in the Dust (1956)
Escapade in Japan (1957)
Lafayette Escadrille (1958)
A Fistful of Dollars (1964; U.S. 1967)
For a Few Dollars More (1965; U.S. 1967)
The Witches (1965; U.S. 1979)
The Good, the Bad, and the Ugly (1966; U.S. 1968)
Coogan's Bluff (1968)
Hang 'Em High (1968)
Where Eagles Dare (1968)
Paint Your Wagon (1969)
Kelly's Heroes (1970)
Two Mules for Sister Sara (1970)
The Beguiled (1971)
Dirty Harry (1971)
Play Misty for Me (1971)
Joe Kidd (1972)
Breezy (1973)
High Plains Drifter (1973)
Magnum Force (1973)
Thunderbolt and Lightfoot (1974)

The Eiger Sanction (1975)
The Enforcer (1976)
The Outlaw Josie Wales (1976)
The Gauntlet (1977)
Every Which Way but Loose (1978)
Escape from Alcatraz (1979)
Any Which Way You Can (1980)
Bronco Billy (1980)
Firefox (1982)
Honkytonk Man (1982)
Sudden Impact (1983)
City Heat (1984)
Tightrope (1984)
Pale Rider (1985)
Heartbreak Ridge (1986)
The Dead Pool (1988)
Pink Cadillac (1989)
The Rookie (1990)
White Hunter Black Heart (1990)
Unforgiven (1992)
In the Line of Fire (1993)
A Perfect World (1993)
The Bridges of Madison County (1995)
Absolute Power (1997)
True Crime (1999)
Space Cowboys (2000)
Blood Work (2002)
Million Dollar Baby (2004)
Gran Torino (2008)

■ Eastwood as Director (1971–2011)

Play Misty for Me (1971)
Breezy (1973)
High Plains Drifter (1973)
The Eiger Sanction (1975)
The Outlaw Josey Wales (1976)
The Gauntlet (1977)
Bronco Billy (1980)

Firefox (1982)

Honkytonk Man (1982)

Sudden Impact (1983)

Amazing Stories (1985) TV series, aka *Steven Spielberg's "Amazing Stories"* (1985; U.S. complete title; episode "Vanessa in the Garden")

Pale Rider (1985)

Heartbreak Ridge (1986)

Bird (1988)

The Rookie (1990)

White Hunter Black Heart (1990)

Unforgiven (1992)

A Perfect World (1993)

The Bridges of Madison County (1995)

Absolute Power (1997)

Midnight in the Garden of Good and Evil (1997)

True Crime (1999)

Space Cowboys (2000)

Blood Work (2002)

The Blues (2003) TV miniseries (episode "Piano Blues")

Mystic River (2003)

Million Dollar Baby (2004)

Flags of Our Fathers (2006)

Letters from Iwo Jima (2006)

Changeling (2008)

Gran Torino (2008)

Invictus (2009)

Hereafter (2010)

J. Edgar (2011)

■ Note

As editor I am indebted to Richard Schickel, *Clint Eastwood: A Biography* (New York: Vintage, a Division of Random House, 1996), for much of the information about Eastwood as an actor. For details on each film, see pp. 505–15. I am also indebted to Raymond Foery for sharing the information about Eastwood as a director.

CONTRIBUTORS

■ William Beard is a professor and Film Studies Program director in the Department of English and Film Studies at the University of Alberta, where he has taught since 1978. He is the author of three scholarly monographs: *Persistence of Double Vision: Essays on Clint Eastwood* (2000), *The Artist as Monster: The Cinema of David Cronenberg* (2006), and *Into the Past: The Cinema of Guy Maddin* (2010), as well as articles and book chapters on various topics in Canadian and American film.

■ Drucilla Cornell is a professor of political science, women's studies, and comparative literature at Rutgers University and also a visiting professor at Birkback College in London and the University of Pretoria in South Africa. She has a J.D. from the University of California, Los Angeles, Law School, and prior to her life as an academic, she was a union organizer, working for the UAW, the UE, and the IUE in California, New Jersey, and New York. She was a National Research Foundation Chair in Customary Law, Indigenous Values, and the Dignity Jurisprudence at the University of Cape Town, Law faculty. Her books include *Moral Images of Freedom* and *Clint Eastwood and Images of American Masculinity*. Her latest book, coauthored with Ken Panfilio, *Symbolic Forms for a New Humanity: Cultural and Racial Reconfiguration of Critical Theory*, was published in spring 2010. Cornell is also a playwright, with plays produced nationally and internationally.

■ Leonard Engel, a professor of English at Quinnipiac University, Hamden, Connecticut, was selected "Outstanding Faculty of the Year" in 1989. His edited collections include *The Big Empty: Essays on the Land as Narrative* (University of New Mexico Press, 1994), *Sam Peckinpah's West: New Perspectives* (University of Utah Press, 2003), *Clint Eastwood, Actor and Director: New Perspectives* (University of Utah Press, 2007), and *A Violent Conscience: Essays on the Fiction of James Lee Burke* (McFarland Press, 2010). He has also published numerous articles on American literature, Western fiction and film, and detective fiction and film.

■ Raymond Foery, a professor of communications at Quinnipiac University, wrote his dissertation on Louis Lumière and the invention of cinema. He has also written extensively on the American avant-garde and on European cinema and contributed a chapter on Eastwood's film *The Bridges of Madison County* to *Clint Eastwood, Actor and Director*. He has recently completed a book on the making of Alfred Hitchcock's *Frenzy*, published in spring 2012.

■ Philippa Gates is an associate professor of film studies at Wilfrid Laurier University, Canada. Her publications include *Detecting Women: Gender and the Hollywood Detective Film* (2011) and *Detecting Men: Masculinity and the Hollywood Detective Film* (2006), as well as articles on gender and genre film in the *Journal of Film and Video*, *Framework*, *Post Script*, the *Journal of Popular Film and Television*, the *Journal of Popular Culture*, and the *Quarterly Review of Film and Video*.

■ John M. Gourlie, a professor of communications at Quinnipiac University, teaches film and media studies and has a special interest in the Western. He has written numerous articles on American fiction and film and has collaborated with Leonard Engel on introductions in *The Big Empty*, *Sam Peckinpah's West* (he also has chapters on Peckinpah in each book), and *Clint Eastwood, Actor and Director* (with a chapter on *Million Dollar Baby* as well). He also has a chapter on James Lee Burke in Engel's recent collection of essays, *A Violent Conscience*.

■ Richard Hutson is an associate professor, emeritus, of English at the University of California, Berkeley. He writes on Western films and has contributed to *The Big Empty*, *Sam Peckinpah's West*, and the first volume of *Clint Eastwood, Actor and Director*. He has also written essays on John Ford's *My Darling Clementine* (in *Representations* 84 [2004]) and on Teddy Blue Abbott's trail-driving memoir *We Pointed Them North* in *Western Subjects* (University of Utah Press, 2004). He is currently working on essays about authors who wrote in and about the West during the Progressive era, 1890–1917.

■ Brad Klypchak teaches a variety of interdisciplinary courses at Texas A&M University–Commerce. He has published and presented scholarly works across multiple entertainment realms including music, sport, film, and theater. This marks Klypchak's third collaboration with Leonard Engel, having previously contributed chapters to *A Violent Conscience* and the first volume of *Clint Eastwood, Actor and Director*.

■ Robert Merrill is the Foundation Emeritus Professor of English at the University of Nevada, Reno. He is the author or editor of books on Norman Mailer, Kurt

Vonnegut, and Joseph Heller, as well as (with John L. Simons) *Peckinpah's Tragic Westerns: A Critical Study*. He has published over fifty articles and reviews in major journals, including half a dozen film studies.

■ Kathleen Moran is the associate director of the American Studies Program at the University of California, Berkeley. She has presented papers and published numerous articles on American political/cultural theory and popular culture.

■ Stanley Orr is a professor of English and chair of the Humanities Division at the University of Hawaiʻi–West Oʻahu, where he teaches courses in literature, film studies, and cultural studies. Orr is coeditor for a textbook entitled *The Pearson Custom Library: Introduction to Literature* (2006; rev. ed. 2008) and has published essays in *Jouvert: A Journal of Postcolonial Studies*, *Literature/Film Quarterly*, *Paradoxa: Studies in World Literary Genres*, and *Post-Script: Essays in Film and the Humanities*. His most recent publication is the book *Darkly Perfect World: Colonial Adventure, Postmodernism, and American Noir* (The Ohio State University Press, 2010).

■ Edward Rielly is a professor of English at Saint Joseph's College of Maine. He is the author of twenty books, including eleven volumes of poetry. His recent nonfiction books are *Football: An Encyclopedia of Popular Culture* (University of Nebraska Press), *Murder 101: Essays on the Teaching of Detective Fiction* (McFarland), and *Sitting Bull: A Biography* (Greenwood). Forthcoming is *Legends of American Indian Resistance* (ABC-CLIO). He teaches a course on the Western that includes Clint Eastwood films.

■ Craig Rinne is a doctoral candidate in English and film studies at the University of Florida. Paraphrasing John Ford: "My name's Craig Rinne. I study Westerns." He primarily researches texts relating to the American frontier myth, ranging from captivity narratives to "spaghetti Westerns" to his dissertation topic, the boom (and quickly bust) cycle of Western motion pictures in the late 1980s and early 1990s, beginning with *Lonesome Dove* and *Dances with Wolves* and ending (arguably) with *Dead Man*. He has published on the 1992 version of *The Last of the Mohicans*.

■ Dennis Rothermel is a professor of philosophy at California State University, Chico. His recent publications about cinema include articles in the *Quarterly Review of Film and Video* and several book chapters. He has coedited a volume of essays authored by members of the Concerned Philosophers for Peace, which is forthcoming from Rodopi. He is working on two monographs, one on Westerns and one on Gilles Deleuze's two-volume essay on cinema, and also a coedited anthology, *A Critique of Judgment in Film and Television*.

■ John L. Simons, a professor of English and film studies at Colorado College, specializes in modern American literature and film with particular focus on the Western. He is the author of articles on William Carlos Williams, Nathanael West, John Berryman, Philip K. Dick, Thomas Pynchon, Kurt Vonnegut, the film *High Sierra*, Mike Nichols's *Catch-22* (with Robert Merrill), Sam Peckinpah's *The Wild Bunch* and *Ride the High Country*, and Billy Wilder's *Double Indemnity* and the entries "Plains Westerns" and "Gary Cooper" for the *Encyclopedia of the Great Plains* (University of Nebraska Press). He is the coauthor (with Robert Merrill) of *Peckinpah's Tragic Westerns: A Critical Study* (2010).

■ Robert Smart is a professor in and chair of the English Department and director of the Writing Program at Quinnipiac University. His publications include books on writing (*Direct from the Disciplines*, *The Nonfiction Novel*), essays on Irish studies (in *Caliban*, *Postcolonial Text*, *Ireland's Great Hunger*, and *History Ireland*), and essays on Gothic literature (in *Money: Lure, Lore and Liquidity*), and he is the founding editor of the *Writing Teacher* (National Poetry Foundation).

■ Mike Smrtic is an independent scholar and freelance writer, living in Brooklyn, New York. His interests include the films of André de Toth and Jacques Tourneur, as well as the intersections between film noir and the Western.

■ Matt Wanat is an assistant professor of English at Ohio University, Lancaster, where he teaches writing, literature, and literary and cultural theory. His scholarship examines intersections of narrative, genre, and culture in the areas of American literature and cinema studies. He has published articles on film and literature, including essays on the work of Sam Peckinpah, Jack Schaefer, and Clint Eastwood. Wanat currently continues to explore the Western, along with questions concerning narrative rhetoric and the agrarian.

■ Brett Westbrook is an independent scholar living, working, and teaching in Austin, Texas. Recent publications include essays in *A Violent Conscience: Essays on the Fiction of James Lee Burke* and in *Clint Eastwood, Actor and Director*. Other areas of research and publication include film adaptation studies, masculinity in pirate movies, and the plays of Lillian Hellman. Westbrook is a native-born Austinite and a member of the American Pie Council.

INDEX

Abeel, Erica, 221n5

Absolute Power (2000), 182–84

Achenbach, Joel, 187n12

actors and acting: Eastwood's identity as, 92, 173, 224; *Rawhide* and Eastwood's development as, 78; Siegel as in *Play Misty for Me*, 50n1. *See also senior persona; specific films*

African Queen, The (1951), 98–99, 108, 120n59, 124, 126

age and aging: and demography in U.S., 186n5; and Eastwood as contemporary icon of masculinity, 9–10; and generational difference in *Midnight in the Garden of Good and Evil*, 198–201; and growth of Eastwood as storyteller, 2–3; and *senior persona* of Eastwood in later films, 131, 135, 139, 142, 145, 146, 168–86

Allen, Woody, 93–94, 177

Alphaville (1965), 96

Ambrose, Stephen, 239

Apple, Jeff, 142

Aristotle, 204

artist. *See* creativity; performance

audience, and Eastwood as director, 95

author and auteur theory, 99, 128

Bacon, Kevin, 217, 219

Bailey, Cameron, 180

Band of Brothers (2001), 12, 239–40

Baseball (television documentary), 239

Basilone, John, 248n14

Baumann, Paul, 172

Beard, William, 11–12, 37, 38, 44, 48, 55, 74n5, 121, 153, 157, 163n8, 168, 182, 187n11

Beguiled, The (1971), and exploration of gender and power relations in, 6, 36–50, 74n4

Benjamin, Jessica, 47

Bennis, Warren, 177–78

Berendt, John, 190, 192, 200

Bernanos, Georges, 238

Beverly Hills Cop II (1987), 170

Big Sleep, The (1939), 150

Billen, Andrew, 50

Bingham, Dennis, 39, 39, 40, 41, 43, 44–45, 48, 49, 55, 74n5

Bird (1988): and characterization, 127; and exploration of creativity and performance, 7, 98, 99, 111–13, 116, 117–18

Black, Dustin Lance, 293

Blaikie, Andrew, 177

Blazing Saddles (1974), 152–53

Blood on the Moon (1948), 148–49

Blood Work (2002), 181–82

Bradley, James, 234–36, 249, 250–57, 263, 265n1

Bradley, John, 236, 237, 251

Bresson, Robert, 238

Bridges of Madison County, The (1995): and characterization, 128; and Eastwood's on-screen persona, 173, 174; and patterns of gender relations in Eastwood films, 37, 48

Brinegar, Paul, 77

Brokaw, Tom, 278

Brombert, Victor, 277

Bronco Billy (1980): and exploration of
  creativity and performance, 7, 98,
  100–105, 114, 115, 116, 117–18; and
  landscape, 94; and mythology of
  hero, 11, 224–27, 234, 246
Brooks, Mel, 152–53
Buchanan, Patrick, 8, 135–36, 137
Burke, James Lee, 222n10
Burns, Charlene P. E., 211, 213
Burns, Ken, 12, 239, 240, 248n13
Buscombe, Edward, 160, 163n16
Bush, George, 136
Butler, Judith, 169–70, 175

Cabal, Robert, 77
Cavell, Stanley, 20–21, 23
Cawelti, John, 152–53
Chandler, Raymond, 150, 163n10
Charley Varrick (1973), 72–73
Chaucer, Geoffrey, 20
Chollet, Derek, 135–36
cinematography, and characteristics of
  Eastwood as director, 91
Citizen Kane (1941), 291–92
Civil War, veterans of as characters in
  Westerns, 23, 33n4
Civil War (television series), 239
Clavan, Andrew, 181
*Clint Eastwood, Actor and Director: New
  Perspectives* (Engel 2007), 1, 16n1
Clint Eastwood: A Cultural Production
  (Smith 1993), 130
*Clint Eastwood and Issues of American
  Masculinity* (Cornell 2009), 5–6
Clinton, Bill, 136–37
Cold War: and sociopolitical context of
  1990s, 135, 137; and view of history in
  Flags of Our Fathers and *Letters from
  Iwo Jima*, 264; and Western television
  serials, 20
Collins, Al, 221n3
Combs, Richard, 173
comedy: and *Coogan's Bluff*, 66; and explo-
  ration of aging as social issue, 178,

179; in *Gran Torino*, 271–72; in *Heartbreak Ridge*, 227
conformity, and Western genre, 22
conservatism, and sociopolitical discourse
  in 1990s, 136
Coogan's Bluff (1968), 6–7, 63–66
Cooper, Frank, 56
Cooper, Gary, 232
Cornell, Drucilla, 5–6, 46, 48, 49, 50n6, 55,
  248n18
Costner, Kevin, 145, 187n12
Cowboy (1958), 154
Coyne, Michael, 81
creativity, issues of in *Bronco Billy*, *Honkytonk Man*, *White Hunter Black Heart*,
  and *Bird*, 7, 90–118
crime. *See* detective novel; police procedural; violence
Crime in the Streets (1956), 74n1
Cruise, Tom, 134
Cullinan, Thomas, 42

Dances with Wolves (1990), 130, 137, 145
Davis, Richard & James, 175
Dead Pool (1988), 168, 185, 186n1
deconstruction, of heroic persona in *Flags
  of Our Fathers*, 245–46, 248n18
Deleuze, Gilles, 96, 97–98, 113, 116, 117
Del Valle, Jaime, 56
Denby, David, 204, 206, 208
Desert Storm (1991), 140
detective novel, *Mystic River* and genre
  conventions of, 206, 216–17. *See also*
  police procedural
Dicaprio, Leonardo, 292
Die Hard (1988), 170, 171, 186n1, 186n4
Dimendberg, Edward, 162n2
director: as author, 128; characteristic
  traits of Eastwood as, 91–96; Eastwood compared to Woody Allen as,
  93–94; and Eastwood's relationship
  with Siegel, 50n1; *Rawhide* and Eastwood's learning process as, 24, 78–79.
  See also specific films

Dirty Harry (1971): and Eastwood's collaboration with Siegel, 66–72, 75n6; and image of masculinity, 168; as political film, 66–67, 72, 74n5

Dixon, Wheeler W., 149–50, 163n13

documentary, and narrative approach in *Invictus*, 280, 282, 284

Don Siegel: Director (Kaminsky 1974), 55

Dorval, Madison, 170

DreamWorks, 12, 239, 240, 248n13

Duffield, George C., 80

Eastwood, Clint: and characterization in *J. Edgar*, 290–94; as contemporary icon of masculinity, 168–86; and culture of South in *Midnight in the Garden of Good and Evil,* 190–202; exploration of creativity and performance in *Bronco Billy, Honkytonk Man, White Hunter Black Heart*, and *Bird*, 90–118; films of in sociopolitical context of 1990s, 130–41; gender and power relations in *The Beguiled* and *Play Misty for Me*, 6, 36–50; heroism and leadership in *Invictus*, 277–85; and history in *Flags of Our Fathers* and *Letters from Iwo Jima*, 249–64; influence of Siegel on body of work by, 53–73; introduction to discussion of works as actor and director, 1–16; and learning curve from *Rawhide* to *Pale Rider*, 76–88; and mysticism in *Hereafter*, 286–89; and *Mystic River* as tragedy, 204–20; mythic reinvention of hero from *Rawhide* to *A Fistful of Dollars*, 5, 18–32; mythology in cinema of, 224–46; and new mythology of *Gran Torino*, 266–75; repetition of themes in *White Hunter Black Heart*, 121–29; and *Unforgiven* as noir Western, 148–62

Ebert, Roger, 192

editing strategy, for *Invictus*, 281

Eliot, Marc, 276n1

Enforcer, The (1976), 37, 74n4

Engel, Leonard, 1, 12–13, 16n1, 33n6, 55, 209–10, 214, 221n3

environmentalism, in *Shane*, 86–87

Escape from Alcatraz (1979), 54–55, 73, 247n3

ethnicity, and new mythology in *Gran Torino*, 13, 271–72, 274, 275. *See also* race

Every Which Way but Loose (1978), 96, 100

fabulation: and *Bronco Billy*, 101–2, 104–5, 117, 225; as distinct from fantasy, 97–98. *See also* fictionality

family: and cultural values in *Letters from Iwo Jima*, 260–62; emphasis on in *Gran Torino*, 12–13, 266–75, 276n1; and father-daughter relationship in *Million Dollar Baby*, 183–84, 268; and figure of father in *Absolute Power*, 182–84; mother and character development in *J. Edgar*, 291; portrayals of and growth of Eastwood as storyteller, 3, 4

fantasy: and *Bronco Billy*, 102; as distinct from fabulation, 97–98

Faulkner, William, 205

feminism, and change in social attitudes toward masculinity, 170

Feschuk, Scott, 178

F for Fake (1973), 97

fictionality: and mythology in *Flags of Our Fathers*, 244–45, 246; and theatricality of *Heartbreak Ridge*, 228, 230. *See also* fabulation

film noir: and *The Lineup*, 75n6; and Western genre, 9, 148–62, 225

Fincher, David, 161

Firewall (2006), 187n12

Fistful of Dollars, A (1964): and family, 266; and mythic landscape, 31, 33n9; progression of mythic reinvention of hero from *Rawhide* to, 5, 18–32; title of, 33n8; and Western noir, 150

Fitzgerald, F. Scott, 1

Flags of Out Fathers (2006): age and image of masculinity in, 186; and conceptions of heroism, 12, 238; and growth of Eastwood as storyteller, 2–3, 4; and history, 11, 12, 249–58, 264; and mythology, 11–12, 224, 234–46

Flaming Star (1960), 66, 74n1

flashbacks, and narrative of *J. Edgar*, 292

Fleming, Eric, 19, 23, 77, 80

Foery, Raymond, 13–14

Ford, Harrison, 185, 187n12

Ford, John, 31, 94

For a Few Dollars More (1965), 232

Frayling, Christopher, 19, 28, 29–30, 55, 63, 74n4, 75n6

Freer, Ian, 192

Friedman, Roger, 241

Fukuyama, Francis, 8, 135–36, 137

Gagnon, Rene, 236–37, 251

Gallafent, Edward, 21–22, 29, 32

Gates, Philippa, 9–10

gender: and cultural war against aging, 177; and Eastwood's collaboration with Siegal, 74n4; and generational differences in *Midnight in the Garden of Good and Evil*, 199; performance of, 170, 175; portrayal of in Eastwood's films as major critical issue, 5–6; and power relations in *The Beguiled* and *Play Misty for Me*, 6, 36–50. *See also* masculinity; misogyny

genres. *See* comedy; detective novel; film noir; police procedural; political film; tragedy; Western

Geraghty, Christine, 193

Gibson, Mel, 170, 171, 186n4

Godard, Jean-Luc, 96

Goldgeier, James, 135–36

Good, the Bad, and the Ugly, The (1966), 30

Gordon, Dexter, 120n64

Gourlie, John M., 1, 12–13, 14, 16n1, 33n6

Gran Torino (2008): and Eastwood's senior persona, 184; and emphasis on

family, 12–13, 266, 276n1; and gender relations, 37; as mythic narrative, 4; and new mythology, 13, 266–75

Grapes of Wrath, The (1940), 94

Great Depression, 243

Great Train Robbery, The (1903), 32

Greenaway, Peter, 97

Grenada, U.S. invasion of, 133–34, 227, 228–29

Grey, Zane, 163n11

Gross, Terri, 91, 92

Guardian, The (2006), 187n12

Gulf War, 136

Gunsmoke (television series), 20

Haaken, Janice, 38, 39, 40

Hackney, Sheldon, 191, 201

Hammett, Dashiell, 150, 153

Hancock, John Lee, 192

Hanks, Tom, 240

Hardy, Thomas, 267

Hawks, Howard, 99–100

Hayes, Ira, 236, 241, 251, 252, 253

Hearst, William Randolph, 292

Heartbreak Ridge (1986): and mythology, 11, 227–31, 234, 246; as redemptive narrative, 8; view of history in sociopolitical context of 1990s, 132–34, 146

Helgeland, Brian, 206–13, 218–19, 221n5–6

Hemingway, Ernest, 123, 125

Hendrickson, Nancy, 210, 211

Hepburn, Katherine, 120n62

Hereafter (2010): and growth of Eastwood as storyteller, 4; and mysticism, 286–89; and themes of isolation and silence, 14, 287

Heroes of Iwo Jima (television documentary), 238, 247–48n11

hero and heroism: and comic book superhero, 247n6; and figure of Western antihero in film noir, 150, 151, 277; and leadership in *Invictus*, 13–14, 277–85; and masculinity, 170; and mythology in *Flags of Our Fathers*, 11, 12, 233, 238,

245–46, 248n18; and new mythology in *Gran Torino*, 272; and presentation of character in *J. Edgar*, 15; progression of mythic reinvention of from *Rawhide* to *Pale Rider*, 5, 18–32; representation of in *Bronco Billy*, 101, 102, 104, 226, 246; and theme of aging hero, 8, 11, 175–76, 185, 231, 246

Herring, Gina, 38, 39, 41

Higham, Charles, 50n5

High Plains Drifter (1973): and nihilism, 83; and Western antihero in film noir, 150, 155, 232; and Western genre, 138

Hirsch, Brett D., 209

Hirsch, Foster, 38

history: challenge to conventional views of in *Flags of Our Fathers* and *Letters from Iwo Jima*, 12, 249–64; Eastwood's films in sociopolitical context of 1990s, 130–41; and growth of Eastwood as storyteller, 3, 4; reworking of in post-Cold War era, 8–9

Hitchcock, Alfred, 283–84

Hluchy, Patricia, 180–81

Holmlund, Chris, 172, 178, 185

homage, to formulaic Western in *A Fistful of Dollars*, 29, 31–32

homosexuality: repressed in *J. Edgar*, 293; and Southern society in *Midnight in the Garden of Good and Evil*, 199, 200

Honkytonk Man (1982): and exploration of creativity and performance, 7, 98, 105–7, 115, 116, 117–18; and landscape, 94

Hoover, J. Edgar. *See J. Edgar*

Hoppenstand, Gary, 162n1

Houser, Dan, 31

Howell, Peter, 169

Huemann, Joe, 87

Huston, John, 98–99, 107, 109, 115, 120n59, 120n62, 122, 126–29

Hutson, Richard, 7–8, 15

hysteria, as marker for misogyny in *The Beguiled* and *Misty*, 38–40

identity: and image of hero in *Flags of Our Fathers*, 254, 255; and Southern culture in *Midnight in the Garden of Good and Evil*, 198–201

ideology: and loss of faith in *Bronco Billy*, 225; and narrative in *Heartbreak Ridge*, 229; and patriotism in *Flags of Our Fathers*, 239, 240, 241, 245

Indiana Jones and the Kingdom of the Crystal Skull (2008), 185

Ingrassia, Catherine, 163n18–19, 164n21

intertexuality, of *White Hunter Black Heart*, 128–29

In the Line of Fire (1993): and sociopolitical context of 1990s, 141–44; and theme of aging hero, 8, 175–76, 185

Invasion of the Body Snatchers (1956), 74n1

Invictus (2009): and exploration of heroism and leadership, 13–14, 277–85; and growth of Eastwood as storyteller, 3, 4

Ireland, John, 77

isolation, as theme in *Hereafter*, 14, 287, 289

It Happened One Night (1934), 226

Japan, and portrayal of cultural values in *Letters from Iwo Jima*, 258–59, 263

Jazz (television documentary), 239

J. Edgar (2011): and growth of Eastwood as storyteller, 4; concept of hero and presentation of character in, 15, 290–94

Jeffords, Susan, 171

justice, in *Dirty Harry*, 172

Kael, Pauline, 50, 74n5, 170

Kaminsky, Stuart M., 55

Kamp, Irene, 42

Kay, Karyn, 36, 37, 38, 39, 40

Kelley, Robert, 86

Kennedy, John F., assassination of, 141, 142, 146, 176

Killers, The (1964), 57

Kimball, Arthur G., 163n11

Kitses, Jim, 162n1

Klypchak, Brad, 10–11, 157

Knapp, Laurence F., 39, 46, 126

Knee, Adam, 44, 48

Korean War, 132, 227, 228, 270, 273

Kubrick, Stanley, 248n15

Kurosawa, Akira, 19

Kuwait, U.S. invasion of, 136

Laine, Frankie, 77

landscape: and Eastwood as director, 94; as language in *A Fistful of Dollars*, 31, 33n9. *See also* environmentalism

language: and ethnicity in *Gran Torino*, 271–72; and noir Western, 156, 158, 159

leadership, and image of hero in *Invictus*, 13–14, 277–85

Lefebvre, Henri, 192

Legend of Jesse James, The (television series), 59

Lehane, Dennis, 204, 206, 210–14, 218–19, 221n4, 221n7–8

Leone, Sergio: limits of Eastwood's relationship with, 93; and *Rawhide*, 25; and renewability of Western mythos, 24, 232; and Western noir, 150, 225, 231. *See also A Fistful of Dollars*

Leone, Vincenzo, 25

Lethal Weapon (1987), 170, 171, 186n4

Letters from Iwo Jima (2006): and concept of honor, 12; and conventional views of history, 258–64; and growth of Eastwood as storyteller, 2–3, 4; and Japanese cultural values, 258–59, 263; as tragedy, 220n1

Levin, W. C., 175

Liénard-Yeterian, Marie, 195, 196, 198

Lineup, The (1958), 56–59, 75n6

Little Big Man (1970), 155, 156

Live Free or Die Hard (2007), 185

Lonesome Dove (1989), 137

Lynch, David, 97

Madigan (1968), 59–63

Maguire, Jeff, 142

Mainar, Luis Garcia, 200

Mains, Susan, 194, 202

Malpaso (production company), 94, 130, 132

Maltz, Albert, 42

Mandela, Nelson, 278. *See also Invictus*

Mann, Anthony, 149

Man Who Shot Liberty Valance, The (1962), 154–55, 163n13

Man Who Wasn't There, The (2001), 161

Marlowe, Philip, 150

masculinity: association of with violence, 49–50; Eastwood as contemporary icon of, 9–10, 168–86; fantasy of in *Bronco Billy*, 101; and hero in *Unforgiven*, 231; view of as under siege in *Play Misty for Me*, 44–45. *See also* gender

Matheson, Sue, 149

Maverick (television series), 32n2

Mazumdar, Rajani, 193

McCarthy, Todd, 177, 202

McGilligan, Patrick, 78, 81

McVeigh, Stephen, 85

Melville, Herman, 129, 157

Memento (2000), 161

Merrill, Robert, 11, 222n10

Metty, Russell, 59

Metz, Walter, 131

Midnight in the Garden of Good and Evil (1994), and representation of Southern society, 10–11, 190–202

Million Dollar Baby (2004): family and father-daughter relationship in, 183–84, 268; and flat characterization, 100; and growth of Eastwood as storyteller, 4; and tragedy, 11, 220

mise-en-scène: characteristics of Eastwood's, 91; of *Riot in Cell Block 11*, 54; and *Unforgiven* as noir Western, 160

misogyny, and gender relations in Eastwood films, 36, 38, 40, 74n4

Modleski, Tania, 170

Moran, Kathleen, 15

Mr. Ed (television series), 78

Mulholland Drive (2001), 97

Murdock, James, 77

Murphy, Audie, 149–50

Murphy, Eddie, 170

Murphy, Kathleen, 175

Murray, Robin, 87

music: and Eastwood's recordings, 77; generational difference and Southern identity in *Midnight in the Garden of Good and Evil*, 198; and images in *Heartbreak Ridge*, 132, 146; and opening song of *Rawhide*, 77; and score of *Dirty Harry*, 70; and score for *A Fistful of Dollars*, 28; and symbolism in *Flag of Our Fathers*, 241. *See also* opera

My Darling Clementine (1946), 94, 148

mysticism: in *Hereafter*, 286–89; in *Pale Rider*, 83, 87

Mystic River (2003): and family issues, 267–68; and growth of Eastwood as storyteller, 4; shooting script of, 221–22n5–9; as tragedy, 11, 204–20

mythology: examination of in *Flags of Our Fathers*, 11–12, 224, 234–46; in *Heartbreak Ridge*, 227–31, 234; and hero in *Bronco Billy*, 224–27, 234; mythic reinvention and progression of hero and heroism from *Rawhide* to *A Fistful of Dollars*, 5, 18–32; new form of in *Gran Torino*, 13, 266–75; in *Unforgiven*, 231–34

Naremore, James, 151

narrative: crystalline and images in Eastwood's films, 96, 97, 113–17; documentary and approach to in *Invictus*, 280, 282, 284; and flashbacks in *J. Edgar*, 292; mythic form of in *Rawhide*, 21–22; organic structure of in Eastwood's films, 96–97, 113–17

Nash, Jay Robert, 294n1

Nathan, Ian, 43

nationalism, and sociopolitical context of 1990s, 136. *See also* ideology

Neale, Steve, 176

near-death experience (NDE), and mysticism in *Hereafter*, 286–89

Neibaur, James, 49

New Man, and social attitudes toward masculinity, 170–71

Nixon, Richard, 294

No Name on the Bullet (1959), 150

Oates, Joyce Carol, 18

O'Brien, Daniel, 74n5

O'Connor, Flannery, 195, 214

Once Upon a Time in the West (1968), 93

opera, and aesthetic of *A Fistful of Dollars*, 26–27, 28

Orr, Stanley, 9

Outlaw Josey Wales, The (1976): and Confederate background of character, 33n4; and Eastwood's growth as director, 80–81; and family, 266; hero and American ideology in, 225; and Western genre, 138, 156, 247n7

Ox-Bow Incident, The (1943), 148

Pacific, The (2010), 12, 240

Pale Rider (1985): Eastwood's development as actor-director from *Rawhide* to, 7, 76, 80–88; and family, 266–67; and organic narrative, 96–97

Parker, Charlie, 112, 114, 115

patriotism. *See* history; ideology; nationalism

Peckinpah, Sam, 55, 155, 231

Penn, Sean, 212, 214

Peoples, David Webb, 140, 152

Perfect World, A (1993): and family, 267; and redemptive persona of aging hero, 9; and sociopolitical context of 1990s, 144–46

performance: fictionality and theatricality in *Heartbreak Ridge*, 228; of gender, performance: fictionality and theatricality in *Heartbreak Ridge* (*cont'd*) 170, 175; and issues of creativity in *Bronco Billy*, *Honkytonk Man*, *White Hunter Black Heart*, and *Bird*, 7, 90–118

Petersen, Wolfgang, 142

Pfeil, Fred, 171

Phillippe, Ryan, 248n12

pilgrimage formula, and Western television serials, 20

Play Misty for Me (1971), exploration of gender and power relations in, 6, 36–50

police procedural: *Coogan's Bluff* as, 63–66; *Dirty Harry* as, 67–72; *The Lineup* as, 56–59, 75n6; *Madigan* as, 59–63. *See also* detective novel

politics: *Dirty Harry* as political film, 66–67, 72, 74n5; and Eastwood's films in sociopolitical context of 1990s, 130–41. *See also* ideology

Poseidon (2006), 187n12

Post, Ted, 78

power: and gender relations in *The Beguiled*, 6, 36–50, 74n4; and sexual irregularities in *J. Edgar*, 293–94

Prakash, Gyan, 192–93

predictability, of Western genre, 22

Prokofiev, Sergei, 28

psychic communication, and mysticism in *Hereafter*, 286–89

race, and portrayal of Southern society in *Midnight in the Garden of Good and Evil*, 195–96, 197–98, 199, 201. *See also* ethnicity

Raines, Steve, 77

Rambo (2007), 185

Rambo: First Blood Part II (1985), 134

Rawhide (television series): as crucial period in Eastwood's career as actor and director, 76–80, 88; and progression of mythic reinvention of hero from *Rawhide* to *A Fistful of Dollars*, 5, 18–32; *Pale Rider* and Eastwood's development as actor/director, 7

Ray, Robert, 128, 143

Reagan, Ronald, 227, 230

realism: and *Rawhide*, 79–80; and *Unforgiven* as noir Western, 151–52, 158–59, 161; and Western genre, 22

Red Dead Redemption (video game), 30–31

Red Harvest (1929), 150

Redmon, Allen, 212

Reflections in a Golden Eye (1967), 107

reflexivity, in Eastwood's films, 121

rehearsal, and Eastwood as director, 91, 115

Reiner, Robert, 74n5

religion: and new mythology in *Gran Torino*, 273, 274, 275; and symbolism in *Mystic River*, 213–14, 221n9; and symbolism in *Pale Rider*, 83, 84, 85–86. *See also* mysticism

revisionism: and *Unforgiven* as noir Western, 151, 172–74; and Western genre in 1990s, 137, 141

Ride the High Country (1962), 155

Rielly, Edward, 7

Rifleman (television series), 20

Rinne, Craig, 8

Riot in Cell Block 11 (1954), 53–54, 59, 73

Robbins, Tim, 211

Rocky Balboa (2006), 185

Rookie, The (1990), 134–35, 140

Rosenthal, Bob, 142

Rosenthal, Joseph, 235, 247n10, 250, 252

Rothermel, Dennis, 7, 204, 206, 212, 216–17, 221n5

Round Midnight (1986), 120n64

Rovin, Jeff, 80

Rubin, Martin, 151, 153, 162n4

Ruiz, Dina, 276n1

Russell, Kurt, 187n12

Rutherford, Jonathan, 171

St. Jacques, Raymond, 77

Sands of Iwo Jima (1949), 263

Saving Private Ryan (1998), 12, 239, 245

Schickel, Richard, 22, 24, 25, 41, 78, 82, 120n67 , 128

Schiesel, Seth, 30

Schifrin, Lalo, 70

Schrag, Calvin O., 161

Schwarzbaum, Lisa, 184

Schwarzenegger, Arnold, 171, 247n6

Scorsese, Martin, 26

Scott, A. O., 178, 220n1, 221n3

Scott, Randolph, 155

Seidler, Victor Jeleniewshi, 38–39

Seiler, Sonny, 200

senior persona, and "auteur-father" status of Eastwood in later films, 131, 135, 139, 142, 145, 146. *See also* age and aging

separation, and editing strategy for *Invictus*, 281

September 11, 2001 terrorist attacks, 239

Seven (1995), 161

sexuality, exploration of in *Beguiled*, 41–42. *See also* gender; homosexuality

Shakespeare, William, 210, 215–16, 219–20, 267

Shane (1953), 81, 82–83, 86–87

Siegel, Don: as actor, 50n1; analysis of influence on Eastwood's work, 53–73; *Coogan's Bluff* and Eastwood's collaboration with, 6–7, 63–66; *Dirty Harry* and Eastwood's collaboration with, 66–72, 75n6; limits of Eastwood's relationship with, 93; and misogyny, 36–37, 40; and scripts for *Two Mules for Sister Sara* and *The Beguiled*, 42–43, 50n5, Western noir and figure of antihero, 150

silence: and heroism in *Flags of Our Fathers*, 254, 255, 256; as theme in *Hereafter*, 14

Silliphant, Sterling, 56

Silver, Alain, 148, 149, 150

Silverado (1985), 145

Simmon, Scott, 154

Simons, John L., 11

Singer, Bryan, 161

Siskel, Gene, 81

16 Blocks (2006), 187n12

Slattery, John, 242

Slotkin, Richard, 20, 24, 134

Smart, Robert, 5

Smith, Paul, 37, 38, 40, 41, 48, 55, 74n5, 86, 87, 130, 134

Smrtic, Mike, 6–7

society: comedy and exploration of aging, 178, 179; Eastwood's films in sociopolitical context of 1990s, 130–41; feminism and change in attitudes toward masculinity, 170; representation of Southern in *Midnight in the Garden of Good and Evil*, 10–11, 190–202

South: and cult of womanhood in late nineteenth century, 41; representation of society in *Midnight in the Garden of Good and Evil*, 10–11, 190–202

South Africa, and *Invictus*, 279, 282

Space Cowboys (2000), 178–79, 186n6

Spacey, Kevin, 161, 192

Spielberg, Steven, 12, 239, 240, 245, 248n13, 248n15

Sragow, Michael, 192

Stagecoach (1939), 154

Stallone, Sylvester, 133–34, 171, 185

Star in the Dust (1956), 169

Stoddard, Karen, 177

storyteller, and growth of Eastwood as actor-director, 1–4

Strank, Mike, 253

Sudden Impact (1983), 36

symbolism: and music in *Flag of Our Fathers*, 241; and photographic imagery in *Flags of Our Fathers*, 254; and religion in *Mystic River*, 213–14, 221n9; and religion in *Pale Rider*, 83, 84, 85–86

Taubin, Amy, 184

Tavernier, Bertrand, 120n64

Taylor, Charles, 192
television: and Siegel as director, 59; and
    Western serials, 19–20. *See also*
    Rawhide; *Wagon Train*
Theoharis, Athan, 294n1
Thomas, Louisa, 18
Thumim, Janet, 151
Toimkin, Dimitri, 77
Tompkins, Jane, 156, 162n7
Top Gun (1986), 134
tragedy: *Letters from Iwo Jima* as, 220n1;
    and *Million Dollar Baby*, 11, 220n1;
    Mystic River as, 11, 204–20; and
    Unforgiven, 11, 205–6
Treasure of the Sierra Madre, The
    (1948), 126
Trouble with the Curve (forthcoming), 1
True Crime (1999), 127, 179–81
Truffaut, François, 99
truth: and mythology in *Flags of Our*
    Fathers, 237; and organic narrative,
    97. *See also* realism
Tulse Luper Suitcases, The (2003–4), 97
Turan, Kenneth, 192
Turner, Frederick Jackson, 32
Two Mules for Sister Sara (1970), 37, 42

Unforgiven (1992): association of mascu-
    linity with violence in, 49; and char-
    acterization, 100, 127–28; dedication
    of to Leone and Siegel, 73; and family,
    267; and film noir, 9, 148–62; and
    lighting, 79; and mythology, 231–34;
    and shift in Eastwood's persona,
    171–72; and sociopolitical context of
    1990s, 130, 131, 138–41; and theme of
    aging hero, 8, 11, 231, 246; and trag-
    edy, 11, 205–6; and Western genre,
    148–62, 172–74
Usual Suspects, The (1995), 161

Van Peebles, Mario, 133
Van Praagh, James, 289n2
video games, 30–31

Viertel, Peter, 108–9, 120n62, 122,
    124–26, 129
Vietnam War, 134, 227, 228, 239
violence: association of masculinity with,
    49–50; critique of in *Unforgiven*, 139,
    140, 141; depiction of in *Unforgiven*
    as noir Western, 151, 152, 153, 232;
    pervasiveness of in *Mystic River*,
    209–10, 215
Virginian: A Horseman of the Plains, The
    (Wister 1902), 154

Wagon Train (television series), 19, 20, 80
Waller, Robert James, 173
Walsch, Neale Donald, 289n2
Walsh, Raoul, 221n2
Wanat, Matt, 6–7, 74n5
war: deconstruction of heroism and
    deglamorization of in *Flags of*
    Our Fathers, 248n18; and view of
    history in Eastwood's films, 264.
    See also Civil War; Grenada; Gulf
    War; Korean War; Vietnam War;
    World War II
War, The (Burns 2007), 12, 239, 240
Ward, Elizabeth, 148, 149, 150
Warner Brothers, 94, 126–27, 128
Warren, Bill, 22, 23
Warren, Charles Marquis, 76–77, 80
Washington, Ned, 77
Wayne, John, 149, 232, 263
Wegner, Phillip, 137
Weiss, Brian, 289n2
Welles, Orson, 92, 97, 292
Westbrook, Brett, 6
Western: and Confederate veterans as
    characters, 23, 33n4; and *Coogan's*
    Bluff, 63; and film noir, 9, 148–62,
    225; and *Gran Torino*, 273–74, 275;
    In the Line of Fire as, 143; and mythol-
    ogy, 232; and *Pale Rider*, 81–82,
    138; and *A Perfect World*, 145; and
    Rawhide, 19–25; and representation
    of heroes in *Bronco Billy*, 101, 102; and

revisionism in 1990s, 137, 141, 172–74; Sergio Leone and remaking of in *A Fistful of Dollars*, 25–32; and socio-political context of 1990s, 135–41; and *Unforgiven*, 148–62, 172–74

Westerner, The (1940), 148

White Hunter Black Heart (1990): and exploration of creativity and per-formance, 7–8, 98, 107–11, 114, 116, 117–18; and repetition of past themes, 121–29

Wilkinson, Rupert, 169

Willis, Bruce, 170, 171, 185, 186n4, 187n12

Winchester '73 (1950), 155

Wise, Robert, 148–49

Wister, Owen, 154

Wollen, Peter, 99, 100

Wooley, Sheb, 77

Wootton, Adrian, 211

World War II, 239–41, 244, 246, 247n9, 248n12, 249, 262, 264

Wuntch, Philip, 43

Yeats, William Butler, 16

Yojimbo (Kurosawa), 19

Zanuck, Darryl F., 94

Žižek, Slavoj, 149, 162n4